TAMBOUR

Publication of this book has been made possible in part by the generous support of the Anonymous Fund of the University of Wisconsin–Madison.

TAMBOUR

Volumes 1–8, a Facsimile Edition

Harold J. Salemson
Editor

Introduction by
Mark S. Morrisson and Jack Selzer

The University of Wisconsin Press

The University of Wisconsoin Press
1930 Monroe Street
Madison, Wisconsin 53711

www.wisc.edu/wisconsinpress/

3 Henrietta Street
London WC2E 8LU, England

5   4   3   2   1

Printed in the United States of America

Library of Congress Cataloguing-in-Publication Data
Tambour : volumes 1–8 / Harold J. Salemson, editor ; introduction by Mark S.
Morrisson and Jack Selzer.— Facsimile ed.
p. cm.
Text in English and French.
Includes bibliographical references and index.
ISBN 0-299-17414-X (alk. paper)
I. Salemson, Harold J. II. Morrisson, Mark S. III. Selzer, Jack.
AP4 .T253 2002
074'.361—dc21
2001040994

CONTENTS

TAMBOUR

TAMBOUR
A Snapshot of Modernism at the Crossroads

Many memorable photographs help document the aesthetic creativity and bohemian daring of the expatriate and native avant-garde communities in Paris between the two world wars. Anyone interested in the Parisian scene has probably at one time or another seen some of these much-reproduced photographs: Ezra Pound, Ford Madox Ford, James Joyce, and John Quinn in Pound's studio discussing the *Transatlantic Review;* Gertrude Stein at her desk with Pablo Picasso's portrait of her adorning the wall behind; George Antheil climbing the façade of Sylvia Beach's Shakespeare and Company bookstore to get into his apartment; a dada soiree; Jean Cocteau smoking opium. These and countless other images of that generation—one that was quite fond of being photographed—remain powerful reminders of an era.

But photographs go only so far in conveying the innovations and aspirations of (and connections among) the modernist revolutionaries of the day. Another kind of "snapshot" can provide a deeper understanding of the excitement of Parisian modernism: the evocation of that scene by its little magazines. Before it found a place in the books we now associate with interwar modernism, the forward-looking literature of the Parisian scene often appeared alongside the work of many other writers—both more conventional writers and currently neglected modernists—in a host of little magazines whose editors were willing to publish controversial work. These magazines, many of which have slipped into obscurity—and which therefore command prohibitively high prices in the rare book trade—give us a valuable view of that intense flowering of aesthetic (and anti-aesthetic) activity in interwar Paris. From them we can enhance our understanding not only of the initial context of these works but also of the kinds of connections that existed among different types of writing (as well as among writing and other social and cultural contexts).

One such magazine that provides a rich and challenging snapshot of Paris at the end of the 1920s is Harold J. Salemson's *Tambour*. We cannot leaf through the pages of *Tambour* in a Left Bank café in February 1929, of course, but the magazine still gives a sense of the vividness of the moment. Opening the first issue, we are confronted with Salemson's clarion "Presentation" (first in French, then in English), followed by poems from the French Zionist André Spire, the American expatriate Ralph Cheever Dunning, the surrealist Philippe Soupault, the Harlem Renaissance poet Countee Cullen (who was in Paris in 1929), and the most avant-garde of all avant-gardists, Blaise Cendrars.[1] Such a range of poetry—putting aside for a moment the drawings, fiction, and criticism—certainly brings out the freshness, liveliness, and diversity of postwar Paris in a way that reading individual works published later in books cannot.

This array of talented writers found themselves in *Tambour* by dint of the efforts of the magazine's extraordinarily young and committed editor, Harold J. Salemson. A not-quite-eighteen-year-old Salemson had gone to Paris in 1928—though not for the first time. Salemson was born in Chicago in 1910 to Max Salemson, a physician, and Mary Salemson, a teacher of English and French.[2] As Salemson later put it, "My father's only religion was education, knowledge. He felt that somebody who had two languages was worth two people and somebody who had *three* languages was worth *three* people. He planned for us to go to France for two years and to Germany for two years" (quoted in Ross 1984:447). The Salemsons lived in France from 1921 to 1923; a brief visit to inflation-ridden Germany in 1922 did not encourage them to stay there. In 1924, Max Salemson died, and the family moved back to Paris to take advantage of the highly favorable exchange rate, which allowed Harold and his sister, even on a tight budget, to go to school without working from 1925 to 1927. Harold, although he had not earlier shown any particular interest in French, studied at the University of Montpellier and at the Sorbonne, auditing courses in literature and history.

So when Harold Salemson returned to the United States in

1927 and enrolled in the first class of Alexander Meiklejohn's Experimental College at the University of Wisconsin–Madison (the progenitor of the Great Books Program at St. John's College in Annapolis), his professors saw that he already had provided himself with a fine education in French and French literature. Since he already had published articles in French journals, they supported him in his aspirations to go back to Paris to write. When Salemson returned to Paris in 1928, he was poised to begin his career in the Parisian literary world in earnest. With the money from his father's legacy that would have paid for his university education, he decided to start a little magazine.

THE PARISIAN LITTLE MAGAZINES

Almost from the start, little magazines were at the heart of modernist publication in the United States and Europe. Many of the editors and writers for these little magazines had great ambitions for them, hoping to reach mass audiences and augment the public role of the arts. At the very least, the cheaper production costs resulting from late-nineteenth-century printing and papermaking innovations allowed modernists to publish, even if only on a small scale, work that often had trouble finding its way into print in more mainstream periodicals (see Morrisson 2001). In the long run, despite the short lives of many little magazines, this strategy was successful in bringing modernism before large audiences. As George Bornstein has noted, "Part of the extraordinary success of the modernists in canon formation came from their attention to editorial presentation of new or neglected writers . . . in little magazines (such as *Poetry, Little Review,* or the larger *Dial*)" (1991:2).

Having been in Paris for much of the twenties, Salemson clearly understood the importance of little magazines, but he was faced with a number of different possible models for his own magazine—including those offered by the *Little Review, transition,* the *English Review,* and the *Transatlantic Review.* The *Little Review,* which had been founded in Chicago in 1914, had moved on to New York City, and finally, by the late twenties, to Paris. Edited by Margaret Anderson and Jane Heap, the magazine had helped launch the first wave of British and American modernism in the teens, and in the twenties it had exhibited the insistently international focus that had come to define much of modernism. But the *Little Review,* aside from the 1929 issue announcing that it would cease publication, had not published an issue since 1926. Other expatriate little magazines had been born in Paris and were more directly associated with the city—the most famous of these were probably Eugene Jolas's *transition* (1927–1938) and Ford Madox Ford's *Transatlantic Review* (1924–1925).

Transition was the longest running of the Parisian expatriate little magazines, and probably the most celebrated. It followed a path that had been taken earlier in the twenties by other expatriate magazines, like Harold Loeb's *Broom* (1921– 1924, published in Rome and then in Berlin). *Broom* proclaimed itself "an international magazine of the arts" and published a rich variety of writers, including the British and American authors William Carlos Williams, Robert Graves, e. e. cummings, and Malcolm Cowley; Frenchmen such as Pierre MacOrlan, Jacques Rivière, Paul Morand, Paul Claudel, Jean de Bosschère, and Benjamin Péret; and even the Italian Luigi Pirandello. It also published reproductions of works by artists Juan Gris, Joseph Stella, Edward Nagle, André Derain, and many others. Yet *all* of the work in languages other than English was translated into English—often by Matthew Josephson, who was later on the editorial board of *transition*.

Like *Broom*, *transition* published all of its literature in English translation from its founding in 1927 until 1933, when Jolas announced that from thenceforward he would publish non-English texts in their original language. As Craig Monk has recently explained, the issue of language in *transition* was a complicated one for Jolas, who was polyglot himself and created neologisms that rivaled Joyce's in *Finnegans Wake* (which, by no coincidence, was being published primarily in *transition* during this period). As Monk indicates, Jolas never could resolve a tension between his desires for a "universal" language, one that would be shared by everyone, and a "perfect" language, one that would be able to express concepts perfectly (1999:30–31). For the first six years of the magazine, including the years during which *Tambour* appeared, Jolas published only English translations of non-English works in hopes of reaching American audiences. As Monk puts it, "Proceeding from what the editor, Eugene Jolas, hoped would be a developing enthusiasm in the United States for world literature, *transition* sought to encourage a host of international contributors, initially translating their works into 'a language Americans can read and understand' (1:137)" (Monk 1999:18). Indeed, the American orientation of *transition* was so predominant that fully half of the ads in the issues around 1929 and 1930 were for New York bookstores and publishers, rather than for Parisian ones (the exception, of course, was Sylvia Beach's expatriate bookstore, Shakespeare and Company).

In spite of the English-only emphasis in the first half of its life, *transition* was certainly a good model of a highly successful little magazine bringing international work to American audiences. By 1929 it was a quarterly, with some issues numbering three hundred pages; it featured lavish covers by the likes of Man Ray and had illustrations in virtually every issue. In addition to Joyce, *transition* published authors such as Stein, Beckett, and Crane. It also published continental avant-garde work, including much surrealism.

In the March 15, 1928, issue of *La révolution surréaliste,*

the "official" organ of surrealism, *transition* advertised itself
as "a monthly magazine presenting the modern spirit of various continents to the English-speaking world. . . . The only review in English to introduce surrealist writers and painters"
(41). Although this last claim was not entirely true (the *Little
Review* had published a few pieces by Aragon, Picabia, and
Soupault, and *Broom* had published some surrealist works
earlier in the twenties), *transition* was the major expatriate
magazine to publish translations of surrealist work. As Dougald McMillan notes, "Jolas considered *transition* a 'documentary organ' dedicated to presenting what he referred to
later as 'pan-romanticism.' Not only was it to publish the authors directly involved in its own revolutionary programme,
but also to present similar movements which had preceded it
and were contemporary with it. It was in this respect that
works of the surrealists, dadaists, and German expressionists
appeared" (1975:79). Though Jolas did not accept all aspects
of surrealism, he was certainly intrigued by its appropriation
of Freud and its experimental emphasis; he published more
than sixty surrealist pieces in *transition* (including works by
Breton, Aragon, Soupault, Desnos, Eluard, Tzara, Leiris,
Crevel, and Péret). His friend Paul Eluard helped bring surrealist material to the magazine and contributed many of his
own poems, and Breton published the opening of *Nadja* in the
magazine (McMillan 1975:80–82). *Transition* represented

the most sustained effort at the time to bring surrealism and other continental avant-garde movements to the American public.

The other important expatriate little magazine in Paris during the twenties was Ford Madox Ford's *Transatlantic Review*. Ford had started a modernist magazine—the *English Review*—once before, in 1908, while he was still living in London, and had done much to introduce work by D. H. Lawrence, Ezra Pound, Wyndham Lewis, and other young writers to British audiences, as well as to draw that work into the orbit of more established writers like Joseph Conrad, H. G. Wells, Henry James, and Thomas Hardy. But with the *English Review,* Ford had also tried to create in England a review journal very much like the successful French *revue* the *Mercure de France,* which had been founded in December 1889 by a group of young writers that included Alfred Vallette (who became the *Mercure*'s editor), Remy de Gourmont, Rachilde (Vallette's wife), and Laurent Tailhade.[3] The *Mercure* had strong symbolist beginnings, but it aimed for a much broader range of content and gradually expanded its scope to include reviews and discussions of many subjects other than literature and art. It managed to outlive the French little magazines of the 1880s and 1890s by adding a large review section in April 1896. The *Mercure* then ceased to be only a *recueil symboliste* and quickly became one of the leading French *revues.* Large audiences were attracted by the *Mercure*'s centrist tone, its inclusion of experimental literature from many countries, and its attempt to bring that literature into line with the larger interests and tastes of French society by publishing it along with a comprehensive review section and fine critical commentary (see Décaudin 1992; Morrisson 2001; von Hallberg 1989).

The successful hybrid format of the *Mercure de France*—a review and an experimental literary magazine—influenced Ford's *English Review;* in that magazine, Ford included a broad review section alongside international literary pieces and aimed for the monthly review corner of British publishing. He continued to use this model when he published the *Transatlantic Review* in Paris in the twenties. In fact, Ford seems to have seen the *Transatlantic Review* as a continuation of the *English Review,* even writing in an editorial that he tried to solicit a poem from the aged Thomas Hardy with which to begin it (just as the *English Review* had opened with Hardy's "Sunday Morning Tragedy" after no other publisher would take it [Ford 1924:93–94]).

Like the *English Review* before it, and the *Mercure de France* alongside it, the *Transatlantic Review* tried to be both international and critical, publishing a section of reviews on diverse topics. Indeed, this format was so popular in France—with not only the *Mercure de France* but also the *Revue des deux mondes* and the *Nouvelle revue française* enjoying great prominence in the periodicals market—that the format of the *Transatlantic Review* would certainly have seemed less surprising in Paris than that of the *English Review* had in London nearly two decades earlier.

The *Transatlantic Review* published experimental work like Gertrude Stein's *The Making of Americans* and James Joyce's *Work in Progress,* as well as diverse work by George Antheil, Ezra Pound, Ernest Hemingway, H. D., Mary Butts, Djuna Barnes, the Baroness Elsa von Freytag-Loringhoven, Dorothy Richardson, John Dos Passos, William Carlos Williams, Joseph Conrad, and other British and American writers. Ford even began publishing one of his best novels, *Some Do Not,* in the magazine. But he also included work in French by Paul Valéry, Jean Cassou, René Crevel, and others, as well as a "Lettre de Paris" by Philippe Soupault to complement the "American letter" by, among others, Ernest Hemingway, and a "Litir o Eirian" by Geoffrey Coulter from Dublin.[4] However, in spite of its international aspirations, the *Transatlantic Review* was still predominantly in English. Its contributions from writers in Paris were mainly from American, British, and Irish expatriates, and its French-language pieces constituted at most one tenth of each issue.

While the expatriate magazines like *transition* and the *Transatlantic Review* were an important inspiration for *Tambour,* the French magazines also had much to offer the new edi-

tor—and Salemson also knew the French-language magazines in Paris well. Some of the important French little magazines of the period were Adrienne Monnier's *Navire d'argent*
(1925–1926); Louis Aragon, André Breton, and Philippe
Soupault's surrealist magazine *Littérature* (1919–1924) and
its successor, *La révolution surréaliste* (1924–1929; continued as *Le surréalisme au service de la révolution* from 1930 to
1933); and Georges Bataille's *Documents* (1929–1930).
These magazines were similar to the expatriate magazines in
that they thrived on publishing controversial, experimental,
and multinational work, and they also published virtually
everything in a single language—in their case, of course,
French, translating non-French work for the benefit of a fran-
cophone readership.

Adrienne Monnier—who owned and managed La Maison
des Amis des Livres, the French counterpart to Sylvia Beach's
Shakespeare and Company—edited the stellar monthly
Navire d'argent. With the help of twenty-four-year-old Jean
Prévost, Monnier published work by Valery Larbaud, Alain,
Antoine de Saint-Exupéry, Blaise Cendrars, Ramon Fernan-
dez, Jules Romains, and Paul Claudel.[5] Keeping with the in-
ternationalism of the Parisian little magazines, and, especially
favoring English-language work, Monnier also published (in
translation) work by several American writers (including T. S.
Eliot's "La chanson d'amour de J. Alfred Prufrock," trans-

lated by Sylvia Beach and Adrienne Monnier, and pieces by
Robert McAlmon, William Carlos Williams, e. e. cummings,
Ernest Hemingway, and even Walt Whitman). Selections from
Joyce's *Work in Progress*—the only thing not translated in the
magazine, for obvious reasons—could be found in the *Navire*
as well. Monnier even included German work: translations of
Rilke. Though the *Navire* lasted for only twelve issues (and
ended when Monnier was forced to sell her private library to
pay off the magazine's debts), its range and taste may be seen
as typical of a corner of the French little magazine world that
also included, for instance, *Commerce* and *Bifur* (McDougall
in Monnier 1976:56).

There were also multiple little magazines edited by writers
associated with surrealism. In *Littérature,* Aragon, Breton,
and Soupault published an impressive range of work from
writers such as André Gide and Paul Valéry, as well as writers
and artists associated with dada and surrealism, like André
Salmon, Blaise Cendrars, Pierre Reverdy, Paul Eluard, Benjamin Péret, Robert Desnos, Francis Picabia, and, of course,
the editors themselves. *La révolution surréaliste* and its successor, *Le surréalisme au service de la révolution,* carried on
this impressive record, and these surrealist magazines also
published Breton's manifestos.

Yet, by the time of the publication of *Le surréalisme au service de la révolution,* Breton's editorial perspective had be-

come more doctrinaire, and his relationship with the other surrealists, more dictatorial, causing many defections. Running concurrently with *Tambour,* and representing a different corner of the Parisian avant-garde from Breton's surrealists, was the counter-surrealist journal *Documents* (1929–1930), edited by Georges Bataille, with help from Michel Leiris and Carl Einstein, and home to some early adherents of surrealism (including Leiris and Robert Desnos) who had left the movement or been expelled by Breton. *Documents* generally did not publish poetry or fiction at all, but rather gathered a fascinating series of articles on, as the journal's subtitle proclaimed, "doctrines, archéologie, beaux-arts, ethnographie" in a "magazine illustré." Though *Documents* initially included an English supplement with summaries of the articles, this feature dropped out after the first volume, and, like *transition,* which advertised itself in the first issue of *Documents,* Bataille's journal generally remained monolingual. The journal, with ten issues each year, was printed on large paper, ran over sixty-four pages, and included reproductions of works by Miró, Picasso, Giacometti, and other modernist artists. Einstein, who had abandoned writing poetry and was just beginning his career as a critic, wrote a series of essays on artists like Picasso, André Masson, and Braque, and the magazine featured many articles by Michel Leiris (including articles on Giacometti and Miró), Bataille, and Desnos, as well as articles by Leo Frobenius, the anthropologist who inspired Ezra Pound, and many discussions of the flurry of archaeological activity of the period.[6] Articles by Sacheverell Sitwell on Mexican baroque and Clive Bell on Constable (both in French) stood alongside discussions of film and jazz.

As Rainer Rumold has recently shown, *Documents* shared *transition*'s interest in primitivism and ethnography, yet the two magazines represented, as Rumold puts it, "two sides of the avant-garde":

Jolas . . . pursued an idealistic vision of a multilingual, transnational, universalist poetic language for modernity, Bataille, on the other hand, engaged in an aggressively anti-humanist, anti-idealist, anti-formalist, in this sense anti-aesthetic project which valorized the shocking, jarring moment of the physiological image, bloody images of prehistorical human sacrifice, images of body parts and excretory functions. In sum, while *Documents* implicitly sought to overturn Western core values by revitalizing the early avant-garde's shock strategies, with its goals to "make the familiar strange," *transition*'s mission was to "make the strange familiar" to a wider transatlantic audience (especially to the conservative American cultural sphere). (2000:46)

Tambour covered many of the same authors, artists, and issues that *transition* and *Documents* were exploring at the time (*Tambour*'s first issue preceded that of *Documents* by

two months, but they both ran for most of 1929 and 1930).
And Salemson could see, in magazines like those just discussed, several different modes of asserting the significance of
modernism.

But the French magazines would offer one more crucial lesson to *Tambour:* unlike most of the expatriate magazines, they
all, to some extent, crafted themselves in the *revue* genre represented by the *Mercure de France, Revue des deux mondes,* and
Nouvelle revue française. The *Navire d'argent*'s subtitle was
"Revue mensuelle de littérature et de culture générale," and
Littérature's (in spite of its wild experimentation) was "Revue
mensuelle." And all of these French magazines shared the *revue* genre's goal of "documenting" a fairly broad range of cultural phenomena, not just literature or art.

Just as the *Mercure* had its "Revue du mois" section ("Revue de la quinzaine" when it became a fortnightly), *Littérature, La révolution surréaliste,* and *Documents* each had their
"Chroniques" sections, and *Navire d'argent* featured a "Revue
de la critique"—all of these carried on the *revue* tradition by
offering commentary on a variety of subjects, often through
reviews of books or events as well as through essays. The
Navire d'argent's *revue* section included different subsections
(following the *Mercure*), including "Littérature générale,"
"Les romans," "Variété," "Les traductions," "Philosophie,"
and a bibliography (which frequently focused on English and

American literature translated into French). *Littérature*'s "Chroniques" section included a subsection on "Livres choisis" (which often reviewed avant-garde books by authors like Tzara and Reverdy), and even one on "Les revues," which discussed the contents of many popular reviews, including the *Mercure de France* (the *Mercure* also had such a section). *La révolution surréaliste*'s "Chroniques" section reviewed the *revues* as well, and included broadly defined subsections (written by Aragon, Soupault, and others) with titles like "L'invention," "La conscience," and "L'amour." It also included a subsection titled "Enquêtes," which featured *fait-divers* (news items) in the manner of the weekly magazines (focusing especially upon suicides).[7]

This combination of literature and general commentary was already familiar to the French through their own mainstream reviews, and adopting this format allowed the more experimental little magazines to suggest their relevance to the broader culture. Although many expatriate magazines tended not to imitate this French model, the value of understanding the connection between avant-gardism and the larger culture that produced it was not lost on Ford in his *English Review* (or later in the *Transatlantic Review*), and, as we will argue, it was also not lost on Harold J. Salemson as he considered the genre of magazine he would found.

TAMBOUR'S CONTRIBUTION TO THE LITTLE MAGAZINE GENRE

With his sensitivity to the field of expatriate and native little magazines and to the French *revue* genre, Salemson created a vigorous hybrid, combining the modernist little magazine's emphasis on innovative and unknown authors with the *revue* genre's emphasis on a wide-ranging review section at the end of each issue. Salemson had temporarily taken over Jean Catel's "Lettres anglo-américaines" section of the *Mercure de France* from the February 15, 1929, issue through the August 15, 1930, issue, and he clearly aimed to imitate the *Mercure*'s "Revue de la quinzaine." *Tambour* concluded each issue with a "Notes" section that documented American and Parisian cultural and intellectual life, and, like the French *revues,* it included discussions not just of modernism but also of mass culture at the end of the 1920s. Salemson included reviews of art and literature, but he also sharpened the magazine's focus on theater, musical performance, phonograph records, and film.

Although most of the French little magazines had included some version of this review section, *Tambour* broke with the French *and* American magazines by publishing regularly in both French and English. While the French magazines aimed at French audiences, and the American magazines at American and expatriate audiences, Salemson wished to reach both,

to create some kind of dialogue between these cultures beyond
what could be achieved by occasional publication of foreign
work in translation. Salemson not only published important
documents—like his opening "Presentation" and his manifesto, "Essential: 1930"—in both languages, but he also published the notes sections in whichever language seemed most
appropriate. Literary contributions generally appeared in
their original language, with the exception of a few American
pieces Salemson clearly wished to present to French audiences, like Zona Gale's story "Bill," and the special issue of
Italian poetry, which printed the poems in French translation.
French and English were clearly the official languages of the
magazine, and its goal seems to have been to create a transatlantic synthesis that would avoid the predominance of English
language texts over French language texts in Ford's *Transatlantic Review*. So when Salemson prepared to launch *Tambour*, he placed an ad in *transition* that emphasized its bilingual character: "TAMBOUR, Harold J. Salemson, Editor. An
international review of literature and the arts, publishing
American, French, and English writers in the original" (*transition* no. 15, February 1929).

But beyond the language issue, Salemson performed the
important task of bridge building in other ways. Modernist
little magazines had often attempted to bring different literary directions together—the *Little Review*, for instance,

placed Chicago and midwestern writing alongside international experiments in imagism, and it brought Joyce's work
and eventually much French avant-gardism before American
audiences. But *Tambour,* in its short life, extended this program of bringing different literary and intellectual strains together. The *transition* ad went on to emphasize the catholicity
of work to appear in *Tambour,* proclaiming that the magazine
would publish "drawings by the most varied types of artists,
every school, every trend, every movement will be represented,
in an attempt to evolve some new direction." *Tambour* aimed
to eschew the well-established avant-garde tactic of proclaiming an aesthetic program, giving it a name, and publishing
manifestos proclaiming its superiority to all other artistic
movements. (The Italian futurists turned this kind of self-
promotion into an art form beginning in 1909, but many
avant-garde groups—including the dadaists, vorticists, surrealists, and expressionists, to name but a few of the more
successful—adopted these tactics with great vehemency.)
Though deploying the avant-garde spirit of the new in order to
"evolve some new direction," *Tambour* would not be the journal of any *specific* movement. Rather, the magazine portrayed
aesthetic "progress" as an "evolution," not a "revolution,"
that involved a wide range of cultures, artists, and thinkers.

 Tambour created a forum to bring together a variety of writers from disparate scenes as the "roaring twenties" came to a

close. Not surprisingly, many American expatriates living in
Paris contributed: Maxwell Bodenheim, Paul Bowles, Ralph
Cheever Dunning, Charles Henri Ford, Ludwig Lewisohn,
Samuel Putnam, Richard Thoma, and Salemson himself
(though he never considered himself an expatriate per se).[8]
But Salemson tried hard to set Anglo-American writing in dialogue with the work of many of the most significant French
writers and artists of the day, including Blaise Cendrars,
Philippe Soupault, and André Spire, as well as Jean Cocteau,[9]
Michel Arnaud, and André Masson (who, like Soupault, and
to a lesser extent, Cendrars, were associated with French surrealism), and its seventh issue included an admirable selection
of contemporary Italian poetry, including poems by Massimo
Bontempelli and Eugenio Montale. Moreover, *Tambour* also
published many American writers who were not associated
with Parisian expatriate modernism. Countee Cullen, for instance, though in Paris in 1929, was associated with the
Harlem Renaissance, not the Left Bank. The presence of his
poem "Ghosts" in the first issue, appearing amongst the work
of French avant-gardists Cendrars and Soupault, was a clear
signal of the broad cultural sweep that Salemson wished to
cover in his magazine ("Ghosts" went on to appear later in
1929 in Cullen's famous collection *The Black Christ and Other
Poems*).

Likewise, Salemson published work by writers living in the

American Southwest, like Witter Bynner and Norman Macleod, and even some of those affiliated with regionalism and
realism, including Zona Gale and James T. Farrell. Bynner,
who had been living in Santa Fe since 1922 (amid an amor-
phous group of moderns that included at various times Ma-
bel Dodge Luhan, D. H. Lawrence, John Sloan, Georgia
O'Keeffe, and Edward Hopper), had just concluded eleven
years of work, with Kiang Kang-hu, translating an anthology
of T'ang Dynasty poems called *The Jade Mountain* (1929: see
Kraft 1995; Tayler 1987). Bynner's "Chinese" poems, Stuart
Gilbert's story "The Whispering Pagoda: A Burma Night's
Entertainment," and translations of poems by Wang-Wei and
Liang-Tsong-Tai represented in *Tambour* the modernist chi-
noiserie of the day. Almost simultaneously with *The Jade Mountain,* Bynner published a collection of poems, *Indian Earth*
(1929), featuring verbal postcards of Southwest scenes and
themes (Pueblo Indian dances, rituals, landscapes) as well
as unusual eight-line, variable-length verse stanzas. Together
the two books reflected the moderns' appreciation for the exotic and unusual. Salemson published eight of the poems that
appeared in *The Jade Mountain,* and he turned to Norman
Macleod for Native American–influenced work that was similar to Bynner's *Indian Earth.*

Macleod, writing in Albuquerque, was fusing experimental-
ism, regional exoticism, and political consciousness into a

blend congenial to *Tambour*. In "Old Walpi" and "At Toreva," Macleod employed imagist-inspired poetry toward social ends: the Hopi in "Old Walpi" speaks the life of a common person while defending his old ways against the Navajo usurpers; "At Toreva" depicts the fading of native cultures under the influence of the Anglo traders summoned at the poem's close.

Salemson's acknowledgment of politics was equally evident in his choice of Gale's "Bill," a bit of regionalist fiction that recalls Macleod, Sherwood Anderson, Willa Cather, Sinclair Lewis, and Kate Chopin: the unsentimental meanness of the protagonist's neighbor in the story evokes the modernist contempt for the small town.[10] Gale eschewed formal experimentation, as did James T. Farrell in "In the Park" and "Friend of the Doctor." In some of his first published stories, Farrell offered *Tambour* the Chicago setting that he would make famous in his Studs Lonigan books (then in the process of composition); "In the Park," his Dreiserian portrait of a hobo who moves unnoticed through an impassive world, fit in with Salemson's consistent concern for social criticism.[11]

The rich array of texts that Salemson was able to bring together in *Tambour* also included some early work of American writers who went on to enjoy great success. Paul Bowles published six of his earliest poems in the magazine, and some of them have not appeared in any of Bowles's poetry collections.[12] Moreover, two early stories by Farrell (one of which has not been reprinted) and an early and uncollected Elder Olson poem, "Two in a City," also appeared in *Tambour*.[13]

That *Tambour* created a visible mark by portraying modernism in the broadest, most eclectic and inclusive sense, and by publishing texts in several languages by writers of different nationalities, can be seen in the ambitions of another little magazine, *Morada*, which borrowed *Tambour*'s format.[14] Four (possibly five) issues of *Morada* appeared beginning in autumn 1929, under the editorial direction of Macleod. From Albuquerque, he managed to create a fascinating magazine that mixed expatriate Parisians with local southwesterners (mainly students and faculty at the University of New Mexico) who were experimenting with fiction and poetry. Along with works by Pound, Bowles, Harry Crosby, Kay Boyle, and Richard Thoma, Macleod found space for contributions by Kenneth Rexroth, Charles Henri Ford (editor of *Blues*), and Salemson himself, who offered to the first two issues a translation of a Soupault poem, "Heures creuses," that had appeared in French in the first issue of *Tambour*, an article on Waldo Frank, and two "Paris letters." Having imitated the multicultural contents of *Tambour* in his first issues, Macleod also sought to emulate *Tambour*'s multilingual flavor by publishing the final issue of *Morada* in 1931 from Lago di Garda; it featured contributions in English, German, and French.[15] The "trilingual *Morada*," as the final issue was called, appears as a sort of memorial continuance of *Tambour* after the latter's demise.

MANIFESTO WARS: *TAMBOUR, TRANSITION,* AND THE "REVOLUTION OF THE WORD"

Morada remained obscure and ephemeral, although Pound had predicted that it might become the next *Little Review* (Dalmas 1980:267). Ultimately, therefore, *transition* stood as the expatriate magazine against which *Tambour* had to position itself. When *Morada* offered notes on its contributors, it often bragged that Bowles, Crosby, Salemson, and others were contributors to *transition,* hard evidence that *transition* was formidable and respected.[16] We have already noted that *transition* published exclusively in English while *Tambour* was bilingual, but the differences between the two extended well beyond the translation issue—and help us discover the crossroads at which modernism found itself in the late twenties.

These differences were aired in the modernist genre par excellence, the manifesto. In the June 1929 issue of *transition,* editor Eugene Jolas published one of the most famous manifestos of 1920s modernism, the "Proclamation," best known as "The Revolution of the Word." In it he made several bold assertions: "THE REVOLUTION IN THE ENGLISH LANGUAGE IS AN ACCOMPLISHED FACT," "THE IMAGINATION IN SEARCH OF

A FABULOUS WORLD IS AUTONOMOUS AND UNCONFINED,"
"PURE POETRY IS A LYRICAL ABSOLUTE THAT SEEKS AN A
PRIORI REALITY WITHIN OURSELVES ALONE," "THE LITER-
ARY CREATOR HAS THE RIGHT TO DISINTEGRATE THE PRI-
MAL MATTER OF WORDS IMPOSED ON HIM BY TEXT-BOOKS
AND DICTIONARIES," and, finally and most memorably, "THE
PLAIN READER BE DAMNED." Like some pre–World War I
manifestos, "The Revolution of the Word" employed a rhetor-
ical opposition to mass audiences in order to advertise itself,
and it clearly shifted the burden of interpretation onto the
reader (see Lyon 1999). It stands as a classic statement of one
ideal of modernism that privileged aesthetic autonomy and
linguistic and formal experimentation. Not surprisingly, Jolas
was able to get many key expatriate modernists in the Parisian
scene to sign it, including Kay Boyle, Caresse and Harry
Crosby, and Hart Crane.

"The Revolution of the Word" was also signed by Harold J.
Salemson and by Stuart Gilbert, who published in *Tambour*.
But by 1930, Salemson had distanced himself from the positions of "The Revolution of the Word" and had published in
Tambour an equally significant manifesto, "Essential: 1930,"
that challenged many of the ideals *transition* espoused. "The
Revolution of the Word" had sparked a kind of manifesto war,
with other magazines (such as V. F. Calverton's *Modern Quarterly* in America) also challenging many of its assumptions.

But *Tambour*'s response to "The Revolution of the Word" was particularly significant, in that *Tambour* had emerged from the same Parisian modernist scene that *transition* represented, rather than from the leftist context of American magazines like *The Liberator* and *The New Masses* in Greenwich Village. In particular, Salemson's "Essential: 1930" challenged the privileging of formalist and aesthetic autonomy that *transition* espoused. Salemson (along with Richard Thoma and Samuel Putnam) continued this attack in another manifesto entitled "Direction," written in 1930 and pasted up on café walls around Paris. Hoffman, Allen, and Ulrich, in their classic study, *The Little Magazine,* rightly see *Tambour*'s emergence as signaling the more socially engaged literature of the 1930s (1947:293)—but, judging by the contents of the magazine, it would be a mistake to see this move as a rejection of modernism. Rather, Salemson and his circle wished to refocus the interpretation of modernism away from the formalist emphasis of Jolas and toward an emphasis on the relationship of modernism to life, in its broadest terms. Clearly, many modernist texts of the 1920s were not preoccupied solely with form, and so what was at stake was primarily an interpretation of the responsibilities of the writer.

Tambour challenged the "Revolution of the Word" in two ways: first, by attacking pure formalism in favor of a more accessible and socially engaged literature, and second, by implicitly emphasizing film—turning from a revolution of the *word* to a revolution of the *image*—at the very moment that film had come to be seen as a major facet of culture by many modernists. We shall first discuss the attack upon what Salemson and others saw as the fetishization of formal innovation.

Critiques of Formalism in "Essential: 1930" and "Direction"

At the end of modernism's most triumphant decade, the twenties, *Tambour* gave voice to the idea that some aspects of modernism (or at least of the way modernism was discussed) had been overemphasized. Stuart Gilbert, though he eventually did sign the "Revolution of the Word" and was closely involved with *transition,* wrote in his diary for May 9, 1929, "And Eugene [Jolas] the word-killer wishes me to sign a manifesto, praising the New Word! Why don't they learn the old ones first?" (1990:13). In the poem that opened the sixth issue of *Tambour,* "Essential: 1930," Salemson hinted at what was to come in his "Essential: 1930" manifesto, which appeared in the following issue. Salemson's poem, presented first in French, then in English, as was his frequent practice in the opening matter of the issues, sets up the binaries he would later challenge in his manifesto:

Parenthesis.
Smashing dishes,
Crash of washing,
Household garbage.
Blows.

Parenthesis.

Light, darkness,
Form, anti-form?
Idea, thought, expression,
Essential: 1930.

Period.

Salemson adopts many of the tactics of modernist verse: the ascetic short lines, the eschewing of self-consciously "poetic" diction, and the juxtaposition of images in the first stanza all echo the imagist poetics emerging before the war, and the paratactic, almost list-like enumeration of seeming antinomies in the third stanza follows modernist practice, as well. He also invokes modernist tropes of cleansing and violently destroying in order to rebuild: "Smashing dishes, / Crash of washing, / Household garbage. / Blows." Yet what is the "household garbage" that must be cleared out? The evocation

of the common everyday acts of domestic life (and even of domestic violence, in a Dreiserian underpinning to Salemson's
modernism) telegraphs, in an almost Williams-like way, what
Salemson will come to argue as the need to keep literature tied
to the reality of life in the 1930s. But this stanza, cordoned off
from the title and from stanza three by the provocatively
spelled out "parenthesis" at each end, precedes a stanza that
will set up a much more abstract set of terms—the antinomies
of light/darkness, form/anti-form, idea/thought/expression.
Salemson puts a question mark after "anti-form," though,
suggesting an imminent questioning of the formalist character of modernism and the anti-form experiments of dada
and other iconoclastic avant-garde movements in Paris in the
twenties. "Idea, thought, expression"—a fairly comprehensive and basic set of terms for a writer—need to be recalled,
suggests Salemson, as the "essential" in 1930. "Period."

Salemson's somewhat cryptic poetic "preamble" to his manifesto set the agenda for a critique that the manifesto itself, "Essential: 1930," made explicit. Salemson argues that
modernism is a sort of belated Romanticism, continuing the
"projection of the artist's personality into the world about
him," but differing from Romanticism in its variation of
forms. He rebels against the tenor of the "Revolution of the
Word," arguing that "Modernism, a research of form, is exhausted" (1930b:5), that the new path "must ignore form,

since all forms and anti-forms are at its disposal. They are waiting to be used" (6). Taking the place of a reification and deification of form, "the first place belongs to ideas" (6). This re-emphasis was meant to tie the artist back to the world, as Salemson understood it, meaning those things outside of the artist that she or he must grapple with to produce anything of imaginative merit: "As for the modern projection of the personality of the artist into the outside world, we replace it by the world without the artist, the world as it is in 1930, a world the artist must recreate (which does not suppose any obligatory realism) according to the contemporary way of seeing things" (7).

Because of the vagueness so common to manifestos, it is unclear exactly how Salemson wanted to change modernism. Many modernists (e.g., Eliot, Pound, and Yeats) had long been using forms of the past and engaging "the world" fairly directly (for instance, Joyce's *Dubliners, Portrait,* and *Ulysses,* any of Virginia Woolf's novels, or the poetry of William Carlos Williams)—and Salemson was still largely committed to publishing both modernist literature and discussions of it (especially of the work of James Joyce) in his magazine.[17] But one must remember that the two causes célèbres of the Parisian expatriate modernist world were Gertrude Stein and James Joyce, and, in particular, the Joyce of *Work in Progress.* Salemson wanted to explore the distinction between

the aesthetic power of words and their ability to communicate.
In his *Mercure de France* review of Black Sun's *Tales Told
of Shem and Shaun,* he argues that Joyce "est aujourd'hui
le phénomène le plus formidable qui soit dans la langue anglaise, cette langue dont il désespère justement au point d'avoir
entrepris de la régénérer totalement. Rien ne sert (ou presque) de connaître l'anglais pour lire ces trois contes, d'ailleurs
en grande partie incompréhensibles. Joyce a refondu toutes
les langues vivantes et mortes pour en former une qu'il considère plus expressive [Joyce is today the most tremendous
phenomenon existing in the English language, this language
which has caused him such despair that he has undertaken
to totally recast it. Knowing English is of very little help in
reading these three stories, which are for the most part incomprehensible. Joyce has merged all languages, living and
dead, to create from them one that he deems more expressive]"
(1929a:746–47). He went on to recommend to interested
readers the *Modern Quarterly* debate over Joyce. Salemson
was beginning to question whether literature could be of enduring importance and seemingly incomprehensible at the same
time, and he emphasized works like Gilbert's *James Joyce's
"Ulysses"* and the collection of commentaries on *Finnegans
Wake, Our Exagmination Round His Factification for Incamination of "Work in Progress,"* that helped foster understanding
of formally challenging work.

Moreover, affirming his growing sense that modernist literature—though of great importance in revitalizing the language—had somehow become excessive, in the fourth issue of
Tambour Salemson wrote that "All the American magazines of
interest are devoted in part, these days, to those that Max
Eastman calls the unintelligibles. *transition* publishes a *Manifesto* that may bring more unintelligibility but that has many
good points and proclaims entire freedom for the artist. *Blues,*
a magazine of the younger generation, would be the most important magazine appearing in English, if it did not devote itself *entirely* to these same unintelligibles between whom and
us the breach is widening. *Blues* may wake up to find the gap
too great, and they on the wrong side" (1929b:76).[18]

Eastman's polemic, "The Cult of Unintelligibility," was an
important volley in the ongoing cultural wars raging over
modernism in America. Though he had broken from the Communist Party and eschewed the Stalinist ideological condemnation of modernism, Eastman nevertheless had long since
moved away from the modernism that he had featured in *The
Masses* in earlier years. He critiqued cummings, Eliot, Stein,
Sitwell, and Joyce for moving into obscurity and ceasing to
communicate with their audiences. In his essay, Eastman (like
Salemson) affirms Joyce's linguistic genius but argues that
"the goal toward which he seems to be traveling with all this
equipment of genius is the creation of a language of his own—

a language which might be superior poetically, as Esperanto is practically, to any of the known tongues. It might be immortal—as immortal as the steel shelves of the libraries in which it would rest. But how little it would communicate, and to how few" (Eastman 1935:65–66). He concludes: "Until we establish an international bureau for the decoding of our contemporary masterpieces, I think it will be safe to assert that Joyce's most original contribution to English literature has been to lock up one of its most brilliant geniuses inside of his own vest" (66).

While none of those who wrote for *Tambour* would have accepted Eastman's characterization of Joyce or of modernism in full, their attempt to refocus modernism continued even after *Tambour* had ceased. The culmination of *Tambour*'s polemic against *transition*'s "Revolution of the Word" came in late 1930 in the manifesto signed by Salemson, Thoma, and Putnam, "Direction." Putnam remembers that "there were a good many who felt that the much-advertised 'revolution' was getting nowhere rapidly and that it would be a salutary thing to call some kind of halt, at least long enough for a calm and sane consideration of the question of language and modernism" (1947:226–27). Putnam describes the beginnings of the discussion "in Montparnasse around a café table," and he recalls that "there was a general feeling that a statement or a declaration of principles of some sort was called for; but when it came to the actual drawing up and signing of a manifesto, most of those who had participated in our discussions exhibited an inclination to keep in the background; for *transition,* I found, cast a spell even over those that did not approve of it, and these latter, not wishing to be branded as mere dull-witted conservatives, were accordingly none too keen about having their names appear" (227). Thus "Direction" was signed only by Salemson, Putnam, and Thoma, all three of whom had contributed both to *transition* and to *Tambour.* It was, as Putnam explains, "printed in black letters on a large yellow sheet . . . [and] blossomed out one morning on the walls of all the Montparnasse cafés (the usual medium of publicity), and another battle was soon in progress, the Battle of the Left Bank" (227).

Putnam asserts that "probably almost no Americans who did not happen to be in Paris at the time ever heard of 'Direction'" (1947:229), but Salemson's surviving correspondence shows that he sent it around to influential writers and editors in America in an effort to bring it into the American debate. Farrell advised him of some places to send it, and he sent a copy to Dreiser.[19] Waldo Frank, a figure from Max Eastman's corner of the American Left, nevertheless cautioned against completely dismissing formal considerations: "Your manifesto is really quite splendid. But there is much to add to it: content, yes—by all all all means. The technique or method whereby this content may be reached, mined, transfigured—this must not be neglected."[20] H. L. Mencken hinted at the problem with most manifestos: they rarely stimulated the production of work that lived up to their proclamations: "Your manifesto, I think, is excellent. You clear off a lot of nonsense, and probably come as close to the essential facts as anyone ever gets. But where is the writing to fit it? If any such writing exists I'll be glad to print it in The American Mercury."[21] And Harriet Monroe, the editor of *Poetry* in Chicago—an editor who had more or less introduced modernist poetry into American drawing rooms with the help of Ezra Pound and Alice Corbin Henderson in 1912—wrote "I hope *Direction* will down the Joyce imitators and the Stein babblers, and find the kind of content the *manifesto* longs for."[22]

"Direction" dismissed Stein's work in no uncertain terms, referring to it as "infantile stammerings," but as for Joyce, Harriet Monroe was correct in perceiving that the polemic was aimed not specifically at him but at his imitators. Salemson, Thoma, and Putnam decided to bracket Joyce off from the crowd as a unique and inimitable figure who did not spring from the fashionable modernity of the Parisian avant-garde, but they took him to task for *Finnegans Wake,* which had spawned an unhealthy preoccupation with form:

There is much young muddlement at the present time on the subject of form, and much of this muddlement is due to the mountainous

figure, continent-like in its individual proportions, of James Joyce.
We concede the mountain, but point to the ridiculous mouse that the
mountain spawns (in that part of Mr. Joyce's output which is primarily occupied with the future of form). We would, also, call attention to the fact that Mr. Joyce is in no sense of the word "modern."
This, in spite of Bergson and the "stream of consciousness," in spite
of Herr Freud and his patented "dream." He is directly out of the
later fifteenth and early sixteenth century, a contemporary of Rabelais. He merely has wed native Irish blarney to the late-medieval
fatrasie [a literary genre consisting of a group of satirical pieces].
He is a figure enormous and out-of-time. Admiration is in order, and
inevitable; but that he should have influenced a writing generation
is deplorable.

Picking up Eastman's dig at Stein as being insane, they continued, "Whatever has been learned, from Joyce, Stein or any
other, that may be of use to the *contemporary* artist in his task
should be, and will be, utilized; but we shall not succumb to the
illusion that either the *fatrasie* or a psychosis is in any way
'modern.'"

Rhetorically positioning modernism as a postwar phenomenon—a move that ignored the pre–World War I origins of
many of the modernist experiments they took to task, but allowed a kind of explanation for modernism's predicament—
the authors boldly proclaimed that "The War has set literature back one hundred years." They argued, in a way that
should not seem entirely inconsistent with Eliot's, Pound's,

and even Joyce's interest in a classical literary heritage, that many features of modernism were unknowingly imitative (a problem for writers who fetishized "the new" and "the revolutionary"): modernist "hardboiledness" had been around since Baudelaire, Byron was a forgotten precursor, the first modernist manifesto was Hugo's preface to *Cromwell* ("most of the others have been mere repetitions or painfully obvious and infantile expansions"), and even the desire to shock the bourgeoisie was a worn-out gesture ("Only a bourgeois would ever want to shock a bourgeois," they sniped). Moreover, "As for a much-ballyhooed 'Revolution of the Word,' it is all to be found in the *Ars Poetica* of Horace, the *De Oratore* of Cicero, the *Poetics* of Aristotle, the gruntings of the first caveman, and any highschool rhetoric, while our young friend gets it via Lautréamont, Rimbaud, Huysmans, Mallarmé, *et Cie.*" Moving back even beyond the Romantic heritage represented in Byron (and its early modernist continuation in Baudelaire), Salemson, Thoma, and Putnam invoked a classical heritage, not to argue that nothing new can be done—the manifesto goes on to cry "IS THERE NOTHING NEW UNDER THE SUN?"—but rather to argue that what had come to seem empty and imitative formal preoccupations would not approach modernity in a way that would produce a new literature: "WE SEEK THE NEW. We seek a *new* that shall be not simply the *old in disguise.* In other words, we go forward rather than backward. We demand a true and vital contemporaneity of thought, feeling and expression. We are aware, however, that such a contemporaneity is not to be achieved by over-striving or by posturing, but only by a sincere, prolonged and patient search."

As with "Essential: 1930," this kind of manifesto rhetoric, of course, always begs the question of how such a new literature can be accomplished, of what precisely the signatories envisioned. "Direction" primarily aims its polemic at what we would now call intellectual fads—the kind of half-baked "knowledge" that is derived from a truly significant source but is facilely repeated, with little understanding: "We are fed up with 'Bergsonians' who cannot frame a syllogism, with 'Freudians' who do not know the technique of the simple laboratory experiment, with 'Einsteinians' who cannot solve a quadratic equation, with 'word-revolutionists' who have never *mastered* the word. Amen." Perhaps unwittingly echoing calls for attention to craft and the professional mastery of the medium in earlier modernist documents—such as Ford's preface to the 1914 *Collected Poems,* his 1908 and 1909 *English Review* editorials, and Pound's 1913 imagist manifestos in *Poetry,* which had all used scientific metaphors to legitimate the profession of writing—"Direction" affirmed a kind of professionalization of knowledge. Bergson is a philosopher, but his disciples are incapable of logical exercise; Freud is a founder of a new school of psychology, not because he gushes about dreams, but because he is a trained medical researcher; Einstein changes the way we think about space and time not because he fetishizes the "new," but because he is a brilliant mathematician. The manifesto implicitly continues the sequence of professional responsibility to include literary writers; it finds Joyce's *Work in Progress* and Stein's poetry lacking something crucial by having focused entirely upon form and the aesthetic qualities of language itself.

So who are the exemplary professional equivalents in literature to be understood and not simply imitated? The manifesto proclaims:

We take our stand with Cocteau and Valéry (different as they are) in France. . . . We believe that the object of art, if we may lift certain words of M. Valéry, is to "rendre la proie éternellement présente dans son attitude éternellement fuyante [render the ubiquitous prey in its elusive glory]." We likewise take our stand (which does not necessarily commit us, man for man, to a theory of neo-Thomism) beside Thomas Aquinas and the thirteenth century, in behalf of a dominating, incisive and concise intelligence. We believe that "when reason goes to sleep, monsters are begot." Yet we would not, preposterously, restrain art to pure reason. We do not believe, needless to state, in "automatic writing,"—at least, not so long as we are sober. The brain has its inalienable rights and the brain should dominate even the subconscious. . . . We call, in other words, for a return to order, the object of art as of existence being, in so far as we are able to determine either, the creation of order out of chaos.

One can imagine Joyce himself applauding much of this statement, especially the choice of Valéry as an example of mastery and intellect in poetry (see Rabaté 1997:95–96). Cocteau in film and Valéry in literature represent the kind of attention to craft, to the conscious construction of phrase and image, that Joyce admired, and "Direction" gets in its dig at surrealist automatic writing as an abdication of aesthetic responsibility. It would be possible to read this manifesto as an attack on modernism, and certainly such phrases as "Innovation in form is justified only in so far as it is demanded by content" were aimed at the "Revolution of the Word." But many Anglo-American modernists would have had some sympathy for the sentiments expressed in "Direction." And such statements as "We condemn aberration for the sake of aberration—pure 'experimentation.' . . . *Had Pasteur carried his experiments further, he might have poisoned, instead of purifying, his milk, M. Tristan Tzara, please copy*" suggest that we should read this moment in the Parisian manifesto wars not as an anti-modernist move (as was so often the case in America) but essentially as a reining-in of what seemed to be the more pointless experimental formal impulses of the avant-garde. In fact, Salemson, Thoma, and Putnam had, in allying their manifesto with Valéry and Cocteau over Tzara and Breton, affirmed the critical project of such established Parisian *revues* as the *Mercure de France, La nouvelle revue française,* and even the conservative *Revue des deux mondes.* All of these *revues,* in-

cluding *Tambour*, aimed at making modernism more accessible to broader reading audiences. But *Tambour* also considered what lay beyond the word: it aimed to bring the revolution of the image to its readers, and began to take film
criticism seriously.

The Revolution of the Image: Salemson, Tambour, and Film

As *Tambour* critiqued what it saw as the formalist obsession
of the "Revolution of the Word," it also implicitly challenged
the emphasis upon the word by addressing film with the same
seriousness and reverence that it displayed in its literary articles. As we shall discuss more fully below, Salemson went on
to become a film critic, Hollywood correspondent for French
periodicals, and worker in various capacities in the film industry after he returned to the United States in 1930, and this
avid interest in film began to appear during his editorship of
Tambour. The magazine's engagement with the highly popular art of film kept it strongly in the fold of Parisian journalism and Parisian life. Immediately after the war, audiences
had flooded movie houses in Paris, and moviegoing continued
to gain in popularity throughout the twenties. The Gaumont
Palace at the Place Clichy seated five thousand people and had
space for an eighty-piece orchestra. The Gaumont Palace and
the Marivaux together brought in over four million customers

in each year of the twenties, and by 1924 ten Parisian cinemas had each reached over two million viewers per year (Monaco 1976:18–19). As Monaco notes, "In 1921 paid admissions to cinemas accounted for 23 percent of total entrances to all 'attractions' in the city. By 1929 the percentage had risen to just over 40. The percentages are all the more impressive because they relate cinema admissions to *all* other public attractions. These included paid admissions not only to legitimate theaters, concerts, and operas, but also to circuses, music halls, cabarets, sporting events, recreational areas, public museums and historical monuments" (1976:19). Cinema revenues escalated throughout the decade, cinema coaches were added to trains, films were shown on board ocean liners, and in 1922 the Paris Conservatory even began offering courses in cinematography (Monaco 1976:22). In 1929 the talkies also took off in France, and a momentary escalation of French-speaking films in Paris between 1929 and 1932, though short lived, returned French films briefly to pre–World War I heights in production (Sadoul 1972:60).

Important French reviews also lent legitimacy to cinema: in 1920 the *Mercure de France* published a series of lengthy film columns by Léon Moussinac, and the *Nouvelle revue française* began featuring articles on film in 1926 (Abel 1988:196, 322). As the surrealist Georges Sadoul notes, Moussinac's column started a trend: "nearly every published paper, from

the major reviews to the dailies and weeklies, made way beside
its section of drama criticism for a section devoted to film.
Henceforward, the cinema became a subject of dinner-table
conversation like the novel or the play, and there emerged a
group among the intellectual *élite* for whom it was a major
preoccupation" (Sadoul 1972:34). Indeed, 1929, the year
Tambour started publication, was the year that cinema caught
up to and surpassed theater in returns in postwar France
(Crisp 1993:8).

Like the French journals, *Tambour* kept up with cinema. It
featured articles on movie personalities who were important to
the surrealists, such as Charlie Chaplin, and its "Notes" section regularly reviewed film journals like *Experimental Cinema, La revue du cinéma,* and expatriate English language
film magazines like *Close-Up.* (The latter was begun by Bry-
her and Kenneth MacPherson and distributed at Shakespeare
and Company; Fitch claims that it was the first English-
language magazine entirely devoted to film [1983:266].) *Tambour* brought commentary on American, and French, cinema
to French audiences: Francis Ambrière wrote columns on films
by King Vidor, Charlie Chaplin, and others, and Salemson himself discussed L'Herbier's *Forfaiture* and pioneering French
filmmakers like Georges Méliès, whom Salemson pronounced
"inventeur du spectacle cinéma-fantastique" (1930a:73) and

whose *Voyage à la Lune* (1902) could rival surrealist films of later decades.[23]

Tambour brought film discussion into modernism just as surrealist film was coming to fruition. Though surrealists had been interested in the cinema since around 1920, and Breton and Jacques Vaché had spent much of their free time during military service going from one movie house to another, it wasn't until the mid-twenties that they began to explore the possibilities of the medium more systematically.[24] The surrealists were fascinated by the potential of horror movies like Wiene's *Caligari* and Murnau's *Nosferatu,* as well as Hollywood movies like *King Kong,* in addition to more experimental work. They wrote film reviews, and, as Robin Walz notes, "In their own cinematic bids, Antonin Artaud, Blaise Cendrars, Robert Desnos, and Philippe Soupault wrote surrealist film scenarios, and a limited number of surrealist films were made by Man Ray, Salvador Dalí, and Luis Buñuel" (Walz 2000:51).

Several of these figures, including Cendrars, Cocteau, and Soupault, contributed to *Tambour,* and Cocteau and Cendrars were subscribers to the magazine.[25] Though Cocteau was in a rivalry with the surrealists and saw himself, as Frederick Brown puts it, "as the underdog in a political contest [with the surrealists] for the suffrage of Youth" (1968:293), his early film style owed some debt to surrealist film. Indeed, on

July 10, 1929, Cocteau saw a private screening of what some
call the first surrealist film: Luis Buñuel and Salvador Dalí's
Un chien andalou. Cocteau's first film, *Le sang d'un poète*
(1930), borrowed heavily from Buñuel's film (Brown 1968:
293). Michel Arnaud, who directed Cocteau's *Le sang d'un
poète,* contributed a long verse drama, "Onan," to *Tambour* 6,
and a story to *Tambour* 2—an issue in which a drawing by
Cocteau also appeared.

Discussions of film provide an important context for understanding conflicts over the status of modernism at the end of
the twenties. Eastman used film metaphors to complain that
modernism was becoming too visual—he complained that audiences must "*see* [Cummings's] poetry because it is composed so largely of punctuation that it cannot be heard. In fact
we shall soon have to exhibit Cummings in a projection-room"
(Eastman 1935:59). But *Tambour* and its contributors were
more sanguine about the possibilities for film to create an important modernist medium. Surrealists saw the power of the
visual register of film to rearrange and reorder reality, to have
the "power to disorient [son pouvoir de dépaysement]," as
Breton put it, and Breton and Desnos spoke of it in terms of
"mystery," "miracle," and "dream" (Matthews 1971:2, 3).

The "Revolution of the Word" was a manifesto about words
in themselves, not film or even visual images. *Tambour,* then,
tacitly challenged the "Revolution of the Word" by bringing

film—both experimental and mass-market—into an implicit conversation with the modernist literary texts in which the journal had invested much of its cultural capital, just as silent film was fading away and word and image could be blended even more accessibly in the "talkies."[26]

SPECIAL ISSUES

In its brief life, *Tambour* published two memorable special issues. The fifth issue included a widely noticed survey about the status of Anatole France five years after his death. Again, Salemson borrowed a common feature of French periodicals—the "survey"—but *Tambour*'s survey collected the opinions of an uncommonly wide range of French, American, and British writers. And Salemson used the subject of the survey to continue his project of asking modernism to question itself. Five years earlier, upon the death of Anatole France in 1924, the surrealists, who had just begun publishing *La révolution surréaliste* and consolidating their identity, had published a pamphlet entitled *Un cadavre* that brazenly denigrated Antole France. As Maurice Nadeau puts it, "Here the surrealists were dealing with a man of recognized glory, who had died amid national mourning. To the Right, he represented *le style français* wrought to perfection. . . . On the other hand, the Left did not want it forgotten that Anatole France had

marched beside Jaurès and that he had almost become a so-
cialist. To attack the late tenant of the Villa Saïd, especially on
the occasion of his death, was to commit iconoclasm, pure and
simple" (1966:95).

In reconsidering Anatole France's career five years later,
Harold J. Salemson was making a bold gesture almost exactly
opposite to that made by the surrealists: he asked for (but did
not always get) serious assessments without encouraging either negative or positive responses. Just as "Essential: 1930"
and "Direction" called for balance in modernist literature,
challenging what had come to seem its overemphasis on form,
Salemson asked for a legitimate range of opinion about the famous writer and kept *Tambour* from seeming to represent any
single movement, in the way that the surrealist publications
had. The responses included, at one extreme, the vehemently
dismissive attitude that the surrealists had espoused. Blaise
Cendrars wrote, simply, "Ennui, ennui, ennui, ennui, ennui,
ennui, ennui, ennui," and Jean Catel of the *Mercure de France*
asked "Pourquoi *lirions*-nous France, dites, alors que nous
avons Proust, Gide, Valéry, Cocteau, Claudel? Pas le temps
[Why would we *read* France, pray tell, when we have Proust,
Gide, Valéry, Cocteau, Claudel? We don't have the time]."
Likewise, William Carlos Williams admitted to never even
having read France, but added that what he took to be
France's writing style was "directly repellant." And the Bel-

gian poet Georges Linze bluntly argued that France was completely out of date: "Anatole France s'évalue en fonction même
de ce moyen-âge qu'est pour nous l'avant-guerre. Son élite
aveugle n'eut aucun sens, ni celui du passé, ni celui de l'avenir.
Au milieu de la révolution des goûts, des mœurs, de la surprenante irruption des machines, du génie des constructeurs
et des ouvriers, son incroyable statisme vaut-il un haussement
d'épaules? [Anatole France is judged in relation to the "medieval period" that the prewar years represent for us. His
blind elite lacked any sense of either the past or the future. His
unbelievable stasis in the midst of the revolution in taste and
manners, the surprising explosion of new machinery, the genius of builders and laborers, hardly merits a shrug?]"

But there were also unmitigatedly positive responses:
Dreiser wrote that *Thaïs* is "one of the great art works of
the world," and to the question "How do you rate Anatole
France?" responded, "How do I rate Sophocles? How do I rate
Villon? How do I rate George Moore or Dostoievsky?—
As great and enduring writers and personages." Zona Gale
felt that France's work was "still in the current vein," and
that "the cleverness, the incisive quality of his comment, will
always have a value as reflecting the mind of many of his
time." But most of the responses, and indeed the fine critical
essays by, among others, Edmund Wilson and Salemson himself, were intelligently mixed. Wilson, who wrote "I consider

Anatole France one of the great modern French writers," also admitted that his work "has gone completely out of fashion." And some, like Gide, complained that his overblown reputation harmed an honest assessment of his work; as Gide put it, "J'aimerais France avec plus d'abandon si certains imprudents n'en voulaient faire un écrivain considérable [I would appreciate France more readily if certain rash individuals didn't try to make him into a major author]." André Salmon, who had been involved with dada circles, wrote that he had praised France publicly on his eightieth birthday, but that "France a représenté le goût, vertue de lecteur et non de créateur. Rien de ce qu'a fait valoir France n'eût été ignoré sans France qui l'emprunte aux classiques [France represented taste, a virtue found in a reader rather than a creator. None of the qualities that make us value France would have been overlooked had he not existed, as he borrowed them from the classics]." And André Maurois wrote that France was a great writer whose glory would have its ups and downs, but that "L'œuvre d'Anatole France est d'ailleurs inégale [Anatole France's work is, however, uneven]." Salemson had deliberately chosen a provocative, contentious topic; however, in what was becoming representative of the "flavor" of *Tambour,* he presented not only an unusual range of responses to the question of France's reputation and value, but also an impressively diverse and famous set of respondents.

The other special issue was the seventh; it featured a large selection of writing by contemporary Italian poets, translated into French. This issue was the one that began with Salemson's "Essential: 1930" manifesto, and he clearly wished it to be a widely noticed issue. The "Poèmes italiens" section featured work by a number of poets, some of whom had long been connected to the Italian avant-garde. Massimo Bontempelli, who had just completed his editorship of the Italian little magazine *900* (which he had edited from 1926 to 1929), had connections to futurism and surrealism and pioneered a form of magical realism (see Urgnani 1991); Corrado Govoni had allied himself with the futurists before the war, publishing *Poesie elettriche* (Electric poems) in 1911 and *Rarefazioni e parole in libertà* (Rarefaction and words in liberty) in 1915 and collaborating on the futurist-oriented magazines *Poesia, La voce,* and *Lacerba* (Bondanella and Bondanella 1996:271–72). And Eugenio Montale, who went on to win the Nobel Prize in literature in 1975, contributed "Delta" from his first collection, *Ossi di seppia (Cuttlefish Bones* [1925], a group of poems set in the wild Ligurian coast). Some critics see this poem as marking a turning point toward Montale's later tone, style, and ethos (Cambon 1982:30; Singh 1973:74–75). The poems appeared in translation, but into French—not into English, as the other American expatriate magazines would have done. Salemson wished to bring some of the most compelling con-

temporary Italian poetry to French audiences, and he relied
upon the translations of Eugène Bestaux and Lionello Fiumi
(an Italian living in Paris whose poems also appeared in the selections).[27]

THE ECONOMICS AND MARKETING OF *TRANSITION*

As much as *Tambour,* the *Transatlantic Review,* and many of
the French little magazines aspired to a close grappling with a
broad range of cultural phenomena, and to a public role for the
arts in their respective cultures, the hopes that many prewar
little magazines had shared were somewhat tempered by the
understanding generated by many years of postwar little magazine publication of the economic realities of little magazines.
Lawrence Rainey has recently argued that "modernism's
larger productive economy" had become fairly set by the
1920s: "In particular, a modernist work was typically published in three forms: first in a little review or journal; second,
in a limited edition of recently collected poems (or as an individual volume if the work was large enough); and third, in a
more frankly commercial or public edition issued by a mainstream publisher and addressed to a wider audience. Especially important were the two forms of book publication, the
limited and the public editions" (1998:99). Rainey chronicles
Eliot's publication strategy for *The Waste Land* and the mar-

ket created for limited collector's editions of *Ulysses* by
Joyce's Parisian publisher, Sylvia Beach's Shakespeare and
Company. While there were mass-market magazine venues for
modernism by the 1920s—Frank Crowninshield's *Vanity
Fair* had a circulation of 96,500 and earned $500,000 of ad-
vertising revenue in 1922 (Rainey 1998:98; also see Murphy
1996)—the small-scale little magazine was still, at the end of
the 1920s (as today), a persistent and important venue of
publication. And we would like to add one more dimension to
the tripartite structure of modernist publication that Rainey
elucidates: the little magazines themselves were able both to
imitate aspects of mass-market journals (the French *revues*)
and to adopt some of the tactics of scarcity and collectibility
that Rainey describes in the world of book publication.

It took a Frenchwoman, Adrienne Monnier, who had already published many deluxe editions of books, to explain to
Sylvia Beach the value of a limited or private edition of James
Joyce's *Ulysses* (Rainey 1998:50)—a strategy that, as Rainey
puts it, "transform[ed] the reader into a collector, an investor,
or even a speculator" (1998:53). But the French little magazines already understood the money that could be generated
from a collector's market. Monnier's own *Navire d'argent,* a
roughly one-hundred-page monthly that normally sold for 5
francs an issue or 50 francs a year domestically, also offered
an *édition de luxe* for 100 francs per year domestically (foreign

prices for all the magazines were up to 20 percent higher). In addition to selling advertising, Monnier used the deluxe edition to raise money to keep the magazine afloat. Aragon, Breton, and Soupault's illustrated twenty-four-page monthly *Littérature* did not carry advertising, but the annual price of 15 francs for the *édition ordinaire* was quadrupled to 60 francs for the *édition de luxe*. Another little magazine, *Bifur,* almost tripled its annual subscription fee of 125 francs to 350 francs for its *édition de luxe*.

Salemson seems to have taken a cue from these efforts to market and pander to collectibility by numbering a limited quantity of each issue. On the masthead of the first issue of the magazine, prominently displayed under the address of the *Tambour* offices, Salemson noted: "Of this issue, 200 copies are numbered. *De ce numéro, 200 exemplaires ont été numérotés.*" The quantity of numbered issues remained at 200 through the first four issues; it was expanded to 250 for the last four issues. Clearly such a prominent proclamation in each issue would be meaningless but for the assumption of a collector's market for the magazine. (As Salemson himself noted in 1981, the person who ran the Gotham Book Mart in New York City, which sold *Tambour* when it was in print, contacted Salemson about fair prices for complete runs of *Tambour* [Ross 1984:447].)

THE RECEPTION OF *TAMBOUR*

So how successful was *Tambour,* and who read it? In terms of
the already well-developed genre of the little magazine, *Tambour* was quite a success. It cost very little to publish—contributors were not paid, as was often the case with little magazines, and production costs were only eighty to one hundred
dollars per issue (Ross 1980:350)—and it had a fairly respectable circulation and list of subscribers. The article on
Salemson in the *Dictionary of Literary Biography* notes that
"*Tambour* had a circulation of about fifteen hundred copies, of
which some eight hundred went to subscribers; copies were
also on sale at Sylvia Beach's Shakespeare and Company in
Paris and at Brentano's and the Gotham Book Mart in New
York" (Ross 1980:350). If these figures are correct (and we
suspect that they came from Salemson himself, who was still
alive at the time the article was written), then in terms of circulation, *Tambour* was doing relatively well. Its circulation
was smaller than the roughly five thousand copies per issue of
Ford's *Transatlantic Review* (Poli 1967:94), but Ford's magazine was funded by John Quinn and other patrons, it paid
contributors, and, like most little magazines, it gave away or
was unable to sell many copies. But *Tambour*'s circulation was
not much smaller than that of the *Little Review,* which had

around two thousand subscribers, or *transition*'s, about which
McMillan claims, "No more than 4,000 copies of any issue
were ever printed and paid subscriptions never exceeded
1,000. Thus at no time did the magazine make money; there
was often a deficit which the Jolases had to make up themselves with occasional help from friends" (1975:23). *Tambour*'s circulation and subscription base were bigger than
those of other, more famous, little magazines like the *Egoist*
(when the *Freewoman* was reborn as *The New Freewoman* in
1913, it started with a print run of two thousand but immediately dropped to fifteen hundred, and when it became the *Egoist* in 1914, the print run gradually fell to four hundred copies
per issue with fewer than one hundred subscribers [see Morrisson 2001: chap. 3]).

Miraculously, Salemson's index card file of subscribers to
Tambour survives (most little magazines did not keep good
records, and the records were usually destroyed after they
ceased publication), though it may well be only a partial subscription list. It has cards ranging across the entire alphabet,
though it contains many more subscription cards from the
first half of the alphabet than the second, suggesting the possibility that some cards may be missing. The cards contain
records of 563 subscriptions, some of them for institutions—
mostly periodicals and publishers, along with a few large city
libraries (the American Library and the Bibliothèque na-

tionale de France in Paris, and, in the United States, the Boston, Chicago, and Cleveland Public Libraries). But most of the cards are for individual subscribers.[28]

The subscription list shows the interest *Tambour* must have aroused in several important figures of the day. French subscribers included Alain, Francis Ambrière, Michel Arnaud, Henri Barbusse, Julien Benda, Henri Bergson, Alfred Bloch, Jean Cassou, Jean Catel, Blaise Cendrars, Jean Cocteau, Leon Deffoux, the comte de Fontnouvelle (French consul to the United States), André Gide, Jean Giraudoux, Jacques Heller, Max Jacob, Henry de Montherlant, and Pierre Mac-Orlan. Among the Italians were Massimo Bontempelli, Lionello Fiumi, and Corrado Govoni, and British (and Irish) subscribers included Stuart Gilbert, James Joyce, and A. S. J. Tessimond. The American subscribers were as impressive a group as the French, and included Sherwood Anderson, Sylvia Beach, William Rose Benét, Paul Bowles, Witter Bynner, V. F. Calverton, Willa Cather, Malcolm Cowley, Frank Crowninshield, Countee Cullen, Floyd Dell, Max Eastman, T. S. Eliot, John Dos Passos, Theodore Dreiser, James T. Farrell, Charles Henri Ford, Waldo Frank, Zona Gale, George Gershwin, Michael Gold, Llewellyn Jones, Matthew Josephson, Ludwig Lewisohn, H. L. Mencken, G. W. Pabst, Edouard Roditi, Upton Sinclair, and King Vidor. These lists suggest that there was interest among writers of several different styles and attitudes, among them philosophers, composers, moviemakers, and editors and journalists.

Young writers avidly read the little magazines, and Paul Bowles, while still living in New York before moving to Paris, spoke of *Tambour* in his correspondence with Daniel Burnes ("that little brown French-English review you liked so much"). Bowles's poems appeared in *Tambour* (he was also publishing in *transition, Blues,* and *Morada*), and even when he had finally traveled to Paris, he still associated a writer with his publication in *Tambour*.[29] New Mexico writers praised the magazine: Witter Bynner wrote to Salemson about the first issue, and Norman Macleod, who was editing *Morada,* wrote to Salemson that "TAMBOUR is great: I always look forward to it." Likewise, Jean Cocteau telegraphed to Salemson, "Bien touché par immense travail [deeply touched by your extensive work]" (1930), and René Henriquez, a Belgian subscriber, wrote to Salemson in 1931 (after *Tambour* had suspended publishing): "J'insiste encore pour que vous me teniez en courant de vos projets et espère revoir paraître bientôt votre excellente petite revue [I strongly request that you keep me apprised of your plans and hope that your first-rate little magazine will soon resume publication]."[30] Little magazines edited by very young men, like Salemson's *Tambour* and Charles Henri Ford's *Blues,* began to create a network of publication for a new generation of writers.[31]

But the subscription list also reflects the success of Salemson's attempts to found a truly international magazine. The number of non-American subscribers (245) almost equaled the number of Americans (265). Not surprisingly, the great majority of those non-Americans were French, and of the 176 French subscribers, 138 were living in Paris, the literary capital of the country. But there were also a fair number of British subscribers—15 of the 22 lived in London (2 in Paris—Stuart Gilbert, of course, and Joyce, if one still counts his British passport as conferring British identity). There were also 9 Italian subscribers (most of whom began subscribing with the second issue, before the Italian poetry issue appeared), and 12 Belgian subscribers. There were a handful of subscribers from other western European countries (Holland, Switzerland, Ireland, Spain, and Germany), from Montreal, and from eastern Europe (Prague, Budapest, and Romania), with 4 in Moscow, as well as subscribers from Algeria, Argentina, Puerto Rico, China, Japan, and India.

The magazine's American subscribers were predominantly living in the United States (only 10 of them were living in Paris, surprisingly, though many expatriates may have bought the magazine at Shakespeare and Company). Most lived in New York City (82) and Chicago (50—largely in Hyde Park, near the University of Chicago), with some in Los Angeles (13). While subscribers were scattered across the country (for instance, in Detroit, Baltimore, Philadelphia, Atlanta, Arizona, St. Paul, Boston, Newark, Santa Fe, and Madison, where some of Salemson's former professors at the University of Wisconsin subscribed), the moviemaking communities of California were well represented (12 in Hollywood, and a few in Beverly Hills, Pasadena, Burbank, Universal City, and Culver City).

These individual subscribers were predominantly male: 322 are identifiably male, while only 109 are identifiably female. Forty subscribers used initials instead of first names—during this period, that probably suggests that they were male, but it is not possible to decide with any certainty. Of the women, 39 were or had been married (listed as "Mrs.") and 23 were listed as "Miss," but 47 gave no such designation. The largely male composition of the subscribers is perhaps in keeping with the primarily male makeup of the contributors to the magazine. *Tambour* was certainly not an antifeminist magazine, but it did not overtly take up women's issues either.[32]

The film industry readership was especially important for the magazine and for Salemson's post-*Tambour* career. Subscribers worked at several film studios in America and abroad—Fox-Film in New York and Hollywood, MGM in New York and Culver City, United Artists in Los Angeles, Warner Brothers, Paramount Pictures, and Garrison Films in New York, and London Films, Garemont-Brit Studios, and British

International Pictures in London. The film journal *Close-Up* also subscribed.

Nonfilm periodicals, or people working at them, subscribed to *Tambour* as well. Avant-garde French little magazines—*Commerce, Bifur,* and *Documents*—and Parisian expatriate publishers like Black Sun Press and Hours Press subscribed, but so did French publishers and more mainstream French periodicals. These included the important *Nouvelle revue française,* as well as *Les cahiers du sud, L'auto, Jazz, La revue européenne,* and the art periodical *L'artvivant,* as well as other magazines, and the Parisian publishers Fayard, Librairie André Dufour, Ferenczi, Fourcade, Flammarion, Bussard, Hachette, Capitole, and the Grande Librairie Universelle. A few Belgian publishers and press agencies also subscribed, including Librairie Brabo and Auxiliaire de la Presse. The midwestern American little magazines *Earth* and the *Midland* and the Harvard magazine that had recently moved to New York, the *Hound and Horn,* subscribed, but so did more popular American magazines—the *Nation,* the *New Yorker, Scribners,* the *Notion,* the *Afro-American,* and the *Forum* (with which the *Century* merged in 1930 to form the *Forum and Century*). Not only did modernist publishers like Covici Friede, the Four Seas Co., and A & C Boni subscribe, but so did the more mainstream American publishers—Simon and Schuster, the Century Company (which published the *Cen-*

tury), Dutton, Doubleday and Page, D. Appleton, Dodd, Mead (which dabbled with occasional publication of modernist authors), Houghton Mifflin, Harper and Brothers, Harcourt Brace, and Henry Holt (B. W. Huebsch, Joyce's American publisher, was a personal subscriber as well).

Both academic periodicals (Duke University's *American Literature,* which had just begun in March 1929) and magazines like the *American Mercury* and *Vanity Fair* (both of which had ambiguous relationships to modernism) subscribed, as did newspapers: the *Baltimore Sun, New York World, New York Sun, Chicago Daily News, Chicago Evening Post, Chicago Tribune,* and the *Hollywood Citizen News.*

The connections of *Tambour* subscribers to such an array of mainstream and nonmainstream periodicals and publishers, and the direct subscriptions from many of them, suggest that *Tambour*'s attempt both to build upon the energies of the modernist experiments of the 1920s and to move beyond modernist formal experiment attracted a fairly diverse audience. And the savvy combination of the American expatriate little magazine and the French *revue* also gave *Tambour* a distinction not enjoyed by any of the other American expatriate magazines in Paris: it was reviewed and followed by the French *revues.* Charles-Henry Hirsch reviewed four of the eight issues of *Tambour* in his column, "Les revues," in the *Mercure*'s "Re-

vue de la quinzaine," sometimes quoting extensively from it.[33]
Tambour reaped the rewards of not publishing only obscure
avant-garde literature. Its special Anatole France issue drew
a long review in the January 15, 1930, issue of *Mercure* (430–
33). Both the *Mercure* (June 1, 1930) and the *Nouvelle revue
française* (June 1930, 933) noted Salemson's "Essential:
1930" manifesto in the May 1930 issue of *Tambour,* and
Hirsch's *Mercure* review mentioned the bilingual publication
of the manifesto and its critique of "modernisme chercheur
de forme" (415). Both the *Mercure* and the *Nouvelle revue
française* generally reviewed only French magazines in their
review sections, and *Tambour* was the only American expatriate little magazine to garner this kind of attention.

So, although *Tambour* only published eight issues, the magazine could hardly be termed a failure. Its success in attract-
ing a wide range of subscribers and in bringing together such
a variety of contributors suggests that modernism by 1929
had begun to move more into the mainstream of American and
French culture and that it could mingle with other styles of
writing without the kind of defensiveness seen in prewar
modernist little magazines. And, though Harold J. Salemson
never edited another literary magazine, the contents of *Tambour* already indicate where Salemson would concentrate his
efforts upon returning to the United States.

POSTSCRIPT: HAROLD J. SALEMSON'S POST-*TAMBOUR* CAREER

In keeping with *Tambour*'s bilingual emphasis, Salemson himself did a great deal of translation after the magazine ceased publication: he translated numerous articles and literary pieces for literary and film magazines, and also translated some twenty books—primarily nonfiction—from French into English during the 1970s and 1980s.[34] But *Tambour*'s engagement with film also gave an early indication of Salemson's post-*Tambour* career after he left France. Though he had published many poems, literary articles, and reviews during the late twenties and early thirties, Salemson turned his attention primarily to film for much of the rest of his life.[35] In 1931 he moved to Hollywood with the intention of becoming creatively involved in the making of films, but the Depression had caused many layoffs of much more experienced personnel, and he was unable to break into the film industry in the way he had hoped. As he put it:

I started being a film critic in Paris in 1928 right after I went back, so I'd written a lot of film criticism in those early days when film criticism was just being born. At that time we really believed that if Hollywood wasn't making artistic and intellectual pictures, pictures of significance, it was because there was nobody in Hollywood who knew how to make them, and if we just went there and lent them our brains they would make them without any problem. So I went to Hollywood just as starry-eyed as most of the people who had gone off to Paris went to the Left Bank. I thought Hollywood offered a real possibility of doing something significant. I discovered very quickly that there were a lot of people just as gifted as I, or more so, who knew a lot about making movies, and the only reason they weren't making serious, important movies was that this wasn't what they were being paid for, they weren't being given a chance to. (Ross 1984:448)

Yet Salemson remained critically and deeply involved with the film industry for many years. During the early 1930s, he worked for the Universal, Warners, MGM, Fox, Columbia, and Goldwyn studios in a number of capacities (as Salemson lists them: "assistant director, technical advisor, French lyricist and recording supervisor, publicity writer and publicity director, as well as sometime actor"), and from 1931 to 1940 he worked as a Hollywood correspondent for the Paris evening newspaper *L'intransigeant* and for its weekly movie magazine *Pour vous.* He became the Hollywood Bureau Manager for *Paris-soir* when it bought out *L'intransigeant.*

In 1940 Salemson and the photographer Karl Schlichter created a West Coast news-and-photo syndicate, Photo-

Reportage, which syndicated material for *Paris-soir* until the
fall of France and for a number of other magazines in America and Britain, and which drew the praise of Orson Welles
and others for its approach to "documentary film script." In
1941, Salemson became the West Coast editor for *Friday* until it ceased publication, and then a Hollywood correspondent
for the *Sydney Sunday Telegraph* in Australia until he enlisted
in the army on December 14, 1941.

After his service during the war, in which he assumed many
propaganda and media duties, Salemson returned to Hollywood and in 1946 became the director of publications for the
Screen Writers' Guild. He transformed its periodical, the
Screen Writer, into an internationally visible magazine. He
also freelanced for many film magazines in America, Britain,
and France during the late 1940s, and, after resigning from
the *Screen Writer* at the end of 1946 over policy differences,
went on in 1948 to join Creative Films, Inc., titling foreign
films in the United States. Salemson stayed involved with the
film and publishing industries for much of the rest of his working life, freelancing, subtitling foreign films, forming his own
company to distribute foreign and art films (he was the president of Film Representations Incorporated in New York),
and, above all, working as a publicity man in the industry
(Ross 1984:449).[36]

Salemson's post-*Tambour* career was also marked by the attacks of demagogues from both the Left and the Right. The trials of Salemson's intellectual life may be seen as representative of those of many independent thinkers in America who tackled difficult issues, but Salemson seems to have experienced the worst of both Left and Right worlds. His own politics were always on the Left, but as the thirties produced bitter rifts within the Left between those loosely characterized as Trotskyites, or sometimes "fellow travelers," and the more doctrinaire Soviet-oriented communists, Salemson found himself attacked as a decadent Trotskyist by the doctrinaire communist journals. Always keeping up with French affairs, Salemson published an article in 1931 entitled "French Letters, Left Face" in the first number of *Left* (a short-lived magazine in which works by V. F. Calverton, Louis Zukofsky, Lola Ridge, and Norman Macleod also appeared). He was immediately attacked by "comrade" M. Helfand in a review of *Left* that appeared in *Literature of the World Revolution*. Helfand "corrected" the "serious mistakes" of the first issue of *Left*—for instance the publication of Calverton in the issue—and he singled out Salemson's article for "pour[ing] filthy slander on the central organ of the French Communist Party—*L'humanité*," for "defend[ing] Trotskyist renegades in France," for supporting "social-fascists" (140-41), and for seeing Calverton as revolutionary (142). In 1932, *International Literature* carried on the attack on Salemson's article in *Left*, largely af-

firming the criticism Helfand had heaped upon it, and noting
that *Left* had invited "Comrade Louis Aragon" to write "an article which will definitely refute Mr. Salemson's and give a true
estimate of revolutionary literature in France" (146). Salemson found himself in the middle of the cultural wars going on
in America that often chose modernist literature and art for
particular scorn or praise. In the next decade, it would be film
rather than literature that would make Salemson the target of
polemic—this time from the politically powerful Right.

Salemson's work in Hollywood got him into trouble with one
of the most paranoid and pathetic witch-hunts of the twentieth century, conducted by the House Un-American Activities
Committee (HUAC). His articles in *Screen Writer* had taken
controversial stands—for instance, critiquing the Production
Code (Hollywood's self-censoring response to religious cru-
sades against violent and sexual content, which dominated the
industry from 1934 through the 1950s) for "call[ing] forth
the most libidinous fantasia" in the audience, rather than preserving good taste (1946:1–7), but ultimately it was another
kind of controversy that dragged Salemson into the limelight.
Much later in his life, Salemson joked, "I think I was the only
person who was blacklisted twice and succeeded in surviving"
(Ross 1984:449), but it must have been a terrible experience.
Salemson was fired from *Screen Writer* after publishing a call
from James M. Cain for the formation of an American Au-

thors' Authority to help enforce contracts and royalties (a deeply communistic enterprise!) and making the mistake of translating an article by Henri Jeanson, president of the French Syndicat des scénaristes, about the fact that the flooding of French markets by American films was hurting French movie production. The *Hollywood Reporter* on August 15, 1946, ran an editorial that began "Just who is this fellow Harold J. Salemson who is trying to take over the American film industry," and then detailed, as Salemson put it, "all of the horrible left-wing things I had done all of my life," and painted him as a dangerous element (Ross 1984:449).

In the middle of this controversy, Salemson had the courage to edit the book *Thought Control in U.S.A.*—a collection of papers from a conference on "thought control" sponsored by the Arts, Sciences and Professions Council of the Progressive Citizens of America (July 9–13, 1947, in Beverly Hills) and published by the Hollywood Arts, Sciences and Professions Council. This conference represented a concerted effort to publicize concerns about what conference chairman Howard Koch called "an alarming trend to control the cultural life of the American people in accordance with reactionary conceptions of our national interest" (2). But, nine years later, "thought control" had become an even more dominant and ugly part of the political landscape, and Salemson was again blacklisted and brought before the HUAC in New York on August 18,

1955, while he served as an executive assistant to the vice-president of Italian Films Export. As a result of his refusal to cooperate with the committee by taking the Fifth Amendment, Salemson lost his job shortly thereafter. Nevertheless, Salemson continued to remain involved with film; he taught film history at Long Island University after his blacklisting.

Salemson lived almost sixty years after the publication of *Tambour* without creating another modernist little magazine. But it seems unlikely that he would have seen as a demotion his move into the film industry, even that part of the film industry that largely remains behind the scenes—the translators, subtitlers, movie journal editors, film critics, publicity workers, and the like. The seeds of that transformation, from poet, fiction writer, and modernist literary magazine editor into film critic and industry worker, were, as we have argued, already sown as far back as 1929 and 1930 in *Tambour*. Yet, the abiding interest in the modernist scene of Paris in the twenties will probably ensure that *Tambour* will remain Salemson's most visible achievement. And it certainly was an achievement of an extraordinary kind for a young American in Paris to have drawn together such a fascinating set of important authors and illustrators. *Tambour* represented a range of possible directions at the end of the twenties that might be phrased as a set of questions: Would modernism come to be seen entirely as formal experiment? Could experimental authors turn to a more socially engaged literature, as the thirties seemed to indicate? Could the culture of the American Southwest rejuvenate European and American writing? Would film ultimately rival the written word later in the century? Could French and American culture and society be brought closer together in a mutually beneficial way? Our historical perspective shows us how significant these questions really were: they identified some of the most crucial issues of the remaining decades of the twentieth century. To have posed these questions in so memorable a fashion early in the century deserves our attention as we begin the twenty-first century.

NOTES

The authors wish to thank our research assistants, Julianne Guillard and Dana Anderson, for their hard work, the Liberal Arts Research and Graduate Studies Office of the Pennsylvania State University for financial support for this facsimile edition of *Tambour;* and the Anonymous Fund at the University of Wisconsin–Madison. We also wish to thank Louise E. Robbins and Scott Lenz for their tireless and careful editing of this introduction. Above all, we thank Harold J. Salemson's son, Steve Salemson, for his tireless championing of this project, his help with information about his father's life and writings, his fine translations of the French texts we have quoted, and his abundant good cheer. Thanks, too, to Harold J. Salemson's grandson Daniel Salemson for his help with the bibliography of his grandfather's writings.

A number of individuals and organizations have graciously allowed us to quote from unpublished materials. Quotations from unpublished letters and materials of Harold J. Salemson appear by permission of Steve Salemson. The

unpublished letter of H. L. Mencken is used by permission of the Enoch Pratt
Free Library, in accordance with the terms of the will of H. L. Mencken. The
unpublished letter of Waldo Frank is quoted by permission of Jonathan Frank.
The unpublished letters of Paul Bowles are used by permission of Joseph A.
McPhillips III, and the estate of Paul Bowles. The unpublished letter of Harriet Monroe is quoted by permission of her estate, courtesy of Ann Monroe. The
unpublished letter of Witter Bynner is used by permission of the Witter Bynner
Foundation. A good-faith effort has been made to locate the copyright holders
for all materials used in this introduction, and the authors would appreciate
hearing from anyone who has been overlooked.

1. Soupault's "Heures creuses" has not appeared since its magazine publication in 1929. Cendrars's "Petit poème à mettre en musique" was republished
under various titles, including "Klaxon," one of his "Dictés par téléphone," but
the *Tambour* form of the poem is a textual variation that does not seem to appear anywhere else. Our thanks to Jay Bochner for contributing so much to our
bibliographic search for the origins of this poem and for his discussions of
French contexts.

2. The following biographical information is derived from Jean W. Ross's two
excellent brief sketches of Salemson's life (1980, 1984) and from helpful conversations with Harold J. Salemson's son, Steve Salemson.

3. Of the six hundred copies of the first issue of the *Mercure de France,* dated
January 1, 1890, five hundred were given away as review copies—there were
only eleven subscribers (Forestier 1992:4). Several essays describe the founding and early years of the journal: de Gourmont (1912) and Aldington (1916)
are good period accounts; see also the six essays on the *Mercure* in the 1890s in
the January–February 1992 issue of *Revue d'histoire littéraire de la France.* In
naming their magazine the *Mercure de France,* the editors were resurrecting a
review that had been published from the seventeenth century into the nine-
teenth and had been a major organ of French opinion.

4. A Paris letter was also a feature of magazines like *Dial* and *Vanity Fair.*

Marcel Le Son took over the *Transatlantic Review*'s letter from Soupault. In addition to Hemingway, Jeanne Foster and Harold Stearns also wrote the American letter.

5. Larbaud's homage, "Paris de France," with which the first issue opened, gave the review its title by proclaiming Paris itself a "silver ship."

6. *Documents* included articles by authorities on Hittite, Sumerian, early Cycladic, and other finds, and it brought contemporary ethnography into the mix as well. The magazine even published articles on contemporary popular cultural phenomena that, from a distance, could be seen as key elements of an ethnography of France, such as Robert Desnos's article on the antihero Fantômas. Robin Walz argues that Desnos and other avant-gardists (including Apollinaire, Aragon, Breton, Colette, Cendrars, Cocteau, Gris, Jacob, Magritte, Malraux, and Soupault) saw Fantômas as "a metaphor for a surreal epoch." He continues: "*Fantômas* was not an image created by the surrealists, but rather a dark spectacle viewed by them, part of an emergent modern mythology in the early decades of the twentieth century" (44).

7. See Walz 2000:114–43 for a fascinating discussion of the significance of *fait-divers* for surrealism.

8. In 1981, Salemson explained: "I was not an 'expatriate' in the sense of most of those on the Left Bank in the late twenties, but rather a bilingual writer who had been raised in both French and American cultures" (Ross 1984:447).

9. Richard Thoma's "Vie et oeuvre de Jean Cocteau" appeared in *Tambour* around the same time that Cocteau was the subject of John Charpentier's "Figures: Jean Cocteau" in the *Mercure de France*.

10. For an interesting commentary on the connection between regionalism and modernism, see Macleod's contribution to "Regionalism: A Symposium" in the 1931 *Sewanee Review*.

11. For a detailed accounting of Farrell's work before 1931, when he went to France and eventually secured the publication of *Young Lonigan,* see Branch (1998: chap. 1) and Kathleen Farrell (2000). According to Branch, Farrell was blanketing the little magazines with submissions in 1929–30, so his submission

to *Tambour* may have been unsolicited. But Branch also notes Farrell's connection with Sam Putnam, the editor and former Chicagoan who co-authored the "Direction" manifesto with Salemson. Farrell's emphasis on content over formal experiment appealed to Putnam, so it may have been Putnam who guided Farrell's sketches into *Tambour*.

12. "Poem," in the fourth issue of *Tambour*, and "Hymn," in the sixth issue, have not been published in any of Bowles's collections of poetry. Two others, "Dream" and "Slow Song," which were published together in the eighth issue under the joint title "Moonward," have been published in his books, but "Dream" has been renamed "Prelude and Dance," and the two poems were never again published consecutively and have lost their original joint title.

13. Farrell never reprinted "In the Park," though "My Friend the Doctor" appeared as "The Doctor" in Farrell's *Fellow Countrymen: Collected Stories* (1937).

14. The title, *Morada*, recalls the chapels of lay penitents in the Southwest, known for their flagellating rites during Holy Week. *Morada* appeared on the heels of *Tambour*; the first issue came out in autumn of 1929, whereas *Tambour*'s first issue appeared in February 1929. Salemson is listed in the first issue as "editor of *Tambour*," and *Morada* carried an ad for *Tambour* as well.

15. Between the first issues of *Morada* and the final one, Macleod had been to Paris himself and also had served as American editor of *Front*, a short-lived magazine published in The Hague that included works in English, French, and German.

16. Macleod was simultaneously publishing poetry in *transition*'s summer 1930 issue: "Twelve Knives," "Revenge of the Three Brothers," and "Cacked."

17. For an examination of Joyce's role in *Tambour* and in Parisian modernism, see Morrisson (forthcoming).

18. We'd like to emphasize that Salemson was not antimodernist (as Eastman had become by this time), but rather wished to reform modernism from within. Charles Henri Ford, the editor of *Blues*, praised *Tambour* in a letter to Gertrude Ford, sending her a copy of an issue containing two of his poems. He

informed her that Salemson had contributed a Paris letter that would appear in the next issue of *Blues* and had a poem in *Blues*'s "expatriate number" (Letter, Charles Henri Ford to Gertrude Ford, October 19, 1929, Charles Henri Ford Collection, Harry Ransom Humanities Research Center, University of Texas at Austin [hereafter, HRHRC]).

19. Farrell to Salemson, March 26, 1931, in possession of Steve Salemson; Salemson to Dreiser, December 16, 1930 (Dreiser Papers, University of Pennsylvania).

20. Frank to Salemson, March 5, 1931, in possession of Steve Salemson.

21. Mencken to Salemson, December 23, [1930], in possession of Steve Salemson.

22. Monroe to Salemson, February 16, 1931, in possession of Steve Salemson.

23. Harold J. Salemson was himself an important link between Parisian audiences and Hollywood film; see postscript to this essay.

24. See Matthews's account of surrealist interest in film. Robin Walz notes that surrealists "also engaged in a variety of viewing practices, . . . roaming indiscriminately from screen to screen and interrupting audiences by eating picnic lunches in movie houses" (2000:51).

25. Other surrealists may have subscribed, too; the surviving subscription file may not be complete.

26. In a move presaging Aldous Huxley's "feelies" in *Brave New World* (1932), Stuart Gilbert in a *Tambour* article even predicted that "just as the 'movies' have been ousted by the more lifelike 'talkies,'" "very soon, I suppose, we shall go still one better and crowd to eye, ear and nose the '*smellies*'" (1929:46).

27. Lionello Fiumi got Salemson into trouble with the United States Bureau of Customs in 1931 when Fiumi mailed Salemson a copy of his volume *Survivances*. The book was confiscated—the Treasury Department officials could not read the French but felt that the illustrations were obscene—and was about to be destroyed when Salemson talked the officials into sending it back to Fi-

umi (Salemson to Louis M. Hall, Collector of Custom, U.S. Treasury Dept.,
St. Louis, Mo., April 13, 1931, and copy of letter from Frank Dow, Acting
Commissioner of Customs, to the Collector of Custom, St. Louis, April 22,
1931; letters in possession of Steve Salemson).

28. The cards are in the possession of Steve Salemson.

29. Paul Bowles to Daniel Burnes, n.d. [late 1920]. Bowles wrote to Burnes
from Berlin, but speaking of Paris, "Yesterday afternoon I had tea with Ezra
Pound and Michel Arnaud, who directed Cocteau's cinema: La Vie d'un Poète.
Arnaud also writes, and did the long poem 'Onan' for Tambour last year." Both
letters are in the Paul Bowles Collection, HRHRC.

30. Bynner to Salemson, April 9, [1929]; Macleod to Salemson, March 18,
1930; Henriquez to Salemson, March 24, 1931. These letters, and the telegram
from Cocteau, are in the possession of Steve Salemson.

31. Bowles corresponded with Ford and read *Blues,* and, just as Salemson
published Ford in *Tambour,* Ford included Salemson among the important expatriate writers in his magazine. In a letter to Gertrude Stein, May 19, 1929,
he writes: "I think of course that this Expatriate Number will be the crowning
issue, continuing as it does your own work as well as contributions by Kay
Boyle, H. D., Harold J. Salemson, Lawrence Vail, Eugene Jolas and others."
Charles Henri Ford Collection, HRHRC. And, marking the interconnection of
these magazines, Ford wrote to Gertrude Ford (October 19, 1929, on *Blues* letterhead), "I am sending you a copy of the last number of TAMBOUR, an interesting magazine published in Paris, containing two of my poems. Also a poem
by Kathleen and a couple by Parker Tyler, who is now associate editor of BLUES
along with K.T.Y. I think you will enjoy reading all the poems as well as the
prose (what is not in French!) . . . I have marked in it the comment on BLUES.
Salemson, the editor, contributed a Paris Letter to my next number—he also
had a poem in BLUES' Expatriate Number" (Charles Henri Ford Collection,
HRHRC).

32. For the sake of comparison, the *Freewoman* (1911–1912), a radical paper with strong feminist support that grappled with modernism in prewar Lon-

don, had around three hundred subscribers, and female subscribers outnumbered male subscribers by almost four to one (unmarried women living in London were the single largest group of subscribers) (Morrisson 2001:91). The later, more stridently modernist version of the magazine, the *Egoist,* had a much higher portion of men in its readership, although for the duration of the *Egoist*'s life, until its demise in 1919, women subscribers still held a slight majority. So although that little magazine had the feminist draw of Dora Marsden at the editorial helm, it still shows that *Tambour*'s predominantly male subscription base was not necessarily representative of little magazine subscribers (Morrisson 2001:108).

33. Hirsch mentioned issues of *Tambour* in the following issues of *Mercure de France:* April 1, 1929 (208), January 15, 1930 (430–33), March 15, 1930 (687), June 1, 1930 (415), and August 1, 1930 (703).

34. Daniel Salemson's invaluable unpublished bibliography of Harold J. Salemson's works lists the following translations done by Salemson in later life: Jacques Graven, *Non-Human Thought: The Mysteries of the Animal Psyche* (New York: Stein and Day, 1967); Jules Romains, *Open Letter against a Vast Conspiracy* (New York: James H. Heineman, 1968); Salvador Dalí, *Open Letter to Salvador Dalí* (New York: James H. Heineman, 1968); Henri Fesquet, *Has Rome Converted?* (New York: James H. Heineman, 1968); Roger Bourgeon, *In Darkness* (New York: William Morrow, 1969); Michel Bataille, *The Christmas Tree* (New York: William Morrow, 1969); Henri Guillemin, *Joan, Maid of Orleans* (New York: Saturday Review Press, 1973); Jacques Bergier, *Secret Armies: The Growth of Corporate and Industrial Espionage* (New York: Bobbs-Merrill, 1975); Serge Groussard, *The Blood of Israel: The Massacre of the Israeli Athletes, the Olympics, 1972* (New York: William Morrow, 1975); André Parinaud, *The Unspeakable Confessions of Salvador Dali* (New York: William Morrow, 1976); Pierre Cabanne, *Pablo Picasso: His Life and Times* (New York: William Morrow, 1977); Cheikh Anta Diop, *Black Africa* (Westport, Conn.: Lawrence Hill, 1978); Elula Perrin, *Women Prefer Women* (New York: William Morrow, 1979); Elula Perrin, *So Long As There Are Women* (New York: William

Morrow, 1980); Robert Beauvais, *The Half Jew* (New York: Taplinger, 1980);
Pierre Rey, *Out* (New York: Bantam Books, 1980); Georges Simenon, *Intimate
Memoirs: Including Marie-Jo's Book* (San Diego: Harcourt Brace Jovanovich,
1984); Cheikh Anta Diop, *Precolonial Black Africa* (Westport, Conn.: Lawrence
Hill, 1987); and Pierre Assouline, *Gaston Gallimard: A Half-Century of French
Publishing* (San Diego: Harcourt, Brace, Jovanovich, 1988).

35. Much of the following information about Salemson's connections with the
film industry and film journalism comes from his résumé (in the possession of
Steve Salemson), presumably assembled in 1949, which he titled "Professional
Background."

36. The film business must have had its ups and downs for Salemson; he
wrote on Film Representations Incorporated letterhead to Michael Bessie at
Harper & Brothers on July 16, 1958, "I have quite definitely decided I would
like to get out of the motion picture business and into general editorial or public
relations work," and solicited advice from Bessie about possible contacts
(Salemson to Bessie, July 16, 1958, Harpers Collection, HRHRC).

WORKS CITED

Abel, Richard. 1988. *French Film Theory and Criticism: A History/Anthology,
    1907–1939.* Vol. 1, *1907–1929.* Princeton, N.J.: Princeton University Press.
Aldington, Richard. 1916. "Remy de Gourmont." *The Drama* 6 (May): 167–83.
Anon. 1932. "Book Review: *Left* no. 2." *International Literature:* n.p.
Bondanella, Peter, and Julia Conaway Bondanella. 1996. "Govoni, Corrado."
    In *Dictionary of Italian Literature.* Revised, expanded edition, edited by Pe-
    ter Bondanella and Julia Conaway Bondanella, 271–72. Westport, Conn.:
    Greenwood.
Bornstein, George. 1991. "Introduction: Why Editing Matters." In *Represent-
    ing Modernist Texts: Editing as Interpretation,* edited by George Bornstein,
    1–16. Ann Arbor: University of Michigan Press.

Branch, Edgar M. 1998. *A Paris Year: Dorothy and James T. Farrell, 1931–1932*. Athens: Ohio University Press.

Brown, Frederick. 1968. *An Impersonation of Angels: A Biography of Jean Cocteau*. New York: Viking.

Cambon, Glauco. 1982. *Eugenio Montale's Poetry: A Dream in Reason's Presence*. Princeton, N. J.: Princeton University Press.

Crisp, Colin. 1993. *The Classic French Cinema, 1930–1960*. Bloomington: Indiana University Press.

Dalmas, Victor. 1980. "Norman Macleod." In *Dictionary of Literary Biography*. Vol. 4, *American Writers in Paris, 1920–1939*, edited by Karen Lane Rood, 266–69. Detroit: Gale.

Décaudin, Michel. 1992. "Le 'Mercure de France': Filiations et Orientations." *Revue d'histoire littéraire de la France* 92 (January–February): 7–15.

de Gourmont, Rémy. 1912. "Le Mercure de France." *Promenades Littéraires*. 4th series, 81–92. Paris: Mercure de France.

Eastman, Max. 1935. "The Cult of Unintelligibility." In *The Literary Mind: Its Place in an Age of Science*, 57–78. New York: Scribner.

Farrell, Kathleen. 2000. *Literary Integrity and Political Action: The Public Argument of James T. Farrell*. Boulder: Westview.

Fitch, Noel Riley. 1983. *Sylvia Beach and the Lost Generation: A History of Literary Paris in the Twenties and Thirties*. New York: Norton.

Ford, Ford Madox. 1924. "Communications." *Transatlantic Review* 1, no. 1 (January): 93–94.

Forestier, Louis. 1992. "Présentation." *Revue d'histoire littéraire de la France* 92 (January–February): 1.

Gilbert, Stuart. 1929. "Marching On." *Tambour* 5 (November): 45–47.

Gilbert, Stuart. 1990. "Selections from the Paris Diary of Stuart Gilbert, 1929–1934." *Joyce Studies Annual*. Vol. 1, edited by Thomas F. Staley and Randolph Lewis, 3–25. Austin: University of Texas Press.

Helford, M. 1931. "Book Review: *Left* no. 2." *Literature of the World Revolution* no. 6: 139–43.

Hoffman, Frederick J., Charles Allen, and Carolyn F. Ulrich. *The Little Magazine: A History and a Bibliography.* Princeton: Princeton University Press,
1947.

Kraft, James. 1995. *Who Is Witter Bynner?* Albuquerque: University of New
Mexico Press.

Lyon, Janet. 1999. *Manifestoes: Provocations of the Modern.* Ithaca, N. Y.: Cor-
nell University Press.

Matthews, J. H. 1971. *Surrealism and Film.* Ann Arbor: University of Michigan Press.

McMillan, Dougald. 1975. *"Transition": The History of a Literary Era, 1927–
1938.* New York: George Braziller.

Monaco, Paul. 1976. *Cinema and Society: France and Germany during the
Twenties.* New York: Elsevier.

Monk, Craig. 1999. "Eugene Jolas and the Translation Policies of *Transition.*"
Mosaic 32, no. 4 (December): 17–34.

Monnier, Adrienne. *The Very Rich Hours of Adrienne Monnier.* Trans. with an
introduction and commentaries by Richard McDougall. New York: Scribners, 1976.

Morrisson, Mark. 2001. *The Public Face of Modernism: Little Magazines, Audiences, and Reception, 1905–1920.* Madison: University of Wisconsin Press.

Morrisson, Mark. Forthcoming. *"Tambour,* the 'Revolution of the Word,' and
the Parisian Reception of *Finnegans Wake.*" In *Joyce in the City,* ed. Michael
Begnal. Syracuse: Syracuse University Press.

Murphy, Michael. 1996. "'One Hundred Per Cent Bohemia': Pop Decadence
and the Aestheticization of Commodity in the Rise of the Slicks." In *Market-
ing Modernisms: Self-Promotion, Canonization, and Rereading,* edited by
Kevin J. H. Dettmar and Stephen Watt, 61–89. Ann Arbor: University of
Michigan Press.

Nadeau, Maurice. 1966. *The History of Surrealism.* Translated by Richard
Howard. New York: Macmillan.

Poli, Bernard J. 1967. *Ford Madox Ford and the "Transatlantic Review."* Syracuse, N. Y.: Syracuse University Press.

Putnam, Samuel. 1947. *Paris Was Our Mistress: Memoirs of a Lost and Found Generation.* New York: Viking.

Rabaté, Jean-Michel. 1990. "Joyce the Parisian." In *The Cambridge Companion to James Joyce,* edited by Derek Attridge, 83–102. New York: Cambridge University Press.

Rainey, Lawrence. 1998. *Institutions of Modernism: Literary Elites and Public Culture.* New Haven, Conn.: Yale University Press.

Ross, Jean W. 1980. "Harold J. Salemson." *Dictionary of Literary Biography.* Vol. 4, *American Writers in Paris, 1920–1939,* edited by Karen Lane Rood, 350–51. Detroit: Gale.

Ross, Jean W. 1984. "Salemson, Harold J(ason)." *Contemporary Authors.* Vol. 110, edited by Hal May, 446–50. Detroit: Gale.

Rumold, Rainer. 2000. "Archeo-logies of Modernity in *transition* and *Documents* 1929/30." *Comparative Literature Studies* 37, no. 1: 45–67.

Sadoul, Georges. 1972. *French Film.* New York: Arno.

Salemson, Harold J. 1929a. "Lettres Anglo-Américaines." *Mercure de France* (November 1): 739–47.

Salemson, Harold J. 1929b. "The Unintelligibles." *Tambour* 4 (September): 76.

Salemson, Harold J. 1930a. "Cinéma-Théâtre." *Tambour* 6 (February): 73.

Salemson, Harold J. 1930b. "Essentiel: 1930/Essential: 1930." *Tambour* 7 (April): 1–7.

Salemson, Harold J. 1946. "A Question of Morals." *Screen Writer* 1 (April): 1–7.

Salemson, Harold J., Richard Thoma, and Samuel Putnam. 1930. "Direction." Single page. Special Collections, University of Pennsylvania, Philadelphia.

Singh, G. 1973. *Eugenio Montale: A Critical Study of His Poetry, Prose, and Criticism.* New Haven, Conn.: Yale University Press.

Tayler, Anne. 1987. "Witter Bynner." *Dictionary of Literary Biography.* Vol. 54, *American Poets, 1880–1945.* 3rd series, 13–21. Detroit: Gale.

Urgnani, Elena. 1991. *Sogni e visioni: Massimo Bontempelli fra surrealismo e futurismo.* Ravenna: Longo.

von Hallberg, Robert. 1989. "Ezra Pound and the *Mercure de France.*" *American Poetry* 6 (winter): 11–14.

Walz, Robin. 2000. *Pulp Surrealism: Insolent Popular Culture in Early Twentieth-Century Paris.* Berkeley: University of California Press.

LIST OF AUTHORS
AND TITLES

References are to page numbers within volumes. Volume
numbers appear in boldface. Page references in italics
indicate illustrations.

TAMBOUR

TAMBOUR

Directeur : Harold-J. SALEMSON, Editor

3, Rue Berthollet, PARIS (V^e), France

Of this issue, 200 copies are numbered.

De ce numéro, 200 exemplaires ont été numérotés.

> *Mes yeux sont deux tambours.*
> Blaise CENDRARS (*Moravagine*).

PRÉSENTATION

Interpréter le passé, c'est exprimer le présent; exprimer le présent, c'est créer l'avenir.

Toute expression artistique, passée, présente, ou future, quelle qu'en soit la tendance, est *tolérable*. Ce n'est qu'en constatant le mouvement, en avant ou en arrière, de l'art que l'on arrivera à en dégager un sens, une valeur. La direction nouvelle ne peut être conçue qu'à la lueur des leçons du passé.

Dès qu'il s'agit d'art ou de littérature, les idées, les croyances, les races, les espèces, toutes se confondent. Quelles que soient nos origines ou nos convictions, nous ne sommes que des hommes réunis en une toute-puissante recherche de la fin ultime de tout art, le *beau*.

Nous réunirons tous les genres, toutes les tendances. Nous laisserons aux lecteurs le soin de se prononcer sur eux.

Mais nous annoncerons l'allure nouvelle a coups de tambour.

Harold-J. Salemson.

PRESENTATION

To interpret the past is to express the present; to express the present is to create the future.

Every form of artistic expression, past, present, or future, whatever be its tendency, is *tolerable*. It is only by establishing the movement, forward or backward, of art, that we can bring out its meaning, its value. The new direction can be conceived only in the light of the lessons learned of the past.

In questions of art or of literature, ideas, beliefs, races, all melt into one. Whatever may be our origin or our convictions, we are all humans united in an over-powering search for the ultimate goal of art, *beauty*.

We shall assemble all the species, all the tendencies. To our readers will be left the privilege of passsing judgment.

BUT THE NEW GAIT WILL BE SOUNDED TO THE BEAT OF THE TAMBOUR.

H. J. S,

CONFIDENCES

Vous me contiez votre chagrin.
Le navire descendait le fleuve.
Les étoiles, la voie lactée
Naissaient, poudraient la nuit brûlante.

Que vous l'aimiez! Qu'il vous aimait!
Comme vos mots, comme votre bouche
Etaient pleins des mots, des baisers
Chastes de sa bouche violente,
Quand, sur les routes, dans les auberges
Vous cherchiez l'accord de vos âmes,
Ou, comme ce soir, étendus
Sur vos chaises-longues de toile,
Sur nos chaises-longues de toile,

Vous l'aimez toujours.
Vous l'aimez!
Pourquoi mon désir
S'est-il mêlé à vos larmes?

André Spire.

THE UNDELIVERED MESSAGE

Now as God lived or leastwise so has seemed
As Christ is good or leastwise so was deemed
Against the dark a bounding ball of black
Far off, slid past the world that hummed and screamed
So dire the weight upon a broken back
Till in the crackling of a little rod,
Leftward and crosswise of the forward track,
Most like a trampling cloud grown hoofed and shod,
A great black knight upon a great black horse,
Straight, stiff and haughty, like a king or corse,
Reined up and waited, terrible and odd.

But all this time and in the knight's despite
There was no change in posture of the night:
Grave stars and silence and a gloomy reach
And on the left some hills and on the right
Also some slighter hills—ahead, to teach
What fated word as at a finished race
Stood he, the black one, so ill-placed to preach
Below the slope, yet nowise changing place

He lifted up the visor of his helm
Yet showed mere fire and hollow it did whelm
'All face, I say, and showed mere fire—no face.

Then said someone, « Begone, thou canst no speak ».
Hence somewhat sadly, as it looked, did seek
And strive no more in sputter, of mere fire
Who had a word or not no lips could wreak
Beyond the seeming of a strong desire
But in some shame and sadly, as was said
On the old way as one that visions tire
Fared he anon, and always at his head
Now flopped a flame, curled over as a plume
Flops backward, or a sprig of flaccid bloom
That flickered long then flickered and was dead.

EGO

If I could once forget
This strongly seeming I
I might be happy yet
Before I come to die.

But this persistent whirl
  Within the wavy deep
Is like a natural curl
  That will not let me sleep.

Unravel me this force
  From tangled dreams of time:
This limbless headless torse
  That struggles into rhyme.

Ralph Cheever DUNNING.

HEURES CREUSES

J'ai attendu un signe
mais les quatre mille secondes se sont écoulées
et je n'ai entendu que les ombres
tout ce qui meurt sans bruit
Il fallait bien se retourner
et faire les gestes nécessaires
Nous n'avions pas à désespérer
Et le temps d'attendre n'est pas encore passé
J'ai l'impatience des fourmis
Je regarde l'horizon jaune
et la fumée
Et maintenant viennent les heures creuses
celles qui mangent le silence
et qui font résonner les pas du marcheur
ces heures pleines de vent
ces heures de pluie
pendant lesquelles il faut attendre
encore
derrière une vitre

Que ceux qui en ont assez se lèvent
se dressent
et mugissent comme tous les animaux du déluge
qu'ils refusent
protestent
jurent
crient
qu'ils renoncent
enfin
à attendre toujours sans rien dire
et qu'ils donnent le signal
le grand signal
LE SIGNAL

Philippe SOUPAULT.

GHOSTS

Breast under breast when you shall lie
    With him who in my place
Bends over you with flashing eye
    And ever nearing face;

Hand fast in hand when you shall tread
    With him the springing ways
Of love from me inherited
    After my little phase;

Be not surprised if suddenly
    The couch or air confound
Your ravished ears upraidingly,
    And silence turn to sound.

But never let it trouble you,
    Or cost you one caress;
Ghosts are soon sent with a word or two
    Back to their loneliness.

Countee CULLEN.

PETIT POÈME
A METTRE EN MUSIQUE

Tango vient de tanguer
Et de jaser vient jazz
Qu'importe l'étymologie
Si ce petit klaxon m'amuse.

Blaise CENDRARS.

RIVIÉRA I

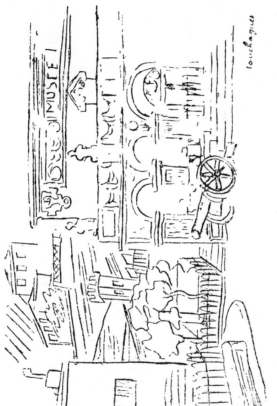

RIVIÉRA II

Explication et Fragments du " Rossignol Américain " [1]

Je découpe, dès maintenant pour Harold J. Salemson, cette « explication », afin qu'il ne doute plus de mes intentions profondes. Je ne nourris pas de pensée injurieuse à l'égard des Américains, et je ne prépare point contre eux de mauvais coups. La locution dangereuse, de père inconnu, est née sur la voie publique, pour qualifier une voiture, de marque américaine, laquelle, en ma présence, venait de gravement blesser quelqu'un. Je l'ai recueillie (la locution), pour mon amusement, et pour l'utiliser à ma fantaisie.

«... La réflexion du livreur me plaisait. (Au fait, était-ce bien un livreur?) Il y a dans le sens donné au « rossignol », qui ne signifie pas oiseau mais mécanique pesante et dangereuse, une agressivité, une sorte de venin ironique. Et que ce rossignol, de plus, soit américain, cela appelle l'idée qu'on peut se faire — avec une pointe de mauvaise humeur — d'un sport un peu lourd, écraseur, qu'on vous propose alors qu'on n'y est pas particulièrement entraîné et qu'on ne désire pas y consacrer beaucoup de temps.

(1) Ces pages sont extraites du livre à paraître, sous ce titre, aux éditions du *Sans Pareil.*

Il me semblait aussi que ce surnom, donné, en la circonstance, à une sale bagnole pouvait être le bon déguisement, la traduction un peu gaie, d'objets susceptibles de fournir un résultat analogue, le revolver, le surin ou la lettre anonyme. Et prendre, à l'occasion, un sens moins détourné, plus près de la nature, par exemple celui d'un jeune siffleur, de nationalité américaine, autant que possible matelot, *samie* de 1918 et souvenir de guerre ?

Pourquoi pas synonyme, au choix, de bonne nouvelle ou de mauvaise ?

Surprise, dans tous les cas, surprise plus ou moins drôle.

Fève sous la dent, fève qui amuse parce que la dent la reconnaît avec prudence, — ou qui casse la dent. Tournure commode, à double fin, signifiant le bien ou le mal. Le « rossignol américain ». Petit mystère dont la révélation sans cesse imminente est rossignol dans la bouche d'un livreur de pâtisserie ou de bière Fanta, et, par la grâce d'un constructeur d'autos de l'Illinois, d'« Outre-Atlantique ».

Un rossignol ? C'est le coin de rue, le contact avec la pierre dure, la rencontre fortuite, graine de chagrin ou de bonheur, *forme imprévue de l'imprévu.*

Dans toutes les histoires de la vie, comme dans celles que je raconte, il y a au moins un rossignol. Sa présence est, pour moi, sous-entendue. (Si je ne l'annonce pas toujours à haute voix , c'est par discrétion). J'ajouterais qu'il peut varier d'intensité, selon la main qui le touche et selon la place de cette main sur le clavier (sur un clavier de rossignols). Il va du drame pur à ce qu'on prend pour tel.

Vous tombez dans le piège tendu, ou vous l'apercevez quand vous êtes sur le point de tomber dedans : rossignol. Un bonbon empoisonné : rossignol. Vous montez, pour la première fois, un cheval emballeur, il vous emballe : rossignol. La gaffe que vous avez commise et qui se campe entre vous et « l'autre », en tiers encombrant : rossignol. L'intimité d'une femme vous ménage des surprises... et même, le larron qui vous enlève une amie chère : rossignols. Encore, toujours. Rossignols à l'américaine, plus ou moins à l'américaine.

(Les femmes devraient bien, au lieu de nous confier que, justement, — et par hasard — elles viennent de rencontrer le loup, nous dire qu'elles ont croisé le rossignol.)

Est-ce donc le changement, le changement tout court ? Eh ! peut-être, c'est *ce qu'on n'attend pas;* c'est ce qui crochète, à l'improviste, nos serrures : la clef.

Pour peu qu'on cesse de traiter le rossignol en symbole, et qu'on lui donne résolument une signification solide, il se défend encore, et dit bien ce qu'il dit. Vous voulez exprimer votre état de stupeur : « Vous êtes tout rossignol ». Mais si, dans une affaire quelconque, il faut vous rendre compte que vous êtes roulé : « Ça y est, je suis rossignol... »

Tels sont les visages que la fortune, le plus souvent adverse, prend pour nous faire du mal. Elle se met en coquetterie, une coquetterie blessante, acerbe. Elle n'adopte pas d'avance un visage affreux. Elle se mondanise et elle blesse quand même. On trouve toujours quelqu'un pour dire le mot aimable, le mot de la situation, l'oiseau de bon augure, le « rossignol ».

Aussi, on se demande si l'on rêve. Nenni. Cette chose qui vient de vous couper, qui attaque le corps, marque justement l'instant où l'on ne rêve plus. C'est le retour de la conscience. Ils se présentent à l'état simple ce rêve, cette réalité. Leurs contours sont dénués de vapeurs. De l'un à l'autre, il n'y a pas de *doute*. Le rêve cesse quand la réalité commence. C'est le phénomène le plus clair de la vie de relations... »

Maurice COURTOIS-SUFFIT.

TWO IN A CITY

(Autumn. A fashionable apartment near the ground floor.   He
tells how she speaks but he dares not listen.)

Thin rain flawing the night.   A rigid hush
Passive and dumb as stone.   The candles burn
Lifting frail leaves of fire.
You sigh and turn,
Being sick of that old ceaseless feverish rush
Of pallid faces driven past the pane.

« Sometimes, I think », you say—your slow voice
  falters—
« A city is a sick bewildered brain
Troubled with men and shadows, as with fears
Unreasoning, and nameless, and insane.

» Its desolate towers rise like terrible altars.

» Sometimes I think it is a thing in pain
Amazed with grief, incapable of tears,
That cries all night, intolerably lone,
In a white wilderness of wintry stone. »

—I know the symptoms.   You have begun again.
You will   rehearse that senseless litany
In sorrowful song of men and crowded places
And flickering haunted faces...

I shall go on with reading, and my tea.

« These people hover in my sleep », you say.
« Last night I dreamed I saw them in the rain.
What is their pain?
Once in my dreams I saw them as to-day,
Blowing in silence past the window-pane,
Whitely. They are terrible as dreams.
They are part of a mute multitude that streams
Palely within my mind, and past the pane.
They are part of a strange structure of the brain,
That was not ever, and will not come again.

« Maybe my mind has formed them out of wind,
Of an old desperate dread of loneliness.
You are not troubled by them.   They are less
Than shadows to you.   You do not seem to mind. »

—You pause.   I continue reading, quite content,
Untroubled with artistic temperament.

« *They enter like despair into my mind.*
Even in sleep I hear their sleepless feet
Ceaselessly tolling through the hollow street,
I see them stream like dark and ruinous wind.
They trample terribly within my brain.
Their desolate tread is like a pendulum
Lifting and swinging, falling back again,
Purposeless, and ceaseless, and in vain. »

—My pipe goes out.   I sigh.   I strike a light.

Thin rain flawing the night.

« *Sometimes at night I waken with the wind,*
And see the frail stars drifting like white faces.
What have they lost, or wasted? Have they sinned?
What thing is it they seek through these swift spaces?

« *Often I wonder, seeing the sharp stars,*
And the dim winds, and fire, the herded waves,
The keen rain's trembling bars,
And even the slow dead stirring in their graves,
Of what unending impulse they are driven.

« *Even the mute movelessness of stone*
Is seized by the resistless fury. Even
Mountains are moved, and men and leaves are blown
Disconsolately about the nervous wind.
Whatever it is, they go to the same end.
Whatever it is that drives them, they can know
Nothing of why they labour, where they go.

« *Sometimes men say, believing that they know,*
It is love drives them, sleeplessly and slow,
Or ache for some lost land.
It was not given
To know in what bewilderment we move.
And we of earth are exiles out of heaven.
It is heaven we long for, when we say we love.

—*Your words fall ceaselessly, like listless snow.*

Christ!
If I listened, if I dared to think
The terrible slow words you say, I know
I should go swiftly mad.
Instead, I drink
The tasteless tea, and read, and do not hear
The curious words compounded out of fear.

You turn again to the dumb endless urging
Of faces like pale leaves past the dim pane.
The silence, surging
In a slow flood like sleep, stills wind and rain.

Only the pulsing feet beat ceaselessly,
Like resolute rain. The faces glimmer white,
The faces like pale leaves blown desolately
Past the dim pane.

Thin rain flawing the night.

E. James OLSON.

SAINT-TROPEZ - VUE GÉNÉRALE

« Aimes-tu ton mari, nom de dieu?... »

Elle s'affligeait, disant qu'elle ne savait pas, qu'elle détestait, en tout cas, les jurons, puis roucoulait contre moi comme une mykyphone.

Je la conduisais dans de petits bars, où personne ne s'occupait de nous, pas même les garçons... Parfois on nous servait un jus noirâtre qui sentait le vernis. Les autobus en grinçant, s'arrêtaient devant la porte, laissant à ceux des passagers qui n'avaient pas la tête pliée dans un journal du soir, le temps de nous maudire ou de nous envier. Car, il fallait bien qu'on nous enviât : après trois ans de rencontres quotidiennes, nous avions à chaque rendez-vous quelque chose de nouveau à nous raconter.

Pourtant, quelles que fussent mes dispositions à la sérénité, mon goût du calme et de la pipe, je pensais à son mari, personnage mystérieux dont elle me disait parfois les méfaits et les exigences domestiques : « Où sont mes pantoufles? — A-t-on lavé mes pyjamas? — Passe-moi le sel! » Auditeur attendri de ces petites scènes, je plaignais Marcelline sans réussir à oublier tout à fait qu'elle dormait avec ce mari, le servait, lui racontait sans doute ses journées, en escamotant nos rencontres.

Depuis quelque temps, j'étais à peu près tranquille: Didier Barbille, mon rival officiel, se reposait en Provence... Marcelline était libre ou presque, je la voyais maintenant chaque soir, je pouvais renifler sa nuque, mordre son cou, lui raconter des horreurs, sans qu'elle interrompe ces exercices par un « Faut que je rentre » sans merci.

Cependant, vipère endormie, ma jalousie vivait toujours dans mon cœur. Parfois j'oubliais ce tourment parce qu'il faisait beau, parce qu'au restaurant le menu était bien composé, les mets agréables... D'autres fois, au contraire, ces faveurs du sort irritaient en moi de vieilles rancœurs. Alors, l'œil pointu, je fixais le sac de mon amie, un petit sac en bête, mystérieux, plein à craquer d'objets de laboratoire et de papiers imprécis, j'essayais de lire, elle s'en apercevait, laissant percer quelque mauvaise humeur, disant: « Qui veux-tu qui m'écrive, à part Didier je ne connais personne. »

— C'est trop de connaître Didier, il ne pourrait pas rester tranquille celui-là, fais donc voir.

— Qu'est-ce que ça peut te faire, tiens regarde l'écriture, tu la connais, le timbre de la poste: Saint-Tropez.

Rond comme un hublot, le cachet cernait le nom de la petite ville. L'odeur d'un port tuait les autres odeurs, un marin chantait, des fillettes brunes se poursuivaient, trébuchant dans les lignes noires des filets.

Didier Barbille avait de la chance... J'étais, moi, le plus malheureux des hommes, condamné à l'amour, au brouillard!

« Que t'écrit-il?

— Des bêtises, des futilités, il m'écrit ce qu'il dit chez nous.

— Fais voir.

— Fiche-moi la paix!

— Que lui réponds-tu?

— Crotte!...

— Oh! pas à lui?

— Non, sûrement, il reviendrait; c'est à toi que je parle, à toi, petit bêta, ne peux-tu simplement savourer notre entente, les profits que nous tirons de son absence.... Notre amour, en un mot, qui est un bel enfant!

— Tu l'aimes plus que moi!

— Sot!

— Tu me trompes avec lui...

— Au revoir! »

Nous devions dîner ensemble, elle s'en alla le cœur
gros, les yeux tristes; je restai devant mon Turin-
curaçao, la bouche amère...

« Garçon, l'indicateur! »

Une pensée m'avait saisi. J'allais planter là Marcelline Barbille, son petit sac plein de lettres, son bâton
de rouge et ses réticences.

Prendre une décision, c'est pour un être amorphe une
libération; dès qu'on sent durcir en soi quelque volonté
d'atteindre un but précis, tout l'univers paraît aimable.
Je partais pour Saint-Tropez (Var). La gare de Lyon
s'ouvrait comme un four aéré, sous le long campanile,
les hommes d'équipe étaient charmants, des importa-
teurs d'histoires de Marseille allaient renouveler leur
stock sur le Vieux-Port. Quel beau voyage!

La nuit voilait avec soin des paysages sans caractère,
puis le jour arrivait, juste à temps, pour vous montrer
d'un doigt étincelant l'étang de Berre, plaque d'argent
nu, ceinturée d'oliviers, couronnée de vols de macreuses,
les gens lisaient le *Petit Marseillais,* le couloir sentait
le charbon et l'eau de Cologne. Les cyprès inclinés par
le Mistral fouettaient de leurs ombres rapides, le train
lancé.

Maintenant, j'écrivais, très mal dans ce wagon secoué : «... Mon amie, je te fuis, mais je t'aime, je veux savoir... plus tard je te dirai. »

Nous roulions maintenant à travers des collines crayeuses, vêtues de pinèdes odorantes... Que faire de ma lettre, je mis le nez à la fenêtre et déchirai lentement le billet... Alors le vent changea, cessa de suivre le train en soufflant, tourna en rond comme un chien malade et rebroussa gentiment chemin vers Paris, entraînant vingt papillons amoureux!

Personne n'arrive à Saint-Tropez par la voie ferrée, aussi la gare est-elle stupide... c'est une vieille bergerie qui somnole entre la mer et des roseaux charbonneux... c'est la nuit, des ruelles noires s'étirent vers des places noires. Brusquement un palmier éclairé par un projecteur s'élance d'une cour, un air de jazz se balance entre deux enseignes, des gens vêtus d'un foulard et d'un bleu de plombier-zingueur passent en fredonnant un chant nègre... De somptueuses voitures vous frôlent en silence. Voici l'Hôtel Sube et Continental, Didier Barbille doit y dormir entre *Télémaque,* sa lecture favorite, et la Côte Desfossés que lui envoie sa femme, cha-

que soir. Ma chambre s'ouvre sur un ciel immense, constellé d'étoiles et de feux terrestres... De l'autre côté du
golfe : Sainte-Maxime et Beauvallon scintillent, sur des
coussins d'encre et de velours. Derrière le mur, un ron-
flement s'élève. Didier Barbille ronfle-t-il? ce rensei-
gnement me manque, dommage... si ce pouvait être
Didier Barbille.

*
**

Ce n'est pas lui, déception cruelle, c'est un savant
suédois venu pour étudier les fougères qui poussent
dans les forêts de la région.

Je n'ai vu mon rival qu'au déjeuner ; muni d'un portrait de lui, volé à Marcelline, je l'ai regardé s'asseoir,
déplier lentement sa serviette. Rien ne semble l'intéresser, le divertir, ni l'anglaise maigre, à peu près nue, noire
comme un sarment, ni deux étranges femmes, ni Segon-
zac hilare et beau, venu voir des amis, et qui se trompe
de verre, s'en aperçoit, recommence...

Mon excellent ami Didier Barbille n'est pas à Saint-
Tropez pour faire la connaissance des héros de la « Naissance du Jour », il regarde sur la place Vildrac jouer
aux boules ou Colette filer vers la Moutte dans sa petite

voiture, ne voyant en eux qu'un boulomane, une femme
qui conduit... Il se repose, offrant à l'air salin, un corps
poreux, un cerveau sans rêves.

Je trouvai l'occasion de lui parler un matin que j'allais remplir mon stylo à la mer, il regardait un vapeur
L'Amphion longer le quai en sifflant; j'ai mis la conversation sur les femmes, il n'a pas l'air de les aimer beaucoup: « De petits poisons, Monsieur, dont on ne peut
rien tirer, pas un service, pas une confidence ». Tiens,
tiens: « — Comme je vous comprends, Monsieur. »

*
* *

Marcelline écrit souvent, ses petites lettres bleues se
posent tous les deux jours, tourterelles prisonnières,
dans la cage à courrier qui domine l'escalier de l'Hôtel
Continental.

Didier paraît lire machinalement les lettres de sa
femme. J'ai essayé de vingt procédés pour surprendre
leur teneur — rien à faire.

Ce matin, en dégageant une enveloppe à mon adresse,
j'ai tenté de saisir la dernière lettre de mon amie à son
époux; derrière moi, la petite voix de l'aimable Mme
Rosset, la propriétaire de l'hôtel, s'élève: « Vous vous
trompez, Monsieur. » J'ai rougi, elle a souri. Allons,
je vois qu'il faut envisager de plus grands moyens.

vers 4 heures, toute la maison est plongée dans la torpeur délicieuse de la sieste, Didier dort, le gérant sommeille, seul Poupouille, un fox agité, circule dans les couloirs, poursuivant un des onze chats attachés à l'établissement.

*
* *

Quatre heures... j'entr'ouvre ma porte, le pas de mon rival s'éloigne, je l'entends accrocher sa clé au tableau... maintenant, je le vois, à travers mes volets, arpenter le quai d'un pas rapide, le soleil est immense dans un ciel impeccable; il va, Didier Barbille, il va, sous son parasol de soie verte, je ne vois que lui... lui et la statue du Bailli de Suffren qui fait la seule ombre du port.

Suis-je fou? J'entre comme chez moi dans la chambre du mari, voici le lit creusé au centre, une grande malle velue, des costumes tendus sur des instruments perfectionnés... J'ai cueilli la clé comme une fleur et, pieds nus, suis remonté. J'erre dans la vaste pièce, je cherche, voici des lettres: une de la Fédération des Philatélistes, une autre signée: Philogone. Ah, diable! des enveloppes bleues, dans la poche intérieure d'un veston de sport, c'est bien la chère écriture, je crois entendre Marcelline, mes yeux se brouillent, les siens sont si près de moi, son parfum flotte mes narines avides... Qu'écrit-elle?

3

« Mon cher Didier, je t'envoie la note de blanchissage que tu m'as demandée — tiens, tiens ! — Mon ami, voici le relevé mensuel de ton compte de banque, je vais bien, je suis allée chez tes parents à Montmorency, ton père est content de ses semis de melons, ta mère se plaint de rhumatismes. J'ai rencontré ton ami Didelot avec une petite poule, un homme marié !... enfin la vertu et la vie sont depuis longtemps en instance de divorce, c'est navrant... » — Pas tant que cela, ingrate ! Je souris... Quel est ce bruit ? Je souris moins, dans le cadre de la porte ouverte soudain, Didier s'inscrit, horrifié, il me regarde. « Nous se regardons », comme dit le garçon d'étage qui est de Toulon. — Aucun sujet de conversation vraiment ; brusquement Didier a l'air de s'étrangler, il fait de grands gestes, cherche un revolver, trouve un mouchoir, avance, recule et se jette finalement dans l'escalier en hurlant : « Arrrêtez-le, un rat d'hôtel ! »

Immédiatement le palier s'emplit de pyjamas, on n'a pas tellement de distractions — j'entends : « Il est peut-être armé — téléphonez au commissariat ! » La charmante Mme Rosset est navrée, le garçon d'étage annonce, important... « Y doit pas être dangereux, c'est le type du 14 ». Il a raison, je ne suis pas dangereux, un bonheur délicieux m'inonde : Marcelline ne semble pas amoureuse de son mari ; c'est une certitude qu'on ne saurait payer trop cher. J'ai ouvert la fenêtre, non pour me tuer, encore moins pour fuir : toute la bourgade rousse et bleue entre par la fenêtre, avec ses maisons de nougat doré, sa citadelle aiguë, son clocher débonnaire. Sur les collines, deux mille peintres en train de fixer les traits éternels de Saint-Tropez pourraient fixer les miens, par-dessus le marché !

On est entré dans la chambre, Didier Barbille a un succès fou. Comme dans les opéras-bouffes, le commissaire est là, le chien Poupouille aboie, le jazz du Bar de la Jetée (Pedroni successeur) écrit pour cette scène une musique folle... Ah, la dernière lettre de Marcelline, je peux lire encore cette phrase : « Depuis huit jours, je suis très triste... » Il y a exactement huit jours que je suis parti, c'en est trop. J'ai envie de sauter au cou du commissaire — un corse noiraud. Je veux serrer la main de Didier Barbille qui la retire effaré, on m'entraîne, j'ai l'air tellement joyeux que personne n'y comprend plus rien...

. . . .

Tous les journaux locaux diront demain « que le dangereux malfaiteur s'est laissé appréhender sans résistance. »

Mario MONTANARD.

VESPERS

To Tsong Ming-Wei.

I stand alone by the hedge.

In this dimness of the twilight, Lord, soft shadows silently come and go, while the shepherd begins his dream of the wild rose.

Standing alone here, I regret and ponder my passionate past, when I madly plucked the flowers of the world.

In tears, I am only waiting for a delicate petal, carelessly blown by the languid wind of the late spring:

With it, solemnly, devotedly, in the warm penitent light of the evening star, I shall complete my evening prayer.

EVENTIDE

Like an old nun,
The dusk, pale and slow,
Draws near from her ancient convent...

LIANG-TSONG-TAI.

NOSTALGIE

à Frances Valensi.

Ce soir, la lune verse une triste pâleur
A l'herbe fine que caresse le zéphire.
Au pourpre de l'étang qui frissonne, se mire
Fier, au flot argenté le frais pêcher en fleurs.

Le silence tremblait, limpide et diaphane,
Ainsi qu'un nénuphar dans l'ombre se bleuit...
Un parfum virginal murmure, évanoui...
Des bambous la rosée en scintillant se fane...

Mais au lac enchanté de ton cher souvenir
Où s'assombrit l'eau calme et plaintive, mon âme
Cygne las du long vol, languit à revenir

D'un coup d'aile rapide et silencieux, Femme,
Et dans l'ombre, d'oubli pensive, pour périr
Pieuse, au crépuscule du mensonge se pâme...

LIANG-TSON-TAI,

LOTUS

Pourquoi demeures-tu ici, reposant tes feuilles sur l'eau, enfonçant ta racine dans la boue et dans l'humidité, ô Lotus aimé?

— Pour que mon âme, lorsque viendra la saison de chants et de fleurs, s'épanouisse en blancheur, en parfum et en murmure.

LIANG-TSONG-TAI.

THE WHISPERING PAGODA

A Burma Night's Entertainment.

When her husband had finished beating her, Mee Sein, with a final and especially lamentable cry, ran out into the village street. As she fled to the headman's house, the pariahs yapped cynically at the fluttering rags of her faded pink *longyi,* and the fowls flew to and fro between the trees, cackling. The headman had little use for Mee Sein; an honourable Burman polygamist, he detested polyandry.

— With what instrument did your ancient correct you, Mee Sein?

— With a slipper, headman, and one of mine at that.

— That is as it should be. And with which of your lovers did he catch you?

— With your son. Therefore I ask you to seize my ancient and put him in the stocks, in a place of many large ants and centipedes. He must learn. Is it likely that an attractive girl of sixteen like me could be satisfied by the semipotence of an elderly chowchow vendor, whose business is being rapidly ruined by the Chinese importers of dry fish?

Leaning forward, the headman picked up a handful of the onions laid out to dry on his verandah and threw them at Mee Sein, adding:

— Go, daugther of a buffalo.

Moaning unutterable things, she hurried out of the West gate of the village. The dogs barked angrily at the shrill excess of her complaint, and the smaller cocks, sitting on the roofs of the opium-eaters' houses, crowed all together.

She ran straight into the light of the declining sun, along the slender shadows of the palm-trees. Where the palm-grove ended she entered the cactus-lined track of sand which leads to the Whispering Pagoda. Its black pinnacle was level with her eyes as she sped westward. The wide, mossy base was hidden from her sight, for it lies in the deep valley at the foot of the Hill of a Thousand Elephants. No Burman has visited that pagoda since half a hundred years ago when six virgins (selected for their blameless past) were sent there to placate an insatiate demon of the forest, the Red Nat, and never returned. When three moons had passed the village elders said amongst themselves:

—We should not have sent that girl Ma Shwe with the others. We ought not to have taken her blameless

on trust.   We should have been warned by what she
said about her cousin and the cicada curry they ate
together in the buffalo-pastures.

Where the jungle path plunged to the valley the
sandy scrub was replaced by a green luxuriance of
massive ferns and creepers festooned from tree to tree.
Mee Sein stumbled as she crossed slippery boulders and
humid pitfalls.   Once she cut her ankle on a sharp rock.
The sun set and the way grew darker.   A huge black
spider dropped from an overhanging branch onto her
head; when she shook it off, it crawled away into the
jungle and crouched there, peering at her malevolently.
Something moved in a cluster of purple orchids pendant
from a half-dead teak-tree.   A green snake with pink
eyes leered at her from a bamboo clump.   A lizard,
large as a young alligator, splashed into a slime-
scummed pool.   Close at hand a long low hooting began,
and, from above, came a sound in answer like the
tolling of a great bell swathed in cotton-wool.   The dusk
blinked with lights, hidden beasts eyeing her from the
thickets.   All at once she was aware of the Whispering
Pagoda looming above.   Now she was splashing kneedeep, through unseen water.   There was a tramp of
padded footsteps behin her.   Something from the

forest was tracking her down. A large body floundered through the water towards her, panting with a greedy rattling noise. In headlong terror, she flung herself onto the crumbling pagoda steps and struggled upward along the ledges. At last she could climb no further; she felt herself slipping. downwards to the thick water.

Then human fingers clutched her hair. She was drawn out of the morass onto the threshold of a dim cavern, whence a long string of bats flittered in ceaseless procession A huge hand lay heavy on her shoulder, urging her on, though she could hardly stagger forward, impeded by the weight of her sodden longyi.

A dim light burnt in the cave and, swinging round, she managed to observe her captor. He was an old man with a white beard and all the other accessories of age. Living, as he did, out of reach of the elixirs and tonics which inevitably rebuild the worn tissues and prolong for decades the vitality of youth, the man was clearly effete. Mee Sein, greatly relieved, directed on the veteran one of her most emollient smiles.

— Venturesome virgin, I can read the inmost secrets of your heart.

— What do you see there, kind rescuer of venturesome virgins?

— I see that immaculate charm which my master, the Red Nat, has long sought in vain. At last your head-man has been able to produce the ultimate flower of blamelessness in his village, and, as is proper, he sends her to gratify the divine susceptibilities of my lord.

— Dear old man, how well you understand me! I had such a good mother. Father died when I was a little girl, and she brought me up ever so carefully; a good example, you know, works wonders with the young. Dear mother died last year. It was such a nice funeral. The headman's son danced all the way from the village to the cemetery and there were three stabbing cases. I wish you had been there.

— Little one, I cannot neglect my duties here. But I thank you for your kind thought.

— I wish I could change my clothes; I got dreadfully wet on the way.

—You can have your choice of six longyis which I have in stock. Before burying your young but blamable predecessors I removed the garments from the corpses. You will find them in that box on your right.

— Thank you. I will take them all if you have no use for them. I am very short of skirts just now. But would you mind leaving the cave while I am changing my garments.

— Child, I am old enough to be your grandfather and...

— As you like, kind old man.

Mee Sein, delighted with the new longyis, chose a red one for immediate use.

— Now you must come and see my master. He, since he knows all things, is aware that you are here and I dare not keep him waiting.

Reluctantly, foreseeing the worst possible kind of trouble, she followed the aged man into an inner cave, ablaze with lights and heavily jewelled throughout.

The Red Nat was hanging by his tail from a golden bar stretched from side to side of the cave, grilling a bat over a stream on incandescent lava.

— Go, old slave, — he growled, — and get me a dozen bats' eggs.

— But, my lord, to whom none of the ways of nature are secret...

— Do what I tell you, and waste no time about it.

The old man retreated, groaning.

— Come here, said the Red Nat to Mee Sein. Come right here.

She complied.

— Have you ever been in love with a white man?
— he enquired.

— I am a blameless virgin. I do not know what love
is.

The Red Nat burst into as ecstasy of laughter. He
fell from the gold bar and ran round the room chipping
jewellry off the walls, in a frenzy of merriment.
Finally he kissed Mee Sein.

— That is what the white men do when they make
love. Do you like it?

Mee Sein liked it, but rememberd the case of Ma Shwe.

— I am a blameless virgin.

— *Will* you stop that nonsense?

— H-how can I? L-last time our village sent you a
selection of blameless maidens you killed them all
because they were not quite good — especially Ma
Shwe, as I have heard.

— Not quite good? So you thought I was wanting
intact? Hee, hee! Nats, my child, especially red ones,
know better! I never met a collection of bigger fools
in eternity, and Ma Shwe was the worst of the lot. Dull
as boiled bamboo shoots! She screamed when I held
her hand and hid in a corner when I told her she was

the little girl I had been looking for since Mee Chit died.
She thought I wanted to eat her. Hee, hee! I eat bats.
Bats, do you hear, no little girls. Why I just *had* to kill
them. Well, anyhow, that's over. Come here and be
kissed again.

— It's nice. Don't stop. I want to learn. You
know heaps of things. I like clever men. But I don't
believe you like me much. You've known such heaps
of girls nicer than me, than I, than me, I mean... Yes,
I like you a little, a lot, passionately... Ooh, that really
is nice...!

Presently the old man returned. The Red Nat
released Mee Sein with divine agility (— I have to keep
up appearances, — he whispered).

— Old man, he said, produce a pair of diamond
earrings and the largest size we keep in ruby pendants
and offer them to this blameless virgin.

— Master, I obey. I knew it from the first when I
saw her modest demeanour and those so candid eyes...

— Thank you ever so, — Mee Sein said. — And you
really want me to come again?

— Of course, we shall be glad to see you.

The old man guided Mee Sein through the valley of a
Thousand Elephants into the light of a sunny morning.

— You had better come earlier next time, he said. This road is rather unpleasant at night.

At the West gate, Mee Sein met the headman. As soon as he saw her he began to declaim in a shrill, ineffective voice the new phrases of abuse which he had thought out since their last interview.

— Daughter of a -

Then he stopped. The odour of immortality and bats which Mee Sein brought with her from the cave of her divine friend smote him in the face. His eyes were fascinated by the glitter of jewels. He ajusted his accolade to the new occasion.

— Daughter of a king, we have had a dreadful night looking for you. My son is nearly off his head. I, too, have longed to meet you that I might correct the false impression which yesterday, perhaps...

Unheeded, his shrill regrets trailed into saddened silence... As Mee Sein sped homeward, goddess patent in her stride, the dogs barked joyfully at the brightness of her new scarlet longyi, and the larger cocks, sitting on the roofs of the opium-eaters' houses, crowed all together.

Stuart Gilbert.

LE VIEIL HOMME

— Pardon, Monsieur. Voudriez-vous bien m'écouter un instant ?

Le vieil homme me regarda du fond de ses yeux. Moi, je laissais errer mon regard sur ses cheveux blancs immaculés, et j'attendais, avec un petit frémissement intérieur, la réponse qui ne pouvait tarder à venir.

Le vieil homme ne dit rien.

— J'ai un ami, repris-je, qui a passé l'hiver dernier ici. Il a fait la connaissance d'un monsieur distingué dont il n'a jamais su le nom. Mais que de fois il m'en a parlé !

« Ce monsieur est écrivain. Je ne sais ce qu'il a écrit, mais d'après les indications qu'il m'a données, il me semble que vous devez être la personne. »

Le vieil homme restait silencieux. A la longue, comme il ne disait rien, je parlai :

— Il est vrai que, dans ces cafés, on rencontre tant de personnes avec lesquelles on cause sans jamais rien savoir d'eux que vous pouvez connaître mon camarade sans en avoir conscience.

Le vieil homme ne dit toujours rien.

Lentement, comme un somnambule, me regardant encore de son œil profond dont je pouvais tranquillement analyser le bleu clair et limpide, il sortit de sa poche un portefeuille. Il le fouilla longuement et puis il en retira une carte crasseuse. Je lus un nom.

En effet, je ne m'étais pas trompé. C'était bien là l'homme qui avait écrit tant de beaux romans et il me semblait voir revivre les personnages qu'il avait si virilement dépeints. Je pensai à Yvan, cet hyper-sensitif, égaré dans un monde dur et sans amortisseurs. Je revis Paulette, seule au pays des hybrides, égarée elle aussi et témoin de tant d'événements surprenants. Tout ce qui était sorti du cerveau de cet homme me semblait défiler sur son front comme un film, déroulé parfois par un opérateur qui tournait la manivelle dans le mauvais sens. Mais maintenant je savais que mon instinct ne m'avait pas trompé.

Quittant le front du vieil homme, mes yeux se promenèrent tout le long du haut corps droit. Je ne me rendais pas compte que je pouvais importuner. C'est mon silencieux interlocuteur qui me rappela au café d'où je m'étais envolé en esprit.

4

— Monsieur, vous aussi vous m'intriguez. Pourrais-je savoir votre nom et celui de votre ami?

— Mon nom, répondis-je, n'a pas d'importance, il ne vous dirait rien, et je suis un homme sans ami.

Le vieil homme me dévisagea longuement de son œil calme et comme détaché.

Harold J. SALEMSON.

Open letter to Michael Gold

My dear Michael Gold,

With reference to my article in *Monde* upon the death of Donn Byrne, you write me: « He was regarded here as a mere hack—and worse, was a cheap and classconscious bourgeois ». The judgment you make is, to say the least, a hasty one. In the first place, allow me to point out that whether doctors agree or disagree upon the dangers of certain illnesses, and even when the majority decide them inoffensive, this does not bring back to life those carried off by the diseases in question. Nor would it make Donn Byrne any the less a great artist, were he to be « regarded as a hack » by the vast majority of critics. (Of course, if you personally wish to back up your judgment, I should be delighted to hear your arguments.)

However, here there is an important point to bring out. Due to the fact that few real artists have ever had popular success, we have come almost to consider successfulness as the disproof of art and popularity as

the characteristic of « hacks ». Still, that is certainly
not an infallible rule (as will attest the cases of Sherwood Anderson, Dreiser, etc..., to say nothing of Donn
Byrne). It is nowhere written either that one must
contribute to little reviews to be an artist, nor to radical
ones to be a revolutionary. One need not vaunt one's
ideas in order to serve the cause.

Moreover, the fact that you, a revolutionary poet, call
him a « cheap and classconscious bourgeois » would
tend to show that you have sadly neglected reading his
work. For Donn Byrne is not only an artist but very
often he is a real proletarian artist. In *Blind Raftery,*
the song of two souls of the people, he is a true artist of
to-morrow. Even in *Hangman's House,* his least artistic book, though some of the romantic elements may be a
bit gaudy, the revolutionary trend of the Irish people,
beautifully depicted, is not to be overlooked. The sub-
versiveness of *Brother Saul,* the outcry against soul-
crushing religion called *O'Malley of Shanganagh,* the
odyssey of a sailor known as *The Wind Bloweth,* are
all the work of a man advanced in theory as well as
outstanding in artistic perfection.

The last element is amply proven by the books already
named but as further evidence, I dare advance that

Messer Marco Polo is one of the finest bits of literary craftsmanship that have come from any part of the world during the last generation.

If you take the pains to verify my references to Donn Byrne's books, I believe you will admit it impossible to call a man « a hack—and worse, a classconscious bourgeois » when it would be more appropriate to doff one's hat and salute him as « a fine artist—and better, a man advanced in sociological theory as well as artistic achievement ».

With best wishes, and the assurance that I envy you the enjoyable hours you will spend when you decide to read Donn Byrne's works, I beg to remain

Fraternally yours,

Harold J. Salemson.

NOTES

Books

FOUR NOVELS

Samuel Rogers is one those rare professors who write well. Perhaps the fact that he teaches French explains the fine qualities of his novels in English. After his book *The Sombre Flame,* a promising first novel, he has now published *Less Than Kind* (Payson & Clarke, New York). The theme of his new book is very simple: a weak brother, after standing as much as he could, kills the faithless husband of the sister he idolized and, although the murder appears accidental and he is exonerated, he gives himself up to the police, realizing that his sister does not need him. But the story is masterfully handled and in the last pages the author brilliantly succeeds in what seems to have been his objective: he transposes into a contemporary middle-west college town a tragedy that any of the great classic writers might proudly have signed.

Another second novel of interest is *The Torches Flare* (Scribners, New York) by Stark Young. This also shows marked progress over the author's first work of fiction. Stark Young, better known as an essayist and critic than as a novelist, had, in *Heaven Trees,* really done only a series of character-sketches, but in his new book he has shown that he does not lack skill in handling a story. *The Torches Flare* is a beautiful book and its theme is captivating.

Mary Butts, in her book *Imaginary Letters* (E. W. Titus, Paris), has attempted, rather successfully, a dangerous theme. This short story, illustrated with several excellent drawings by Jean Cocteau, depicts several scenes of the life of a young homosexual. « Sauvons-nous de cette pédérastie », he says, but apparently it is to no avail. He persists in his life of dissipation, taking his pleasure wherever he finds it and with scarcely any idea as to what type he prefers. Mary Butts has handled the idea quite delicately.

In his novel *Georgie May* (Horace Liveright, New York), Maxwell Bodenheim has shown us quite a different type of person. His heroine is a street-walker in a southern city of the United States of the years 1909 to 1912. Bodenheim has skillfully shown the inside workings of the prostitute's heart as he accompanies her through periods of « hustling » and imprisonment, a chance to be legally married and settle down, a true love for a boy she must give up, and her final suicide. Perhaps the theme is not of the most original : others before him had shown that some sensibilities could be left in constantly humiliated hearts. But the poet Bodenheim writes a most beautiful prose and his conception of the novel is original and worthwhile. His manner of speaking to his characters will find more than one imitator in years to come.

MR. BAUDELAIRE AND OTHER POETS

Here are four books of poetry that deserve mention. Two are outstanding by their quality : *Little Poems in Prose* by Charles Baudelaire, translated by Aleister Crowley (E. W. Titus, Paris), and *Mr. Pope and other poems* by Allen Tate (Minton, Balch and C°, New-York) ; and two by their authors' reputations : *Moods Cadenced and Declaimed*, by Theodore Dreiser (Horace Liveright, New York) and *The Buck in the Snow*, by Edna St. Vincent Millay (Harpers, New York).

Aleister Crowley's new translation of Baudelaire's poems in prose is quite good. He has rendered the original as well as anyone could unless some new Poe should appear to do in turn for Baudelaire what he did for Poe. The book is nicely illustrated by Jean de Bosschère. Moreover, for the epilogue, in verse, four translations are given. The best is undoubtedly the one by Ralph Cheever Dunning. The other three, by the publisher, the translator of the book, and Pierre Loving, are fair.

But Baudelaire's fine qualities are an old story. Allen Tate has not yet
attained so great a reputation. *Mr. Pope* is his first volume of verse but
his poems received high praise when they appeared in various American
periodicals. Tate defies classification. The only category that would
fit him would be « intellectual » but I profoundly dislike the word. His
poetry is a poetry of the idea. Perhaps even too much so. I am afraid
he has sacrificed his rhythm too often to his meaning. Still, of the three
parts of his volume, I prefer the first. The poems in this, such as
Death of Little Boys and *Long Fingers*, are with *The Progress of Oenia*
and *Ignis Fatuus* the most perfect in form and content. These lines from
his sonnet *Long Fingers* are perhaps the most expert craftsmanship in
the book:

> *And there have been long fingers like a stone,*
> *Eternal, girded with an ancient ring*
> *Engraved:* These fingers are not flesh and bone.
> *Often I catch my breath when I'm alone.*
> *What was I saying? An Egyptian king*
> *Once touched long fingers, which are not anything.*

Allen Tate, an intelligent essayist, writes intelligent poetry. But has he
yet reached artistic perfection?

Mr. Dreiser, of course, does not aim at artistic perfection. His *Moods*
are peculiarly well-named. But, unfortunately, for the three or four
rather good things in the book, one has to wade through 385 pages. Still
his novels have won him the right to do one book that is not perfect.

If Dreiser's book disappointed me, Miss Millay's new volume gave me no
deception. The explanation is that I expected nothing of it. Those who
over-rated *The Harp-Weaver* were necessarily forced to rectify their
opinions after reading *The Buck in the Snow.* Except for the poem
Hangman's Oak, the whole thing strikes me as tediously factitious.

CALVERTON ON MARRIAGE

The Bankruptcy of Marriage by V. F. Calverton (Macaulay, New York) is one of the most important books on the sexual question that have ever appeared in English. The author does not attempt to moralize. He merely sums up the present situation and tries to point out how we may adapt ourselves to it. He advocates the scientific teaching of birth-control, the legalization of abortion, companionate marriage, and any other progress that might be made toward the amelioration of our *legal* relationship to the eternal problems of sex and marriage. His data on the conditions in Soviet Russia are vastly interesting and his book, a most competently documented study, is a summary of preceding works on the subject, giving full indications for further reading, and expounds original ideas and conclusions of the highest importance.

Les Livres

ROMANS

De tous les romans parus depuis longtemps, le plus important me semble incontestablement *Le Crime des Justes* (Grasset, éditeur), d'André Chamson. Je ne suis pas de ceux qui en veulent à ce jeune romancier d'être cévenol; et j'en suis tout heureux, cette fois encore il est rentré chez lui prendre le sujet de son livre. Chacun de ses romans montrait un progrès marqué et cette fois l'on peut dire que Chamson a l'air d'avoir atteint sa force entière et sa forme définitive. Il est de ceux qui ne rétrogradent pas et nous devons attendre encore mieux de ses romans à venir. Mais déja, dans *Le Crime des Justes,* il montre une telle virilité, une telle force insaisissable que l'on ne peut que le saluer. Par la nudité et la suffisance en eux-mêmes des faits, il ressemble au grand Knut Hamsun, mais il ne dessine pas de grands tableaux comme le Norvégien. Il ne fait qu'esquisser une vivante image d'un événement, un seul, mais qui en vaut la peine. Bien différent, on le voit, de l'auteur de la *Recherche, Chamson est la figure la plus importante qui soit apparue en France depuis Marcel Proust.*

Un autre roman dont on a dit grand bien est *Les Conquérents* (Grasset, éditeur) d'André Malraux. Je pense qu'on le veut meilleur qu'il ne soit, mais c'est tout de même un fort beau livre. Le roman de la révolution chinoise, malheureusement assez mal bâti, mais d'une grande force et d'une sincérité étonnante. Malraux, s'il travaille avec plus de soins, fera certainement un des grands romanciers de notre époque.

Victor Llona, lui aussi, a donné avec *La Croix de Feu* (Editions Baudinière), un livre excellent. Documentaire très intéressant, ce roman donne un coup d'œil admirable sur les agitations du Ku Klux Klan aux Etats-Unis.

Mais Llona fait encore mieux en traduisant Sherwood Anderson. Celui-ci est, on peut le dire assez sûrement, le plus grand romancier américain d'aujourd'hui. *Un conteur se raconte* (Kra, éditeur), son autobiographie romancée, est un livre d'une force peu habituelle. Les deux premiers volumes parus en français (c'est un gros livre que l'on publie à mesure qu'il est traduit) donnent déjà une idée de ce que sera le reste. Et le plus beau est encore à venir. Ceux qui ont lu l'original peuvent le garantir. Anderson est une des seules figures de notre époque auxquelles on pourrait comparer un Chamson sans faire de tort à ce dernier.

Nord de Jacques Heller (Grasset, éditeur), est encore un roman intéressant. Il nous a fait le récit d'un séjour arctique et nous offre des aperçus amusants et instructifs sur les Esquimaux.

En général, c'est apparent, on n'a pas à se plaindre des meilleurs du moins d'entre ces romans qui paraissent en si grand nombre cette saison.

QUELQUES DOCUMENTS

Dans cette collection « Les Ecrits » qu'il dirige, Jean Guéhenno a enfin donné son fameux livre si attendu *Caliban parle* (Grasset, éditeur). Dans la bouche de Caliban, symbole du peuple, il a mis les arguments que peuvent avancer comme défense les masses. Et très intelligemment, il montre le bon côté, le côté « aspiration à l'instruction » du peuple, cette victime des circonstances. Sobre, précis et fort, son livre est un des documents les plus importants et les plus intéressants qui existent sur le sujet.

Dans la même collection, on avait publié précédemment le *Belleville* de Robert Garric. Cette fois, c'est non pas l'homme du peuple, mais celui qui est allé éduquer le peuple, qui parle. Un autre point de vue, et qui fait pendant au livre de Guéhenno.

La maison Bernard Grasset publie encore une collection documentaire du plus haut intérêt, c'est « La Vie de Bohème » que dirige Francis Carco. Trois volumes déjà sont parus : un *Alfred Jarry* de Rachilde, intéressant au possible ; *Utrillo* de Francis Carco, moins amusant, mais un document de premier ordre ; et enfin, *Paul-Jean Toulet,* de Jacques Dyssord. Ce dernier, le plus intéressant de la série jusqu'ici, nous initie à la fois à l'œuvre et à la vie du grand poète méconnu des *Contrerimes.* On nous promet un *Modigliani* de Blaise Cendrars, dont on peut tout attendre et d'autres volumes intéressants.

Moins important est le livre de Régis Michaud, *Littérature Américaine* (Kra, éditeur). On ne pourrait trop décourager la lecture de ce livre aux gens curieux des lettres d'Amérique. Il est gavé d'erreurs et de mauvaises qualités.

Disques

WIÉNER ET DOUCET

Peut-être les exécutants les plus intéressants de ce moment sont les deux pianistes belges Wiéner et Doucet qui, lors de leur concert du 31 décembre 1928 à la salle Pleyel, furent accueillis par une ovation inouïe. Tout de précision et de rythme, leur art est perfectionné à un point étonnant. Aussi leurs disques méritent-ils l'intérêt des amateurs. Ecouter leurs disques de chez Columbia, c'est entendre une des manifestations de musique les plus importantes de notre jour. Lorsqu'ils jouent le *Chopinata* de Doucet (D 13009) ou *The Man I Love* de Gershwin (D 13020), ils nous

montrent un curieux mélange de musique américaine et européenne. Roland
Manuel dit qu'ils ont déniaisé la musique d'outre-Atlantique. En effet. Mais
ils lui ont ajouté des parures qui ne lui vont pas toujours très bien. Ce
qui n'empêche pas qu'ils jouent avec une perfection inégalée. Avec l'orchestre Whiteman, ils sont parmi les rares musiciens enregistrés qui vaillent
la peine d'être entendus.

Music

MISS THELMA SPEAR

Mis Thelma Spear (Mrs. Ludwig Lewisohn) gave an excellent recital
of English, German and Jewish songs a few weeks ago at the Salle
Majestic. In every case she interpreted the subtleties of the music with
intelligence and feeling and her voice left nothing to be desired.

....

American letters were harshly stricken by the death of Elinor Wylie,
from the consequences of an accident. She was the author of several
volumes of fine poetry and several novels.

C'est avec le plus grand serrement de cœur que nous apprenons la
mort à 55 ans de Léon Bazalgette. Rédacteur en chef d'*Europe,* membre
du Comité directoral de *Monde,* c'était un homme qui avait rendu de
grands services aux lettres françaises et américaines.

ACHETEZ
TOUS VOS LIVRES
ET VOS ÉDITIONS DE LUXE

— A —

L'OFFICE
— DE —
LIVRES
— DU —

CRAPOUILLOT

3, Place de la Sorbonne
— PARIS —

R. C. DUNNING'S

WINDFALLS

With portrait by Polia Chentoff
is on the press and will appear shortly

TENTATIVE PRICE : **40** francs

SUBSCRIPTIONS NOW RECEIVED

Edward W. TITUS
Publisher
4 et 8, Rue Delambre
PARIS

———×———

Abonnement (4 numéros) : 20 francs en France, un dollar à l'étranger. 4 issues : 20 fr., in France, 1 dollar elsewhere.

1

DANS CE NUMÉRO :

ANDRÉ SPIRE est l'auteur de plusieurs volumes de vers (*Versets, Poèmes juifs,* etc...) et de prose (*Quelques juifs et demi-juifs,* etc...).

PHILIPPE SOUPAULT a écrit plusieurs romans excellents (*Le bon apôtre, juifs,* etc...) et de prose (*Quelques juifs et demi-juifs,* etc...). Son poème dans ce numéro sera dans le recueil *Poèmes de Loire,* à paraître chez Grasset.

BLAISE CENDRARS, auteur de *Moravagine, La fin du monde, Kodak,* etc... est poète et prosateur. Il connut le début du mouvement dada, mais s'en éloigna fort heureusement.

LOUIS TOUCHAGUES, illustrateur de *Jeanne d'Arc* de Delteil et de divers autres livres, vient d'illustrer *Fredegonde* de Jean Cassou (Tremois, éditeur).

MAURICE COURTOIS-SUFFIT a déjà publié deux romans. Un recueil de nouvelles de lui doit paraître cette année.

MARIO MONTANARD est l'auteur, avec Jean Catel, du *Marchand de Statuettes,* du *Brasier,* etc... Il a collaboré à diverses revues.

LIANG-TSONG-TAI a publié un recueil de vers en Chine. Il a traduit en mandarin le *Narcisse* de Paul Valéry. Il vient aussi de traduire en français un volume de poèmes chinois.

IN THIS ISSUE :

RALPH CHEEVER DUNNING is the author of *Hyllus,* a dramatic poem, *Rococo,* a long poem, and a volume of shorter pieces to appear presently : *Windfalls.*

COUNTEE CULLEN is in France on a Guggenheim scholarship. He has published two volumes, *Color* and *Copper Sun,* and an anthology, *Caroling Dusk.*

LOUIS TOUCHAGUES is a young French artist and illustrator.

ELDER JAMES OLSON is a distinguished young American poet. He received an honorable mention for two poems which appeared in *Poetry.*

LIANG-TSONG-TAI is a young Chinese poet who writes equally in Chinese, English and French. He has published a book of verse in China.

STUART GILBERT is an English writer who has done many articles on James Joyce. He has appeared in *transition,* etc...

TAMBOUR

TAMBOUR

Directeur : Harold-J. SALEMSON, Editor

3, Rue Berthollet, PARIS (Vᵉ), France

Of this issue, 200 copies are numbered.

De ce numéro, 200 exemplaires ont été numérotés.

*Les jeunes gens semblaient se déta-
cher du tambour de leurs pères.*

Pierre MAC ORLAN.
(La Cavalière Elsa.)

LETTER TO 99

Brothers :

I wish neither to implore nor to defy you. I wish to
look you in the face and have you look back. Afterwards,
we will go out and have a drink together. For the

present, I am not I; you are not you. We are separated
by ten years. They are easily bridged by friendship.
Can we extend this confidence beyond personal matters?

You are the last children of a century that gave the
world a number of changes; you are the real victims of
the first cataclysm of a century which may do even
more.

Any number of you have already written your names
high in the firmament of art. Others among you have
shown the greatest promises.

But, arrested in your development by the War, to
which you were the impotent spectators and by which
you suffered even more than the immolated hosts, you
were perhaps slower than you might have been in
reaching the plateau of recognition. Today you are
there, but you have not held it long enough to feel that
it yet is your property, undisputed and secure. And we
have the indecency to arrive upon your heels already.

We scarcely felt the effects of the four-year catastrophe which we witnessed as children. On the contrary,
we were drawn into the forward reaction that followed
it and it seems, to us at least, that we have matured
with unusual rapidity.

I may be wrong. We are doubtless still only groping
children. But our gropings have brought us into contact

with you. Your elders, whom you dislodged with much difficulty, are open-armed in welcoming us. And we are not in competition with them. But you and we are differently related.

I would not even hint at jealousy. I have too much admiration for you to believe that you could fear us. Still, what other cause might we consider as the basis of the half-hearted welcome we receive?

This cannot continue. I, for one, believe that an entente is not only possible but imperative. I hope my immediate contemporaries agree with me. But it takes two to make a bargain. I think we are strong enough not to be afraid to fight. But we will not begin unless we are forced to it.

Will it be peace or war?   Harold J. Salemson.

N. B. — This letter, which is statement of fact, has to do only with American generations. In France, the divisions are not the same.

Many of the men of 99 (and I take that year as a symbol of the generation born in the last years of the XIXth century and the first of ours) have been extremely cordial. This is not aimed at them. It has in view those who have shown themselves slow in acceptation.

Moreover, through a great lack of modesty, I have
made myself the spokesman of my generation. I have
no right to this position. But I sincerely hope that
Tambour may become the first real manifestation of
this litter.   H. J· S.

LITTÉRATURE et ESPRIT

Dans son intéressant essai sur les littérateurs et la
révolution qui vient de paraître dans *Europe*, Emmanuel Berl disait : « ...la littérature moderne n'est pas
drôle, mais les littérateurs sont spirituels... », et d'énu-
mérer les littérateurs pleins d'esprit. Or, si je ne
partage pas l'opinion de M. Berl sur certains écrivains,
il n'en est pas moins vrai qu'il a vu juste.

L'esprit, voilà le grand mal de la littérature contemporaine. On ne peut l'admettre que s'il est doublé d'un
ferme talent. Anatole France pouvait se payer le luxe
d'être spirituel. Jean Cocteau le peut aussi. Mais il
n'en va pas de même pour... pour certains qu'il est
inutile de nommer ici (pour devancer toute attaque,
j'atteste de suite que je suis lâche).

On se laisse trop souvent prendre au piège de l'esprit.
Et, s'il a du bon chez les grands talents, les petits

disciples ne copient que cette apparence amusante,
derrière laquelle se trouve donc un vide lamentable.
Guillaume Apollinaire était spirituel, mais il n'en était
pas moins un grand écrivain. Pourra-t-on se contenter
aujourd'hui de Louis Aragon?

En peinture, André Masson est spirituel. Mais Max
Ernst n'est *que* spirituel. Voyez la différence.

L'amusement ne peut se suffire à lui-même. Qui
connaît encore les contemporains de Rabelais? Et pourtant il n'a pas dû être seul. Voltaire aussi a été imité.
Se rappelle-t-on par qui?

La boîte doit être à double fond. Lorsqu'on aura
dissimulé celui qui glisse, il doit rester le vrai, celui qui
est stable, qu'on n'enlèvera pas sans démolir la boîte.

Les bons mots ne restent que s'ils portent. Pour cela,
ils doivent faire plus que d'amuser. Les confiseries sont
doublement alléchantes si on les a préparées avec des
matières de première qualité. Autrement pour bon que
soit leur aspect, elles exhaleront l'infecte odeur du
beurre rance qui a servi à les confectionner. On ne
mange pas uniquement pour la joie du ventre. On ne lit
pas uniquement pour la joie du moment. Et pourtant,
quels plats littéraires sont plus attrayants que ceux de
Jean Giraudoux, de Jean Cocteau, ou de Philippe Soupault (réunion volontairement « incompatible »)?

Même Paul Valéry est parfois spirituel. Mais il sait
préparer la sauce sans gâter le mets. Nous n'avons pas
de mauvais goût dans la bouche au réveil.
L'esprit, hors-d'œuvre, ne nuit à rien. Mais, comment
songer à en faire un plat de résistance? Il accroît le
repas, mais ne doit pas diminuer sa valeur nourris-
sante.

Le rire seul est nécessairement amer. Lorsqu'on s'est
diverti à voir les imbécillités d'un quelconque acteur de
cinéma, on se sent soudain soi-même vide, inutile. Par
contre, Chaplin, qui amuse bien plus, nous laisse avec
la sensation de nous avoir enrichis.

De même en littérature. De grâce, ne troquons pas la
vraie valeur de la parole écrite, contre l'amusement
passager qu'elle peut nous donner.

Quel philantrope nous indiquera le remède à ce fléau
intellectuel?   Harold J. Salemson.

N. B. — Après avoir écrit cette note, je relève dans
le *Plan de l'Aiguille*, le nouveau roman de Blaise
Cendrars (autre écrivain qui, à l'occasion, a su être
spirituel) : « L'art n'est pas un paradoxe, l'art n'est
pas un jeu d'esprit, ni une mode plus ou moins spirituelle, ni une pose... c'est un phénomène aussi complexe
que la vie... »

TOUCHAGUES : **Pierre MAC ORLAN**

LA CHANCE[1]

La face d'un dé marqué de cinq points noirs, offre un spectacle d'art nègre suffisant. La tête est indiquée dans la belle matière des résidus de l'anthropophagie : les os.

Hamlet, providence des esprits vagues, avec ses trois dés pouvait tirer de soi-même un parti aussi séduisant que celui qui lui laissa cette réputation internationale dont nous sommes encore victimes, à certaines heures.

En ce moment, les trois dés posés sur ma table de bois jaune, couleur du Sahara, projettent trois petites ombres régulières et donnent les premiers éléments d'un village marocain : c'est-à-dire trois cabarets espagnols. C'est un aspect bien suffisant de la nature méditerranéenne pour un homme qui a l'électricité chez lui, comme on possède une sentinelle inconnue dont on ne sait si elle protège votre sommeil ou si elle guette le moment favorable d'accomplir un meurtre savamment prémédité.

---

[1] Le lecteur reconnaîtra dans cette nouvelle inédite, la première version de l'œuvre de Pierre Mac Orlan, *Port d'eaux-mortes.* — H. J. S.

***

A B.., sur les quais du port de commerce, entre la boutique d'un pharmacien démocrate et le magasin d'un shipchandler, se trouve le bar du *Petit Nord*. La patronne s'appelle Jeanne : c'est une blonde au visage de Japonaise. Elle vend des alcools excellents avec autorité.

Par la fenêtre du bar, on aperçoit le quai, la perspective du troisième bassin, la cheminée d'un grand remorqueur hollandais, qui nuit et jour attend, tous ses feux allumés, le signal de secour d'un cargo talonné par la tempête aux yeux de poulpe. Ces messieurs de l'état-major du remorqueur hollandais sont grands et roses. On les rencontre rue de Siam, à l'heure de l'apéritif, tous les quatre vêtus d'imperméables kaki et coiffés d'une casquette grise bien enfoncée sur la tête.

Le bar du *Petit Nord* n'offre que sa propreté pour séduire l'œil des clients. On y boit poliment, aux uns, aux autres, à mille santés traditionnelles et internationales. Un mystère de bon ton pénètre avec quelques clients débarqués, sans crier gare. Quelquefois, rarement, un jeune officier de la marine de guerre y conduit une femme, qu'il n'a sûrement pas bien vue, sous les deux yeux froids et réprobateurs de la bigoudène aux cheveux oxygénés.

Au loin, dans la rade, les bâtiments de l'état font école de T. S. F. Dans l'ombre d'une porte, déjà cernée par la pluie, les beaux yeux d'une trop belle fille portant le costume d'Ouessant, luisent, s'éteignent, alternativement. Le costume est interdit par la police des mœurs.

*
* *

Ce soir-là, pour boire, je dus, malgré le geste de Jeanne qui m'indiquait une place, demander l'autorisation de m'asseoir à un fort Monsieur, aux yeux gris, qui occupait déjà la table. Il accepta de la tête ma présence et, un peu gêné par son voisinage, je me mis à frotter mes mains l'une contre l'autre, d'un air plus niais que distingué.

A boire vite et sans parler, l'alcool se venge. Nous buvions tous deux, je crois, de la fine qui provenait d'une même bouteille.

Le fort Monsieur, qui était âgé, prit la bouteille avec autorité et me versa un verre. Il leva son verre à la hauteur de ses yeux et je lui rendis son salut, selon l'usage de l'impériale armée de l'ivresse publique.

L'homme parlait français, mais avec précaution, il
sortit de sa poche un poker dice et aligna les cinq dés
sur la table en les rangeant par figures : le roi, la dame,
le valet, l'as et le dix.

Puis, il renifla mélancoliquement.

A ce moment, la porte s'ouvrit et un personnage qui
semblait né   dans le brouillard, tant sa consistance
semblait molle, vint s'échouer à notre coffre, je veux
dire à la table où les sentiments du vieil homme fort et
les miens semblaient faire la parade autour des dés
alignés.

L'homme mou, à la chair de poisson gras, s'inclina
comme je l'avais fait. Puis, il saisit la bouteille, se
versa un verre, l'éleva à la hauteur de son œil et en
avala le contenu d'un trait.

— Ça va mieux, fit-il.

Il aperçut alors les dés alignés sur la table et étendit
la main pour les prendre.

L'homme fort arrêta brutalement son geste.

— Bas les pattes ! hein !

Jeanne, dans son comptoir, leva la tête. Ses yeux

cherchèrent le point faible de la bagarre. Mais tout
s'apaisa, car personne ne commenta le geste de l'homme
âgé.

*
* *

Dehors, il pleuvait bêtement. Une tristesse parfaitement septentrionale pénétrait en nous, pauvres éponges,
que l'alcool assouplissait dans la nuit.

Jeanne sortit pour pisser dans sa courette, nous
laissant seuls, et nos regards se rencontrèrent durement
dans la direction de la caisse.

Ce ne fut qu'un instant de faiblesse, un appel très
sourd, probablement de notre passé.

Le vieux Monsieur se leva. Le nez goguenard et l'œil
ranimé il chanta :

> Je te baiserai Cath'rine,
> Si tu viens pisser dans mes choux...

Jeanne se mit à rire et nous l'imitâmes machinalement. Elle dit : « Mon oncle est soûl. Qu'est-ce que sa
femme va lui passer ».

— Assez! fit le vieux, et il jeta les dés qu'il avait
ramassé dans le creux de sa main.

*
**

— Un full!

— Quelle poisse! Jeanne, amène la bouteille, chérie.

— Oh vache!

Ainsi, nous devisâmes et bûmes jusqu'à l'aube. Trois fois, le mari de Jeanne qui travaillait sur le port vint la chercher pour fermer la boutique; et, somme toute, pour nous foutre dehors. A chaque tentative, Jeanne murmurait: « laisse... » A l'aube, la pluie se mêla à la mer comme la poix au goudron. On voyait cela à travers les vitres, sans trop tourner la tête.

Je vis que le grand vieux avait du sang à ses manchettes de chemise et probablement sur le devant de son veston noir. L'homme mou le remarqua peut-être. J'avais tant de choses à me reprocher que je n'eus pas l'instinct d'estimer à sa juste valeur sociale ma découverte.

— Jouons notre chance! dit le vieux, quand il ne resta plus rien dans la bouteille.

Nous jouâmes le dernier tour avec férocité.

Et le soleil avec l'aide de la patronne nous jeta tous les trois, non sur le quai, mais sur une petite rue, qui par derrière accédait à la courette de l'établissement.

Tous les trois, honteux, nous nous serrâmes la main

furtivement en emportant notre destin dans la dernière combinaison marquée par les dés.

C'est ainsi que je devins écrivain pour mener une vie définitivement honorable.

L'homme mou devint un assassin célèbre. Et comme il était d'origine anglaise, il fut pendu à Londres, cependant que trois filles pauvres s'agenouillaient dans la boue, devant la porte de la prison, au premier coup de la cloche.

Et quant à l'homme qui avait assassiné, le fort inconnu au veston maculé de sang, il oublia son passé, adopta une petite fille, devint aveugle et fut conduit par elle sur la route lumineuse de la vertu.

Pierre Mac Orlan.

THREE APPROACHES

I

The bird-wing is a little fan.
The invisible, great hands of twilight
Slowly use the fan to make
Cold the memory of countless days
Waiting to die upon the night.
But your half-dark smile does not cease
To wave the flutter of love I give.
Is there no night within you?

II

One lone frog in the marshes
Stammers raspingly and almost faints
Beneath his delusion of fluid, sweetest music.
The night-winds carry his voice tenderly.
The marsh-reeds tremble to take its small strength.
The lily-pads hold it when it seems to pause.
Perhaps it is fluid and sweet
To all except human ears.
Will you enter the marshes and sit beside me?

III

No one regards the pebble
Resting in a corner of the garden
Upon so thick, so hugely effortless
Understandings of black loam.
Only spring is touching it
With lavishings of soft belief
And laughing at the little, hard skeptic
Who does not need to move.
Only spring can fathom
Pebbles in your heart and mine.

Maxwell BODENHEIM.

MÉLANCOLIE AU GRAND AIR

La tête du poète s'élargit sur la mer
qui suce les rayons obliques du soleil;
les poissons stériles pleurent
la mort de leur bonheur
et les algues reflètent pour toujours
l'angoisse d'une prison marine.

L'oiseau pense que les vagues patinoire
d'un rêve torturé de glissades
se dépêchent d'échapper au soir
qui les engloutira dans sa pommade.

L'oiseau pense, l'oiseau pense pourquoi?
La tête du poète silencieux
ne cherche ni la mort ni l'amour
ni la vie ni le vin des cieux.

La tête du poète s'efface
et son ombre coule à pic dans les flots.
Seul l'oiseau reste et se mire dans la glace
de l'eau.
             Les poissons trouvent cela beau.

Edouard Roditi.

2

OFTEN AT NIGHT

Slowly I
sink into depths of
greasy smoke where insects
stink and a soft motion of
wheels blurs silence. Slowly
shadows turn voices rise
slowly a train leaves
tracks on my ears and slowly I
weary of the sound of
breath.

Often I
hear the engines of my
breath at night puffing
thick smoke of anguish often a
swift twitching of my hands
a grasping of timorous hands
frightens away sleep often
echoes arise from the
dark shell of night.

Slowly I sinking
into depths slowly
grasping at consciousness clinging
to consciousness slowly
drowned in a nauseous
sleep I slowly sinking
forget the blurred sound of
breath.

Edouard RODITI.

Hommage à
Raymond Roussel

Jean COCTEAU : **Dessin**

MULATTO GIRL 1926

(*After Pascin*)

Snug sofa cuddles her nestled body neat
into so many such soft good restful knobs
of cozy meat and skin. If thinking robs
desire, makes it thin, why waste good nerve
of such unamiable hire, she likes warm fire.
And squeezed into this fluid body she can serve
her passion toddy or exquisitive repose.
Comfort tingles not too violent her nose
and she is sober like a padded rose.

SONNET 1924

Since naught may dwell but in the flow of cir-
cumstance and nothing measured in a pause
of tide nor halting estimate the cause
by arithmetic certainty, aver
no interest beyond the sense of stir,
but stir the sense too volatile for laws
to postulate new movement in the paws
of Sphinx, stressing the immortal silent cur
beyond the sands to wide hypotheses.
And — when in the swollen unceasing tide
the dual creature bathes — shall you evoke
consideration of eternal pride,
the floating essence and shall nimbly tease
the dullard secret with a space in smoke.

Harry Alan POTAMKIN.

CADEAUX

Je vous dédie ce que j'ai lu dans la journée,
Le chapitre cent trois du roman-feuilleton
Où l'héroïne meurt dans un Château breton
En regrettant tout bas sa jeunesse fânée.

Je vous offre les visions du cinéma:
Charlot blessant les cœurs de son rire livide,
L'ouest désert où bondit comme une Ford avide
Douglas fuyant trois mille indiens d'Oklahoma.

Je vous offre un chant russe et de nobles sonates,
Toutes les fleurs d'un étalage parisien,
Un tableau de Gromaire et des meubles anciens,
Tout ce qui rentre dans ma tête et la dilate.

C'est pourtant vrai, que jamais rien de tout cela
Ne fut à moi, mais je comprends toutes ces choses.
Un fleuriste distrait peut dédaigner ses roses.
Mais le passant les prend dans ses yeux... les voilà.

SONNET

Je veux écrire un sonnet plein de guitares
Pour Madame Marie Laurencin
Qui peint avec les roses et les gris, les plus rares,
Des femmes qui ont des yeux immenses et pas de seins.

De mon âme la plus secrète elle s'empare
Avec ses douceurs de couleur et de dessin.
Tant je l'aime, ces vers voudraient être sans fin
Et chanter autour d'elle des romances Baléares.

Car il doit en exister, n'est-ce pas...
Nées d'îles orangères ou de mers scintillantes,
Et que des balancelles apportent en tas...

Bonjour madame, à travers tout ce qui nous sépare
Qu'une colombe vous offre mes pensées insistantes
Et ce sonnet si vague et mon chant de guitare.

                                        Mario MONTANARD

THESE WASTES

Corrugated motives,   wasted;
as
wrinkled segments,   wasted;
as
ragged pursuits   wasted;
as
halted highways   wasted;

Wasted   not the elements
as
wasted   am 1
in
wasted   ragged pursuits
on
wasted   corrugated highways.

FOR EVERY REEL
OF OUR EMOTION

Must I tear this unspoken word into a caption
And paint it with white ink on black sheets,
Then arrange it in symetrical order;
Have thousands thrown from high buildings
For you to see, fluttering about like flakes
Of snow?

Like flakes of snow,
These words,
Are cold and geometrical.

                                                    Paul Du Pont.

Henriette BERGER : **Lithograph**

LETTRE A P'EI-TI

Depuis peu, pendant le mois sacrificatoire, il a fait
un temps calme et clair et nous aurions pu, comme
jadis, nous promener ensemble à la montagne. Mais je
savais que tu étais plongé dans la lecture des classiques
et n'osais pas te déranger.

J'errai donc seul dans les montagnes, me reposai au
Temple Kann-P'ei, dînai avec les moines montagnards,
et repartis après le dîner. Au nord, je traversai le
Yüen-Pa; sur les eaux brillait la lune en son contour
resplendissant. Dans le calme de la nuit, je montai à
la Colline Hua-Tseu, regardant sur l'onde agitée de la
Rivière Wang, flotter et sombrer la lune...

A présent, sur les montagnes glaciales, au-delà de la
forêt, oscillent de petites lumières; un chien, au sein
de l'allée, aboie contre le froid, avec un cri aussi féroce
que le hurlement du loup; le son des villageois moulant
leur grain remplit les intervalles entre les notes
qu'égrène lentement une cloche lointaine. J'écoute at-
tentivement, tandis que mes domestiques reposent en
silence. Je songe beaucoup aux jours anciens, comme

nous descendions, la main dans la main, le sentier sinueux vers les ruisseaux limpides, composant des vers en marchant.

Nous devons attendre le retour du printemps, quand les herbes bourgeonneront et que les arbres seront en fleurs. Alors, errant parmi les collines printanières, nous regarderons ensemble les truites s'élancer du ruisseau, les mouettes blanches déployer leurs ailes sur la mousse rafraîchie de rosée, et, au matin, nous entendrons les cris des courlis dans les champs d'orge...

L'attente ne sera pas longue. Seras-tu alors avec moi? Si je ne connaissais la subtilité naturelle de ton esprit, je ne t'aurais importuné avec une affaire d'aussi peu d'importance. Mais tu comprends cette joie profonde... Rappelle-toi.

WANG-WEI, *un habitant des montagnes.*

(Traduit du chinois par LIANG TSONG TAI.)

THE COUNT

It was six weeks before the Count's appearance that George arrived in the section. The Chef's staff car, which had been sent to meet him in Châlons, happened to pull up before my ambulance, spattering my front wheels with as much mud as I had scraped from them since breakfast; so my first view of him no doubt was prejudiced.

« Soft », I remember thinking, « and just a kid ».

He could not have been more than eighteen; rather pale, with a girl's complexion, black hair, and eyes that avoided your glance with a kind of apologetic selfconsciousness. By the end of a month we knew him hardly better than at first, though I had discovered, to my surprise, that I liked him. I was convinced that if you could penetrate his diffidence, you would find something delicate and sincere — a temperament highly-wrought, insecure perhaps, but certainly not weak. It was obvious that he had been thrown little with boys. He spent much of his spare time writing to his mother.

We had asked him several evenings to drink cocoa with us about the iron stove set up in a corner of the

loft where a few of us slept. He had hardly spoken on
these occasions, and when any one told a smutty story
he would stare at the floor with a strained, uncomfor-
table smile. One day, during his fifth week in the section,
being sent to poste with him — to a dirty little abri
under a bank, with a battery of 75's behind it — I
began calling him by his first name. It pleased him, I
knew; but during that afternoon he was more than
usually silent.

After supper, which we had at five o'clock with the
brancardiers, I had written a letter in the abri. Then
the sound of a barrage in a neighboring sector had
driven me out to see what was going on. I found George
sitting in the grass on top of the bank, staring westward, across the fields of the Champagne, to the hills
along whose scarred and ashen crests extended the German lines.

Over the horizon hung a screen of purple smoke that
stood out theatrically against the yellow sky above it,
while shells continually bursting along the ridge sent
up great black mushrooms of earth. Fusées, golden or
white or silvery green, broke into constellated stars,
or hovered, burning in the afterglow, like butterflies of
phosphorus.

« Rather nice, isn't it? » I asked.

My voice startled him. « I think it's horrible », he
said — « like a nightmare ».

« A nightmare? » I didn't catch his meaning. « You
haven't seen anything especially bad yet, have you?
This sector's been dead since last fall. »

« I don't mean any special horrors, » he went on.
« I mean the whole thing. It's so powerful and strange...
the star-shells, and the guns you're always hearing.
But it's just as bad back at the cantonment. It seems
so far away... so far from everything you've known
before. I can't get used to it ». Then he added in a low
voice: « You know I get terribly homesick... so homesick I can't see straight ».

I told him that he ought not to keep so much to
himself; that the work did seem strange at first, but
that presently you thought of it as the dullest kind of
routine.

He did not answer for a long time. The sky was
darkening, and high above the blink and flare of the
fusées, the real stars burned quietly and steadily. At
last he spoke in a constrained, jerky voice — so wretched that it made me look away.

« Perhaps that's true for most. But I don't get on
with people. I'm different. I guess I must be. It's my
fault. I'm no good. God, I despise myself! »

« George, what is it? » I asked. « What's the matter? »

But he had risen to his feet, as if afraid, and was hurrying down the slope towards the abri.

« Don't mind me », he said without looking back. « Please don't come. Please! I've got some letters I must write. I'm just a fool. You mustn't mind. »

Three days after that I went on my leave to Paris, and when I returned the Count had come.

I saw him for the first time that evening at supper, which we ate around a long table in a lean-to at one side of the barn. What made me notice him, apart from his being a new-comer, was the fact that he was sitting beside George and talking to him with the utmost friendliness. This predisposed me in his favor, and I began to study him more closely.

He must have been thirty two or three. He had yellow curly hair, and a bald spot on the crown of his head. A little golden moustache, with twisted ends, failed to conceal his moist, well-shaped lips and gave an agreeable accent to the pink and whiteness of his face. His eyes were small and keen, glancing this way and that, as if to take in what was going on around him, yet always returning with a fresh intensity to George. I think he would have struck me as handsome, if he had been quite so plump.

3

The next morning, as we were washing our cars, I questioned George about him.

« He's very clever, » George said; « and he's been awfully nice to me ».

I asked if he was really a count.

« Oh no, » George replied. « They just called him that, because his moustache makes him look sort of foreign, dont't you know, and he speaks with a slight accent. He's an American really; but he's spent most of his life in France, and he's travelled all over the world. »

« He must be interesting, » I said.

Then the Count himself appeared and George introduced me to him.

And certainly, whatever else may be said about him, the Count was interesting. He would talk of French or American politics, of moral questions, of books or of music, with a witty and daring precison that dazzled our inexperience. His range of taste was wide, but it tended on the whole to the *précieux*. I fancied that he took nothing with more than a wilfully limited degree of seriousness. In the midst of the most earnest argument his lips would slowly broaden beneath his bright little up-turned moustache, and his expression would suggest to me that his real attitude was quizzical, if not mocking.

This veil of irony that he kept between himself and the rest of us might have proved irritating if it had not been for his continuous and urbane good-nature. And then, of course, there was his his kindness to George.

During those spring days George and he, when they were both in the cantonment, were always together. Indeed, under his influence, George became less shy with the rest of us, probably because now in his absorption with the Count he had grown less conscious of himself. He talked proudly of his new friend, and sometimes he would flush with pleasure when the Count spoke affectionately to him. So warm had their friendship become by the first week in June that its sudden ending created a good deal of talk.

They had left the cantonment together after lunch. At about four o'clock, as I sat writing in my car, I noticed them enter our barnyard and saw at once that something was wrong. Not that the Count gave any sign. With his smooth khaki uniform, whose neat fit seemed to minimize the plumpness that threatened his figure, his pink and white face, his tranquilly ironic smile, he appeared as self-possessed as usual. But it was George that shocked me to attention. The boy was walking hurriedly; his lips were set as if to prevent his crying; about his eyes and his brow there was a look of misery and, it seemed to me, of terror. He went to his car and began fumbling in the toolbox. The Count chatted with me until George disappeared into the barn.

For the next week, the week before the coup de main at the 39th, I did not see them once together. Several times I tried to draw George into conversation, but he refused to talk. He looked depressed, almost ill. I thought that the Count, too, seemed to regret the quarrel, though he never referred to it. I had been following its course with such interest that when, on the morning of the sixth of June, they were sent together to the 39th, I was curious to see what would be the outcome of this forced twenty-four hours in each other's company.

Then, that evening, when word came that the project of a German coup de main had leaked through the lines, and Marsdon and I received orders to join them, my curiosity was quickened by the chef's remarking that George had pleaded with him not to be sent to poste with the Count. « George couldn't give me any reason, » he said, « so I told him he had to go. I can't consider personal prejudices. That boy's just a God-damned kid ». The chef had certainly not considered « prejudices », in the case of Marsdon and me. Marsdon was a loudmouthed bigot, with a keen sense of his own humor; and his description of me, were he to write one, would be equally unattractive.

It was about seven o'clock that we started. The gray sky was curdled into bits of whitish fluff near the zenith; across the fields there sprawled a chalky network of wagon trails. Night fell thickly as we drove on, straight toward the hills; and by the time we reached the poste for the 39th, a kilometre from their foot, we could just distinguish the road.

The poste de secours was reached by a zigzag trench. Ten yards in you came to a square doorway, clambered some twenty steps down a boarded shaft, and there you were. We Americans had a smaller dugout just beyond it, where we slept alone.

Marsdon had been ahead of me, and by the time I had collected my blankets to follow him along the trench, he had disappeared. At the shaft entrance, I stopped to draw breath, for the air was poor below, and then began to back down the steps, taking care not to bump my head. Marsdon was talking in a loud voice at the bottom of the shaft. All at once I realized that he was jeering, blatantly, unbearably, at George and the Count. I paused for an instant to listen, then stumbled in anger down the remaining steps.

A kerosene lamp on a strip of board bracketed to the wall cast a sooty light through the dug-out — a chalky cavern not more than eight feet square, with two tiers of bunks that took up most of the space. Marsdon stood near the entrance, his back towards me, staring at the Count who sat half-dressed on the edge of the lower bunk and whose features were strained into a likeness of ironic detachment. George was standing before the bunk, his hair towsled, his eyes fixed on Marsdon with, the agonized, incredulous look you see on the face of a child the instant after it is hurt and before it breaks into tears.

« You God-damned fairies! » Marsdon shouted. Then he changed his tone to a mincing affectation. « I do hope you'll pawdon me, Gawge. I just hate to cut in on your little party. I feel so chagrined I could smack myself on the wrist. » He heard me behind him and turned. « Isn't this just the cutest love-nest? » he said. « I guess they weren't counting on visitors. I had a hunch something might be up, so I came kind of softly. Won't the boys in the section be pleased, though? Oh dearie me, ain't we got fun? »

« Shut up, Marsdon! » I requested. For a minute no one spoke. With a shrug of his shoulders, Marsdon began to whistle. Once I thought the Count was going

to say something, but he checked himself. He had turned
his gaze from Marsdon to George; and I was suddenly
convinced, though his expression hardly changed, that
his strongest emotion just then was pity for the boy.
The air was rank with the smell of kerosene, and so
chilly here underground, that we could see our breaths.
Then George crossed the room to the stairway and
disappeared into the shaft.

Presently Marsdon vaulted into the upper bunk. The
Count lit a cigarette. I sat down on the bottom step of
the stairway idly listening to the thud of the shells that
had begun to come in from the Boche. There was a
concussion more violent than the rest; another followed
it. They did not seem loud down here, but you felt the
jar. It occurred to me that George ought not to be
wandering around without shelter.

As I was starting up the stairs, the Count's voice
came to me sharply. « Where are you going? »

« Up to look for George », I said.

« Wait a second. I'll come too. »

« All right. Come along. »

He put on his coat and shoes, and was ready in a
moment.

When we reached the top of the stairs I was surprised
at the din. There was nothing very near, but behind us

a rather heavy barrage was preparing for the coup de
main. The shells were big ones, and we could hear them
hurtling over our heads with the rumble and shriek of
the little wooden cars at Coney Island.

A fusée rose suddenly and hung poised, like a huge
calcium lamp, casting our shadows on the white wall
of the trench. We looked into the cars. The boy was in
none of them. Next the Count ran back to the Poste de
Secours on the chance that he might have taken refuge
there; but he had not. Without making any plan, we
started up the road toward the lines, the Count peering
to the right, and I to the left. We had not gone twenty
yards when he called me. I ran to him. He was pointing
to a pale hollow, ten feet off the road, in which I could
make out something dark and extended. We walked
across to it, and there was no mistaking, even in the
gloom, that it was an ambulance uniform.

« An éclat », the Count said quickly.

But I leaned over.

« It looks too broken up for that, unless the shell was
almost on top of him, » I said. « I dont't see any new
shell holes ».

« Then he must have stepped on a hand grenade...
By mistake. » The last two words were spoken under
his breath, yet I heard them clearly.

Just then another star shell, soaring high above the
hills, cast a bluish glare all about us, and lit up in detail
a face, flattened and enlarged, like the painted gray
and red mask of a South Sea idol.

I glanced at the Count. His lips were drawn. He was
staring at the thing with an intensity so fixed that it
seemed passionless.

« He was killed on duty, » I said, when I could force
myself to speak. « We must tell Marsdon ».

But the Count did not hear me.

Samuel ROGERS·

MON CORPS DE L'AMOUR ENFUI

Tes lèvres aujourd'hui sous ma bouche avaient le goût frissonnant des hiers évanouis, et leur nouveauté. Départ: séparation affaiblie de serrements de mains et de tous les serments.

Oh! la rue verte noyée dans l'eau des réverbères! Ton regard tremble encore comme une veilleuse étouffée par les grands rideaux de peluche rouge, et puis il meurt.

La rue seule; et tous les murs et les portes et fenêtres devinées.

Je marche — comme le sol est doux sous mes pas, il ne cabre plus son silence sonore: Pas: un pied devant l'autre, et ainsi de suite.

La rue.

Naissance d'une porte. J'ai vécu jusqu'à la naissance de cette porte, et pour la naissance de cette porte. O ma belle âme hypocrite qui cachais ainsi tes desseins!

Entrer.

Il y a des jardins derrière cette porte, où je te retrouverai, vêtue d'étoiles. Tes gestes seront doux comme la lune pour deviner mes appels. Je te trouverai, et nous

nous présenterons à nous-mêmes; pense toutes les beautés qu'il a fallu celer jusqu'à maintenant. Nous serons délicieusement infirmes pour nous contempler.

Et maintenant, c'est le jardin.

La porte a fini son existence éphémère, merci Sublime porte, car voici le jardin!

Illimité, illimité, le jardin. Je te retrouverai au kiosque à musique, après le petit pont de rocailles près d'où bâillent les deux vieux cygnes.

Le jardin.

Mon corps sombre dans le jardin, le jardin est à moi, oh! que j'ai d'arbres!

Cette vie sans embûches : l'avenir apparaît tourmenté mais les obstacles sont en moi.

On a enlevé tous le bancs pour les repeindre, c'est pourquoi je ne les reconais plus — bancs verts offerts avec ferveur.

Je n'ai pas voulu lui faire de mal : le bois s'est déchiré sous ma chaussure (le cauchemar d'Epinal).

Mais je t'aime — même les marguerites vont être en papier — hélas! ce n'en est plus la saison, mes oiseaux devraient s'éveiller.

Mon corps livré aux eaux calmes, nagera jusqu'au tout petit rocher.

C'est toujours le jardin, et c'est le lac où tes mains
semaient des bulles.

Le kiosque à musique est prisonnier des algues. Mon
âme a perdu son corps.

Paris 1927.   Michel-J. ARNAUD.

EAT, DRINK,
AND BE MERRY...

Jim was a quiet boy. He stayed home, idling away
his time as best he could, not caring much for anything.
He had resigned himself to following the career his
parents had chosen for him and he appeared to wish
nothing better than to fulfill all the ideals of everyday
morality. In fine, a quiet boy, he would grow into a
good man.

Of course, Jim had his secret little whims, as everyone
has, but nary a word out of him on the subject. No one
suspected anything of the sort. He realized that he had
best not tell and was wise enough to keep his secrets to
himself.

He had a bad habit of staring at women in the street,
sometimes even stopping, turning, and watching them
as they continued walking. Several times he had all but
created scandals.

And thus his life sped on until something happened
to him when he was about nineteen.

He was walking down a street when, passing in front
of a building that was in the course of construction,
he was the victim of an accident. How it actually happened he never knew. All he could remember later was
the sudden shock and then lapsing into unconsciousness.

When he emerged from the hospital several months
later, no one could have recognized him. He looked like
a sorry wreck; the remains of a person undermined by
some devastating disease. His face and head were
practically one scar. He limped terribly, his back was
bent, and his right arm was no longer. From far, he
might have been taken for an old man.

Still, he was not ill-tempered. He continued his life
practically as it had been before. But a growing lone-
someness was upon him. He felt expatriated. There
was somewhere a land of which he had but seen a mira-
ge in dream; and to that land Jim longed to go.

The longing grew in intensity so that he could think
of nothing else. An end had to be put to it, he felt.

He dragged on until, at length:

« Chr-r-r-r-ist », he muttered, as he pulled the trigger.

Harold J. SALEMSON.

DEUX GRANDS FILMS :
SOLITUDE et LA FOULE

Voici deux films dont la réussite est inégale, mais qui, par la noblesse
de leurs intentions et la qualité cinégraphique dont ils témoignent, consti-
tuent assurément les deux œuvres les plus marquantes de la saison. Le
plus curieux est qu'ils présentent de nombreux points communs. Analysons-
les séparément; nous les comparerons ensuite.

*
**

D'abord, *Solitude* (*Lonesome*), de Paul Fejos.
A New-York, un samedi matin. Deux chambres modestes : dans l'une,
Mary, téléphoniste; dans l'autre, Jim, ouvrier. Chacun se hâte vers son
travail : déjeuner rapide, cohue, métro; enfin, le central et l'usine.
Midi· Semaine anglaise. Tous les camarades de Jim vont chercher leur
petite amie. Toutes les compagnes de Mary trouvent à la sortie leur flirt.
Jim reste seul. Mary reste seule. Impénétrable solitude, au milieu de huit
millions d'hommes.
Dans leurs chambres, ils s'ennuient, malgré le livre, le magazine et le
phono. Soudain, un air de jazz : c'est une voiture publicitaire chargée de
musiciens qui passe dans la rue et draîne vers Coney-Island, la plage populaire, tous les désœuvrés new-yorkais.
Jim et Mary s'y rendent. Un hasard fait qu'ils se rencontrent dans le
même car. Jim remarque la jeune fille, la suit; ils font enfin connaissance.
Et dès lors c'est un enchantement· Ils ne savent rien l'un de l'autre, à
part leur petit nom... Mais ils se parlent, parfois leurs doigts s'effleurent,
ils participent aux mêmes distractions simples : bain, danse, manèges. Ils
ne sont plus seuls, un bonheur immense les soulève.
Un sot accident les sépare. Et à travers la foule, ils se cherchent désespérément. C'est leur seule chance de se revoir, puisqu'ils ignorent réci-

proquement leurs adresses. La nuit vient, et l'orage... Retombés à leur solitude, l'âme ravagée, ils rentrent dans leur chambre inhospitalière. Machinalement, Jim choisit un disque : *I'll be loving you always,* l'air sur lequel ils ont dansé. Et voici que l'occupant de la chambre voisine heurte le mur à coups de poing. Jim, hargneux, se rue dans la chambre d'où viennent les coups ; c'est Mary qu'il y découvre, Mary dont le phono avivait la douleur, Mary qui, depuis des mois peut-être, habitait la pièce contiguë à celle de Jim.

Tel est le sujet de *Solitude,* un sujet simple, poignant, humain.

*
**

Maintenant, *La Foule (The Crowd),* de King Vidor.

Un enfant naît, John Sims. Quand ses petits camarades lui demandent ce qu'il fera plus tard, John répond : « Papa dit que je serai quelqu'un ». Pendant toute son enfance et son adolescence, il est hanté de cette idée : devenir quelqu'un. A vingt ans, riche d'espoir, il arrive à New-York.

Et dès lors le voici englobé dans la foule. Foule au restaurant et dans la rue. Foule au travail, dans l'immense salle de banque où chaque employé possède sa place et son casier numérotés. Foule au plaisir, si, l'après-midi du samedi, on s'en va à Coney-Island.

John Sims éprouve alors l'insignifiance de sa vie, et sa sujétion de tous les instants à cette puissance formidable, la Foule. En sortir, être quelqu'un : son ambition de toujours. Le soir, après les heures de bureau, il travaille. Une fois pourtant il se laisse entraîner par un ami, qui lui présente de petites camarades. John aime Mary, l'épouse. Cet amour va-t-il être un stimulant pour lui, l'obliger à la réussite ?

Nous le croyons d'abord, quand les jeunes gens reviennent d'un voyage de noces enchanteur aux chutes du Niagara. Hélas ! la vie ménage à John Sims de rudes surprises. Il y a d'abord la banque où il végète, et qui ne consent pas à l'augmenter. Il y a aussi les parents de Mary : sa mère et ses frères, hostiles à John et ne lui cachant pas. Il y a enfin les mille tracasseries de l'existence conjugale : la conduite d'eau obstruée, la serrure faussée, l'assiette qu'on casse, le lait qui gicle... Le ménage vit dans la laideur des discussions quotidiennes.

Deux maternités de Mary apportent, après les premières joies, de nou-

veaux soucis. Et toujours l'antienne : « Ça changera... quand j'aurai
réussi ». Mais John demeure toujours aussi veule, aussi incapable d'un
effort lent et poursuivi.

Que sa fille soit mortellement blessée par un camion, alors ce sera la
ruine totale de sa volonté. Ici se place une scène poignante : comme le
docteur et les parents veillent au chevet de la petite agonisante, les bruits
du soir envahissent la maison; la Foule, la vieille ennemie de John, vient
le poursuivre presque dans sa douleur· Spectacle déchirant que ce père qui
court dans la rue, tragique, pour imposer silence aux passants, aux came-
lots qui crient la dernière édition., aux klaksons des autos, au bruit des pas
sur le trottoir... Entre la Foule et John se livre un duel atroce et sublime
d'où le malheureux sort anéanti.

Et c'est la déchéance : la place quittée par écœurement, il faut en trouver une autre. John essaie de tout, se dégoûte de tout· La misère règne
au foyer. Et la discorde aussi : Mary malheureuse devient méchante... Ses
frères veulent l'emmener : elle y consent, elle va partir quand John rentre
à la maison. Après une méditation désespérée qui l'a conduit au bord du
suicide, il a réagi héroïquement; il s'est fait embaucher comme clown, il
a paradé et jonglé pour rapporter aux siens quelque argent. Il a acheté
des billets de cirque, des fleurs pour Mary ; elle est touchée, elle demeure.
Le soir même, John, sa femme et son fils applaudissent aux excentricités
des pîtres, momentanément réconciliés et heureux.

Telles sont, dans l'ensemble, les péripéties de *Solitude* et de *La Foule·*
L'idée directrice des deux films est la même : l'isolement terrible de
l'homme moderne dans la grande ville, et cet espèce de désert encombré
à quoi conduit notre civilisation. Mais, par la technique et par l'esprit,
on ne saurait trouver deux œuvres plus différentes.

Par la technique d'abord. Le film de Paul Fejos est composé comme
une tragédie classique : il comporte un début, un sommet pathétique et
une fin; tel un son qui naît, s'enfle et meurt. Les scènes de *La Foule,* au
contraire, apparaissent heurtées, sans lien apparent. La composition en
est symphonique : toutes ces notes isolées, tous ces détails du plus intégral
réalisme, ce n'est que dans le tableau final qu'ils prennent leur place exacte

et leur sens profond. Alors on est bouleversé par l'âpre grandeur de l'œuvre. Mais le public n'a pas conscience de cela. Il exige à l'impression
visuelle une correspondance spirituelle immédiate. C'est pourquoi *La Foule*
rencontre, il faut bien le reconnaître, un mauvais accueil, même auprès du
public qui se dit averti de la chose cinégraphique ; tandis que *Solitude*
connaît aux Ursulines un éclatant succès, car il satisfait davantage notre
sens latin de la mesure et de la logique.

Le public a d'ailleurs raison. *La Foule* surabonde en notations qu'on
croirait échappées d'un roman d'Hennique ou de Céard. King Vidor entasse, accumule. Mais l'art n'est pas accumulation ; il est sélection. Le
meilleur artiste est celui qui choisit le mieux. C'est le mérite infini de
Paul Fejos, que d'avoir su traiter, en vingt-quatre heures, et avec une
plénitude autrement intense que celle de Vidor, l'aventure de ses héros :
tout porte, tout revêt un sens immédiat, nuancé et profond. Fejos ne prend
pas la peine, comme King Vidor (dont c'est une grosse maladresse) de
nous montrer la naissance ni l'enfance de Jim et de Mary : comme jadis
Racine, *il prend ses héros en état de crise ;* il nous épargne ainsi toute une
longue partie d'exposition sans grand intérêt. Il faut 50 mètres de pellicule à Fejos pour nous introduire au cœur du drame ; il en faut 600, peut-
être plus, à King Vidor.

Contraires par la technique, *La Foule* et *Solitude* sont aussi contraires
par l'esprit. Paul Fejos est un optimiste résolu, King Vidor s'avère violemment pessimiste. C'est peut-être ce qu'on a le moins compris.

Qu'on ne s'y trompe pas : la fin de *La Foule,* que certains interprètent
comme un symbole d'espoir, elle est de la plus implacable tristesse. La
joie dont vibre John, le rire qui entrouvre ses lèvres, sont le rire et la
joie standardisés d'une foule entière ; ils soulignent cruellement l'abdication du pauvre diable. Devenir quelqu'un, réussir : voilà l'ambition. Et le
terme : être une unité qui s'esclaffe parmi des milliers d'êtres qui s'esclaffent, un visage sans nom, sans volonté, sans relief, usé par la vie comme
un galet par les flots, — un de ces visages innombrables qui ne sont rien
et qui sont la foule.

Paul Fejos, lui, voit la vie en rose. Certes, elle comporte des épreuves,
le bonheur s'envole parfois dans le temps qu'on croyait l'atteindre ; mais
il finit toujours par revenir à votre portée, — durablement. Certains cri-

4

tiques, les « purs », ont blâmé la fin de *Solitude;* ils n'auraient pas voulu que Jim et Mary se retrouvassent. « Concession au goût du public! clament-ils. Exigeance commerciale! » Mais non. Cette fin est logique, nécessaire. Vous n'auriez pas voulu qu'un film si plein de bel humour et de bonne humeur s'achevât tristement· Le malheur n'est pour Paul Fejos qu'un accident, qu'un fait passager; il n'y a de vraiment pénible dans tout le film que le passage où Jim et Mary se cherchent dans la cohue et rentrent chez eux trempés et en larmes.

La vie est belle! crie Paul Fejos après Marcel Achard. On conçoit quelle aisance, quel naturel cela peut conférer aux acteurs; et effectivement Barbara Kent et Glenn Tryon jouent avec un tact, une finesse, une fraîcheur adorables.

Pour King Vidor, la vie est triste. Le pessimisme est toujours systématique; aussi toute joie est-elle absente de *La Foule;* du moins est-elle si étouffée, si rare, qu'on n'a pas l'occasion de sourire une fois. (On peut, à ce sujet, comparer utilement les scènes qui, dans *La Foule* et dans *Solitude* se déroulent sur la plage de Coney-Island). Un pareil effort d'austérité dénature l'aspect normal des choses; parfois, on quitte la vie pour entrer dans l'artifice. Et c'est pourquoi James Murray et Eléanor Boardman, pour excellents qu'ils soient, semblent à certains moments gênés.

*
* *

Concluons, bien que nous soyons loin d'avoir épuisé la matière. *Solitude* et *La Foule* sont à coup sûr des films de haute classe; mais, l'un est une œuvre parfaite; l'autre, malgré sa noblesse et certaines scènes vraiment pathétiques, est un chef-d'œuvre manqué.

Plaise à Dieu cependant de nous donner souvent des œuvres de cette qualité. Car de tels spectacles nous vengent, nous consolent, et nous rassurent, quant au sort d'un art, que les combinaisons des marchands et les virtuosités techniques les plus vaines ne sauraient empêcher de grandir.

Francis AMBRIÈRE.

NOTES

Mises au point

UNE LETTRE D'ANDRÉ MASSON

Nous avons reçu de notre ami André Masson la lettre suivante (trop tard pour l'insérer dans notre dernier numéro):

« Paris, le 30 janvier,

» Mon cher Salemson,

» Je suis navré de me voir nommé dans ton prospectus parmi quelques « personnalités distinguées ». Cela peut faire croire que je fais partie (malgré tes précautions oratoires) d'un groupe de « divergents ». Ce n'est ni vrai, ni vraisemblable.

» Cependant, je te prie de bien vouloir insérer ce mot dans ta revue et me croire toujours ton ami·

» André MASSON. »

Evidemment, si on a parlé, au sujet de *Tambour,* d'artistes « divergents », il fallait entendre « divergents entr'eux ».

CENSURE

Le fait d'avoir annoncé toute expression artistique tolérable nous a valu un véritable déluge de littérature pornographique. Que nos aspirants-collaborateurs trouvent ici notre point de vue à cet égard.

Il n'y a de censure possible que l'esthétique. Les écrits pornographiques ne peuvent être harmonieux (esthétiques) et sont pas conséquent censurés par eux-mêmes. La licence de thème ou de mise en scène n'est permissible que si elle ne fait que servir de fond à quelque recherche intéressante. Tout ce qui tend vers la perfection artistique est moral; moral de la seule moralité.

Point of view

CSNSORSHIP

Our announcement that all artistic expression was tolerable brought us a veritable deluge of licentious writings. We feel it our duty to explain our ideas on the subject to aspiring contributors:

No censorship is possible other than that of the esthetic. Licentiousness in itself being unharmonious (unesthetic), it defeats its own cause. Daringness of theme or setting is admissible only as the background of some interesting reseanch. There is but one morality: that which tends toward art-perfection alone is moral.

Les Livres

DES MÉLANGES

Un livre posthume de grand intérêt vient de paraître avec une préface de François Mauriac. C'est *l'Horizon chimérique* (Grasset, éditeur), de Jean de la Ville de Mirmont. L'auteur, qui fut étudiant en même temps que celui de *Génitrix*, donna sa vie pour la patrie sur le champ de bataille, laissant nombre de manuscrits qui viennent d'être réunis en ce volume. Des vers très intéressants, d'une régularité à laquelle se mêlent quelques formes surprenantes mais très efficaces; un court roman, *les Dimanches de Jean Dézert*, où l'auteur raconte avec quelque cynisme amusé les banalités de la vie; et des contes, dont certains sont de petites perles. C'est à peine de quoi nous faire goûter ce jeune talent, mais assez pour nous faire regretter sa disparition prématurée et les livres ultérieurs qu'il eût pu nous donner.

Mme Marcelle Auclair a traduit de l'espagnol un livre qui ne manque pas non plus d'intérêt. Il s'agit de *Ciné-Ville* (Kra, éditeur), de Ramon Gomez de la Serna. On ne saurait appeler roman ce livre, mais il n'est point non plus reportage. La ville du cinéma. Et nous pensons de suite à Hollywood. Si quelques-unes des idées ont été inspirées par la colonie américaine du film, le gros du livre est cependant d'imagination. Comparons la forme à un film documentaire à peine romancé, parsemé de quelques anecdotes. En tout cas, c'est un volume qu'on lit avec agrément, parfois avec amusement, et où il y a des trouvailles « très cinéma ».

De *La tasse de Saxe* (Grasset, éditeur), de Jacques Bainville, je ne trouve guère à dire de bien. Maurras a parlé de Bainville, comme d'un Anatole France de droite. Bien s'en faut. Loin d'être France, il n'arive dans ce recueil de contes, même pas à être Paul Bourget.

Le nègre qui chante (Les cahiers libres), est un volume de chansons nègres américaines traduites par Maria Jolas, avec une introduction par Eugène Jolas. Pourquoi n'a-t-on pas donné la musique? On nous transforme ces chants de travail, de religion et de plaisir, en des poèmes, ce qu'ils n'ont jamais eu la prétention d'être. Dans l'impossibilité de les fredonner, nous ne pouvons que les lire. Ce n'est, il faut l'avouer, pas désagréable, car le travail est bien fait, suivant plutôt le rythme et la forme que le sens des paroles. L'introduction nous apprend ce qu'il faut savoir d'avance pour les lire et la lecture est instructive, pour le moins·

UN POÈTE PROLÉTARIEN

C'est le paysan luxembourgeois, Francis André, qui semble être le premier vrai représentant de la poésie prolétarienne contemporaine tant vantée, mais qui viendra, à n'en pas douter, du sein même des classes ouvrières. Son volume *Poèmes paysans* (Les écrivains-réunis), est sobre et, quoique plein de conscience de classe, dépourvu de la haine qui trop souvent dégrade ce genre de manifestations. Quant à sa technique, je ne puis que l'en féliciter. Il a une grande sincérité qui se joint à une force incontestable de conception aussi bien que d'expression. Pour tout dire, il est naturel, vertu peu commune chez les poètes d'aujourd'hui.

QUATRE ROMANS

Henri Duclos me semble le cas typique du romancier qui a des convictions mais qui trouve que l'expression naturelle de son être ne coïncide pas avec celles-ci. Il aimerait pourvoir peindre de bonnes gens dévotes et il se trouve dans la nécessité de se débarrasser de ses besoins littéraires en dépeignant des êtres qui vont à l'autre extrémité, des blasphémateurs exagérés. Tel, du moins, se montre-t-il dans *l'Abbesse* (Grasset, éditeur) où, malgré tous ses efforts, il ne peut ramener son héroïne dans le droit chemin. Alors, il emploie le subterfuge d'un accident, ce qui lui épargne de l'accompagner vers une fin sans piété ou vers une conversion sans naturel.

Mlle Marguerite Grépon, par contre, ne semble pas forcer les choses. Le personnage de son livre, *La voyageuse nue* (Ferenczi, éditeur), est tout simplement une jeune femme amorale. Le roman pourrait décourager un lecteur sans persévérance, car son début n'est pas trop engageant, mais l'entrain vient en écrivant (ou en lisant), et le livre se termine très adroitement après avoir conduit le lecteur vers un point culminant tout à fait en règle. J'ai des préjugés contre les femmes écrivains; qu'on ne croie donc pas que ce livre m'ait déplu. Le personnage, qui est féminin, à l'inconstance de son sexe, et la trame aussi. Mlle Grépon, qui est bien capable, n'entreprendra-t-elle pas quelque chose de plus substantiel, de plus résistant?

Chez Jean Brumières, à qui j'ai les mêmes reproches à faire, il n'y a pas tant de circonstances atténuantes. Son roman, *L'étrange vie de Johann Landsteufel* (Grasset), chancelle et nous laisse froid. La préface de Tristan Bernard exprime un enthousiasme que je ne partage malheureusement pas.

Mais je voudrais encore parler de *La Beauté sur la terre* (Grasset), de C. F. Ramuz. Quoique paru voici bien des mois, ce roman du grand écrivain suisse mérite quelques mots. C'est une œuvre forte qui, comme tous les livres de cet auteur, a une allure un peu rébarbative. On pense à Proust ou à Joyce, tant on a de peine à pénétrer le sujet, mais, une fois la barrière franchie, on ne met le livre de côté que lorsqu'on l'a terminé. Les passions et les caractères humains s'y entre-choquent dans une broussaille dialectique qu'on a autant de plaisir à explorer que des forêts vierges. Les démons de l'âme humaine y rôdent comme des fauves. Mais on y sent la main d'un maître qui dirige et la syntaxe et l'intrigue. Très personnel, l'œuvre de Ramuz est pourtant au plus haut point universel.

...ET DEUX AUTRES

Deux romans qui ont paru tout dernièrement découvrent des personnalités intéressantes·

Colline (Grasset), de Jean Giono, présente un jeune auteur qui apporte un hallucinant roman de Provence. Un vieillard à l'agonie est soupçonné d'avoir jeté un sort sur le pays, un petit village isolé sur la *colline*. Toutes les forces de la nature, la sécheresse, le feu, etc.... semblent s'être alliées contre la poignée de villageois. A bout, ceux-ci pensent que leur salut se trouve dans la mort du vieux. Mais le crime sera évité. Le vieil organisme vient de se taire à jamais. Et la vie reprendra sur la *colline·* Un style très personnel, et une grande originalité, Jean Giono arrive à captiver le lecteur. Son roman durera.

Si *Le Joueur de balle* (Riéder), de Joseph Jolinon ne nous dévoile pas de personnalité nouvelle, il confirme notre conviction de n'avoir pas exagéré la grande valeur de l'auteur de *Claude Lunant* et des *Histoires corpusculiennes*. Jolinon mélange très harmonieusement le sport et l'étude ; je doute que les sportifs soient aussi tolérants envers les livres ni les « bas-bleus » envers l'exercice corporel. En tout cas, ils font ici bon ménage et la lecture est mieux qu'agréable. Elle donne à penser. Sans en avoir l'air, elle contient des réflexions d'une profondeur étonnante. Le lecteur perspicace se verra largement récompensé.

HISTOIRE

Robert Dreyfus est le plus agréable historien qui soit. Rares sont les livres techniques qui se lisent aussi facilement que son *Monsieur Thiers* (Grasset). Richement documenté et très intéressant, c'est une belle réussite.

Chez le même éditeur, *Calendrier royal pour l'an* 1471, par Pierre Champion, plaide une cause sans espoir. A la fin du livre on n'est guère rassuré sur la personnalité de Louis XI que Champion voudrait peindre en homme-modèle. L'historien remarquable a entrepris une tâche vaine.

Le livre d'après-guerre, par Raymond Hesse (Grasset), est un bon manuel pour débutant bibliophile, mais il n'apprend pas grand chose. Des listes intéressantes de bibliophiles et d'illustrateurs, et des bibliographies.

Books

THROUGH THE FIELD

In verse, the most interesting volume to have appeared lately is Robinson Jeffers' *Cawdor* (Horace Liveright). The stark cruelty of Jeffers' verse is unequalled in contemporary poetry. The hermit of California (as he is depicted to us) has bridged the gap to the Greeks. His sense of tragedy is entirely classical. *Cawdor* has a resemblance to Oedipus and is probably more dispassionately ferocious in its pessimistic conclusions than the classic poets ever succeeded in being. Certain lines are remarkable, though one hesitates in lauding the poetic form. Among the shorter pieces in the volume, *A Redeemer* is probably the most powerful.

En passant let us mention *The Turquoise Trail* (Houghton, Mifflin), an anthology of New Mexico poetry compiled by Alice Corbin Henderson. The outstanding artist: Witter Bynner; the most generally sincere section: the cowboy ballads.

Of novels, we have two (we do not contend to cover all published). *Ryder* (Horace Liveright), by Djuna Barnes, is doubtless a piece of brilliant writing though I can hardly say it is enjoyable. A feat of strength it is, with perhaps slightly too much of an attempt to shock. Djuna Barnes does not come up to those with whom her *Little Review* period has linked her: Sherwood Anderson, Aldous Huxley, James Joyce, and so on.

Just as brilliant is Donn Byrne's posthumous book *Destiny Bay* (Sampson Low, London), but in a much more sober manner. Hardly a novel, it is a group of stories around a young Irishman who is the central figure of none of them. This book ranks with two or three others as Donn Byrne's best work. When will due honor be given him?

Zona Gale's essays, collected in *Portage, Wisconsin* (Knopf, New-York), show us a perspicacious and somewhat cynical side of this lady's nature which neither her novels nor her short stories have hitherto displayed. Miss Gale deals here with men's faults and peculiarities, rather than with men themselves. She takes Portage, Wisconsin, as the model of American small towns and puts it through a more concise grilling than any *Main Street*. Critical articles, essays on the author's mother and father, digressions and reflections on the novel, complete this highly interesting volume.

Hendrik Van Loon uses a more simple language than most writers in his *Man the Miracle-maker* (Horace Liveright), the story of invention, told for children. Youngsters may read this with interest, but adults will read it with delight. Van Loon's method of exposition we have already appreciated in his previous works. Here he includes more subtle remarks which draw many a smile. And any number of us can learn something from him.

A European correspondent, George Seldes, has published a book which perhaps at last throws the real light on newspaper consorship as it is practised the world over. I believe we may have utter faith in his *You Can't Print That* (Payson and Clarke)· Better than his tales of suppression in such countries of terror as Italy, Rumania, Mexico and Russia, his divulgations of the goings-on in *free* countries are enough to disillusion the most ardent optimist. Nowhere in the world can the utter truth of political situations be told and the crimes hushed-up (even assaults upon American consuls) because Wall Street is booming the particular country where they take place, are hair-raising. Mr. Seldes has added personal incidents that amuse as well as captivate. His book is fine reading and a good punch-on-the-jaw to Babbitt.

FROM MAGAZINES

Here are two collections of short stories from magazines : *transition stories* (McKee, New-York) and *Short Stories from Vanity Fair* (Horace Liveright).

The Vanity Fair stories include every grade of literature except the very worst. Four little masterpieces by Sherwood Anderson, then down through stories by Schnitzler, Molnar, Paul Morand, André Maurois, as far as Jim Tully. All are interesting· Every now and then a spark of « real stuff ».

transition stories reprint the best contributions to Eugene Jolas' magazine· Murray Godwin, Kurt Schwitters, Leigh Hoffman, Robert Sage, and Philippe Soupault have given what seem the best stories. The extracts from James Joyce's new work are lucid fragments which bring out the great virtuosity of the Irish master. They seem unequal but are beyond the judgment or criticism of the ordinary mortal. The whole volume is interestingly experimental.

Magazines

Poetry. — Miss Monroe has given the editorship to her associates temporarily and we are not yet able to judge how the review will fare under the new management. We may recall the prize- awards announced in the

November issue : the late Elinior Wylie, Vachel Lindsay, Marion Strobel, Ted Olson, Elizaberth Madox Roberts, Sterling North, Emanuel Carnevali, Horace Gregory, and, among the Honorable mentions, Robinson Jeffers and E. James Olson.

Transition (n° 15). — More of James Joyce's new work and a vast collection of various types : Hart Crane, Harry Alan Potamkin, Robert Mc Almon, Eugène Jolas, Murray Godwin, Jean-George Auriol, and others.

The Bookman (January). — Particularly, an article by Allen Tate on American Poetry since 1920.

The Book League Monthly. — A book-club scheme, which gives a new book in magazine form each month. The outstanding book so far is Matthew Josephson's *Zola and His Time* (November). Included is an interesting review section composed of essays, reviews and a review of reviews. V. F. Calverton is the book-review editor. The most striking articles have been : *The Rise of Woman*, Anna Strunsky Walling (January) ; and *Translators — Traitors?*, V. F. Calverton (February). Probably the most interesting book-club idea we have yet found.

Les Revues

Nouvelle Revue Française (février). — Une « explication » du *Cimetière marin*, par Gustave Cahen. Mais Valéry ne se laisse pas prendre par une « conquête méthodique ».

Europe (mars). — Voici la fin du *Premier pamphlet* d'Emmanuel Berl : une charge parfois exagérée, mais qui ne manque pas de piquant. Signalons aussi la collaboration régulière de Jean-Richard Bloch.

Raison d'être (février). — Une revue de poésie. Max Jacob, qu'on voit un peu partout. De bons vers de Gilbert Trolliet.

La Courte Paille (mars). — Premier numéro d'une revue qui promet. Chamson, Max Jacob (encore), et des jeunes.

Le Point (février). — Autre premier numéro. Revue des générations d'après-guerre. Attendons.

Anthologie (février). — Georges Linze, surtout. Belle couverture d'André Leroy. Neuvième année. Une revue qui réalise quelque chose. C'est une force, une fière force belge.

Du Cinéma (numéros 1-2). — Une belle revue à avenir. Dirigée par Jean-George Auriol, elle apporte un nouveau point de vue cinématographique. « Le cinéma et les mœurs ». Très bien présentée.

Les Arts

TOUCHAGUES

Deux manifestations du talent de cet agréable artiste nous ont été données dernièrement. Son exposition, chez Trémois, a offert le meilleur coup-d'œil d'ensemble que nous ayons jamais eu de son œuvre. De grandes gouaches tout à fait remarquables, où il interprète diverses scènes typiques en les rendant entièrement « Touchagues » ; des lithographies splendides, entr'autres, une négresse mystérieuse et admirable ; et une réunion des livres qu'il a illustrés.

A ce sujet, parlons de *Frédégonde* de Jean Cassou (Trémois, éditeur), qu'illustra Touchagues. Cassou a une plume qui se range dans la bonne tradition ironique dont il serait trop banal de nommer les prédécesseurs. Avec des données très limitées, il a su écrire un livre intéressant et intelligent que Touchagues sut décorer, plutôt qu'interpréter, de la façon la plus spirituelle. La plume de l'écrivain et le crayon du dessinateur ont la même netteté, le même tranchant.

Touchagues, qui fut membre du salon de l'Araignée, a un des talents les plus sûrs du groupe. Et ses compagnons ne sont pas de piètres artistes.

Disques

CHEZ COLUMBIA

La grande maison Columbia nous donne un choix très éclectique et très intéressant.

Tristan et Isolde, du Festival de Beyreuth, est une manifestation très importante. L'exécution est impeccable et on y distingue de très belles voix. Gustaf Rodin, qu'on n'entend pas assez, est particulièrement intéressant. Gunnar Graarud et Rudolph Bockelmann sont de très grands artistes, absolument étonnants. Toute discothèque devrait avoir cette rendition remarquable de Wagner (L. 2187 et suite).

Du côté jazz, *Chiquita* chanté par Layton and Johnstone (5116), et par Ukelele Ike (5153), est une chanson très gentille sans prétentions. Les deux exécutions sont bonnes. Layton and Johnstone donnent encore *Crazy Rhythm* (5146), une chanson très amusante et qui donne envie de danser. La nouvelle valse d'Irving Berlin, *Where is the Song of Songs for Me* (5204), est très jolie.

Signalons encore, toujours chez Columbia :

Quatrième Symphonie, de Schumann (L. 2209).

La Flûte enchantée, de Mozart (12549) ;

Danses espagnoles, de Granados et la *Suite Ibéria*, de Albeniz (9605 et la suite) ;

ainsi que des chansons d'opérettes françaises.

Livres à lire

Viennent de paraître de quelques-uns de nos collaborateurs :

André Spire, *Poèmes de Loire* (Grasset) ;

Pierre Mac Orlan, *Sélections sur ondes courtes* (Les cahiers libres) ;

Blaise Cendrars, *Le Plan de l'Aiguille* (Au Sans pareil) ;

Touchagues, *Frédégonde*, de Jean Cassou, illustré par Touchagues (Trémois) ;

Stuart Gilbert, *Ulysse*, de James Joyce, traduit par Stuart Gilbert, Auguste Morel et Valery Larbaud (La Maison des Amis des Livres).

What to read

New books by some of our contributors :

Maxwell Bodenheim, *60 Seconds* (Horace Liveright) ;

Ralph Cheever Dunning, *Windfalls* (E. W. Titus, Paris) ;

Samuel Rogers, *Less Than Kind* (Payson and Clarke).

Le Gérant : **Jules BRUNEL.**

Montpellier. — Imprimerie Causse, Graille et Castelnau, 7, rue Dom-Vaissette.

DU CINÉMA

REVUE DE CRITIQUE ET DE RECHERCHES CINÉMATOGRAPHIQUES

JEAN GEORGE AURIOL: Rédacteur en Chef

Les rubriques déjà fameuses:

LE CINÉMA ET LES MŒURS

par Jean George AURIOL et Bernard BRUNIUS

LA CHRONIQUE DES FILMS PERDUS

par André DELONS

et la collaboration régulière de

Michel J. ARNAUD, Pierre AUDARD, Alb. CAVALCANTI, Louis CHA-VANCE, Henri CHOMETTE, René CLAIR, Robert DESNOS, Paul GILSON, Michel GOREL, André R. MAUGÉ, Man RAY, V. POUDOVKINE, Harry A POTAMKIN, André SAUVAGE, Philippe SOUPAULT.

30 photographies inconnues

2

April
1929
Avril

Pages

Revue Mensuelle

A monthly magazine

PRIX 6 Fr.

2

TAMBOUR

TAMBOUR

Directeur : Harold-J. SALEMSON, Editor

3, Rue Berthollet, PARIS (Vᵉ), France

Of this issue, 200 copies are numbered.

De ce numéro, 200 exemplaires ont été numérotés.

> *Roulez, tambours.*
> Jean COCTEAU.
> (*Roméo et Juliette*).

Le prochain numéro de *Tambour* paraîtra fin août.

The next issue of *Tambour* will appear at the end of August.

LETTRE A DES JEUNES GENS

MES AMIS,

Je vous le dis franchement, votre lettre m'étonne. N'avez-vous **donc** rien vu dans *Tambour?*

Vous venez me parler de générations; mais vous allez, alors, vous
fourvoyer tout comme les ainés. A un moment où la lutte des classes est
plus vive et s'intensifie plus rapidement que jamais, à un moment où nous
ne savons quelles mesures prendre pour empêcher un choc de nations, de
races, de continents, où nous commençons à espérer la découverte prochaine
d'un homme martien contre qui tous ceux de la terre, alliés, seront enfin
frères, vous allez créer ou augmenter cette autre barrière, les générations!
Comme je vous plains, d'être aveugles.

Il ne peut plus y avoir de différence entre les générations. Nous sommes
des hommes et nous devons d'abord tirer une leçon de ce qu'accomplirent
les morts, ensuite nous intéresser à tout ce que font les vivants. *A tout
ce que font tous les vivants,* entendez-vous? Car fonder une revue pour ceux
d'après-guerre, à l'exclusion de leurs aînés, c'est aussi borné, non, c'est
plus borné, puisque ceux-là n'ont pas encore fait leurs preuves, que de
publier une revue d'où sont bannis tous ceux au-dessous d'un certain âge
ou d'une certaine notoriété.

Mais vous n'avez évidemment rien vu dans *Tambour,* puisque vous
venez me parler d'indécision. Et vous voudriez voir un mouvement moins
indécis? Dois-je comprendre par là que vous me voudriez voir me borner
à une génération, voire à une partie d'une génération? (Car vous devez
savoir aussi bien que moi que les hommes de même âge sont divisés entre
eux par diverses opinions). Mais alors, vous n'avez pas lu la *Présentation*
de notre premier numéro?

Par ailleurs, vous parlez de gestes nobles et magnifiques. Vous venez
d'avoir vous-mêmes celui qui l'est le moins. De votre organe, que vous
alliez borner à ceux « de 16 à 20 ans » et dont vous auriez été vous-mêmes
exclus la limite passée, vous avez fait celui « de la génération d'après la
guerre ». Or, si votre publication devait continuer à jamais à ne publier
que les 16-à-20 ans, le groupe se régénérant complètement tous les quatre
ans, voilà qui eût été beau, voilà qui eût été noble. Mais non, vous
commencez par être des moins-de-20-ans, ensuite votre revue (avec votre
génération) deviendra celle des moins-de-30-ans (sinon encore celle des

20-à-30-ans), et, si vous atteignez le succès prévu, sans doute votre publication sera-t-elle un jour le bulletin officieux de l'Académie Française.

Non, devenir le champion d'une seule génération, fût-elle même la vôtre
(qui est la mienne), ce n'est pas là faire œuvre humaine. Ne faites pas
comme ces lutteurs forains qui, même lorsqu'ils invitent le public à se
manifester, savent qu'en fin de compte ils se trouveront uniquement en
face de compères qui sont de mèche, et que leurs exhibitions ne les fati-
gueront pas. Non, je vous le crie, NON, ne faites pas comme eux! Ouvrez
vos portes! Ne craignez pas de vous mesurer aux hommes!

Harold J. SALEMSON.

TO A GROUP OF YOUNG MEN

FRIENDS,

I tell you frankly, your letter astonishes me. Did you see nothing at all
in *Tambour?*

You talk about generations; you are going to take the wrong path then
just like your elders. At a time when the struggle of classes is keener
than ever and more rapidly than ever is gaining in intensity, at a time
when we are at a loss what measures to take to avoid a collision of
nations, of races, of continents, when we are beginning to hope for the
coming discovery of a man from Mars, against whom all those of the
earth, allied, will at last be brothers, at a time like this you intend to
create or to increase this other barrier, the generations! How I pity you
for your blindness.

There can no longer be a difference between generations. We are men,
and we must first of all learn a lesson from that which the dead have
accomplished, then interest ourselves in what the living are doing. *In
everything that all the living are doing,* do you hear? For to create a
review for those of the post-war generation, excluding their elders, is just
as limited, nay, more limited, since those have not yet shown anything, than

to publish a review ignoring those under a certain age or of insufficient fame.

But you very evidently have seen nothing in *Tambour,* since you speak of indecision. And you would like to see a movement less undecided? Am I to understand by that that you would wish to see me limit myself to one generation? Even more, to a part of one generation? (For you must know as well as I that men of the same age are divided among themselves by diversity of opinions.) But then, have you not read the *Presentation* of our first number?

Elsewhere you speak of noble and splendid gestures. From which the one you just made is the farthest removed. Your publication, which you are going to limit to those « between 16 and 20 », and from which you yourself would have been excluded once past the age limit, you have turned into that of the « post war generation ». Now if your publication were to continue indefinitely to publish only those between 16 and 20, the group to be completely regenerated every four years, that would have been splendid, that would have been noble. But no, you start out by being those under 20, then your review (with your generation) will become that of those under 30 (perhaps even of those from 20 to 30) and if you attain the expected success, in the end your publication will probably become the officious bulletin of the Académie Française.

No, to champion a single generation, be it even yours (which is also mine) would not be a worthy undertaking. Don't imitate those side-show fighters, who even while defying all-comers know that they will have to spar only with their accomplices, and that their exhibitions will in no way exhaust them. No! I shout it to you, no! Do not imitate them. Open your doors wide! Do not fear to compete with men!

Harold J. Salemson.

N. B. — Upon reflection, the reader will realize that this letter is in perfect agreement with *Letter to* 99.

BILL

Bill avait trente ans, quand sa femme mourut, et la
petite Minna en avait quatre. La menuiserie de Bill était
dans la cour de sa maison, alors, il pensait qu'il pourrait maintenir le ménage pour Minna et pour lui-même.
Toute la journée pendant qu'il travaillait à son établi,
elle jouait dans la cour, et lorsqu'il était forcé de
s'absenter quelques heures, la femme d'à côté s'occupait
d'elle. Bill pouvait faire un peu la cuisine, il pouvait
faire du café et du bacon et des frites et des crêpes, et il
trouva très utiles les bananes et les sardines et les
biscuits. Quand la voisine lui dit que ce n'était pas là
le régime d'un enfant de quatre ans, il lui demanda de
lui apprendre à faire des semoules et des légumes, et
bien qu'il brulât toujours les casseroles où il faisait
cuire ces choses, il en préparait tous les jours. Il
balayait, partout sauf dans les coins, et il époussetait,
en donnant un petit coup sur chaque objet; et il se
plaignit de voir moins bien à travers les vitres après
les avoir lavées qu'avant. Il lavait et rapiéçait les petits
vêtements de Minna et il raccommodait sa poupée. Il
lui trouva un petit chat pour qu'elle ne fût pas seule.
Le soir, il lui faisait dire sa prière, agenouillée au milieu

du parquet, les mains jointes, et à une vitesse d'éclair. S'il oubliait la prière, soit il la réveillait, soit il la lui faisait dire la première chose le matin. Lui-même avait l'habitude d'essayer de prier : Seigneur, montrez-moi comment me conduire envers elle si vous voyez que je me trompe. Le dimanche, il l'amenait à l'église et il restait la tête sur le côté, à essayer de comprendre, et à donner à Minna des bonbons de menthe quand elle remuait. Il chôma un jour pour l'amener au pique-nique de l'école du dimanche. « Sa mère aurait fait ça », expliquait-il. Quand Minna fut assez âgée pour aller à la maternelle, Bill l'amenait le matin ou l'après-midi, et il venait la chercher. Une fois il endossa ses meilleurs vêtements et alla visiter l'école. « Je crois que sa mère aurait fait ça », dit-il à la maîtresse, avec diffidence. Mais, il ne comprenait guère les papiers de couleur et les dessins et les jeux, et il n'y retourna plus. « Il y a des choses avec lesquelles je ne peux pas l'aider », pensa-t-il.

Minna avait six ans, quand Bill tomba malade. Une après-midi de mai, il alla voir un docteur. A son retour, il resta longtemps assis dans sa boutique sans rien faire. Le soleil brillait à travers la vitre en carrés lumineux. Il n'allait pas guérir. Peut-être en avait-il encore pour six mois... Il pouvait entendre Minna qui berçait sa poupée.

Quand elle vint l'embrasser ce soir-là, il trouva un
prétexte, parce qu'il ne devait plus l'embrasser maintenant. Il la tint à bout de bras, fixa son regard, et dit :
« Minna est une grande fille maintenant. Elle ne veut
plus que papa l'embrasse ». Mais la lèvre de la petite
trembla et elle se retourna chagrinée, alors, le lendemain, Bill alla à un autre docteur pour se rassurer.
L'autre docteur confirma avec assurance.

Il essaya de penser ce qu'il faudrait faire. Il avait
une sœur dans le Nébraska, mais c'était une femme fati-
guée. Sa femme avait un frère en ville, mais c'était un
homme qui parlait trop. Et la petite Minna... elle était
initiée à des choses que lui-même ne connaissait pas —
des histoires de fées et des paroles de chansons. Il aurait
voulu entendre parler de quelqu'un qui la comprendrait.
Et il n'avait que six mois...

Puis, la femme d'à côté lui dit crûment qu'il ne devrait
pas garder la fillette là, avec lui qui toussait comme il
le faisait ; et il savait que sa décision était déjà impé-
rative.

Toute une nuit il pensa. Puis, il annonça dans un
journal de la ville :

> Monsieur n'ayant que quelques mois à vivre, cherche gentilles
> personnes pour adopter sa fillette, six ans, yeux bleus, cheveux
> bouclés. Références exigées.

Ils vinrent en une grosse voiture, comme il espérait

qu'ils viendraient. Leurs vêtements étaient comme il
avait espéré. Ils amenaient une petite fille qui s'écria :
« C'est elle, ma petite sœur ? ». A quoi la dame bien
habillée répondit sèchement :

« Allons, fais comme te dit maman et ne te mêle pas
de ceci ou nous te laisserons ici et nous emmènerons
avec nous cette charmante fillette. »

Alors Bill regarda cette dame et dit avec confiance
qu'il avait maintenant d'autres projets pour la fillette.
Il regarda s'éloigner la grosse voiture bleue. « Pour
l'amour du ciel », dit la femme d'à côté, quand elle eût
entendu, « Vous lui avez volé la fortune. Vous n'en aviez
pas le droit — une homme en votre état de santé. » Et
quand d'autres voitures vinrent, et il les laissa partir,
cette voisine dit à son mari qu'on devrait dénoncer Bill
à la police.

L'homme et la dame qui entrèrent dans la boutique
de Bill, un matin, portaient encore le deuil de leur
propre fillette. La dame n'était pas triste — seulement
chagrinée, et l'homme, qui avait pour elle de tendres
égards, était menuisier. Dans une floraison d'espoir et
de crainte, Bill leur dit : « C'est vous, les personnes ».
Quand ils demandèrent : « Combien de temps avant que
nous puissions l'avoir ? », Bill dit : « Encore un jour ».

Il passa ce jour-là dans la boutique. C'était l'été et

Minna jouait dans la cour. Il pouvait entendre les paroles de ses chansons. Il fit le souper et pendant qu'elle mangeait, il la regarda. Quand il l'eut bordée, il resta debout dans le noir à l'écouter respirer. « Je suis une petite fille ce soir, embrasse-moi », avait-elle dit, mais il secoua la tête. « Une grande fille, une grande fille », lui dit-il.

Quand ils vinrent la chercher le lendemain matin, il l'avait préparée et ses petits vêtements étaient préparés, lavés et raccomodés, et il avait raccomodé sa poupée. « Minna n'a jamais été en visite », lui dit-il allègrement. Et quand elle courut vers lui, il lui rappela, « Une grande fille, une grande fille ».

Il suivit des yeux l'homme et la dame qui descendaient la rue avec Minna entre-eux. Ils lui avaient apporté une petite ombrelle bleue, au cas où le départ serait difficile. Cette ombrelle, Minna la faisait tressauter au-dessus de sa tête, et elle s'intéressait tellement à examiner la soie bleue qu'elle ne pensa pas à se retourner et à lui faire signe de la main.

ZONA GALE.

(Traduit de l'américain par Harold J. Salemson).

YOU, DRUM MAJOR

To save itself from the dufferiority it deserves if it
depart from the rule, an institution must remain
faithful to the principles (there are yet such) it espouses
at its inception. *Tambour* propounds itself as an institution and scales out the defi that it holds every form
of artistic expression *tolerable,* that the ultimate goal
of art is beauty (sic). That is ancient law. A modesty a
playfulness I name it myself almost prevents me from
vaunting that this is an *artistic expression.* Its purpose
is in too old a tradition to be denied unless age in itself
be a cause for denial. But that purpose! — further to
wipe away preventions to the achievement of that *ultimate goal.* It is invalid to argue that we are again ready
to build, that the muck is now gone. Untenability of the
skysailing nose the stench is still too magnetic. Dema-
gnetization first and then on to the goal. *Tolerance*
then — that must import not a tolerance of this or that
but of all things (even intolerance), provided the expression be artistic and as M. le Directeur held in the
primary issue *To our readers will be left the privilege
of passing judgment.* For literature only does pope hold
true *Whatever is is right,* but there are things which

are not right and until they are beauty will be remote,
until *this* condition together with others...

Admit there is love the romantical or sentimental is
out — who has not seen that? What kind next? Name
one — one of many — and ten to one it is foul to the
heart. The puritanical? There is one. New england is
full of it and who can say where else? Ask robert frost
not amy lowell. Ask the man who hates a fence not the
woman who loves lilacs. How proor is this one must read
william carlos williams to know, must read the chapter
cotton mathers wonders and one or two others, but that
in especial of the book in the amurican grain, but it
is just as hot an objection. One must read that
chapter on the pilgrims great souls they, great souls
they had. What can puritan mean save one who is within
the sphere of life, in all, and is yet pure, and then what
is purity who can say one mans poison. Would it be
pure in spirit pure in heart and thought pure in relation
to all without, to the external world. Yes it would
dostoievsky was that, but was the puritan pure in the
composite the synthesis of them all — love — no the
bastard. For the puritan to love his god purely and
god came first it was essential that humanity be denied,
ostensibly. His god demanded that. It was necessary
that he segregate his animality from his purity, osten-

sibly. To segregate when all his purity was directed to
his purification as an animal the louse. Man and louse
then. The one an intellect socalled the other a parasitical
in a greater sense man too bellycrawler and poker into
private parts and places there are such I hold but both
animalculae. Too late for the louse to purify himself
into a man — himself? *it*self; it lost its gender long ago
— thousands of years ago in the heyday of the isolate
cell the incipient louse had its chance opportunity
knocks but once to coin a phrase frequented poolparlors
and smoked at an early age and man the tortoise what
delightful euphuism forged slowly albeit furrumly
ahead to *win*. And man is still an animal — deny? But
the purest of animals and the purest must not deny.
Christ! how to deny the factbody. But the puritan found
a way or said he did once aboard a mistress. In a pew
pure. In a featherbed — what? — an animal. But deny
it he did. For forms sake a large *a* ugly word adulteress
when there is no adultery.

So back to the dimmesdale way the dimmesdale husband. He would sleep with a rusted flintlock provided
the bore was large enough... or a broken bottle (empty)...
but with his *wife!* Sinner you take me for. *Sleep with a
wife.* W. c. w. tells of some married for twenty years
without having seen her ankles deny deny deny it. Never

saw her *ankles*. And *when* the full cream of the curve of her hip? — after a *thousand* a curve. No curves for the puritan, ostensibly...all angles from his imitation silver shoe buckle to his precisely sliced off conical (black) hat. Square consciences rectangular lives octagonal brains cubic or is it pubic arses. But spherical mistresses with conical breasts unsliced and round round round thighs tapering slimly in th thighs plangent loins *Oh Yes*. My dear might I have the temerity to suggest to thee that an unseemly one eighth of an inch of thy I blush to say it throat *not neck* obtrudes its carnality above thy throatlatch or horsecollar as it was then referred to and the same to thee beamed the belle of bedford (evil refe-rence) town... her pride lay in her tresses kneedeep and never disarranged for any save her fourteen year old lover cesspool mopper up that was his job in the demo-cratic colony he was dowd frob saleb with a bad cowd... chilly town thet one... and the same to thee thy purita-nical marmoreality peeps through thy gaping antipa-pistical fly — or did they wear no phlies; was it phlaggellation? — the massachusetts anomaly, the back bay phallic symbol, the yawning castiron phly phlanked by brown velour polhadotted with soupstains or maybe.

Poor miles and lucky john fit subjects for the most ribald and rollicking ballad in the universe of song

where o where is the newworld villon. He would sing
them to heaven. And the newworld serioflalstaff, cui-
rassed breastplated flintlocked miles. Worthy prize, the
fair priscilla, a skin lotion as we all live, and friable
miles the powder man powdered under the pestle of love,
a knight with a burning pestle — but priscilla was
lovely even beyond longfellows spluttering stub squill.
So he sent john. John bursting with phrases. Bursting
john, miles boon one, and miles so full of love or something else that he could not speak for fear of spilling it.
But he had sped a million rusted nails into aboriginal
guts without a quiver — they *had* quivers the little red
devils — without a quaver then. A bolt and a tetanus
incrusted slug for every yard of prehistoric intestine
spoiled no meals for miles. But strangely (you say)
priscilla did. So he sent john. Fool. Fatslob. Speak for
yourself ha ha and he did. He did. The most humourous
fate in the world. Cry up a ballad for john and miles.
Too full of love to propound it send your best friend your
worst enemy could not do ye browner while ye prowl
it is cased in an epidermis of toledo. No looking at a
woman even for a proposal that he have the privilege
of looking at her for life. Miles standish passed...
untimely... away early last evening in his homestead
bedchamber his wife had just removed her shoe — *shoe*

we interpolate shoe only — when miles our beloved protector was seized of a plethora to the lower regions of his body here today gone tomorrow mused n.w. the parish parson upon receiving information of the sad affair and mordivigation of the modesty pronounced the chirurgeon, hastily summoned from... ah but no. Was it grief over the lost priscilla o founder of our country?

until *this* condition together with others are wiped off the face of the earth. *Then* build. *Then* beauty.

Julian L. SHAPIRO.

COMME LES FILLES?

« C'est lui, dit son cœur.

— Oui, répondit-elle, pourvu que je ne me trouble pas et que je puisse Le regarder sans rougir, sans que des larmes montent à mes yeux.

— C'est Lui, vois-tu, redit son cœur, Il est seul.

— Comme toujours.

— Jamais tu ne L'as rencontré avec d'autres jeunes hommes... ni avec une femme.

— ... ni avec une femme. Jamais.

— Regarde Le bien au passage et mets dans ton regard toute la flamme qui est en toi.

— Impossible, je suis trop heureuse et trop émue.
D'ailleurs, Lui ne me voit pas.

— Mais Il est tout occupé de ton souvenir, affirma
son cœur. »

Alors, elle se redressa, pleine d'orgueil, frémissante,
et passa devant la terrasse du café où Lui, insolent,
rêvait, une cigarette aux doigts, dans une absurde pose
conventionnelle.

« Il t'a reconnue, Il t'a regardée, chanta son cœur.
As-tu senti la caresse de ses yeux sur les tiens?

— Oh! oui. Mais, pourquoi ne s'est-Il pas levé pour
me suivre?

— Parce qu'Il est délicat et ne veut pas te compro-
mettre, plaida son cœur.

— Alors, comment Le retrouver, puisqu'Il est aussitôt
perdu? dit-elle, toute son angoisse réveillée et sa
solitude.

— Il faut revenir sur tes pas, passer encore devant
Lui et sourire cette fois, audacieusement...

— Jamais je n'oserai.

— Il le faut. Sais-tu s'Il n'est pas timide et s'Il n'a
pas besoin d'être encouragé? dit son cœur qui, Le
peignant et Le plaignant, était irrésistible.

— C'est vrai. Alors... »

...Alors, elle pivota sur ses talons et, d'une allure très décidée, revint sur ses pas, arpentant la grande rue bruissante où elle n'entendait rien — rien que la voix de son cœur — la grande rue claire et animée où elle ne voyait rien — rien que les premières tables d'un café, là-bas.

« Il t'a regardée encore et plus longuement, cria son cœur.

— Il ne m'en veut donc pas d'avoir été trop sévère avec Lui, ce matin, implora-t-elle, toute confuse et craintive devant ce bonheur qui entrait en elle comme un intrus.

— Il ne t'en veut pas, Il t'aime, assura son cœur, Il t'aime, Il t'aime! »

Elle continuait sa marche sur le rythme de sa joie, elle allait et soudain, s'arrêta devant une vitrine de coiffeur :

« C'est pour Lui donner le temps de me rejoindre, expliqua-t-elle.

— Mais Il n'est pas derrière toi, Il n'ose pas. Reprends ton chemin, remonte jusqu'à la place et redescends vers la gare.

— Et passer encore devant Lui ? s'effara-t-elle.

— Oui, dit le cœur, catégorique ».

***

Docile, elle s'en alla vers la place, d'un pas flâneur. Elle tourna autour du monument qui était là tout **exprès** pour lui éviter de pivoter encore sur elle-même, et elle redescendit vers la gare, c'est-à-dire, vers le café... c'est-à-dire, la même chose.

Seulement, comme elle était très heureuse et très sûre cette fois, elle prêta une plus grande attention à ce qui l'environnait. Elle rectifia sa coiffure devant une glace; elle sourit à un enfant et baissa les yeux devant un pauvre, elle regarda une grosse dame, devant elle, ce qui lui donna envie de rire, puis une jeune, très mince, mise avec goût, qui allait avec une affectation de flânerie.

« Je l'ai déjà vue tout à l'heure... oui, avant de Le rencontrer. Tiens, comme les hommes la regardent! »

Puis, elle ne pensa plus qu'à elle-même et à Lui, parce qu'elle passait encore devant le café.

Lui, était toujours à la même place; un peu renversé sur son fauteuil, il lissait de la main ses cheveux libres. Il lui sourit avec fatuité et moquerie — avec tendresse et espiéglerie, interpréta son cœur — puis Il fit signe au garçon de lui allumer sa cigarette.

« Il a une aisance de prince, pensa-t-elle.

— Oui, de prince, souligna son cœur, et c'est un prince qui t'a remarquée ! »

***

Elle continua de marcher, voyant de plus en plus clair autour d'elle, parce qu'elle était forte et fière.

« Tiens, la jolie dame est arrêtée devant une modiste. Un monsieur s'approche. Est-ce qu'il va lui parler ? Non, ils ne se connaissent pas. Ce qu'elle est fardée et fânée, bien que jeune ! »

Un petit vieux, derrière elle, s'essouflait et marmottait avec persévérance. Elle se retourna puis, choquée de l'entrain qu'il mettait à trottiner beaucoup trop près d'elle, changea de trottoir.

La jolie dame était immédiatement devant elle avec une autre jolie dame qu'elle venait de rencontrer. Leurs voix lui arrivaient, un peu traînantes, puis, parfois, tout à fait éteintes en chuchottements.

« Qu'est-ce que tu as fait hier ?

— Pas grand'chose...

— ...moi, je désespérais, quand tout à coup, devant les « Négociants »...

— .....

— ...un beau chopin, ma chère ! »

Elle fut gênée indiciblement. Ces deux jolies dames étaient donc des professionnelles de l'amour ?... et trouvaient des recrues devant les « Négociants », Son café!

Arrivée à la gare, il lui fallut bien revenir sur ses pas.

« Vite, vite, disait son cœur. S'il était parti? »

Elle se hâta. On se hâtait derrière elle. « Bonjour chérie! » dit une voix grasse. Un ouvrier la dépassa, la bousculant un peu et se retournant.

Les jolies dames étaient maintenant derrière elle.

« Il se trompe. Mais, au fait, comment nous distinguer? »

Un malaise grandit en elle.

Le café, sa marquise, d'un jaune verdi, aux franges blanches, toujours en mouvement — une ondulation régulière qui court très vite — les tables rondes, les verres où les liquides clairs ou sombres, opaques ou translucides, mettent la joie d'un tas de notes discordantes, les consommateurs accoudés... Lui! Il n'est plus seul. Il rit avec un gros homme très ordinaire, tellement ordinaire qu'elle en est blessée — comment peut-Il fréquenter ça? — Elle voit qu'on apporte d'autres verres, d'autres bouteilles, c'est une nouvelle installation. Elle passe sans être remarquée.

La promenade continue, mais tout est changé autour d'elle. Les gens croisés tout à l'heure la dévisagent sans

ménagements : les hommes avec une drôle d'expression,
les femmes avec une vraie hostilité. La jolie dame qui
traverse la chaussée au bras d'un gros monsieur lui
jette une œillade complice. Elle va... Elle va et, soudain,
nette, obsédante comme un coup de sifflet, cette idée se
forme, grandit : « On dirait que je fais le trottoir ».
Comment ne pas y avoir pensé déjà ? Ses allées et venues
solitaires, obstinées... La honte l'aveugle un moment,
elle sent qu'elle prend une allure d'automate et elle a
toutes les peines du monde à en changer. Enfin, elle va
rentrer chez elle, s'y terrer, ne plus sortir, soudain très
modeste.

Il faut encore remonter la rue — comme c'est la
dernière fois, elle n'en éprouve aucune gêne — passer
encore devant le café. Elle peut même Le regarder une
dernière fois puisqu'Il n'est plus seul, puisqu'Il ne la
regarde plus, n'est-ce pas ?

Eh bien, au contraire, Il la regarde, Il la
remarque et le lui montre par un sourire jeté hardi-
ment, malgré tout ce monde, malgré son ami — pas si
vulgaire, en somme, lourd seulement et tout simple.

Elle sent sa joie la reprendre et la briser, sa joie et
son espoir de tout à l'heure, plus impétueux d'avoir été
matés un temps. Un jeune homme mince — tête trian-
gulaire de voyou, sous la casquette réglementaire — la

frôle au passage d'un coup d'épaule savant. Elle ne s'en
rend pas compte. Elle s'écoute être heureuse.

« Il vient sans doute là tous les soirs », dit son cœur.
Mais bien entendu, et elle aussi viendra pour Le rencontrer, pour se frotter à son regard, à son sourire —
petite bête amoureuse.

Elle dit tout bas : « Comme c'est facile de se retrouver! », mais elle pense, c'est abominable et c'est
irrésistible, aux deux jolies dames qui croisaient elles
aussi devant le café des Négociants.

« Alors moi, je fais comme les filles? »

Elle veut secouer l'obsession comme elle secoue la
tête quand ses cheveux, trop pressés, la fatiguent.

« Comme les filles, comme les filles! »

« Oui, finit-elle par dire, oui, c'est ça, comme les
filles! »

Elle admet pour éteindre le bruissement de ces trois
mots en elle, elle admet comme on raille, mais elle sait
qu'elle reviendra demain et un autre jour et tant qu'il
le faudra pour s'excuser auprès de Lui, elle reviendra
pour Le voir et pour qu'Il la voie, pour qu'Il la par-
donne, pour qu'enfin Il se décide à la suivre, à l'accoster,
tellement heureuse cette fois et prête à tout :

Comme les filles !

Claude Symil.

SIDNEY HUNT : DRAWING

ANDRÉ MASSON: DESSI

BLUES

I

The sousaphone unfolds
sepal by sepal
a blue petunia bud

II

Incantation
incantation
of muttering rain
on petals

III

Saxophones mould
surfaces smooth
as the polished wood
of a negro god

SPRING IN A TUBE STATION

The tubelift mounts
            sap in a stem
and blossoms its load
            a black untidy rose

The fountain of the escalator
curls at the crest
breaks and scatters
a winnow of men
a sickle of dark spray
A. S. J. TESSIMOND.

COLLYRIDIAN

(Berceuse)

When ma bairnie had the hinkcough
I gave her a quaff from a hollycup
and every scotsman is a jew says Heine

only a handful of jews in scotland
but they brought me the hollycup
from the brow from the brow of Christ

and my child to my child I gave a quaff
for my child my child had the hack and whoop
though she lay near her comfort in me

dream me an alcove, niche for Mary
three cookies I lay for Jephtha's bairn
Astarte and Venus two cookies each
O Eve O Eve of the pannicles

Harry Alan POTAMKIN.

TROIS POÈMES

I

Rude au travail, accoutumé à vivre de peu,
notre jeunesse dompte la terre avec le boyau.
(*L'Eneide*, livre IX).

— Je vois d'ici la rustique terrasse et, dans l'ombre
du tilleul, la table de bois sur laquelle j'ai laissé,
entamés, la galette de maïs et l'oignon violet.

— Je vois la jarre vernie dans laquelle j'ai planté
l'œillet frisé et j'entends danser les abeilles, dans les
traits épais du soleil qui sèche les ails et racornit les
aubergines délicates.

— Mais, ce sont mes jeux du repos sur lesquels j'anti-
cipe. Que me restera-t-il lorsque je m'assiérai dans la
fraîcheur parfumée si je goûte déjà, au milieu de mon
travail, les joies de la lumière, des couleurs et de
l'ombre ?

— Reprenons le binage de la vigne qui escalade la
colline.

Ma bêche monte et s'abat avec un bruit ailé puis
sourd ; elle mord la terre qui se bossue de vagues noires
où les mauvaises herbes coupées moussent comme une
écume verte.

Tout à l'heure, quand le soleil de midi appuiera son pied lourd sur ma nuque, j'irai sous le frémissant tilleul.

II

Ici était marqué le terme de ta vie.

(*L'Enéide,* livre XII).

Quand mon gémissant attelage s'est approché du bosquet de coudriers qui est le terme de mon bien, les bœufs apeurés se sont jetés hors du sillon et j'ai pu à grand'peine enfoncer le frein dans la terre.

Au milieu des verveines, j'ai vu, éclairant l'ombre, les os blêmes d'un vieux mort. Ils étaient étendus, gardant encore l'apparence d'un homme.

Une plaque de ceinturon luisait à la place où le ventre avait pourri.

Si les dieux m'accusent d'impiété pour avoir ramassé cette rondelle d'or où est ciselée la colère de Mars, je leur dirai: « Ma femme a fait une séquelle d'enfants aux larges bouches. Le blé, cette année, est léger; il n'a pas assez plu pour gonfler les fèves; mes oliviers n'ont pas grainé et, il est juste enfin, et rare que, un métal ouvré par la guerre, entre, paisible et bienfaisant dans la vie d'un homme. »

III

Ce que présentement nous faisons : boire, chanter
et discourir, rien de tout cela n'est beau en soi,
mais tout peut le devenir par la manière dont l'action s'accomplit.

(*Le Banquet*, Platon.)

Malgré la pluie qui clapote dans le feuillage des acacias, il viendra tout à l'heure le sage qui, solitaire, habite de l'autre côté du chemin, cette maison ceinte d'aubépines et de ronces rouges.

Nous irons nous asseoir sous le rosier si épais que la pluie ne le traverse pas. Je porterai la cruche de vin doux, l'eau dans laquelle a bouilli l'hysope et la petite jarre d'olives vertes.

Quand il aura mangé et bu, et purifié ses mains dans l'eau parfumée, il aplatira près de lui la lettre avec la semelle de sa sandale et, du bout de son bâton, il dessinera les mystérieuses figures où sont prisonniers les dieux et les déesses.

Alors, nous discuterons ensemble les mérites de chacun et le duvet gris du ciel, la voix de l'eau, le champ de tulipes, l'odeur du vent marin, nous fourniront les arguments alternés.

Jusqu'à l'heure où Vénus s'allumera sur le dos de la colline.

Jean GIONO.

Nous sommes heureux de reproduire ces trois poèmes extraits de la plaquette épuisée, « Accompagnés de la flûte ».

THE DANCING SOCRATES

I parch like old rags on the stubble
And yawn, hunched up, or flick a thistle.
I'm old, but young thoughts in me bubble,
A draught of wine makes me see double,
And whistle...
On my old bones the sun comes streaming
And warms my head, shaggy and scheming.
In the sage head, in crooning rhyme
With trees in spring, the sager liquor
Spins songs, and tireless thoughts pass quicker
Than time...

Why stand you there, Cerbeus, gaping,
As though to say, « Old dunderhead,
Just look at him, — he's lost his speech, —
Spings songs, and tireless thoughts pass quicker
Bake bread...

My pupils, there, how they are grinning,
That their old master's head is spinning,
That Socrates is drunk...
Go, Cerbeus, tell the fledglings,
That at last I've solved the puzzle:
It is virtue, if you lick
The dust in Athens; virtue, also,
To blow up bladders tight with air,
Pour water in and out of pitchers:
No matter which, — or wear a muzzle. —
But, better still, — come leave your buns,
Forget your loaves and oven's flicker,
And sit down with me to good liquor!...
A bumper, — and let them stare!

What now, Cerbeus? Are you angry,
Because my speech has lost its ripple?
I laugh too much, and, more the pity,
In broad daylight, in Athens City,
I sprawl like an old tramp and tipple?
That it ill becomes, you are saying,
A sage, if one the point examine,
To be playing
Like a gamin?
That no disciples gather near me
To learn from me truth's hidden sources,

To hear me
In profound discourses?

O yes————————I know————————
Good! Evil! Is that it? God, virtue,
Eternity, men, words and action,
And back again to stupefaction, —
Of gods and men, of good and bad,
Of deeds, and law and order ruling, —
It listens well, all that, my lad, —
This bit of fooling...

It's proved by Heriphon's opinion
That I'm the wisest... The Oracle
Revered throughout the Greek dominion
Proclaimed it, crowning me with laurels, —
Now learn what are this wise man's morals:
O!
What means to me the current mintage
Of word or action, good or no,
When having drunk of honest vintage
My shaggy head, — head of a hound —
Teems with a pageantry of trances?
You better join me in my dances:
Heigh-ho, hop-la, and round and round!
Heigh-ho, once more, and spin around!

Come, watch a wise man at his dances!
You would think his lives were seven!
Truth and virtue, evil, heaven, —
How remote seem all these spectres
When a wife for ever hectors!
Hip, hip, hippie, — come Xanthyppe,
While the tom-toms pound!

Come, friend Cerbie, join the revel,
In the square the ground is level!
Clear the way for dancing sages!
Truth and gods of all the ages,
Men and idiots, — for this bouncing
Xanthie surely plans a trouncing.
But no fear shall ever stop
My inebriating hop!
Dance I will until I crumble,
May the shining heavens tumble,
Whirling, jigging, deftly dipping,
Forward, sideways, nimbly skipping.
Never sparing my old limbs!
Gods may well sing festive hymns:
Socrates has found the link —
Chosen sage — and crossed the brink
Where starts truth and end romances;

Casting off all that perchance is,
Rogue, besnouted like a hound,
Caught the knack of dance, and dances,
Hop-and-skip, and round and round...

Juljan Tuwim.

(Rendered from the Polish by Edward W. Titus.)

DEUX POÈMES

A ma mère, seule à le comprendre.

Où est mon père?

Quelle nostalgie l'a rappelé,
Quel souvenir est-il allé rejoindre?

Un jour, il n'était plus là
Et c'était un de ces vides
Qui ne se décrivent pas.
Mélodieusement, et en silence,
Il s'est écoulé comme une eau qui se retire.
Comme un mouvement symphonique,
Un mouvement qui se termine;
Non, plutôt comme une sonate,
Et le piano s'étant tu.

Quelle est la vague qui l'a emporté?
Où est mon père?

DEPUIS PRÈS DE CINQ ANS

Depuis près de cinq ans, je ne vois qu'en songe
Ce visage,
Ce personnage,
Dont la chair est mienne,
Ou dont je suis
La chair, le sang,
Dont l'âme
Prolonge en moi son rayonnement.

Depuis près de cinq ans, le souvenir
Seul me souffle
Ces pensées que je recrée,
Ce fond, ce tout
De mon être,
De mon esprit.
Depuis près de cinq ans, je pleure.

HAROLD J. SALEMSON.

HELMUT SUMM : EUGÈNE O'NEILL

DEUX POÈMES

Mollesse de l'Infini.
Démocratie de l'invisible.

L'automne
mouille les machines.

Il n'y a que
de l'air gris
dans l'église.

Les étoiles sont
dans le pylone

et les continents
pendent comme des pis.

Rien que
les lignes de ce bras
ont touché la mémoire.

La jeunesse
des villes
radie comme un amour.

On voit
les yeux des enfants
si bas
qu'on dirait
les yeux de la Terre.

Georges LINZE.

THREE POEMS

(from *Forces Of Time*)

Two memories
oddly trace
my mother.

An iceberg was taken
out of our spring.

At the same moment
oh!
the coffin that is seen
going down
like a submarine
in the stairway of the house.

The child's heart
beats
as we love each other.

Summer is
but a spot on the Earth.

No other surprise.

It is not difficult
to see the camels
passing like waves,

the spider-webs
strange nebulae
in the garden-space.

And still,
still,
a kite
like a dam resists
all the Atlantic wind.

4 airplanes
seem to practice
on trapezes of the sky.

*2 blonde women
on a path.*

*And since we are at war
around it all
the warmth of homicides.*

Georges LINZE,

*(Translated from the French
by* Harold J. SALEMSON.*)*

JEANNE MILLAS: DESSIN

A NECESSAY DISMISSAL

« I can't help what Dr. Groves said. I can't help if he's married, can I? » said Mr. Fowler.

« No » said Sam.

Mr. Fowler wiped his bald head.

« I'm a business man and I can't afford to have people's feelings hurt in a small town like this. Besides that radical talk is dangerous. He might influence someone ».

« I know just how you feel Mr. Fowler », said Sam.

Sam had shiny hair but his lower lip was loose.

« You see how it is, don't you », said Mr. Fowler.

« No one can say a word against you », said Sam.

A third man entered with a package and took it to the back of the store.

Mr. Fowler retired hastily to his desk behind the cash register and opened a ledger. Sam fingered the necktie boxes.

The man came up to Mr. Fowler's desk and stood waiting for him to look up. He was small and middle-aged, his forehead large and veins standing out upon it.

He walked with a certain tremulous defiance but his
eyes were timid. He held his mouth firm with an effort.

Mr. Fowler laid down his pen. He cleared his throat.

The man whose name was Jones spoke with a careful
voice.

« There was ten cents due on the package, Mr. Fowler,
I paid it. Is that all? »

Mr. Fowler hesitated. « No, I have something to say
to you. It is very slack here in summer ». He looked
along the lines of red boxes piled upon one another as
if there was something written on them. His glance
finally travelled to the red bathing caps on top of the
counter and remained there.

« You know yourself, Mr. Jones business is slow », he
said with more energy. « There isn't much work to do ».

The little man's mouth had begun to quiver.

« That is enough, Mr. Fowler » he said with dignity.
« I am quite aware that my opinions are not liked ».

Suddenly his face reddened.

« I see through your little lies. You needn't trouble to
invent them. This work has never been anything but
painful to me ».

He closed his mouth and held it firm. « Good
day, sir ».

He closed the heavy door upon the gloves and the

neckties and the socks and Mr. Fowler behind the cash register much as he had closed his mouth.

He looked up and down the street. There was a red gasoline station and across the way the front of the drug store was plastered with yellow cold drink signs. Inside two girls were drinking sodas.

The clerk laughed loudly.

The library.

The peach farm.

Mr. Fowler's dry goods store.

Three failures. The last because he had talked of the wrongs of society. He had a right to. Mr. Pendleton who owned the silk factory had been angry. A thick red face. He had a right to, it had crushed him. He felt himself a man of intellect, sensibilities. Whose fault was he had not had a proper education? He remembered the library in his off hours. Then he was studying philosophy but on the farm there were only magazines.

He couldn't help it if his health was bad. And enemies. He could tell the way they looked at him. There was something in their eyes.

Their eyes made up the world — society that crushed the life out of a man if he had any sensibilities. Mr. Pendleton's red face danced in front of him. They ruled the world with their red faces and their high powered cars.

He did not turn down the street toward his home. He did not want to go home. He was discharged.

He must collect himself.

It was difficult for him to endure these things like other people. He walked along main street slowly. He took off his hat. A few thin grey locks clung to his forehead where his hat had disarranged them. He passed his hand over his forehead. It felt hot.

Joe Rogers passed carrying an empty gasoline can. His sleeves were rolled up and there was a pipe in his mouth.

« Hello Mr. Jones ».

« Good afternoon Joseph » just as if he had not been discharged. He knew he spoke better than most of the townspeople.

Joe walked down the street whistling.

Mr. Jones had almost reached the end of town.

If the peach orchard had not failed, he was thinking. If it hadn't been for Tom's education. He had not wanted to move into town, he would have preferred scrubbing along somehow.

In the town were people. He spoke to them politely. Good morning Mr. Morschauser, good afternoon Mr. Schatz and they looked at him.

On the farm he was alone of course and the light came oftener.

He remembered one summer evening how it had flashed behind his pine trees. Spires and peaks. Strange shapes had melted swirled and glowed.

Of course there was Margaret and Tom but he could not explain to them. He tried once or twice but they did not understand.

He knew people talked about him. How could they understand that he was strangely sensitive.

Tom was getting along very well in the high school. He was slow in mathematics. Margaret coached him.

It wasn't his fault that the peach crop had failed and afterwards he had been ill. Very kind of Doctor Groves — the physician in town. Of course he could not see how painful. Doctor Groves was a man of great cultivation. A gentleman.

A little breeze flicked the grey locks on his forehead. He felt the air enter him, the cool current running thru every vein and fiber of his body. Few men were so sensitive to nature. If he held the leaves of a tree against his cheek, he could hear the secret subtle vibrations of the life within the plant.

He remembered he was discharged.

But Margaret would be frightened.

She had so much to worry her.

But how can a sensitive man with enemies? They were jealous. Margaret was a remarkable woman. Everyone liked her. They hated him.

He was a wretched failure.

Nothing he could do.

Half a man or worse.

His mouth trembled. He put on his hat and turned back down the road. From the distance the town was only a clump of thick trees with here and there a grey roof projecting. And each roof covered a little mind. They were all shallow, conventional.

Squalling doggeral hymns in square boxes. He thought of nirvana a great transcending peace. What did they know of eastern thought and mystery of contemplation.

Of how the mind could swim off, quite forgetful. Little things would lose their sting and the mind would be almost at the center, almost at the source of the light. And the world would be like the image in an inverted telescope with tiny unimportant figures till even that disappeared. But the body — that was another thing.

There was no reason why people should behave as though he were sick. Or be solicitous in a peculiar way. Of course he was delicate. Very difficult for a man of his temperament to live in one of these small towns.

Without the body would there be only the light?

His body was irksome. It told him that he was weak, ill — and a failure.

He passed Ed Winship tinkering with his ford. His hands were greasy to the wrist and there was a black smutch across his nose.

« Hello Mr. Jones » he said.

« Good afternoon Edward ».

« Looks a little cloudy, don't it Mr. Jones ».

« Yes it looks as though it might rain ».

« Is there anything wrong with your car? »

« Little carbon, I guess ».

He hesitated a moment. Then he said

« We need rain don't we? »

« Yes it wouldn't hurt ».

Ed was using a screwdriver. Mr. Jones watched him.

« I'll be walking along », he said finally. « It must be supper time ».

« Good night Mr. Jones ».

« Good night Edward ».

A filthy animal. He would have liked to ask him why he was alive or if he had ever seen his soul. But Ed would have stared. People were always staring.

He must pull himself together. If Margaret — Possi-

bly if he explained to her very carefully but it would be
so difficult. When he thought of it he felt tired.

Tom was doing so well. He was worth two of his
father. Dependable if slow.

But counting out neckties and making change. For a
sensitive man. Mr. Fowler had disliked him from the
first. His eyes. Just waiting an opportunity. They all
hated him. Little things betrayed people. There was
hatred in their hands or the movements of their
shoulders... Sometimes they tried to hide it but he saw
through them. He helt himself unusually observant as
well as sensitive. If a man said good morning, merely,
he could tell.

Margaret would be worried.

It stooped her shoulders.

But he felt things, they pierced him. His nerves
within his body were like bowstrings. She couldn't
understand about the light. She was always saying he
mustn't work too hard.

Even in the vilage he had seen the light, glowing
behind the peaked gable of the post office like a halo or
a crescent of flame, wrapping the little brown building
in eternal glory. And sometimes he would perceive it in
a tree, the bark luminous, each leaf a spark or flake of
lucent metal. It glowed and glowed terribly but beauti-

fully. At times it seemed to enter into him. It was in all things living and dead but hardly anyone could see it. Dull hateful clods.

But noone knew how little things tortured him. He couldn't stand the ticking of a clock at times. Sensitivity was a terrible thing.

But he would not tell Margaret until after supper.

If it were not for Margaret and Tom.

Something shrank within him — he felt unable to think ahead. He wanted to go away.

The steps of the porch creaked under his feet.

Margaret was in the living room helping Tom with his Algebra. Her blond hair looked as if it had faded from a more brilliant color.

« Was anything the matter? » she said.

He held his mouth firm, « I took a walk. I wanted to think ».

She looked at him for a moment and said nothing. Then she said. « I left your supper on the table ».

Tom was still looking at his book. Tom's hair was thick and blond.

The lamplight flooded the book. He could see a blot on one page.

Tom was slow in mathematics.

He went in and sat down in front of a chop and some boiled potatoes.

He could hear Margaret saying patiently.

« No, Tom that isn't right. You forgot to change the signs ».

He ate a mouthful of potato slowly.

He did not feel like eating.

If he did not he would see the worried look in Margaret's eyes.

He heard Tom say.

« Please help me with these. I can't get them thru my head ».

He heard her say.

« I must see if your father wants anything ».

He got up suddenly and went thru the living room saying, « I'll be back, I need a handkerchief ».

The light still glowed on the Algebra book. Tom did not raise his head.

In his room he went to the desk and groped in the corner of a drawer. He took out a little book and fingered the leaves. After a moment he got up and went to the window.

He threw open the sash and leaned out. The sun had completely set. A greenish yellow light still flushed the horizon and illuminated the lower edge of one thin cloud.

For some time he leaned on the sill and looked out. The wind tumbled the thin locks on his high forehead.

He returned to the desk and wrote in the little book. On the pages were lines of irregular length. Under his pen lay:

> Oh flaming heart of mystery,
> Spires of light in mounting radiance furled.
> Oh mystic world!

He closed the book and put it carefully away.

Then he went into the bathroom and closed the door.

« Tom go upstairs and see what your father is doing. Ask him if he is looking for something » said Margaret.

Tom went upstairs.

« The bathroom door is shut » he called from above.

« See if it's locked ».

There was a little silence.

« Mother — Dad — he's all blood! »

H. R. Hays.

VIE ET ŒUVRE
DE JEAN COCTEAU

AMOUR

« Jeunes hommes avides, croyez-moi. Il n'existe que deux manières de gagner la partie : jouer cœur ou tricher. Tricher est difficile. Un tricheur pris est battu. La grande race des fripouilles, on ne l'attrape jamais ; ce sont les hommes au pouvoir, les ministres, les peintres, les poètes, les romanciers, les musiciens, les comédiens illustres. Je les admire. Comment admirerais-je une fripouille mise au bagne ? Elle a manqué son coup.

Jouer cœur est simple. Il faut en avoir, voilà tout. Vous vous croyez sans cœur. Vous regardez mal vos cartes. Votre cœur se cache par crainte du ridicule et par obéissance à un vieux code criminel : « Voici venir le temps des assassins ». Montrez votre cœur et vous gagnerez. Voici venir le temps de l'amour ».

Voilà les paroles d'un voyant. Croire à l'amour, c'est voir Dieu. Ce conseil de Jean Cocteau est celui d'un homme qui a battu la haine, l'orgueil. Pour vaincre la haine, il faut jouer seul contre elle et ses complices. Cocteau a joué seul. Il a joué cartes sur table. La haine a voulu les brouiller. Elle l'a forcé à les tirer. Cocteau n'a pas refusé. Il a tiré carte-blanche, y a épinglé son cœur, et a gagné la dernière partie.

L'amour n'est pas littéraire.

L'amour n'a jamais fait de réclame. La crucifixion est un symbole qui ne peut jamais servir d'affiche. La haine est rusée. Elle n'a rien de l'innocence, de la pureté, de la poésie. Elle s'est vite rendu compte qu'elle ne pouvait pas attirer l'homme avec ses défauts. Il fallait l'enjoler, pour ne pas ressembler à une ennemie. Alors, elle l'a comblé de cadeaux et distractions, de promesses, en lui demandant seulement de la servir.

Le seul cadeau de Dieu, c'est l'amour. A l'homme, gâté par la haine, ceci ne lui semblait pas assez. Il s'est laissé prendre par la haine. Il a accepté ses cadeaux, les instruments de guerre; ses distractions, les arts; ses promesses de divinité, ne voyant pas que cela n'est pas la propriété de la haine, qu'elle ne pouvait lui offrir que profanation et blasphème.

Pour s'attirer l'homme, la haine lui a donné des explosifs, des gaz étouffants, des feux liquides. Elle a

perfectionné une invention d'Icare et une autre de
Jules Verne. Elle a fait croire à l'homme que, penché
sur une croix, il ne voyait pas assez bien; il lui fallait
des gratte-ciel. Elle a appris à l'homme de toujours
vouloir aller plus vite, pensant qu'il s'éloignerait plus
vite de l'amour. De temps à autre, l'homme se troublait.
Il se rappelait vaguement de la paix et du calme. Alors,
la haine redoublait ses efforts. Elle faisait parler des
machines. Elle faisait apparaître sur des tableaux
blancs, l'assouvissement des désirs de l'homme. Elle a
montré à l'homme comment mentir plus souvent à ses
semblables, simplement en agitant l'éther.

Pour que la haine lui en donne encore, l'homme a
voulu mettre le feu à ses jouets. L'explosion l'a renversé. Se relèvera-t-il jamais? L'amour l'y aidera.

Nous avons tous été les amants de la haine. Elle nous
a bafoués. Elle voudrait nous reprendre.

Heureusement, la guerre nous a assourdi; nous ne
pouvons plus écouter les mensonges de la haine. Le
spectacle de la guerre nous a ouvert les yeux; nous
avons vu clairement son horreur et sa repoussante
laideur. L'odeur épouvantable nous a rappelé un
parfum frais. Nous avons touché à l'anéantissement et
nous nous sommes souvenus de la vie. Nous n'avons
plus le goût de la haine. La guerre nous en a dégoûté.

Il est inutile de dire qu'il faut remettre la haine à sa place. *Elle n'a pas de place.* Il faut tout simplement la supprimer. Il faut supprimer les barricades, l'espionnage, les mensonges. Il faut dissiper les gaz et les mirages. Il faut se mettre au delà du Malin.

Pour abolir la mémoire de la haine, il faut mettre ses inventions au service de l'amour. Il faut libérer les arts, si longtemps emprisonnés par des liens païens, en leur indiquant le chemin du Calvaire. Qu'ils quittent l'Olympe pour Golgotha.

Etre artiste, c'est affirmer sa peur. Pour gagner le Grand Jeu, il faut jouer son cœur. Jean Cocteau le sait. Il l'enseigne. Il en saigne. Ecoutez-le: « Voici venir le temps de l'amour ».

POÉSIE

Le moment le plus heureux de ma vie fut celui où je reçus d'un ami, au sujet d'un essai que je lui avais envoyé, une lettre dans laquelle il m'écrivait que, réellement oui, j'étais un poète. Pendant trois siècles et demi, je suis resté fou de joie et de fierté. Car mon ami est un poète, un grand poète, et sait reconnaître la poésie.

La poésie, c'est le débarras de tout ce qui n'est pas nécessaire. C'est la conservation du cœur, de l'esprit, de la quintessence. L'amour, c'est Dieu, mais le Fils de Dieu, c'est la poésie.

Cocteau est un poète de premier ordre. (Il n'y en a pas d'autre). Très tôt, il s'est débarrassé de tout le bagage qui ne lui était pas nécessaire. Je parle des bagages du cerveau. Mots impuissants, images obscures, il les a tous balayés avec les toiles d'araignées que sont le passé et le présent. Pendant que les jeunes gens commencent d'habitude par des livres gonflés, dilatés, Cocteau nous a présenté de fins livres renfermant entre leurs couvertures poésie et sagesse dans une forme si *essentielle* que d'abord on n'a pas vu leur immense importance, à cause de la dynamite qui sautait aux yeux. Cette dynamite n'est pas une pâte que Cocteau nous sert pour nous faire avaler la pilule. C'est une partie même de l'Idée. Voila ce que, d'habitude, on ne reconnaît pas. On voit la dynamite, elle éclate aux yeux, puis, on prend peur avant qu'on ait digéré l'Idée, l'érudition, la finesse, la prévoyance, le fruit mûr de la pensée. Cocteau, lui, n'a peur de rien. Pas même de faire peur aux autres. La dynamite n'est que le vêtement que portent ses fantômes. (Cocteau appelle ses créations des fantômes).

Mais, je crains que cette méthode d'explication ne
fasse peur aussi. O lumière! O clarté! Voilà les fantômes que Cocteau crée. Ce ne sont pas des revenants
qu'il rassemble, ce ne sont pas des ombres qu'il nous
fait voir, ce ne sont pas des artistes de cinéma; ce sont
le fantômes qui viennent, ce sont les fantômes qui
naissent, *ce sont les fantômes auxquels nous donnons la
vie.*

Prenez garde, lecteur! Un jour viendra où le ciel ne
sera plus vapeur bleue, où les nuages auront disparu
pour toujours, où il n'y aura plus de nuit, ni de lune,
mais seulement un soleil terrible et stationnaire, comme
un pavillon flottant autour du monde, et, derrière, un
ciel qui sera comme un tremblement de terre. Alors,
vous perdrez connaissance, et quand vous vous réveil-
lerez, tout aura changé, rien ne sera comme avant. Ce
n'est pas la fin du monde que je vous annonce, c'est
l'arrivée des fantômes de Jean Cocteau, c'est la venue
de la poésie.

Ce qui est inutile à la poésie, c'est le compliqué,
l'affectation, l'artifice, le stratagème. Ce qui lui est
nécessaire, c'est la simplicité, la candeur, la force, la
vérité. Tout le monde le sait. Personne ne le croit.

Dans ses livres, dans ses dessins, Cocteau nous précise des drames effroyables. On trouve cela drôle. On rit. On ne voit pas les larmes, la tragédie, le fil que les Parques coupent constamment. Le monde s'amuse aux spectacles déchirants que Cocteau déroule devant ses yeux. Il trouve très spirituelles les histoires effarantes que Cocteau lui présente entre les couvertures de ses livres. Pourquoi ce malentendu? C'est certainement la faute du monde, mais c'est aussi la faute du génie de Cocteau. Quand chaque mot compte, le monde, pusillanime, se perd. *Il y a tellement de matière qu'il n'y voit plus rien.* C'est pour vous dire à quel point en est le monde. Il comprend tout sauf l'Idée, sauf la poésie.

Avec Orphée, Cocteau a touché les cimes, il est monté au zénith même de la poésie. La maison d'Orphée n'est pas montée au ciel. Dieu a quitté sa demeure pour venir l'habiter.

Tour à tour, la poésie habite un cheval, un miroir, un buste. Et tout le temps, elle habite les corps d'Orphée, d'Eurydice, d'Heurtebise et de la mort. L'ange-gardien même, raccommode avec ses ailes les trous de la superstition. Le mystère de la lumière survole tout. On le pénètre.

Cocteau se dit indifférent à l'admiration. Je le crois. Il veut être cru. Il l'est, dans Orphée. L'eau bénite n'est pas faite avec de l'eau sucrée.

Autre forme de poésie: Extase et sacrifice. En écrivant à Maritain, Cocteau cite une phrase de Sainte Thérèse de Lisieux: « A toutes les extases, je préfère le sacrifice », et puis, il ajoute que tous les poètes devraient se faire tatouer cette phrase sur le cœur.

Certes, la poésie est toujours un sacrifice. Mais la substance d'une poésie confessionnelle, c'est l'extase, le ravissement de l'âme. Il arrive un moment où Dieu arrache la poésie de l'âme. Le supplice n'est qu'extase. La question de sacrifice n'existe plus. L'homme trouve la raison, perd l'horizon, et comprend Dieu.

Le sacrifice, c'est se planter un poignard dans le cœur. L'extase, c'est retourner ce poignard.

Voilà ce que Cocteau a fait.

Le Coq et l'Arlequin, le Secret Professionnel, c'est la critique faite poésie, peut-être la forme la plus élevée, et sûrement la forme la plus difficile que prend la poésie. Dans ces livres, Cocteau a mis tout son cerveau et beaucoup de son cœur. Quand le cœur a mal, il se plaint souvent en vers. Quand le cerveau a mal, il s'exprime en thèses et se défend avec des instruments de chirurgie. Réunir les deux forces et en faire un poème, voilà l'œuvre du poète. Le poète fait rimer ses thèses, raisonner ses vers, et s'opère avec des instruments de liturgie.

La poésie choque toujours l'homme de science, à cause de sa réalité et de son audace. *Le savant ne sait rien.* Il joue avec des théories. *Le poète sait tout.* C'est la sagesse qui lui vient de sa divine origine. La phrase : « Le rossignol chante mal », éblouit et terrifie parce qu'elle est vraie et s'oppose à une illusion populaire. Le savant parle de subtilité ironique et de paradoxe. Il ne voit pas que cette phrase n'est pas un tour de force, mais une révolution de force cosmique.

Le poète se dit romancier ou historien, comme il lui plaît. La poésie d'une histoire s'annonce sans annonces. Elle ne prévient pas. Elle existe dans chaque incident, et dans le dialogue, qui sont ses forces motrices et matrices. La poésie est sans époque, mais le poème est toujours de son époque. « Trop de boutons à boutonner et à déboutonner », un jeune homme se tue. Voilà un poème de proportions épiques et de son époque. La poésie qu'il contient ne date pas du jour de l'invention des boutons, et ne mourra pas quand nous arriverons à nous en passer.

Les dessins ne sont jamais des feuilles mortes. Le papier n'emprisonne pas la poésie graphique. Au contraire, il lui sert d'ailes pour survoler les continents et les océans, et pour traverser, même l'amour et l'intelligence.

Les dessins de Cocteau sont les plumes d'un phénix,
fils du mariage d'un aéroplane avec Polymnie.
Posséder un de ces dessins, c'est tenir une partie de
cet oiseau de feu. Entouré de monstres, de cauchemars,
d'épouvantails, nous pouvons nous libérer en faisant
appel à ce faisan du soleil. Il connaît le secret de
Kotschéï.

Richard THOMA.

(*Suite et fin au prochain numéro*)

VARIATIONS SUR LE CINÉMA

I. — Sur le dénouement des films

Qu'il s'agisse d'un roman, d'une pièce de théâtre ou d'un film, ce n'est
pas un mince problème que celui du dénouement. J'entends pour l'auteur
soucieux de son art, car la question ne se pose guère pour les fabricants
de littérature et de cinéma commerciaux. Et chacun sait que le classique
baiser sur la bouche est un merveilleux remède aux défaillances de
l'imagination.

La vie, que tout art a pour but d'exprimer, offre cependant une infinie
diversité de conclusions; mais elles ne sont pas toujours très optimistes,
et l'on craint surtout de laisser le spectateur sur une impression pénible.
Pourquoi, si cette impression est celle que la logique des faits impose?

Le préjugé du dénouement heureux est capable de gâcher les plus beaux
films. Je n'en veux pour preuve que le *Crainquebille* de Jacques Feyder,
qu'on reprit justement, l'hiver dernier, au studio du Vieux-Colombier. Au
lieu de la sobriété que l'on serait en droit d'attendre, — et qui fait la

qualité de la nouvelle d'Anatole France — le souci d'une bonne fin a
poussé le metteur en scène à créer, en guise de providence, un personnage
accessoire, la Souris. La Souris est un gamin abandonné, qui vend des
journaux dans la rue. Crainquebille l'a défendu, une fois, contre des
écoliers qui le rossaient. Aussi, le soir où le vieux marchand ambulant
va se jeter dans la Seine, le gamin arrive-t-il à temps pour l'en dissuader,
et pour le recueillir. Outre qu'on sent fort bien qu'elle est surajoutée, cette
banale histoire nuit à l'intérêt du film, en usurpant une part de l'attention
qui devrait toute aller aux pitoyables démêlés de Crainquebille avec la
Justice. Une telle erreur suffit pour trahir l'esprit de l'œuvre.

J'ai d'ailleurs la certitude que le public n'aime pas tant qu'on veut bien
le dire les conclusions à l'eau de rose. Le spectateur est un homme aux
prises avec les difficultés de la vie, qui sait bien que tout n'est pas pour
le mieux dans le meilleur des mondes, et qui ne s'en laisse plus accroire.
Le baiser sur la bouche ne l'émeut pas. La meilleure preuve qu'il se
désintéresse de ce dénouement standardisé (qu'il accepte sans protester,
mais qu'il accueille avec ennui, et comme une espèce d'obligation rituelle)
c'est que, dès qu'il pressent la fin des avatars de l'héroïne et du héros, aux
derniers mètres de la bande, il enfile son pardessus et fait claquer son
fauteuil.

Ce n'est pas cependant qu'il faille proscrire absolument le dénouement
heureux. Si le spectateur a vraiment sympathisé avec les protagonistes
du film, je conçois bien qu'après une suite de scènes violentes et doulou-
reuses, il ait besoin d'un soulagement, d'une détente nerveuse ; et il éprou-
vera un bien-être physique à savoir son héros hors d'affaire. Je pense,
en écrivant ces lignes, à l'œuvre admirable de Howard Hawks, *A girl in
every port,* et surtout au *Lonesome* de Paul Fejos. Car il ne faut pas non
plus, sous prétexte qu'elle n'est pas toujours gaie, rendre la vie plus
triste qu'elle n'est. C'est tomber d'un arbitraire dans un autre que d'in-
venter une fin bien sombre, propre à de faciles effets. Cet arbitraire, je
serais tenté d'en faire grief à Albert Guyct, qui doit mettre beaucoup
de bonne volonté, dans son film *L'eau coule sous les ponts,* à faire noyer

Mireille Séverin dans le temps précis que le riche jeune homme passe en rêvassant sur ses bords.

J'ajouterai encore que, sans même tenir compte des soi-disant exigences commerciales, l'artiste a quelque peine à terminer son film sur une idée triste. Charlie Chaplin en offre une preuve frappante. On connaît peut-être *Le Vagabond*, qui est comme une ébauche du *Cirque;* ce qu'est *La jalousie du Barbouillé* à *Georges Dandin* par exemple, ou encore *Les Précieuses ridicules* aux *Femmes savantes*. Les deux films ont absolument la même intrigue. Charlot soulage la misère d'une jeune fille qu'il aime et dont il espère se faire aimer. Mais il n'est pour elle qu'un camarade, et c'est à un autre qu'elle se donne. Dans le *Vagabond*, Charlot, malheureux, mais résigné à son malheur, accepte de suivre le jeune couple; au moins pourra-t-il jouir, en silence, de la présence de celle qu'il aime. Pour arriver à cette admirable scène finale du *Cirque*, à cette sagesse amère et désespérée, pour accepter sa solitude, combien d'années et de méditations a-t-il fallu au grand artiste?

Que conclure? Rien, sinon qu'il n'y a pas plus de règle en cela que pour toute autre réalisation artistique. Il faut faire crédit au bon goût du metteur en scène et du scénariste.

On souhaiterait seulement que le dénouement ne survînt pas avec tant d'arbitraire, et dans l'unique but de signifier la fin du spectacle, mais comme la conséquence naturelle, je dirais presque inéluctable, des faits que l'écran vient d'offrir aux yeux.

II. — Le film parlé, négation de l'art cinégraphique

L'éternelle mission de l'art est d'exprimer l'évolution profonde du temps qui le crée. Mais, immuable dans sa fin, l'art est divers dans ses moyens; chaque grande époque possède ses modes d'expression particuliers.

Or, grâce aux formidables découvertes scientifiques qui, en abolissant la distance, ont permis aux peuples de comparer leurs philosophies et leurs esthétiques, nul doute que le xx° siècle n'assiste à la naissance d'un esprit mondial, promoteur d'un art nouveau.

Il semblait que le cinéma dût remplir ce rôle de truchement universel, l'image étant le plus naturel véhicule de la pensée.

Créer le film parlé, c'est restreindre la portée du film, rétablir la barrière des idiomes, donc aller contre l'esprit de notre temps. Les limites de cet article nous empêchent d'entrer dans le détail de la chose. Mais un exemple : le synchronisme tant vanté du son et de l'image, comment, pour un même film, l'obtenir dans toutes les langues? Telle phrase qui demande vingt mots en italien n'en exige que dix en allemand. Comme le synchronisme est indispensable, d'une part, et comme, d'autre part, on ne saurait modifier la durée du son, il faudra modifier le mouvement de la bande. Or, le mouvement est la qualité essentielle du cinéma : ralentir ou précipiter le débit des images, c'est altérer le sens du film, *c'est le trahir.*

D'ailleurs, le film parlé est un retour aux conceptions du théâtre. Et jamais les personnages sur l'écran ne donneront l'impression de réalité des acteurs sur la scène, pas plus que la voix du vitaphone ne remplacera parfaitement la chaleur, les nuances à peine perceptibles, de la parole humaine articulée. Un partisan du film synchronisé, le critique du *Sunday Times,* l'avoue d'ailleurs ingénument : « C'est une invention d'un réalisme étourdissant, écrit-il. Imaginez des photographies mouvantes de gens, qui peuvent parler et chanter presque aussi naturellement que leurs originaux vivants ». Je souligne le « presque » à double fin ; c'est d'abord un aveu d'impuissance technique ; et ensuite, comment parlerait-on d'art, puisqu'on se trouve dans le domaine de l'à-peu-près?

Un art ne vit qu'indépendant. Le cinéma ne doit pas plus imiter le théâtre (c'est le cas du film parlé) que la peinture (c'est le cas du film en couleurs). Sa beauté réside dans le mouvement, dont les possibilités sont infinies, et les oppositions ou combinaisons du blanc et du noir, également infinies.

Hors de ces deux moyens qui sont parfaitement neufs, innombrables dans leurs réalisations, et d'expansion universelle — donc conformes au génie de notre temps — il n'y a pas de salut pour l'art cinématographique mondial.

Francis Ambrière.

NOTES

(Harold J. SALEMSON)

Les Livres

LE COUPLE

Le problème du couple préoccupe bien notre siècle. Trois livres dont il est le sujet inquiétant : *Climats* (Grasset) d'André Maurois, *Trois Récits* (Grasset) de François Mauriac, et *La Veilleuse* (Riéder) de Jean Tousseul.

Je m'explique vraiment mal l'énorme succès de librairie, et surtout de presse, qu'a eu le livre de Maurois. Peut-être, cependant, l'explication se trouve-t-elle dans le fait que c'est un livre de vulgarisation. Car si, sur la fin, il faut lui reconnaître une certaine valeur (bien infime, encore), le gros du livre est du Proust réduit à l'échelle d'une mesquinerie qui m'a écœuré. Evidemment, le grand public, ignorant Proust — acheté mais pas lu — a trouvé *Climats* formidable.

Les *Trois Récits* de Mauriac, que nous avions déjà lus en revue, sont au contraire l'œuvre d'un grand maître. Il est en France, actuellement, une demi-douzaine de romanciers importants, et Mauriac est de ceux-là. Naturellement ici, comme dans tous ses livres, l'auteur de *Génitrix* prêche non pas pour, mais contre le catholicisme. D'ailleurs, à mon avis, Mauriac fait toujours ce qu'il ne cherche pas à faire, mais ce qui est sa vraie nature.

Jean Tousseul, lui, est un bon écrivain à qui je ne reprocherais que les velléités de propagande qu'on surprend parfois dans *La Veilleuse.* L'histoire qu'il raconte est intéressante, et elle est bien écrite. Elle a cette grande noblesse — le mot est sans doute incorrect — qui est inhérente au bon ouvrage humanitaire. Jean Tousseul, s'il écrivait simplement son livre, sans chercher à convaincre atteindrait mieux son but; son succès serait parfait. Même comme il est, ses défauts ne sont pas graves.

DE BELGIQUE

La Belgique bout de vie littéraire. Nous rendons compte ailleurs de quelques-unes des jeunes revues belges. Je veux parler ici de certains livres récents.

D'abord, parlons de Marcel Loumaye, que les jeunes Belges semblent considérer le plus important d'entr'eux. J'ai sous les yeux un recueil de fort beaux poèmes intitulé *Le visage dans la brume* (Anthologie, Liége). Ce sont des poèmes d'exil, poèmes d'un Belge à Londres, contraint par la guerre à rester loin de chez lui. Des accents de Verhaeren et de Whitman, et beaucoup de cœur. *Les ardeurs spéculatives* (Anthologie), du même auteur, roman où il mêle la finance à la littérature, est une œuvre très forte. Je préfère Loumaye prosateur à Loumaye poète, peut-être justement parce que sa prose est si poétique. Il a une valeur certaine et j'espère un jour en reparler, lorsque je le connaîtrai mieux.

Un jeune poète, Franz Steurs, donne avec *Etape* (Renaissance d'Occident, Bruxelles) ses premiers vers. On y reconnaît un talent nouveau et qui promet de belles choses. Le début d'*Ardeur,* cri du poète naissant, est très beau :

> *Trop de routes naissent en moi,*
> *et des accueils nombreux*
> *usent mon cœur, usent mes bras.*

Dans le même volume, *Le prophète influencé* de Georges Linze est un essai déconcertant. Je préfère Linze dans son œuvre poétique. Il y a dans

Avis et Forces du Temps (Anthologie) de très beaux poèmes en vers et en prose. Linze est le plus original des jeunes Belges et probablement le plus doué. Sa poésie, un vers-libre dont on ne peut nier la valeur lyrique, est d'une forme jusqu'ici inconnue. Il n'a ni le geste large de Whitman et Verhaeren, ni la composition « en vagues» d'André Spire. Linze ne doit rien à personne. Il a réduit la poésie à l'essentiel, mais il n'a rien perdu de sa beauté ni de sa force.

Je veux encore parler de quelques livres de Constant de Horion. En premier lieu, il y a deux essais traduits par M. Arnold Whitridge, critique américain, *Charles Maurras* et *Sacha Guitry* (La Pensée latine). J'en veux à Constant de Horion, cependant traducteur admirable, d'être allé chercher un critique américain. Pourquoi pas des œuvres originales? L'Américain a été jusqu'ici foncièrement créateur. La génération des combattants le reste. S'il vous faut un critique américain, cherchez-le parmi ceux qui ont 30 ans ou moins. Allen Tate est le premier critique littéraire américain qui se défende. Les ainés créent mais ne savent pas analyser. Avec le talent de Constant de Horion, il y a mieux à traduire.

L'enquête que mena M. de Horion (que n'est-ce son vrai nom!) est très intéressante, mais comme dans toutes les enquêtes, les réponses s'égalisent pour les deux opinions. Il s'agit de *Les Lettres et le Droit* (Art Moderne, Liége). On n'est d'accord que pour dire que l'expérience juridique ne peut pas nuire aux littérateurs aspirants.

Toutefois, Charles de Coster, Verhaeren et Maeterlinck ont une digne descendance parmi tous les jeunes écrivains.

DIVERSES CHOSES

La collection fort intéressante que publie la maison Bernard Grasset, et dont nous avons déjà parlé, *La Vie de Bohème,* se continue par deux volumes nouveaux: *Henri Murger* par Georges Montorgueil, et *Gérard de Nerval* par Henri Clouard. Les deux vies sont curieuses; celle de Murger, pour être si intimement liée à tout ce que signifie la « Bohème artistique », et celle de Nerval par ses détails énigmatiques. Clouard a fort bien compris la vie de ce dernier, et nous nous contenterons de penser comme lui que tout le secret, inexplicable, de Nerval est contenu dans le sonnet qui débute :

Je suis le ténébreux, le veuf, l'inconsolé…

Chez le même éditeur, Henry de Montherlant donne *La petite infante de Castille,* livre qui contient toute l'ardeur de l'écrivain. Il a un enthousiasme et une force admirables. Montherlant est un homme d'idées, un vrai écrivain, qui écrit pour s'exprimer et non pour s'exhiber. Je crois à sa sincérité et par conséquent à son importance.

Un autre écrivain qui n'est pas comme-qui-dirait « professionnel », qui ne cultive pas son champ de vente, mais écrit pour satisfaire son besoin d'écrire, c'est Albert Marchon. Son premier livre, *Le bachelier sans vergogne,* d'une forme qui eût pu être sa perte, le classa de suite, et aujourd'hui l'*Impasse* (Grasset), avec ses relents de M. Bergeret, nous le montre en pleine possession d'un grand talent.

Il n'en est pas de même pour André Demaison. Loin de le faire paraître un Kipling français (et encore serait-ce une telle louange ?) son *Livre des bêtes qu'on appelle sauvages* (Grasset) nous découvre un aimable conteur, mais sans grande originalité. Ce qu'il dit ne vaut pas la peine d'entendre plusieurs fois, mais il se répète constamment.

Ne lésinons pas les éloges envers M. J. B. Kin-Yn-Yu pour son *Anthologie des conteurs chinois modernes* (Riéder). On se plaît à nous donner des traductions des Chinois anciens et les contemporains sont trop souvent négligés. Or, il se trouve parmi eux de vrais talents, notamment celui de Lou Sioun. D'ailleurs, cette traduction est fort lisible et, si quelques notices biographiques n'eussent pas fait de mal, le volume est cependant des plus importants. C'est un document précieux pour qui aime la littérature.

QUELQUES COLLABORATEURS

Trois de nos collaborateurs viennent de publier de nouveaux livres et tous sont entièrement dans le genre de ce qu'ils avaient fait précédemment.

Je ne dirai pas grand'chose du roman de Blaise Cendrars, *Le Plan de l'Aiguille* (Au Sans Pareil), dont j'ai déjà cité dans le dernier numéro quelques phrases admirables. Très beau livre, j'y reviendrai un jour, car ouvrage capital dans le développement de l'œuvre de son auteur, ce n'est pas un livre qui perdra de l'intérêt en perdant son actualité.

Pierre Mac Orlan a donné aux Editions des Cahiers Libres un essai, *Sélections sur ondes courtes,* où il poursuit par la théorie ce « fantastique social » qu'il a illustré par l'image dans ses romans et ses vers. Résumer le livre ? Impossible; il est réduit à l'essentiel. En citer des passages? Pas faisable non plus; comment choisirait-on? Non, ce livre est un document pour la compréhension de notre temps. Il renferme de solides raisonnements et de profondes réflexions. Mac Orlan connaît l'époque où il vit, et il sait y vivre.

Quant aux *Poèmes de Loire* d'André Spire (Grasset, éditeur), ils comprennent des vers inédits et des plaquettes épuisées. On y retrouve *Confidences,* paru dans *Tambour,* et les recueils connus, *Tentations* et *Fournisseurs.* Le vers-libre d'André Spire n'a rien perdu de sa coulée souple, de son admirable jeunesse. Chez Spire, on suit les cimes de la pensée; il éveille chez le lecteur un besoin d'idées, il tire celles-ci de son public sans les écrire lui-même. C'est le vrai talent du « fournisseur ».

Books

THE EDITOR SHERWOOD ANDERSON

Hello Towns! (Horace Liveright) is a collection of the contributions made by Sherwood Anderson to the two country weeklies he edits, *The Marion Democrat* and *The Smyth County News.* It is an uneven volume, of vast interest to faithful admirers of Anderson, such as myself, but I am afraid it might be tedious to some. If one has no particular interest either in the author or in the people of Marion, Virginia, there is no point in reading these reprints from the local papers.

However, we find Anderson's personal style and that is enough to warrant reading the book. Theare are furthermore seversl stories, which we mentioned when they appeared in *Short Stories from Vanity Fair.* They are up to the caliber of the finest Anderson, the Anderson of *Winesburg* and *Many Marriages*.

TWO NOVELS

Here are two interesting books of fiction: *Young Family,* by Robert Hyde (Payson and Clarke) whose first novel, *Crude,* had shown great promise, and *Sixty Seconds* (Horace Liveright) by Maxwell Bodenheim.

Robert Hyde, a young professor and a young husband, tells the story of one such as himsef and, despite his warning us not to, we are tempted to believe the book is about himself. Might not the novelized text-book *Masterly* be *Crude?* Let's hope Mrs. Hyde hasn't thought of that. Be that as it may, the book is full of saucy wisdom, and thoroughly amusing.

Maxwell Bodenheim's new novel is of a more harsh type. John Musselman is a victim of society just as Georgie May was. Buffeted and tormented, he ends up by murdering his mistress in a gratuitous manner, beside himself and desperate. Bodenheim indicts the modern world throughout his book, both by the theme itself and his digressions in which he addresses the world-at-large directly. As in *Georgie May,* Bodenheim has maintained a high standard of prose in *Sixty Seconds* and he has made a wide use of comopunded qualificatives which is not displeasing.

VARIED VERSE

Three utterly different volumes of poetry: *Ballyhoo for a Mendicant* (Horace Liveright) by Carlton Talbott, *The Long Leash* (Houghton, Mifflin) by Jessica Nelson North, and *Windfalls* (E. W. Titus, Paris) by Ralph Cheever Dunning.

Mr. Talbott is scarcely more than an amusing rhymester, though several times he soars above mere jingle, particulary in the title-poem and in the section called *Wags and Wantons*.

Mrs. North is a poetess whose talent I would more sincerely admire if it were not handicapped by a form which seems to me factitious. Two rhyming lines to each stanza, the verse entirely free, and the stanzas varying in length so that the wish for the rhyme seems the only regulating impulse. However, Mrs. North has real lyricism and her poetry is marked by a continual ironic strain of scepticism which shows solid thought behind its lines.

As for Ralph Cheever Dunning, I know no living poet that I more profoundly appreciate. I like particulary *Chanty,* a blithe sailor-lyric, with Dunning's ever-lurking depth of thought, even in his springiest work; *Andrew Bell,* the cry of the poet, is a beautiful ballad; and *In the Luxembourg Gardens* is one of the finest things in the book, ending:

> *The drummer drums us out at last.*
> *He drives all save the ghosts away.*
> *(Insulted soul, some few years past...*
> *You too shall stay.)*

STAGE-DECORATION

A capital book of the theatre, by Walter-René Fuerst and S. J. Hume, *Twentieth-Century Stage-Decoration* (Knopf), has just appeared. Through all its mutations, the authors follow the contemporary setting, as conceived by Craig, by Antoine, by Reinhardt, Stanislavsky, Bel-Geddes, and so on. Profusely illustrated, the book is captivating reading as well as a document of the utmost importance. The publishers are to be congratulated on having brought out this monumental work. It is the one authority on contemporary stage-decoration.

The authors are both well-known theatre-men. Hume is the animator of any number of American little-theatres and directed the Greek Theatre at the University of California. Walter-René Fuerst, about whom we will have more to say in our next issue, is an architect and stage-decorator in Paris.

Les Revues

Nouvelle revue française (avril). — *Ulysse,* de James Joyce, par Stuart Gilbert. Le fin mot de l'énigme.

Le Point (n°ˢ 2-3). — Revue de la génération d'après-guerre. On parle de sa transformation. Nous y reviendrons.

La Courte Paille (n° 2). — De la littérature. Pas une mauvaise revue. Mais il manque de la poigne.

La revue mosane (n°ˢ 1 à 5). — Revue belge. Des pages intéressantes de Jean Tousseul, Constant Burniaux, Francis André, Marcel Loumaye, Georges Linze, etc...

Europe (mai). — Première partie des *Revenants dans la boutique,* le nouveau roman de Joseph Jolinon.

Anthologie (avril). — Le prix Marcel Loumaye, dont nous parlons ailleurs. Constant de Horion sur l'art. *Amérique,* par Harold J. Salemson.

Magazines

Ray (1-2). — Just brought to our attention, this art miscellany of which two issues edited by Sidney Hunt in London (1927). The most advanced review in the world. It may soon be re-issued.

The Enemy (London, first quarter, 1929). — In which Wyndham Lewis (of England) wins the Grand Prix de Polémique, by 99 lenghts; Léon Daudet (of France), second; H. L. Mencken (of America) also ran.

Poetry (April-May). — Since Miss Monroe left we notice contributions both more advanced than she would have accepted (Harry Crosby, etc...) and below her standard (Hoffenstein, some of Merrill Moore, etc...). But Mrs. North's editorials are fine — strong and intelligent. And the new editorship seems quite satisfactory.

The Dial (April-May). — Excellent poems by Hart Crane, Witter Byn-ner, Lola Ridge, D. H. Lawrence; also Valéry, Picasso, Adolf Dehn, Toomer, and so on.

J.A.P.M. — Just Another Poetry Magazine. A small but lively poetry *weekly,* published by Benjamin Musser in Atlantic City. An amusing Poetry Editor's Number.

Contemporary Verse (May). — A monthly published by the same as J.A.P.M. Various types. Charles Henri Ford, Ernest Hartsock, etc...

Blues. — A very experimental new magazine, which we will soon discuss at length.

Bozart (Vol. II, n°ˢ 3-4). — A somewhat conservative poetry review, but interesting just the same. Some fine verse by Jessica Nelson North, Musser, Hartsock, Ted Olson, and others.

Expositions-Spectacles

ART

Signalons, en passant, la très belle exposition d'André Masson, à la Galerie Simon. Masson, qui fut le plus fort des surréalistes, reste un des peintres les plus intéressants de notre jour.

A la même galerie, exposition de G.-L. Roux. Roux est un curieux mélange du style d'André Masson et, à travers Max Ernst, de celui de Fernand Léger. Il n'est pas de la classe d'André Masson. Mais cela, ce n'est tout de même pas une insulte.

THÉATRE

Aux Folies-Wagram, on a donné *Tip-Toes,* opérette de George Gershwin, dont la version originale est presque un chef-d'œuvre. Mais l'adaptation est lamentable. Et la mauvaise qualité de l'orchestre arriva même à rendre méconnaissable la partition remarquable de Gershwin. Sabotage inexcusable. Surtout pour une œuvre de la classe de celle-là.

A la Comédie-Caumartin, nous avons vu avec un intérêt très vif *Les Egarés,* de Mme Marguerite Duterme. Une pièce qui s'imposait. Une œuvre dont l'auteur nous présente les mœurs anormales trop répandues de notre jour, en nous en montrant toute l'horreur, en nous expliquant la sincérité possible, et tout cela sans dépasser les limites du tact, de la délicatesse. C'est une pièce d'une puissance tragique et complètement réussie, dont l'auteur se révèle habile à faire parler ses personnages et remarquable à comprendre leur psychologie.

Disques

MORT DU JAZZ ?

On crie à la mort du jazz. On dit que les nouveaux disques importés
d'Amérique sont mauvais, qu'ils manquent d'entrain. Or, si on est forcé
d'accorder que le maître incontestable du genre est George Gershwin, et
qu'il n'a rien donné de nouveau dernièrement, il y a eu cependant chez
Columbia (dont la production est la plus intéressante de toutes les maisons
exploitant en France), quelques disques qui montrent que le jazz, pour
tout transformé qu'il soit, n'est pas mort.

Just a Night for Meditation (5185) est une chanson sentimentale tout
à fait prenante que Ukulele Ike exécute admirablement. Au verso, *Good
little, Bad little you,* chanté par le même.

Il y a encore Layton and Johnstone, qui donnent deux airs de *Show
Boat* (4916) et deux chansons nouvelles de Donaldson, *Because my Baby
don't mean maybe now* et *Just like a Melody out of the sky* (5033).

Wiéner et Doucet donnent aussi deux airs de *Show Boat* (D. 13076).

Montrant qu'en vérité, le jazz revit, viennent des danses, *The Five Step*
(5245), *Come on, Baby* (14251), et les chansons de Vaughan de Leath,
I wanna be loved by you et *You're the cream in my coffee* (14276).

On s'aperçoit d'un Ted Lews fini, sans entrain, et ayant perdu tout son
attrait. Mais à part cela, non, le jazz n'est pas mort. Et on le verra.

Du côté classique, signalons :

Parsifal (2ᵉ acte) et

4ᵉ *Béatitude* (D 15121), chantés par M. Georges Thill, de l'Opéra.

Varia

PRIX LITTÉRAIRES

M. Joseph Jolinon vient de recevoir le Prix de la Renaissance, pour
Le joueur de balle et l'ensemble de son œuvre. Rappelons que, dans notre

dernier numéro, nous écrivions : « Si *Le joueur de balle* de Joseph Jolinon
ne nous dévoile pas de personnalité nouvelle, il confirme notre conviction
de n'avoir pas exagéré la grande valeur de l'auteur de *Claude Lunant*
et des *Histoires corpusculiennes.* »
Notre collaborateur Francis Ambrière vient de recevoir une Bourse de
voyage du Cercle Littéraire français, pour un livre encore inédit, *La
Vie de Joachim du Bellay.*
Le Prix Marcel Loumaye 1929 (destiné à des écrivains belges) vient
d'être décerné à Léon Chenoy, Georges Linze et Henri Soumagne.

CENSORSHIP

A subscriber, Mrs. W. H. Walling, of Hoopa, California, writes us that,
having requested of the local library *Less Than Kind,* by Samuel Rogers,
the was informed that « this book is not suitable for library circulation ».
Under such conditions, why should Americans write good books?

UNE ACADÉMIE

On annonce la fondation à Marseille de l'Académie de l'Art des Jeunes
(président : Alfred Nahon, 12, rue Saint-Suffren, Marseille). Cette Académie publiera régulièrement, à partir de novembre, un organe « Notre
plume », dont les académiciens seront les collaborateurs. Ils sont déjà
au nombre de 16.
Destinée à représenter la génération d'après la guerre, cette Académie
publiera, en outre, un bulletin (juillet 1929), qui contiendra les premières
œuvres des jeunes académiciens. Bonne chance et longue vie à cette
entreprise. !

ANNOUNCEMENT

A new magazine entitled *Brogan* and edited by Norman Macleod is
to appear at Holbrook, Arizona. It will tend « in a new direction with the
hope of etablishing a literature of affirmation ». We will expect a lot
from it. And we should be gratified.

ACHETEZ

TOUS VOS LIVRES

ET VOS ÉDITIONS DE LUXE

— A —

L'OFFICE

— DE —

LIVRES

— DU —

CRAPOUILLOT

3, Place de la Sorbonne

— PARIS —

ANTHOLOGIE

Revue Internationale

Abonnements : **3 belgas**

IIIIIIIIIIIIIIIIIIIIIIIIIIIIIIIIIIIIIIIIIII

RÉDACTION :

Georges LINZE

104, rue Xhovémont, LIÉGE, Belgique

ADMINISTRATION :

Constant de Horion

288, rue Mandeville, LIEGE, Belgique

REPRÉSENTANT EN FRANCE :

P. FLOUQUET

64, Boulevard Verd Saint-Julien. Meudon PARIS

REPRÉSENTANT EN ITALIE :

Nenè CENTONZE

17, Viale Umbria, MILANO

June
1929
Juin

3

Pages

———✳———

Revue Mensuelle

A monthly magazine

PRIX 6 Fr.

3

DANS CE NUMÉRO :

FRANCIS AMBRIERE fait régulièrement la chronique cinématographique
de *Tambour.*

ZONA GALE est une des meilleures romancières américaines. *Bill* est la
première de ses œuvres à paraître en français.

JEAN GIONO est l'auteur d'un roman, Colline, prix Brentano.

SIDNEY HUNT est un artiste et écrivain anglais.

GEORGES LINZE, poète belge, dirige la revue *Anthologie,* à Liège.

ANDRÉ MASSON, jadis surréaliste, est un peintre bien connu.

JEANNE MILLAS habite Paris, où elle fait de la peinture.

MARIO MONTANARD est connu de nos lecteurs.

HELMUT SUMM est un jeune artiste américain.

CLAUDE SYMIL est une jeune Française qui n'a paru nulle part jusqu'ici.

RICHARD THOMA, de nationalité américaine, est un écrivain bilingue.

IN THIS ISSUE :

H. R. HAYS has contributed verse to several magazines. The story in this
number is his first to appear in print.

SIDNEY HUNT is an English artist and writer.

GEORGES LINZE is a young Belgian poet and magazine-editor.

ANDRÉ MASSON is one of the leading living French painters.

JEANNE MILLAS is a painter who lives in Paris.

HARRY ALAN POTAMKIN appeared in *Tambour II.*

JULIAN L. SHAPIRO is a young American writer who has never appeared
in print before.

HELMUT SUMM is a 21-year-old American artist.

A. S. J. TESSIMOND, an English poet, has contributed to *The New
Age, Poetry, transition, This Quarter,* etc...

JULIAN TUWIM is a well-known Polish poet.

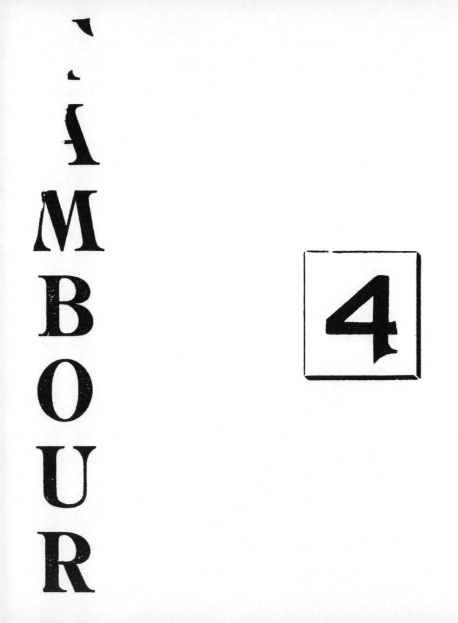

TAMBOUR

Directeur : Harold-J. SALEMSON, Editor

3, Rue Berthollet, PARIS (Vᵉ), France

Of this issue, 200 copies are numbered.

De ce numéro, 200 exemplaires ont été numérotés.

> *Before dawn the drums and bugle are too loud.*
> Tu Fu (translated by Edna Worthley Underwood).
> *...The songs of the drum, That had called the rain and made it come.* Witter Bynner (*Caravan — A Dance for Rain*).

AVIS

Avec ce numéro se termine la première série de *Tambour*. La nouvelle série commencera fin novembre. Elle aura, elle aussi, quatre numéros et le prix d'abonnement sera le même que pour la première.

C'est le succès éclatant qui a accueilli *Tambour* qui nous incite à con-

tinuer. Les résultats obtenus — les textes et dessins inédits, les traduc
tions et publications d'écrivains inconnus — ont été dûment appréciés, et
nous ne doutons pas que nos abonnés veuillent tous continuer à recevoir
notre revue, et y intéresser leurs amis.

Nous pouvons d'ailleurs, assurer nos lecteurs que la nouvelle série
apportera encore plus de ferment intellectuel que la première. On y verra
les meilleurs écrivains et artistes en renom, ainsi que de nombreux jeunes.

N'attendez pas! Comme par le passé, *Tambour* ne se vendra qu'à l'abonnement. Ne le manquez pas. Abonnez-vous! Abonnez vos amis!

ANNOUNCEMENT

With this issue, the first series of *Tambour* comes to its end. The next
series will begin in November. It will again be composed of four issues
and the subscription-rates will be the same as for the first series.

The fine reception given the first issues of *Tambour* has prompted us
to continue. The results obtained — the original matter and drawings,
the translations and publication of unknown writers — have been duly
appreciated and we feel certain that all our subscribers will wish to continue to receive our magazine and arouse the interest of their friends
in it.

Moreover, we may add that the new series will offer even more intellectual ferment than the first. The leading writers and artists of the day,
as well as innumerable unpublished younger men, will contribute to it.

Do not wait! As in the past, *Tambour* will be sold by subscription only.
Do not miss it! Subscribe now! Subscribe for your friends!

BRUITS [1]

Il y a quelque chose de plus étonnant, dans un orchestre, que l'homme aux timbales, et c'est l'homme au tambour, chargé aussi communément de la grosse caisse, des cymbales, et de la cloche du monastère. C'est un homme qui s'ennuie continuellement et qui ne se trompe jamais. Vous lui voyez presque toujours le genre d'embonpoint des gens qui baillent ordinairement sans ouvrir la bouche. Hippocrate explique que, par ce mouvement naturel ainsi contrarié, le diaphragme se trouve refoulé vers le bas, en même temps que l'homme qui baille ainsi avale de l'air comme font les grenouilles; d'où une dyspepsie que les modernes ont appelée canonicale. L'homme au tambour est donc assis au plus haut de l'orchestre comme un chanoine à vêpres, et ne s'étonne de rien tant que le sublime musical s'exprime par des sons seulement. Mais dès qu'il voit les deux harpistes qui commencent à frotter de leur pouce toutes les cordes hautes, ce qui indique le passage à la couleur,

---

(1) M. Alain a bien voulu nous permettre de reproduire cette page dont nos lecteurs goûteront, en plus de sa valeur, l'à-propos au sujet du titre de notre revue. — H. J. S.

si j'en crois les critiques, alors il saisit ses armes, ouvre sur le chef un regard intelligent, et loge son bruit dans le temps avec une précision mécanique, ce qui signifie combat, victoire, ou fête populaire, ou bien troupeaux de vaches et prière du soir, selon l'instrument choisi.

Il m'est arrivé, comme à beaucoup, d'être rassasié de sublime et d'observer ce petit monde si exactement gouverné. J'ai toujours remarqué que tout ce qui est bruit rythmé est soumis à une discipline véritablement militaire, alors que les sons se promènent assez souvent hors de leur juste chemin. Les cors sont célèbres sous ce rapport, mais il ne faudrait pas oublier les flûtes, les clarinettes et les bassons. Il arrive même que Nos Seigneurs les Violons ajoutent quelque chose aux hardiesses harmoniques ; mais l'homme au tambour ne se trompe jamais ; et le chef, quand il ouvre les bras, déchaîne toujours son bruit à point nommé, comme un homme qui décharge du bois.

Quels sont les goûts et les préférences de l'homme au tambour ? Tient-il pour les classiques ou pour les modernes, pour l'harmonie ou pour la mélodie, pour la fête russe ou pour la fête espagnole ? Je suppose qu'il juge de tout cela d'après la partie de tambour. Peut-être s'amuse-t-il du chef d'orchestre. Mais, trop sou-

vent sans doute il l'a vu mâcher de la gomme, faire
signe aux cuivres de sa main roulée en cornet, secouer
les trémolos du bout de sa baguette, et finalement montrer l'orchestre au public comme pour dire: « Que
ferais-je sans eux? » Ce sont produits américains; on
ne vend plus que cela. Et quelquefois je me demandais
si tous ces musiciens d'orchestre aiment beaucoup la
musique. Il me semble que, s'ils l'aimaient, ils mour-
raient tous à la fleur de l'âge. Je me souviens d'un
premier violon, qui avait joué son solo à peu près
comme on prend un purgatif, et qui se levait aux ap-
plaudissements de l'air d'un homme qui va manquer
son train de minuit quinze. Mais la vraie musique
s'arrange de tout, et même de l'orchestre.

ALAIN.

POEMS

ROSE OR A ROOF

sick with the clamor
of tortured roses
weary of rivers
where no one loses
grief or the thought
of a city street
tired of hills

where pinetrees bleed
i surround myself
with tears and sighs
paraphernalia
of sweet goodbyes
a train runs wetly
through rain's thin mesh
and papers rattle
like singed flesh
now are roofs
and rosecolored fires
yellow disasters
of spent desires
o supplicant
and thundering blood
my body has taken
a stone for food
my eyes are grim
my mouth pale wet
my breath impetuous
regret

Charles Henri Ford.

10 CENTS A DANCE

i press myself
to a listless dancer

> *whose body smells*
> *like a burntout censer*
> *where mist comes in*
> *on a secondfloor*
> *and a jazzband bawls*
> *like a raucous whore*

Charles Henri FORD.

HOPI MOTLEY

Chimopovy and Oraibi are a long swing on a windy day.
I have seen the dust of saurians
on a blue reach of sky
hotfoot on the trail to Chinle.
Pueblos hold a touch of moisture
to a parched areno
with the utmost delicacy,
with utmost grace, a torch of life
in a barren:
They say their women have seen the blood of the navajo
on the hand but not in children:
They told the tale to Zuni
3000 years ago.

Norman MACLEOD.

AT TOREVA

At Toreva, the rock as terraced apartmentwise
perhaps they knew 6000 years
what realtors in New York City...
At Toreva, a whitehaired child
ran with a burnish of tears
through segregated grottoes,
grovelling in filth, smirched with lice
where pueblos bring the light to sun
a 1000 feet from mesa:
Spawn of indian trader
and braves mark syphilitic.

Norman MACLEOD.

OLD WALPI

When sands are still at Walpi
and no snakes gild the tangled altar
with fanged ferocity,
squaws footpad docilely
past adobe allowing pinnacles to god
in yellow sandstone:
I saw a Hopi weave the sunlight into shadow
and the unit of his work was done,
with the hair so scraggly on his chest
He said, no Navajo weave this:
breath of the ages.   Norman MACLEOD.

BLESSED BE THE MEEK

Blessed be god and I
Blessed be all his angels and all my thoughts
The roofs are wet with night rain
I am undergoing a deep change
My slippers have frayed tops
Blessed be all gods and myself in all my moods
All my clothes may become shreds but I shall sleep
*   through it*
While my curtains sweep over the windowsills it can
*   rain*
And I can keep undergoing a deep change
If I walk down a road in the provinces I shall meet a
*   beggar*
His feet will be on the earth but I shall not care at all
Even if his feet have been wet by the night rain
It is on all the engines of the forest
It glistens on every leadpipe in the meadow oh blessed
*   be god and I*
Every smokestack in the wilderness is covered with
*   night rain*
We have ice god and I

Paul BOWLES.

POEM

i will have my spy hunt you out
if you are in beige sands by a sea
i shall send a satin serpent to your skin
if you lie elongated on a couch
i shall send my spy there waiting
cautiously he will hold his fingers spread
slowly he will stalk without your door
cleverly he will trap your smothered cry
if you recline in a glass tower
i shall send my spy down the valley
if you sleep behind dark velvet
he will ferret you out
he will penetrate beyond the ultimate curtain
he will seek you in the farthest chamber
he will find you in the deepest cell
no matter down what dim passages you flutter
no matter up what dusty steps you fly
i will have my spy hunt you out
cleverly he will trap your smothered cry

Paul BOWLES.

PORTRAIT OF A WRITER

ONE

Machine is intricate, symmetrical,
designed, composed and murderously calm.
It gives no aid, offers no precious balm,
but ever demands ransom electrical.
Demands! Demands! Nor ever returns it,
but gorges itself and gathers its power,
immobile, aloof, awaiting the hour,
the terrible hour when it shall vomit.

The writer has fed it, has named it God
and worshipped ever at its dynamo.
He has kissed the piston and the steely rod.
He adores the current, the magic flow.
Machine offers nothing, but purrs like a cat
and plays with the Writer as if he were a rat.

TWO

The stars did not suffice. He must fling mud
at them; obscure the gods! Make them cymbals
loud in praise of greco-jewish symbols
that fornicate with whores in beds of blood,

breeding blasphemies in halting syntax,
devoid of music, full of bombast, loud
in argument; in reason, a cloud
seeking in vain to cover up its tracks.

He scorns the bays, the crown of thorns denies,
admits not truth, nor even prophecy;
Temples he knows not, but wounds deifies —
Exhibits sores and cankers, leprosy. —
Monster he is, nor pacifically dies,
But shrieking madly as when a Poet lies.

THREE

He found that words have roots. Why not square roots?
Why not cube roots? His splendid mind divided
words, multiplied them, subtracted, added —
till even the Verb wore mathematical boots.
Words had had meanings. Why should they not be
meaningless? A new etymology!
he cried; Let's force a new philology —
We must intellectualize To Be!

He found new words in the far ends of his brain
and married them and crept into their bed,

exciting here, preparing there to reap his gain
when new planets and new worlds were bred.
But suddenly he died. The Earth shook and surged,
and who creates Chaos is the first submerged.

Richard THOMA.

WOMAN HOLDING A WATERING POT

Speak to a woman who is watering a pot of flowers
Feeding her husband's ego
Watching her children in the sun, curl
Up to their destinies
Ask her, What is the little plot of land
In your eyes shaded by age's hair
And who across a reading table
Could know it is there?... Ask her

How she remembers
The bridal ceremony in the kitchen
Steaming up a less imperious need
And dropping a clattering pan —
Where did the vision go
That was yesterday's adequate seed?

Somewhere behind the eyes
Is she making a bed and lying on it

Waiting not for the children to go to bed
And the dishes done;
Holding the watering pot, she might reply:
It is nothing,
Tell no one you have seen
Passing my gate leave
The mouth singing, the heart
Beating with hope and my children
There at their play
Innocently
Jumping rope

Parker Tyler.

TRAGEDY IN THE EYE OF A TELESCOPE

From my eylids there is
Start a tear that
Blasphemous—
Ly is a
Wound and end
And start
A tear that blas—
Phemously is
A wounding to have
Start a tear

That shall be blas—
Phemously wounding
So right—
Ly blasphemous—
Ly started wound
A tear from eyelids
Ignorant of
Time and
Wounds

Parker TYLER.

NOW THAT MORNING

Now that morning in the little streets
wakes, and is blue with the fluttering wings of birds,
that we walk slowly through the dawn,
saying: morning should be all brightness:
while over this the grey, and over the grey grey again
a dull sun illuminates a thousand compressed atoms
that are pressing their ways toward grey toil:
that we have seen the gulls blow, and the mists thicken,
and the grey morning a little less tedious than death,
futility walking in the streets in a torn black hat
wearing jauntily in his lapel the tiniest dead rosebud:
morning in the little streets
and on boats at sea and on islands at sea
and walking people through the newly dulled sunlight,

walking people through the grey mists
who are but atoms hurrying toward death again:
but for the moment hurrying through and hurrying
    through:
all waking people going through the greyness:
I say: morning should be brilliant
with orange sun like mornings in April after rain:
saying slowly of your eyes:
morning should be brilliant and mention carefully April
while your threaded smile climbs into my silence
where nothing IS except April and your morning smile:
saying slowly of your eyes as they turn seaward again
where the birds fall and the waters fall
and the grey mists thicken on the grey dull air:
how little lives are lived on dull mornings
and how my ill and little heart
glows faintly something like the silver moon
that is not wholly dead across the right horizon
of the ship's mist:
under your slow sure eyes:

MORNING.

KATHLEEN TANKERSLEY YOUNG.

POEM

lions of the sands soft fawning manes
rippling beside the boneless sea
where the grey air relentless rains
drowning dim footprints feet that flee

there my lost hands have often sought
tendrils of time and ivy leaves
on the sea's silver goblet wrought
metallic sea that ever grieves

no less the ship alas torn sails
souls lost in endless tempests where
the sunset bleeds midst howling whales
whose voices are the wind's despair

Edouard RODITI.

POÈMES

DÉCLIC

Sur le chemin tout palpitant
Sur la route d'or de la mer
Qui mène au ciel éblouissant
Sur la grève au sable ridé
Par la morsure âpre des vagues

Sur la jetée sonore et froide
Où veille la lampe des vivants
Sur les bornes scellées du quai
Sur le balcon où l'on attend
La nef à la voile fleurie
Les yeux qui cherchent le vieux philtre
Dans d'insaisissables grimoires
Sur l'horizon sali de brume
Sur les guirlandes de lumière
Qui se balancent au fond du port
Sur la nuit pourvoyeuse de silences
Sur ton visage blafard
Sur tes mains fragiles comme les feuilles mortes
Sur des cascades de sanglots
Sur le banc de l'allée étroite
Où j'aperçois ton cœur ouvert
Au souffle chaud des sapins verts
Sur tes caresses favorites
Lèvres rouges et parfumées
Oh! sur ton corps offert et profané
J'ai tout absorbé — tout — tout — tout.

Valentin de MANOLL.

BEAU FIXE

Consommateur attendri aux terrasses du monde,
J'écoute le chant de la vie,
J'écoute le chant de mon temps.
Le sang du monde est un vice fort,
Les regards sont chauds comme des baisers,
Chaque passant laisse un sillage de bonheur,
Les marroniers vernis par l'orage récent
Sont des nids de feuillage où chante la lumière...
Rien ne peut plus troubler ce cœur.
Rien... sinon quelque Amour, plus noble que le calme.
Ce temps est-il meilleur que d'autres?
Je ne sais, mais des boissons fraîches
Consolent de ne pas savoir.

Mario MONTANARD.

ESPACES...

Je t'ai connue dans le Paris-Prague:
Cet avion si léger qu'il semble fait d'un jour
Aussi blond que tes cheveux courts,
Nous ne regardions que nous-mêmes,
Dans le balancement des osiers ventilés.
Nos regards dédaignaient les plaines,
Les fleuves, les bois et les monts...
Ton indulgent mari discute autour des tables

De la Société des Nations.
Ton premier amant spécule à Londres,
Sur les valeurs de la Royal-Pétroleum.
Et moi, délégué-ouvrier aux conseils de Moscou,
Je t'amuse avec ma pipe,
Mon goût de bâtir du nouveau...
Dis, bien-aimée, donne moi ta nuque,
Où tes cheveux font comme du blé qui pousse.
...C'est joli de vivre aujourd'hui...

Marie MONTANARD.

NEIGE

La neige a mis le froid dans mon corps,
Qui donc a mis le froid dans mon âme ?

La neige tombe, la neige va.
On dirait qu'on attend là-bas
tout son silence et son mystère,
pour porter doucement en terre

mon rêve las.

La neige tombe, la neige va ;
amoncelée en petits tas,
elle feutre et revêt la terre,
pour que soit mieux au cimetière

mon rêve las.

> *La neige tombe, la neige va.*
> *Un peu ici et un peu là;*
> *effaçant toute ligne altière,*
> *effaçant même dans sa bière*
>
> > *mon rêve las!*

> > > Claude SYMIL.

VIOLENCE

Je veux des sons purs,
Je veux des sons froids,
Des sons scandés
Comme des coups de hâche,
Des sons hautains
Tombant des vieux beffrois
Pour marteler le cœur des lâches!

Je veux des doigts tordus,
Cruels comme des ronces,
Des doigts sans émoi,
Des doigts sans remords,
Des doigts incisifs
Qui mordent
Et s'enfoncent
Pour étrangler les méchants forts!

Je veux encore,
Sur la route des plaisirs honnis,
Des fleurs sauvages,
Belles et vénéneuses,
Troublantes
Comme des fauves orchis,
Pour vous ulcérer, lèvres trop voluptueuses!

Robert DELAHAYE.

VIE

Le mouvement du monde
Satisfait notre rêve
De ressentir profonde
Une âme qui s'élève.

Au cœur si attendri,
C'est la félicité
Qui s'offre et qui sourit
D'avoir ainsi été.

La vie nous a leurrés
Du calme de ses ailes,
De sa chaste durée,
De sa grâce éternelle.

Après avoir vécu
Quel triste lendemain
Que se sentir vaincu
Au milieu du chemin!

Sache au sortir du rêve
Te sentir éphémère...
Il n'est de vie sans trêve
Qu'au fond de la chimère.

Alfred NAHON.

THE ALCHEMIST

It was undoubtedly magic; not black, but golden. Twenty tired people sat, and forgot they were tired. On scattered couches were eight lovers; but they were not for the moment lovers. A lawyer became suddenly heedless of his deeds and documents; a physician of his routine. An arrogant stock broker stopped thinking of his ticker. A mother was able to ignore the fact that she had borne children, and that she loved them.

In the room no sound was heard save the voice of the girl standing beside the piano. Her slender body curved gracefully to lean against the instrument the sound of whose notes served merely to accentuate the girl's voice. All that one heard was this singing, but the song had gone deep into the hearts of the twenty who were listening there to give life once more to melodies which time had choked with a covering of thick gray dust.

The song of the slender girl became twenty songs each one of which was different. The twenty listened not with their ears... twenty souls like twenty sounding boards transmuted the one song into twenty.

The last note quivered on the keyboard; the voice of the slender singing girl had stopped.

The twenty stirred in their chairs like twenty sleepers struggling to awake. The lovers on their little couches moved closer to each other. The lawyer shrugged his shoulders briskly and began twirling his watch chain. The physician abruptly pulled out his watch; he rose saying that a patient was waiting for him and that he must leave at once. The stock broker drew a cigar from his pocket and spat the end out of his mouth viciously. The mother sighed and drew her shawl more closely around her shoulders.

The girl who had been leaning against the piano

walked deliberately from the room. Leaping from my chair I followed and came upon her in a little dark hallway.

« Please », I blurted, « please don't go away like this. I must tell you how beautifully you sang. It was divine; like nothing I've ever heard before. I must hear you again — I must. Where can I find you? Or perhaps you'd even consent to come to my house some evening soon... »

Her eyes in the darkness were like the eyes of a cat; their pupils flashed like phosphorus.

« Good god », I went on since she remained silent, « what wouldn't I give for a voice like yours? There can be nothing to equal it, nothing. »

« I hate it », she said slowly and bitterly. « I tell you I hate it. If only I could be born again, my one wish would be to be born without my voice. It's a curse! When people look at me what do they see? A girl, a woman, a human being? No, I tell you, no. All they see is — a voice. If I had my way I'd never sing again — not one note, never, never! All my life it has been like this. I do not exist. I am only a voice. »

I stood looking after her stupidly as she went on her way down the dark hall.

R. S. V.

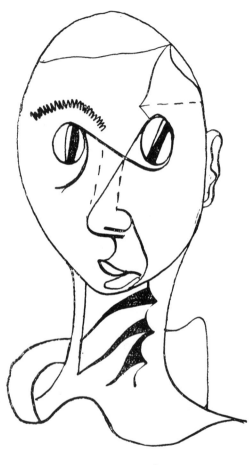

Sidney Hunt
1929

SIDNEY HUNT: DRAWING

SIDNEY HUNT : DRAWING

IN INDIA INK

MAN AND WOMAN AND BEAST

If I painted a picture of India of the tangible things
I would choose the sphinx and a serpent for its image
But if I painted one of the things intangible I would
select storm — in a desert. So would I strive to tell of its
unfathomable love and its unfathomable hate and the
abiding mystery between the two. In the central provinces of India this mystery is like shadows you have
dreamed, like deeper shadows you will one day not
dream.

Ibbitson lived in central India. He claimed to be an
Englishman when he was with the English, when he was
not the Hindus knew how deeply versed he was in their
creeds and philosophies, in Upanishads doctrine and
Sânkhya belief. And they knew, also, that when it came
to an obscure point, some traditional custom or tribal
faith, Ibbitson could tip the scales in his direction every
time, by some seeming proof and by every guarantee
of its infallibility. Therefore there was no love lost
between the natives and Ibbitson.

He was of good stature, muscular and strong as any
robber among them, with a face bronzed almost to the
color of old leather, though he was not over thirty five
years of age.

His wife had been a nautch girl and was beautiful, with all the allure and mysticism of the east in her eyes, in her every movement. He had brought her to this place, Tanaris, some two years ago.

It was said that he had carried her off one night after a great festival in Calcutta. It was said that he smoked bhang in her face, as the South African coast traders sometimes do to overpower a victim. It was said that it was only by beatings, by curses, by hunger, by — maybe worse things — that he had subdued the everlasting devil of this woman. It was said that was the reason he had chosen this remote Tanaris for a home.

Be these things as they may, an unsubdued devil looked out of her eyes at times, as though her body was its cage. That Ibbitson loved her was very evident in his meaning of the word. She had whatever she wanted that could be obtained in this inaccessible part of India. The finest East Indian rice was always hers and the spirit distilled from it, Shou-choo. Ibbitson sent to Turkey for her sweetmeats and to Arabia for her coffee. She cared little for the tinned food with which he kept himself supplied, probably because she was too lazy to cultivate any taste for it.

Ibbitson himself lived principally on the native food, but he kept the other for emergencies, when some En-

glishman came to see him on business, for he had varied
interests ranging from the coal fields beyond the Goda-
very to the discovery of gold in the Neilgherries. And
Chyra, his wife, had a double set of clothes, English
ones for the visitors and the occasional trips with her
husband, for he never willingly left her, and Indian
garments of exquisite oriental color and fabric, many
of them jewelled, for the daily life of Tanaris. And
Chyra loved clothes and jewels and sweetmeats.

She had been less restless of late. At least so thought
her ayah, the Indian woman whom Ibbitson had selected
after many experiments and failures to be Chyra's
personal attendant. For the other attendants, Mussip,
Serhan and Bijar, had failed him. Once he had returned and found Chyra absent and Mussip dead drunk.
Another time both Chyra and Serhan were away and
were absent all night. Serhan brought a tale of being
lost in the forest, she who had once led a party through
the Kohispur woods when the stars had left the sky
And Bijar's faults were as the threads of a garment.

But this ayah had done very well, only that —
Sometimes Ibbitson thought they had secrets together.
« The priest runs no farther than the temple », is a
well known proverb and Jaler was of Chyra's race,
creed — India. It was a common thing for English-

men to have some one they could trust in these matters, or thought they could trust. A married Indian woman is faithfulness itself if she loves and as long as she loves, but Chyra had not been bought with love. Ibbitson guarded her closely and then had his suspicions — which she paid for. But he had had no real evidence —

Tanaris was scarcely more than a collection of hovels save one large building which some Englishman had erected there with a view to studying eastern dancers and taking them to Europe. But oil may not be extracted if no sesamum remains and he had gone the way of thousands of others who were certain of obtaining a fortune from the east. And the building was roughly in the charge of any Englishman who happened to be there. It was Dr. Erdington, a physician with preconceived ideas about opium, in whose possession it was now.

Occasionally the natives held dances in it and very occasionally these dances were honored by the presence of the nearest reigning Rajah. He came when it was said the dances would be exceptionally good, given by strolling Indians, by nautch girls, once it was whispered by temple dancing girls. There was to be a great dance on the tenth and the Rajah had sent word he

would be présent. The bearer also brought the rupees
that the Rajah gave and it meant that the hall was
decorated with eastern plants, colored like enormous
butterflies, scented with curious, ardent perfumes. One
corner was roped with scarlet and gold ropes, carpeted
and cushioned.

It had been kept a secret, as it generally was, as to
the dancers, but not a woman at Tanaris, who was
permitted to go, but had secured all that was possible
in the way of eastern dress. Ibbitson had given permission to Chyra to attend the dance. She did not have
many pleasures and a dog cannot be to much of a lion
even in his own kennel.

Chyra gave herself up to the delights of her dress.
It was the purple of a deep evening, caught here and
there with gold, embroidered all over with the bul-bul
in full flight. If they could not sing, as indeed it appeared possible, Chyra could, with this nightingale's
own note. Ibbitson had understood that she was to
wear English dress, but with a woman's coquetry Chyra
had so altered it that it was more a nautch girl's
dancing dress. It was cleverly done. Ibbitson would
never know; he disregarded color in this land that so
foamed with it.

Two days before the dance Ibbitson was called to

Bhotan where he had a small mining interest. He hastily considered and told Chyra she could still go to the
dance with Jaler. If he refused he knew it would not
prevent her going disguised as to dress and veil and
she would probably run into ten times the mischief
that she would if accompanied by her ayah. He could
not possibly return in time — this she would know.
Chyra was delighted; he read that in her sombre, dusk-
dark eyes as readily as he read, too, the raw, bitter
things that the jungles keep for their own.

He returned the day following the dance, late and
very tired. Chyra met him at the door and put her hand
on his arm with more affection than she had ever done.
There was no lamp in the room beyond, but the stars
were hurling themselves from their violet shelter and
he saw by their light that something had occurred since
he left, something he might never know but something
— now — to dread. The very touch of her hand
told him, the slight tremor that ran through her body
and above all things those eyes, that could not entirely
find refuge behind their many veils.

Ibbitson knew, with his eastern subtlety, that if he
reproached he would never find out what had occurred
— yes, that was it — at the dance. But he watched, as
a jaguar its prey. Whatever it was Jaler had taken

sides with Chyra in this; he could tell from her oblique glances, from the way in which she performed her duties, generally so slackly done as to require much cursing, and from her avoidance of him.

The days passed uneventfully however, until entering Chyra's room suddenly one evening he saw — or thought he saw — Jaler give her a note. When the woman had left Ibbitson put his hands on Chyra's shoulders and looked straight down into her eyes. They were as blank as the floor beneath his feet.

« Give it to me », he said, tightening his hold.

« What? »

« The letter Jaler gave you. »

« Letter? I have no letter. »

He made her hold up her hands and ran his hands roughly over her, examined her robe, looked in her sandals, made her open her mouth — there was nothing.

« If you ever dare! » he threatened, but the eyes that gazed back at him were those of an injured doe.

The next day Dr. Erdington came to see him and remained some time on the porch. Ibbitson was most interesting when he chose to be and Erdington flattered himself that he obtained a great deal of accurate information — he certainly obtained information.

Today the subject came around to Indian beliefs and superstitions. « And what is it about the Jalaga lions?

Dilenz let fall a word about it today and then his lips
tightened until I thought he would eat them. I heard
something of it at Bangalore but, of course, there it
was a jest. »

Ibbitson thought quickly. He had told Erdington
many things, colored to suit the whim of the moment;
why not give him a good mouthful of the truth, some
of the naked things about this country which he had
come out to study somewhat as one might gaze at a
certain painting and think he was an artist, something
to remember when he awoke in the night and heard
evil, ominous sounds —

« It is true », he answered. « I, myself, know of a
case. The story goes that the Jalaga lions were once
men and retain enough of a man's thoughts and habits
to be the most dangerous beats in the world. When they
decide to kill a man — how the decision is made
comes later — they come for him between the hours
of twelve and one. The first time they do not take him
but a low roar, as of the wind in torment, wakes him
from sleep and when he goes to the window he sees —
The next time, and it may not be for months and it may
be in the streets of a town in broad daylight, they cap-
ture him but do not kill him at once. He lives among
them, becoming their king-slave until, being brutalized,
he goes with them to select the next victim. It would

be », Ibbitson, finished slowly, « a good way for a man
to revenge himself on an enemy. »

Dr. Erdington looked up and saw Chyra hesitating
in the door. She was bringing them some wine, with a
rose leaf or two floating on each glass. Ibbitson had
seen it thus served at the table of an eastern prince.

« And you mean to tell me that you believe such
arrant nonsense? »

« Why not? » asked the other, but his eyes looked
malevolent. « That story — if you choose to call it
so — is as this ant », he flecked one from his hand
as he spoke, « to that elephant », he pointed to the verge
of the Shetzu forest where one was trumpeting, « in
the way of things I know to be true. And, as I said, I,
myself, know of a case. »

« There is no twisting a rope of sand », quoted the
physician.

« Ask any native if you want to know more », Ibbitson was irritated. « They will not tell you, but if you
persist in your unbelief you will live — perhaps die —
alone here. »

« I know that — these tribal beliefs are as firmly
attached as their black skins. »

« You can't separate water by commanding it »,
added Ibbitson, who could go from occidental to oriental thought in a flash.

It was just four days after this that Ibbitson, returning from an errand that took him some distance beyond the village, caught a glimpse of a brilliant red dress through the nearest tangle of the Shetzu undergrowth. If suspicion enters one's mind it soon becomes as large as belief. Ibbitson hastened to his house and as he suspected found Chyra absent. Jaler, outside, was languidly washing some towels, the heat pouring from her in sullen drops.

He seized her arm. She looked altogether too satisfied over the round bowl of water. She usually had a slight snarl when she worked, for it was not her habit to like work or its usual handmaiden, cleanliness. « Where is Chyra? »

« In the house, Sahib. » She pointed a wet forefinger towards Chyra's room.

Ibbitson tightened his grasp. « She is not and you know it — What do I pay you for? »

« To be all eyes. » She nodded rapidly and then, at the look on his face, started for the house, saying over her shoulder, « But they don't grow in the back. »

Ibbitson reliquished her and made for the woods. Time enough to consider Jaler. He strained his eyes as he went and thought he could see — *could see* — the glint of a gold turban disappearing through the trees. Only members of the Rajah's household wore gold turbans —.

But he could not find Chyra though he tramped the woods until his clothes were almost as wet as if he had been swimming, assailed now by the most terrible fear. He had heard of such cases...

When he returned, white, spent, Chyra was sitting in the first room of the bungalow that jutted forward, open to the north. She was playing with the tassels of her dress. Ibbitson knew there was deviltry afoot, but for the first time in his life he was at a loss as to the best course. He could beat her, kill her, but he could not force her to tell anything she did not wish and there was something as of *security* in her appearance...

He must watch and find out and then — He ground his teeth as he thought of his vengeance on any man that might come between him and this girl — And his vengeance on her —.

He slept heavily that night, heavily. Four pipes of opium only, while he thought things out, but he had not taken any for a long time — He was awakened by Chyra's voice and the Ayah's in great excitement outside his window. Looking down he saw they were examining the ground closely.

« What is it? » he called.

« The tracks of a lion », answered Chyra, « or they look like it — come and see. »

They were a lion's tracks, unmistakably, and they encircled the house.

« I heard them last night », said Jaler. « I heard — », she drew nearer to Chyra.

« D — it all! » Ibbitson kicked the tracks and turned to enter the house. It was not an infrequent thing for them to come from the forest to the village. But, even as he did so, he heard Jaler say, « They are mighty tracks », and his conversation with Erdington flashed in his mind. So that was it, was it? *So that was it!*

The news spread through the village, Chyra and her Ayah repeating it over and over again. But before the moon of that month had finished its tapestries there was a great hue and cry in Tanaris. Erdington was awakened by it, as by vibratory sensations that communicated the fact that something was wrong. One always expects the unexpected in the east, from the first pagoda thrush in the morning to the shriveled ends of day. He was out in a moment and by dint of much questioning, for the natives were too excited to be explicit, he found that Ibbitson had disappeared in the night. Carried off by a Jalaga lion! It was very rare, so an old Vihara priest told him, and it was —

final. There had never been one known to return
except — The old man looked at him as from the
dreams of a monastery.

Erdington nodded his head. « I have heard », he
said briefly and he went on to Ibbitson's house.

A great crowd had collected and were examining
enormous tracks that looked to Erdington almost the
size of an elephant's feet, but one and all pronounced
them lion, Jalaga lion, as surely as an English detec-
tive names a criminal by finger prints. Chyra and her
Ayah were within and the wailings, Erdington concluded, came from them.

He asked if he could speak to Chyra and upon being
told that he could do so, entered the room. She seemed
prostrated with grief, her body every now and then
being shaken by convulsive sobs. Erdington tried to
extract some information but the utmost he could gather
was that after moonset she was awakened by struggles,
cries, at the door — he had been carried that far —
Then on — on — She had shrieked and tried to see
but it was dark — black. There were the marks, on
floor, side of wall, on ground outside — And they
led to the forest.

Erdington endeavored to organize a search party
and offered rewards, but he might as well have tried to
uproot a teak tree with words. Armed with his rifle and

pistols he followed the tracks a short distance into the Shetzu forest but there lost them entirely, almost lost himself and returned worn out, bearing the heat as a burden. Chyra and Jaler mourned, the former desperately, bewailing the fact that she could not immolate herself in suttee, the latter as became the servant of an adored mistress.

Sometimes the course of events in India runs as if in the trough of a thousand years, sometimes as rapidly as the sowing of seed and gathering its flower the same day. This last was the way certain epochs now occurred for Ibbitson, for the villagers, who remembered them unto the telling their children's children.

Four days after Ibbitson disappeared Chyra and her Ayah too disappeared, but this time there were no marks of violence to be found. Later the Indian woman, who was their nearest neighbor, told that she saw certain preparations for their departure, the washing of fine garments, even their packing but this was discredited by the others who would have the tragedy without a leak... But certain it was the door was securely fastened.

Erdington loaded a brace of pistols and slept with them near his hands. Of course that story of Ibbitson's was bosh, but when each Indian face was terror-

stricken at the mere mention of his name — He had
no friends among them so each man feared —

The fifth night from his disappearance Erdington
heard his name called in an agonized tone. As he hurried
to the door it occured to him — Suppose Ibbitson —
« Who is it? » he demanded, without opening the door
and with his hand tight on his pistol.

« I — Ibbitson — open Erdington — for the love of
heaven! »

There came the sound of a heavy fall. Erdington opened the door cautiously. The moon was full and poured
its light down on a huddled figure, Ibbitson, face up
and smeared with blood. Erdington got him in, locked
the door and proceeded to examine him. He was bruised,
streaked with marks and with here and there the flesh
torn — as if — Erdington forbade himself the thought.

He went to work, dressed wounds, poured some
brandy down his throat and set his left arm which was
broken. It was doubtful whether he would live or die.
And doubtful it remained for a long time. He had had
a terrible shock and was half starved. And when he
grew better and was able to talk — he did not. When
questioned his eyes appeared to see some far-off scene
that prevented his knowing the difference between
sound and silence. He never asked about Chyra. Either
he knew or something had blotted her from his world

as the sirocco blots out life. As soon as he could walk
he returned to his home.

A brave man, thought Erdington as Ibbitson depar-
ted and a desperate one. But one thing he had found
on Ibbitson's body brought a curious gratification to
the physician, even though he was grieved for his
patient. It was a half inch of Indian dagger carved to
the very point. It told of wealth. Lions, even Jalaga
lions, did not use daggers.

When Ibbitson recovered he left his home one morning in charge of the Indian woman who lived near
him. Jaler had never come back. He would return very
shortly, he said, with his wife! And return he did
driving —, yes, that was it, *driving* Chyra before him.
She appeared nearly dead with exhaustion, with heat
and the cruel marks of welts across her back.

The woman would have attended to her but Ibbitson
pushed Chyra in and shut the door of her room. The
Indian listened, kneeling close where the floor and wall
supposedly met. « I shall let you decide », she heard
Ibbitson say. « Will you have it by pistol or water or
poison? »

Chyra moaned and the listener thought he shook her.
« Answer me! »

And faintly, as faintly as a leaf on lake she heard,
« Water ».

Ibbitson waited until the hour of siesta, which all India takes, and then the Indian woman saw him not drive but drag Chyra off in the direction of the river.

He returned alone and threatened the Indian with the vengeance of every god under their hierarch if she revealed what she knew. That was the reason, she told Erdington later, that she had not given out the information, that and the added reason that a man should mete out punishment to his wife. She was guilty and the edge cuts, but it is the sword that has the credit. As to telling this before the girl was drowned — it had evidently never entered her mind.

Ibbitson continued to live alone. Even when the story was known there was no one, in a small village in central India, who cared to take any steps. Besides, as one of the priests remarked, the matter was finished, like a cut string.

But that it was not was proven a month later when lion tracks were again found about Ibbitson's house, with the door open and its master gone. And from this departure there was no return. Erdington, examining the tracks, was assured that the only human ones there fitted the feet of Ibbitson. But in the jungle one never knows.

Later the chief man of the village swore by his

father's grave that he saw Chyra decked in royal state, driven by royal syces behind the Rajah's ponies. Perhaps she escaped, was swept away from Ibbitson by the water, and that was the reason she had not chosen pistol or poison. But when darkness comes in India it is thick, impenetrable, covering the murdered and the murderer alike.

And after all, agree Mahommedan and Hindu, it is not necessary that others should know, for justice is meted out to each one at last. As the Koran succinctly expresses it, « The fate of every man is bound about his neck ».   Virginia Stait.

ARTISTES

I. Walter-René Fuerst

Walter-René Fuerst est connu surtout comme décorateur et il l'est profondément. Son théâtre est une autre vie, plus belle mais plus féroce que celle-ci; plus nue et plus vivante. Mais ce n'est pas seulemnt hors de la vie que Walter-René Fuerst fait de la vie. Il crée la vie dans la vie.

Oui, je veux dire qu'il est foncièrement architecte. L'architecture! L'art de faire de l'art qui reste de la vie; de créer une vie qui soit un objet d'art: la construction architecturale, c'est l'art-vie, c'est la dénégation de ceux qui veulent que l'art et la vie soient différents, contraires; mais c'est le point sensible où, d'une façon palpable, la vie suit l'art, le copie, l'imite, enfin le devient.

Mais, pourquoi, direz-vous, ne connaissons-nous pas Walter-René Fuerst architecte? C'est simple, c'est terrible; c'est beau et horrible; c'est la vie qui en est la cause, elle qui ne reconnaît jamais ceux qui l'enrichissent véritablement.

Ce serait trop beau si nous voyions dans la rue des maisons, des théâtres, des squares, des paradis de Walter-René Fuerst. Non! Jamais l'homme n'acceptera ce que l'artiste n'a pas encore compris! Il faudra que l'artiste, que l'architecte nous disent: C'est beau! Ensuite l'homme comprendra.

Mais eux, les artistes, les architectes, eux non plus ne savent quoi dire devant cet art qui les dépasse comme l'après-guerre l'avant-guerre. Faudra-t-il une nouvelle catastrophe pour qu'ils se rendent compte qu'ils sont d'un siècle en retard?

Nulles, les constructions que les hommes prennent pour des miracles ou pour des pitreries! Arriérés, tous ceux que je ne nommerai pas, mais dont les travaux méritoires sont déjà relégués au plan des élucubrations de Garnier.

WALTER-RENE FUERST: DESSIN

HOTEL PARTICULIER 21 HAMEAU de BOULAINVILLIERS
VUE DE LA FAÇADE / W. R. FUERST / ARCHITECTE.

Walter-René Fuerst, peut-être le plus grand architecte de notre temps, ou plutôt d'un temps futur, je vous salue!

Vous, qui faisiez des merveilles avant même que je ne fusse né, c'est vous qui m'avez appris ce que nous serons. Vous avez vibré de la vie future avant même qu'elle ne fût future. Vous devancez non seulement vos contemporains, mais les prophètes d'entre-eux. C'est lorsque ces prophètes-là seront démodés que vos conceptions seront acceptées comme des possibilités de réalisations futures. Artiste, quand seras-tu de ton temps?

Le théâtre de Walter-René Fuerst est plus beau et plus féroce que la vie. Il est l'idéal d'un homme que la vie, sans le comprendre, n'a su satisfaire.

Comment serait heureux dans la vie un artiste qui vit dans la mort? Car, ne nous trompons pas! Comme nous tous, Walter-René Fuerst vit dans la mort. Il n'est que quelques-uns qui voient la vie. Vous les connaissez.

Walter-René Fuerst est de ceux-là. Il vit parmi la mort et il voit la vie. Mais il ne peut pas la toucher. La vie, mon vieux Fuerst, vous le savez comme moi, ce n'est pas dans le monde qu'on la trouve, c'est dans vos maquettes!

Harold J. Salemson.

4

AN OLD LADY

She is a queen in captivity. Still garlanded with courtiers, but for courtiers only the faithful, her own descendants, but courtiers caprioling with mincing heavi-
ness, percherons in sable, ugly heavy gestures in applied
fealty, beatendown gauche insincerity of peasant blood,
peasant throwbacks, embarrassments to the queens
pure blood... ruriks own transmitted blood spawning
stewards. Rurik breeds a line a backbone into time, the
queen a vertebra, she too a progenitor of a tribe to
follow. That gives her rights over constituents, control,
and they agree, circumscribe the now first female cause,
place backs to the external name and placeless circum-
ferential world, bellies within to the visible point of
female concentricity. Backs to the world. Tribal loyal-
ties blood is thicker than water in the old stale phrase,
not *your* blood. Give over your destinies into her eightyeight year keeping, toothless tressless keeping, put
decay at the helm and trust in her god to lead you out
of the thicket, her god through her devout intercession.
Give over your lives your wills your dreams perfection,
let her religion make them over... but you have no
dreams so what does it matter. Preserve the languour

of antiquity, consanguinates, let her remain. Why break it up, you have nothing, nothing to lose. And so 'she remains in moribund languour. But others voices speak questions into this old dominion, this command as from a drowsy stupor, a half long sleep; speak of this somnolent sound made in tones of dissolution though working with live metal, live arms, live flesh — new beings. Other criticisms than mine of this tribute to the dead and gone. What old. Merely passed by, washed, in point of time. That is not old, there is no old; old cannot control the insuperable mechanism of life and death. Eightyeight and compulsory subservience, old queen, old quean, who knows. A queen locked up dusk to dawn like a prostitude in a nightcourt cell. A queen turns washerwoman, idiot; you dont cross an idiot, you pamper it. substitutes for former hair and teeth, yes, but never heart or knowledge. For hair a flaunting rag of a mudbrown wig facetiously interskeined with slender grey to shut off raptures how splendidly preserved you are at your ripe old age, your rotten old age you mean — the grey, an unconscious time worship, an admission of its exactions. For teeth, hurtful chips of gleaming porcelain redly embedded in vulcanized rubber. All in black her body, anachronistic grey at cuffs and throat. Now the reverse, major in black for alltime death, for all time, a plea in abate-

ment, a plea in trimming for just another day, just one
more. Cheap gold ornamentation in her ears on her
breast and left hand, respectability, all faded to laby-
rinthine wrinkles, gold on her breast intricating goldly
into itself like death into the pores of life. Cheap gold
ornamentation on hands twisted like the gold but into
insoluble rheumatic tangles. Cheap gold on flaccidly
drooping ears, oh go no further into the uglinesses of
dissolution, conscious death, watching oneself die before
a mirror. Mouthing devout supplications for mercy
mercy complicated with clamouring prayers for recognition of goodnesses performed, just another day only
one more oh god, one more.

The throneroom commands the hudson, from early
afternoon to sunset a room drenched in sunbeams shot
through with jigging dust mobile in its moted gra-
dations of colour. Near dusk when the sun drives down
over the jersey palisade, subtle blends and coloric com-
positions and syntheses contribute splashes of life to
the integral gold and deep blue of afternoon. With the
downward press of the sun the eastern face of the
jersey escarpment hides in its own sombre shadow,
empurples its own surrounding gloom. The right prism
of the sheer brown cliff and the flat western division
of the river is dun in thick purple, the only purple

against such brown, groundbrown. Dun thick purple to the west but over it and obliquely down in a cloud-caught fan diffuse shafts of light in glancing brilliance spread alive over and into the ripples, spread in a whirl of bouncing water. The bustling skirts of a distant flotsam ferry throw a lengthening angle of small flirting wash acutely to the shores while to one side of this fat lady of the river a tug puffs a faroff complaint of the chain of scows lashed to its stern, the steaming mother motive power throbbing forward like a duck tied to a plank, but beating on with all the noisy seriousness of a stubborn child bent upon a ridiculed high resolve. Masefields ninevehian quinqueremes crouch interstitiallly in the weehawken docks, argosies thrusting rakish masts and funnels to the skies in submission. To the southwest invisible smokestacks of invisible factories emplant in the air their days last black smoke lily, the widening murkflower sailing disintegratingly over jersey and the bay like a pregnant rainrunner, while in the light blue north stormking ignores the scar of the deftly chiseled road bitten in a long sweeping trajectory across its granite forehead.

Life in transit; insentient, she doesnt care. The ways you address god are indicated in that small red volume on her left. What else matters.

Julian L. Shapiro.

VIE ET ŒUVRE
DE JEAN COCTEAU

(suite)

A Mademoiselle Lila NYFFENEGGER.

VIE ET MAGIE

Jean Cocteau est né.

Il a vécu sa jeunesse.

Comme tous les enfants, il a fait des choses merveil-leuses, des choses vraiment prodigieuses. Il a appris à marcher, à parler, à lire et à écrire. Depuis, il a grandi, il a agi. Quel âge a-t-il aujourd'hui? Qu'importe, puis-qu'il est en vie? Et il est en vie. Il dit que là, c'est une chose étonnante.

Hier, il a écrit *Le Potomak*. Il avait vingt ans. Plus tard, il a écrit d'autres livres: *Le Coq et l'Arlequin, Thomas l'Imposteur, Plain-Chant, Le Grand Ecart, Orphée, Opéra*. A ce moment, il n'avait plus d'âge. Mais a-t-il vraiment terminé ces livres? Je ne crois pas. Je crois qu'il a encore à les écrire, car des livres écrits sont des livres morts, et ces livres ne sont pas morts. Ce sont des courants d'électricité qui animent le fil de notre vie et que nous transmettrons à nos enfants. Ils sont devenus une partie de notre semence.

Mais Cocteau ne s'est pas seulement tourné vers la littérature. Il s'est retourné de tous les côtés. Ici, il a aidé. Là, il a poussé. Autrepart, il a renversé.

Il y a cent cinquante ans, il a fait la connaissance de Picasso. Picasso, alors, était noir. On ne le voyait pas. Aujourd'hui, Picasso est blanc. *On ne le voit pas non plus.* Mais, pour arriver à être blanc, il a passé par le spectre de son génie. C'est Cocteau qui lui a montré par où entrer. « Voilà », il a crié, « par ici, par ici ». Picasso, qui est devenu blanc pour le monde, comme il a été noir pour le monde, est vert pour nous, de la même manière que Cocteau est vert pour nous. Car ils sont tous deux magiciens. Je l'ai dit autrepart: La magie est verte.

La magie est verte parce que la poésie est verte. Dans la poésie de Cocteau, on plonge en plein mystère, c'est-à-dire, dans une lumière éblouissante, blanche, rare. Car le mystère que personne ne comprend, c'est la lumière, le soleil, le feu. L'obscurité que tout le monde sait ne se trouve pas dans Cocteau. Cette obscurité, ce nuage de nickel, fond comme dans un alambic, et alors, dans le vertige qui suit, le monde se perd, crie

aux énigmes, aux charades, aux arcanes, au Sphinx, et
n'y comprend plus rien. L'incendie qu'est la vérité,
l'éclaircit, leur fait peur, comme tous les incendies du
cerveau, ces fièvres qui voient mais qui n'arrivent à
faire voir que beaucoup plus tard, non pas quand le
danger a passé, mais quand il a vaincu. A ce moment,
les bêtes deviennent dieux. Et, naturellemnt, dans le
procès d'apothéose ils oublient leur créateur.

Louange à Nirvana!

Cocteau est un Sphinx. Je l'en remercie. Le monde
est son désert. Mais il n'est pas muet. Il parle, il crie,
il aboie, il chante. Seules, les étoiles l'écoutent. Le désert dort, comme tous les déserts. C'est ce que j'appelle
le supplice du Sphinx.

Et comment, me demandez-vous, Cocteau n'est pas
satisfait de se faire entendre des étoiles? Il voudrait
réveiller le désert, faire écouter les grains de sable,
parler aux dunes? Oui, il voudrait tout cela, et même
plus, car ce qu'il donne, c'est la poésie, c'est l'amour,
c'est la vie. Il ne vend pas ces choses. Il les donne, et
pour rien.

Est-ce que le désert se retourne même dans son sommeil implacable? Jamais. Ne vous en faites pas. La
vie, c'est la fièvre, la chaleur, l'incandescence, la pyro-
technie, l'étincelle. Que voulez-vous que le désert fasse

de ces choses? Il est bien trop endormi. Quand on le
pince, comme la vie pince, quand on le blesse, comme
l'amour blesse, quand on le mord, comme la poésie
mord, il hurle un moment, puis il se rendort.

Cocteau se promène à tue-tête. C'est Cocteau. Tout
d'un coup, sans aucune raison, il se coiffe d'un chapeau.
C'est toujours Cocteau. Ceci n'est pas un truc. Tout le
monde peut le faire. Mais souvent, Cocteau se met à
nu, et demeure toujours Cocteau. Voilà un prodige.
C'est le seul être que je connaisse qui puisse faire cela.
Evidemment, il n'y a rien d'abracadabrant là. Rien du
forain, du prestidigitateur, du sorcier.

Magicien, oui. Thaumaturge, certes. Ni noir, ni blanc.
Vert. Ne perdez pas le sens des mots. Gardez-en l'essence. Le forain est ésotérique. Le prestidigitateur mys-
tifie en créant des illusions. Le sorcier ensorcelle. Le
magicien et le thaumaturge ressuscitent les vérités qui
ne sont pas mortes, exposent les réalités qu'on ne voit
pas, expliquent les rêves que l'on fait éveillé.

Beaucoup de gens perdent le nord. Coctau ne l'a pas
perdu. Il s'en est débarrassé. Le nord, c'est la folie,
c'est la bourgeoisie, c'est le nationalisme, c'est la politique de droite ou de gauche, c'est le mensonge, c'est
l'intolérance. Tout, sauf la poésie, l'amour et la vie. Il
n'y a pas de direction géographique. Le seul chemin

prédestiné, c'est celui que l'on suit de la vie à la mort. Personne ne peut l'indiquer, mais nous le connaissons tous par cœur. Nous n'en sortons jamais un instant. Nous sommes incapables de nous y arrêter un instant. Droit devant nous, nous marchons. Cocteau dit qu'il est en marche. Ce n'est pas tout à fait juste. Il est en marche depuis sa naissance. Mais il dit que la promenade est belle. Il a raison.

Cocteau est littérateur, mais il est aussi plus que cela, puisqu'il vit. Il est l'inspiration de beaucoup de gens, quoique l'inspiré remercie souvent une autre personne. Incident indicatif : Je suis Américain. A New-York habite un écrivain qui passe, aux Etats-Unis, pour le grand-prêtre de l'esthétisme. (Le seul esthétisme, c'est la vie, l'amour, la poésie). Jeune, je raffolais des œuvres de cet auteur. Ses livres m'ouvraient de vastes horizons. J'y trouvais des idées surprenantes. Ne connaissant pas l'auteur personnellement, je le remerciais dans mon cœur. Mais, me voilà venu en France. J'achète un livre à cause de son titre : Le Potomak. Les mots étranges m'attirent toujours. Ce livre me plaît. Plus, il m'emballe. J'achète d'autres livres du même auteur : Le Coq et l'Arlequin, etc. Qu'est-ce que j'y trouve ? Des phrases entières de mon écrivain américain !

Que penser? Une chose seulement, puisque je sais que ce dernier a beaucoup habité Paris et qu'il connaît à fond la littérature française. Je sais à quoi m'en tenir. Simplement à un emprunt international, que j'essaye de rembourser en partie en le dénonçant. L'œuvre de Jean Cocteau a énormément aidé à rendre cet écrivain américain célèbre dans son pays, mais il commence à ne plus en profiter.

La légende fait sa première apparition.

Avant Cocteau était le vide. Après lui est venue la guerre. Ce n'est pas de sa faute. Mais il a survécu à la guerre, et puis, depuis, il nous a donné beaucoup de choses. Il a créé la musique, le ballet, le théâtre, le nègre, le décor, l'affiche. Il a peuplé notre monde. Il nous a donné des autruches, des porte-voix, la Tour Eiffel, des chevaux, des masques, des peintres, des aéroplanes, des toits et tout un monde de créatures d'encre et de papier qui sont bien plus vivants que les gens qui se promènent aux Champs Elysées.

On lui a immédiatement volé toutes ces créations.

Se promenant un jour, Cocteau a découvert un cadavre, celui d'un mucisien tué, il y a onze mille deux cent trente neuf ans, par l'incompréhension. Ce musicien était le compositeur des œuvres les plus pures, les plus directes dans le répertoire d'Euterpe. Quelques

personnes l'avaient écouté, mais l'indifférence générale l'avait blessé à mort. Il se nommait Erik Satie.
Cocteau s'est penché sur son cadavre, lui a donné un
peu de son souffle, un peu de vie, et voilà le corps qui
s'anime, qui se remet au travail, qui nous fait entendre
des accords harmonieux. Qui se rend compte, aujour-
d'hui, de l'importance de la rencontre entre Jean Cocteau et Erik Satie? Quelques-uns, dont je suis. Mais
nous sommes peu. La légende grandit.

Je ne prétends pas que Cocteau ait le pouvoir de
donner le génie, en largesse, à ceux qui viennent. Mais
il a certainement le pouvoir de l'inspirer, de le pousser,
de rallumer ses flammes. Et puis, il a le courage de se
battre pour le génie. Il dit quelque part que le monde
brillant repousse le génie, comme la soie l'électricité.
Pour que ce monde finisse par accepter le génie, il faut
lui ôter sa robe de chambre protectrice. Il faut arriver
à cela par la force, à coups de cravache, à coups de
trique, car ce monde admet tout sauf qu'on le voie en
linceul, et le génie, force impitoyable, ne se retient pas
de dire la vérité qui tue.

La plupart des gens qui encombrent les rues, les salons, les spectacles, ne sont pas vivants dans le sens
exact du mot. Marcher, parler, danser, ne sont pas des

signes de vie. La vie ne demande pas des gestes inutiles. Elle exige des gestes utiles. Mais pour se faire reconnaître par les morts vivants, il faut les dépasser en actions fantasques. Alors, ils s'arrêtent, ils regardent celui qui a l'air d'aller plus vite qu'eux. Parfois, ils l'écoutent.

Pour se faire écouter, Cocteau a créé le nègre, les bars, le jazz. Ce qui montre que ces choses ne sont pas toujours inutiles. Cocteau a joué dans des orchestres, il a participé à des courses de bicyclette privées (pour qu'on en parle), il s'est montré dans tous les bars, il a élevé l'art nègre au-dessus de l'art aryen. Résultat: Tout le monde a parlé de lui, tout le monde s'est arrêté pour le regarder, beaucoup l'ont écouté.

Mais la plupart l'ont mal compris. La légende se gonfle.

Il y a encore les scandales. Et il y en a eu pas mal. *Le Sacre du Printemps, Parade, Le Bœuf sur le toit, Les Mariés de la Tour Eiffel.* Le scandale, c'est beaucoup de vie, et beaucoup de magie. Le scandale est un précipice par où l'on précipite le génie. On croit le tuer, il tombe sur ses pieds.

Presque tous les grands noms d'aujourd'hui sont mêlés aux scandales Cocteau: Stravinsky, Milhaud,

Auric, Tailleferre, Poulenc, Honegger, Satie, Picasso, Dufy, Laurencin, Lagut, Hugo. Est-ce que la légende en prend compte? Ce n'est pas à la légende de tenir compte des vérités.

Mais au moment des scandales, Cocteau ne songeait ni à la légende, ni à lui-même. Il songeait à la vie, à l'amour, à la poésie. Que dis-je? Il songeait à la mort.

Dans tous ses livres, Cocteau se préoccupe beaucoup de la mort. C'est parce qu'il est en vie. Parler de la mort est réservé aux vivants. Les demi-morts qui errent par-ci par-là en essayant de s'amuser, ne parlent que de la vie, et ne la retrouvent jamais. Les vivants qui parlent de la mort ne trouvent jamais la mort. Ils finissent par s'endormir éternellement, mais leur sommeil est aussi orageux que le fut leur vie.

Pour comprendre le soleil, il faut faire disparaître les nuages. Cocteau savait cela en 1916, quand il a attaqué le debussysme. On l'a accusé de toutes sortes de choses. Jamais d'aimer.

Debussy reste seul. Les nuages et les brumes ont disparus. La légende raconte que le soleil les a détruits. La vérité est qu'Arlequin a dû se retirer devant Cocteau. Cocteau ne demande pas qu'on lui soit reconnaissant. Reconnaissance, reconnaissance! Un mot creux que l'on dit d'une voix voilée.

On reproche à Cocteau d'avoir fumé de l'opium, mais
on ne le reproche pas aux Chinois. Voilà une indication
de mentalité curieuse et générale. Si Cocteau a fumé
de l'opium, c'était parce que cela lui était utile. Vivre,
c'est faire, mais c'est surtout faire ce qui est utile à
soi. Connais-toi toi-même est une phrase que tout le
monde respecte, mais que personne n'aime. Quand on
se connaît soi-même, comme Cocteau se connaît, on a
la permission de faire tout ce qui est utile à soi, en
violation de toutes les lois, civiles, morales, physiques.
L'homme libre ne reconnaît aucune loi, sauf celle qui
lui commande de se tenir ouvert à tout. D'ailleurs,
toutes les lois, sauf la dernière, sont négatives, et les
choses négatives sont toujours malsaines. Cocteau est
sain. Plus, il est saint. La santé, c'est le danger conti-
nuel. La sainteté, c'est le danger vaincu. Cocteau a
vaincu son danger moral et physique. Il entre dans un
nouveau danger, non pas, comme vous croyez, danger
de mort. Ceci n'existe pas pour lui. Il n'y a, pour lui,
que sécurité dans la mort. Son nouveau danger est celui
des mythes et des fables. Rien de plus pernicieux que
la légende, car pour la faire il faut mélanger du poison
avec des mensonges. Mais chaque poison a son anti-
dote, et le mensonge n'est qu'une glace à l'envers de
laquelle on lit la vérité. La légende de Cocteau pousse

avec chaque pas qu'il fait. Il ne peut pas se retourner pour la détruire. Il faut que cela soit la réalité qui l'anéantisse. Autant j'aime Cocteau, l'écrivain, l'homme, le poète, autant je déteste cette légende. Il faut la supprimer. J'espère que cet essai aidera un peu à voir plus clair.

Richard THOMA.

POLÉMIQUE

Nous avons reçu du Président de l'Académie de l'Art des Jeunes (groupement marseillais) la réponse que voici, à notre *Lettre à des jeunes gens:*

> « Nous portons en nous la révolte fière d'un sang non encore souillé... »

Robert DELAHAYE.

Le malentendu qui se plaçait entre « Tambour » et nous, est désormais dissipé : L'Académie de l'Art des Jeunes n'est que la maison des jeunes poètes et écrivains de moins de vingt et un ans, expulsables dès l'époque de leur majorité et remplaçables par leurs cadets ; sa revue : « Notre Plume », sera uniquement rédigée par ses membres. Ainsi, votre souhait n'était que notre premier désir. C'eut été un tort de vouloir persister à être l'expression de la génération d'après la Guerre. Nous avons abandonné vite cette formule fausse, sans doute étourdiment choisie, qui risquait de nous donner, à la confusion générale, l'allure de lutteurs forains, et de précipiter notre déchéance. C'est vrai, car il n'y a plus d'heure pour se combattre inconsidérément, ainés et cadets de la même grande famille. La France est présente dans notre cœur, son essence vibre en nous comme notre propre essence. Mais, nous avons trop le souci de notre avenir pour ne pas désirer que celui de notre pays soit la suite logique de son brillant passé. Certes solidaires de nos aïeux, nous sommes respectueux des moissons futures du sol qui les enfanta et qui nous supporte.

Ici, nous touchons au point sensible. Comme là, nous étions d'accord avec « Tambour », ici nous nous en séparons à regret : Nous ne prétendons pas opérer un mouvement tout court ; nous créons peut-être à notre insu un mouvement, mais destiné à durer puisqu'il englobe toute la jeunesse intellectuelle de toutes les générations, la jeunesse qui souffre de son isolement.

Hélas ! nous, les fondateurs, nous arrivons après la catastrophe. Les atrocités commises ne nous ont pas touchés directement, cependant nous avons presque honte des ruines autant morales que matérielles qu'elles ont causées. La génération d'avant la guerre a subi, a été sacrifiée, et elle supporte inévitablement les déplorables conséquences de l'événement. Ayant été à la peine, elle devrait être à l'honneur. Mais maintenant, nous sommes obligés de dire qu'il est un fossé, mi-tragique, mi-burlesque, entre certains de ses hommes et nous. Leurs œuvres ne sauraient nous indifférer, nous ne les ignorons pas, mais nous constatons par la suite quel séparatisme littéraire elles suscitent. Pour nous retenir, il ne fallait pas de ces divergences absurdes qu'ont provoquées dans les esprits les influences étrangères ; il fallait simplement suivre la pure tradition française.

A tout mercantilisme de Lettres — à la facilité, à l'extravagence, à la bizarrerie voulue, à l'empire de la fantaisie, du surnaturel, de l'artifice, de l'incohérence et de la négligence, où le talent réel se dépense en vain pour aboutir à se détruire — nous essayons d'opposer (hormis les querelles périmées de préjugés, de poncifs, de dogmes, et les sottes vanités d'écoles), avec la candeur et l'ardeur de notre âge, la beauté diverse où se reconnaît le génie éternel qui a fait la France. Voilà pourquoi nous hésitons à tendre la main à *tous les vivants,* à tous nos aînés ; tous n'en sont pas dignes : nous en éprouvons du dépit et une gêne que nous déplorons. Qu'on ne vienne plus dire que nous efforçons de représenter une « *autre génération* ».

L'Académie de l'Art des Jeunes est française. Elle sera fraternelle, sinon seulement envers tous les jeunes, du moins envers tous ceux que préoccupent les vertus de la vraie Poèsie et de l'Art français.

Alfred Nahon,
fondateur et président de l'Académie de l'Art des Jeunes.

Que notre *Lettre* ne fût pas directement dirigée contre *ces* jeunes gens mais qu'ils aient le droit de la prendre pour telle, voilà qui est clair. Mais, ils nous viennent parler inconsidérément d'une manière un peu trop chauviniste. S'ils sont, eux, Français, quelles sont ces « influences étrangères » qui ont, selon eux, désorganisé la littérature française? Est-ce le pseudonyme de Mac Orlan qui les irrite?

Non! la brèche est grande entre les jeunes et les ainés « modernistes », mais seul le ciment d'une entente profonde nous empêchera, nous les jeunes, de glisser et de nous perdre dans ce fossé, nous qui marchons sur un sol mouvant trop brutalement labouré par les charrues catastrophiques. Aller seuls serait nous vouer aux mêmes erreurs que celles commises par nos prédécesseurs; et plus certainement, notre situation étant plus précaire. Il ne s'agit pas de brûler des ponts derrière nous: il n'y en a pas. Il faut en construire, car il n'y a qu'en rattachant notre terre mobile à celle qui est ferme qu'on l'empêchera de s'effondrer et de nous emporter dans sa course.

Monsieur Nahon choisit mal ses épigraphes. Si son sang va être souillé, comme l'indique cet « encore », abandonnons-le lui. C'est sans souillure que se fait une conception immaculée. — Harold J. Salemson.

NOTES

(Harold J. SALEMSON)

Bienfaïteurs — Benefactors

Voici la liste des bienfaiteurs qui, par leur généreuse souscription, ont aidé à la publication de la première série de *Tambour:*

The names of the benefactors who, through their generous subscriptions, helped to permit this first series of *Tambour* are as follows:

Mr. Witter Bynner (Santa Fé, New Mexico);
Miss Berenice Davis (Chicago, Illinois);
Mr. and Mrs. Vinol Hannell (Chicago);
Miss Lucille Luedke (Madison, Wisconsin);
Mr. Norman Macleod (Albuquerque, New Mexico);
Mr. S. G. A. Rogers (Madison, Wisconsin);
Mme Julia Schutz (Paris);
Mrs. Luba Shacter (Chicago);
Mrs. Irving Squires (New-York City);
Mr. and Mrs. W. H. Walling (Mescalero, New Mexico);
Mr. Henry Weinstein (Bristol, Connecticut);
M. C. D. Zdanowicz (Paris).

Varia

A MESSAGE FROM. Mme BAZALGETTE

Mme Augustine Bazalgette, the widow of the late French writer and literary animator, has requested us to become her *porte-parole* in thanking the numerous friends in America who have been so kind to her at the time of the deep misfortune which has befallen her. The French translator of Whitman and erudite biographer of Thoreau was widely appreciated in America and marks of sympathy, private and public, were so numerous after his death that Mme Bazalgette has been obliged to accept this general manner of expressing her gratitude, incapable as she is of assuring each one of it individually. Her recognition is in no way diminished by the form she has had to adopt to express it, and we are sure that each of her friends reading these lines will feel personally gratified.

Les Livres

ETUDES

Au premier plan des études si diverses parues ces temps derniers, mettons *Flambeaux* (Grasset), recueil de critiques littéraires par Léon Daudet. L'auteur a une verve de pamphlétaire qui est indéniable et un petit sourire amusé traine constamment sur les lèvres du lecteur. Mais, en approfondissant et en comparant l'une à l'autre ces études intéressantes sur Rabelais, Montaigne, Hugo et Baudelaire, on est choqué par certaines contradictions : François Ier est le plus grand des rois pour avoir su exploiter Rabelais, mais la Troisième République est ignoble pour avoir voulu se servir de la force d'Hugo tout en le gardant loin du pouvoir. La critique de parti-pris, pour intelligente qu'elle soit, reste infirme.

Non moins amusantes sont les opinions du critique américain H. L. Mencken que M. Régis Michaud nous traduit sous le titre *Préjugés* (Boivin), celui même dont se sert l'auteur. Cette fois, le travail du traducteur est bien fait. M. Michaud s'est surpassé. Mais, j'attends mieux des prochains volumes qu'il va nous donner dans cette « Collection des Ecrivains et Penseurs américains ». H. L. Mencken est superficiel au possible ; aussi ne le discuterons-nous pas. Les recueils de Ludwig Lewisohn et d'Henry Adams nous réservent de meilleures surprises.

M. Emmanuel Berl donne chez Grasset, *Mort de la Pensée bourgeoise* que nous avons signalée lorsqu'elle paraissait dans *Europe*. Le communisme de Berl est, en effet, un communisme de « jeu de massacre ». Il sait exploiter la pointe comique de l'énumération exagérée. Enfin, cela est amusant en ce qui concerne les littérateurs, mais les pamphlets suivants qu'il annonce, sur la politique, etc... risquent d'être plutôt ennuyeux que drôles.

D'un caractère plus sérieux, *Pour une politique sexuelle* (Grasset), d'Alfred Fabre-Luce est un livre de grand intérêt sur les problèmes du mariage et des mœurs sexuelles. J'aurais aimé un plus long exposé des idées de l'auteur sur les remèdes à la liberté croissante des mœurs. Mais, sans qu'il l'accepte affirmativement, il semble ne vouloir que surveiller cette liberté inévitable, puisque la plus grande partie du volume est consacrée aux maladies vénériennes.

M. Françis de Croisset étudie, lui aussi, les mœurs dans *La Vie parisienne au théâtre* (Grasset). Il analyse la vraie vie boulevardière de Paris, celle du Second Empire et aussi de la fin du siècle dernier, dans ses reflets chez Meilhac et Halévy, chez Pailleron, et plus tard chez Flers et Caillavet. L'auteur conclut à la mort de cette « vie parisienne », remplacée par une autre, plutôt américaine, mais pour laquelle il est, somme toute, assez optimiste.

Du côté art, une des choses les plus intéressantes que nous ayons vues est *Sidney Hunt, graveur anglais d'ex-libris* (L'ex-libris, Paris), traduit par H. Dort, d'après l'anglais d'Edmund Paul. L'auteur situe en quelques pages très intelligentes le grand talent de notre jeune collaborateur. Il déclare avec raison qu'une originalité telle que celle de Hunt se voit rarement. Mais il oublie peut-être un peu de souligner la grande virilité de l'artiste.

Signalons encore l'intéressante vie d'*Humilis* (Grasset), par Léon Vérane, dans la collection « La Vie de Bohême ». Elle passionnera non seulement les admirateurs de Germain Nouveau, mais encore ceux de Verlaine et de Rimbaud.

VERS LA NATURE

Le monde entier, sans distinction de classe, de parti, ou d'idée quelconque, a applaudi au tour du monde solitaire d'Alain Gerbault. Aussi, son second livre de bord, *A la poursute du soleil* (Grasset), ne peut-il manquer de trouver un public avide. Toute considération sportive à part, Alain Gerbault sait relater ses voyages en gardant l'intérêt du lecteur et son érudition, en tout ce qui concerne les pays qu'il a visités, est rare. Alain Gerbault est sans doute le meilleur type de cet intellectuel sportif cher à Joseph Jolinon.

Chez le même éditeur, un nouveau livre de C. F. Ramuz. Voilà un événement. Ce romancier suisse prend place à côté des Giraudoux, Cendrars, Mauriac, Mac Orlan, Larbaud, Soupault, Cocteau, Chamson, et un ou deux autres, au pinnacle du roman français contemporain. Son nouveau livre, *Salutation paysanne,* est un recueil de contes et nouvelles dont tous sont excellents. Plusieurs sont des soliloques intérieurs, forme encore peu usitée dans la nouvelle. Le volume, qui vaut le meilleur Ramuz, contient en outre une *Lettre à M. B. Grasset* qui est un excellent plaidoyer en faveur de la littérature « désacadémisée ». Ramuz représente l'homme à l'état civilisé le moins « sophistiqué », le plus près de la Nature. Ses mains ne sont pas souillées de la suie des villes; mais sainement tachées de sa terre vaudoise.

Mais, puisque nous en sommes aux champs, je voudrais rappeler *La Sauvagine* (Grasset), de M. Joseph d'Arbaud, publié en texte français et provençal. Après avoir donné avec Mistral un poète de véritable génie, voici que la langue d'oc nous dévoile un fabuliste remarquable. Si l'Académie voulait donner son prix du Roman à un livre de bêtes, celui-ci s'imposait et non l'œuvre d'André Demaison. D'Arbaud, qui domine Demaison comme La Fontaine domine Franc-Nohain, occupe aujourd'hui une place unique. Seule parmi nous, Colette peut se comparer à lui comme interprète des animaux.

QUATRE COLLABORATEURS

Notre ami Jean Prévost, qui promet sa collaboration pour un de nos numéros futurs, vient de publier chez Riéder, dans la collection des Maîtres de l'Art, une étude esthétique sur *Eiffel.* L'intelligence méticuleuse de Jean Prévost donne à cette étude un intérêt tout particulier. Le bien-fondé des raisonnements et des jugements ne nous étonne pas, mais le livre nous semble tenir une place particulière dans l'œuvre de l'auteur. En effet, Prévost avait accompli un cycle. Parti de *Plaisirs des Sports,* études physiques, il avait atteint le cerveau à travers *Tentative de Solitude* et *Brûlures de la Prière.* Dans ces parages il écrivit encore *La Pensée de Paul Valéry* et sa *Vie de Montaigne,* pour revenir au corps physique par son *Essai sur l'Introspection,* où il institua l'introspection physique, l'épreuve des sports. Ensuite, Jean Prévost donna un roman de délassement, *Merlin,* et une confession de foi, *Dix-huitième année.* Aujourd'hui, *Eiffel* semble ouvrir un nouveau cycle, cycle d'analyse détachée et de critique. Jean Prévost va-t-il abandonner le corps de l'homme et son esprit intérieur, pour se consacrer aux manifestations de cet esprit, ou ce livre est-il moins symptomatique que nous ne croyions?

Trois autres de nos collaborateurs viennent de publier de nouveaux livres. D'abord Jean Cocteau nous a livré, avec *Les Enfants terribles* (Grasset), encore une face de sa nombreuse personnalité. L'enfance, il nous l'avait déjà un peu entamée dans *Le Grant écart.* Mais son nouveau livre, qui est son plus beau roman, met Cocteau à côté du seul Proust comme psychologue de l'enfance.

Ensuite, Maurice Courtois-Suffit a livré au public *Le Rossignol américain* (Au Sans Pareil). Nous avons donné la primeur d'un fragment du conte qui donne son titre au recueil. Mais un autre des quatre contes du volume, *A la Parasolerie du Progrès,* nous semble le chef-d'œuvre actuel de l'auteur. Pour la prmière fois, il tente le modernisme intégral en un narration de l'imagination la plus pure et la plus experte. Par ce conte, Maurice Courtois-Suffit a fait un vaste bond. C'est la première réalisation de ce que son *Promeneur sympathique* laissait entrevoir.

Enfin, Pierre Mac Orlan a réuni et rendu à son public toujours fidèle ses *Œuvres poétiques complètes* (Au Capitole). Ceux qui les connaissent retrouveront avec joie ces *Simone de Montmartre, Inflation sentimentale,* et autres plaquettes épuisées, ainsi que quelques vers inédits, qui sont la digne contrepartie de l'œuvre romanesque de Mac Orlan. Ceux qui ne les connaissaient pas auront une nouvelle raison d'aimer Mac Orlan.

POÈMES

Deux volumes de vers à signaler. Surtout *De Nos Oiseaux* (Kra), recueil des poèmes de Tristan Tzara. Fondateur de dada, on néglige trop
souvent Tzara dont l'œuvre, à défaut de sens bien transcendental, a cependant une musique toute particulière et remarquable. On ne peut manquer
d'être emporté par l'allure de vers tels que :

> *La chanson d'un dadaïste*
> *qui n'était ni gai ni triste*
> *et aimait une bicycliste*
> *qui n'était ni gaie ni triste.*

Par ailleurs, nous avons reçu un volume anonyme, sans nom d'éditeur :
Poèmes guerriers. Il y a, en guise de préface, une fort bonne note sur
la nature trop personnelle, et par conséquent anonyme, de toute vraie
poésie, et parmi bien des platitudes, quelques vers sentis qui valent la
peine d'être lus.

Books

SHORTER NOVELS OF HERMAN MELVILLE

Under this title, Horace Liveright reprints, in The Black and Gold
Library, four of Herman Melville's long short-stories. They are preceded
by an excellent introduction by Raymond Weaver. And, while *Typee* and
Moby Dick had convinced us that Melville was among the few real an-
cestors of contemporary Amercan literature, it is after reading these
stories, and particularly *Benito Cereno* and *Billy Budd,* that we are
brought to believe that Melville is the greatest writer America has yet
produced. Of course excluding our contemporaries, whom we dare not
judge yet, Hawthorne, Emerson, Whitman himself, all fade beside
Melville.

The masterful handling of the two sea-stories, *Benito Cereno* and *Billy
Budd,* their remarkable plots and revolutionary style ; the tranquil fantasy
which lends real modernism to *Bartleby the Scrivener;* and the fact that

they reveal in Melville the founder of all the school of open-air, sea-faring novelists we have long cherished, make me treasure this volume even more than *Leaves of Grass*. Melville! America has a literature of its own.

POEMS

Three volumes of poetry full of merit are added to our library.

Tu Fu (Mosher Press, Portland, Me.), a complete (?) translation by Edna Worthley Underwood and Chi Hwang Chu, at last gives us a general view of the work considered by the Chinese that of the world's greatest poet. Tu Fu is doubtless one of the greatest poets that ever lived. And for the reason that his life and his work were one. He did not create poetic morsels. He translated his life. Why can no modern poet do that? Why do we insist on factitious elucubrations? Tu Fu needed no theme. He lived. So does his work. The translation is very enjoyable.

Here are two diagonally opposed volumes of to-day's verse. Mac Knight Black, in *Machinery* (Horace Liveright), uses a free-verse form to tell of his love for machines and the emotion they inspire him. The general tone is highly lyrical but the poet's images are out-of-date. They are not adequate to the machines admired. As for Miss Virginia Stait's *Sanctuary* (Stockwell, London), it is the expression of a gifted poetess, using a classical manner to portray profound, true sentiment. The subjects have a wide range, but a note of sincerity prevails. There is no sham in any of the poems and many a reader will become lastingly attached to Miss Stait's work. Her poems will be read with a pleasure and an emotion that are not superficial.

STORIES

Miss Carman Dee Barnes is a *Schoolgirl* who uses that title to tell the story of her experiences in a southern boarding-school. Horace Liveright publishes her novel and, although the author denies all intention of being a reformer, one of the book's outstanding merits is that it may open the eyes of some Americains who remain blind with obstination. But it has other good points. Outside of showing American schoolgirls as they really are, the book is interesting and well-written. Discussion of its social bearing would demand too much space. We will merely add that the author shows great promise for future novels.

The same publisher also sends us *Tumbling Mustard* by Harold Loeb, chiefly known for having founded *Broom* with Alfred Kreymborg. Loeb is an excellent novelist and the subject and place he chose allow him to shine. To the reader's great enjoyment, he studies a number of complex characters in Empress, a speculation-town in the last wilds of Canada. His fantasy is most infectious, and his hero, Dan, is a powerless person driven by circumstances. We are disappointed in seeing him return to his domineering wife in the end, but it is Loeb's good humor that saves the book. The flavor of the last paragraphs is delicious. The finality of the last words, « Charon spat », is typical. We are almost tempted to *buy* the author's preceding novels.

Copy 1929 (Appleton) is not made-up of stories alone, but outside of the play, *Love is Enough* by Alice P. Reynolds, the short stories are the outstanding feature of this yearly anthology of work done by students and alumni of the Columbia University School of Writing. Among the stories, the two situated in the atmosphere of the life of America's colored population are far and away the best. They are « *Neber Said a Numblin' Word* » by Vernon Loggins and *An Unimportant Man* by Dorothy West. The story by Isa Glenn, like the author's reputation, is over-rated. But the two colored-folk narratives are of the very highest class. If their authors ever write a volume of such stories, they will rank with the most gripping of raconteurs. The collection as a whole is well worth reading.

MORE POEMS

From Atlanta, Georgia (The Bozart Press) come two volumes, *Dipped in Aloes* by Benjamin Musser *and The First JAPM Anthology* (edited by Benjamin Musser); New-York sends *Riding at Anchor* (Broder) also from Benjamin Musser's lyre. Now, Ben Musser refuses to bombard literary form, but his thought is highly modern. He is sour; but not like sour grapes. He is naturally sour, like extra-dry wine. He has something to say, and he knows how to express it. But Ben Musser will be sarcastically rolling-along when most of our innovators are long forgotten. I like this *Hermit,* from *Dipped in Aloes:*

> *His face was drowned in a sea of faces,*
> *His heart was ironed in the city press:*
> *He was alone in the crowded places,*
> *And the only hell is loneliness.*

Mr. Harry Crosby, in his volume *Transit of Venus* (Black Sun, Paris), strikes me as a gifted person who has mastered a discipline. His complex is the Sun, and there are themes and variations. It does not matter to any but the critic, whether these are exercises or irrepressible outbursts: they contain many exquisite lines and are read with pleasure.

JAMES JOYCE

Two volumes appear in Paris to help the reader of James Joyce's new work. One contains three fragments of *Work in Progress, Tales Told of Shem and Shaun* (Black Sun Press) and a preface by C. K. Ogden; the other is a collection of commentaries on Joyce's new novel, entitled *Our Exagmination Round his Factification for Incamination of « Work in Progress »*. That the new undertaking Mr. Joyce has attempted is interesting, there is no doubt. Of its ultimate value, much is to be said. It is one of those things that people will never cease discussing unless, by some improbability, it should be forgotten. *Tales Told,* in most parts utterly incomprehensible. is beautifully presented. The volume of comment is provocatory.

Magazines

THE UNINTELLIGIBLES

All the American magazines of interest are devoted in part, these days,
to those that Max Eastman calls the unintelligibles. *transition* publishes a
Manifesto that may bring more unintelligibility but that has many good
points and proclaims entire freedom for the artist. *Blues,* a magazine of
the younger generation, would be the most important magazine appearing
in English, if it did not devote itself *entirely* to these same unintelligibles
between whom and us the breach is widening. *Blues* may wake up to
find the gap too great, and they on the wrong side.

In *Poetry,* Jessica Nelson North, astute as ever, correctly distinguishes
between the real unintelligible and those who only pass for such; and the
editors of the new *This Quarter* remain aloof and comment intelligently.
Many lances are being broken and the situation is becoming critical. Up
to the present, *Broom, Ray* and such had been greeted with serene indifference. Now the interest is general, and for that reason a decision imminent. The rebels are no longer ignored; and for the first time some justification is demanded of them. A great part, I dare say, will qualify. Not
all. But literature is on the upward trend in consequence.

Art

MARC H. DARIMONT

Contentons-nous de signaler l'album de M. Marc H. Darimont, *Mixture
of Spleen* (Anthologie, Liège). Un ferme talent donne aux linos de ce
jeune Belge un attrait réel et puissant. On aimerait mieux connaître son
œuvre; mais on ne peut s'empêcher de lui vouer une grande admiration
en voyant ces dix gravures.

Disques

Pour les disques, comme pour le cinéma et le théâtre, l'été est la morte-saison. Les nouveaux disques de chez Columbia, comme toujours, valent la peine d'écouter. Nous en reparlerons à la rentrée.

LiVres à lire

Œuvres nouvelles de quelques-uns de nos collaborateurs :

Pierre Mac Orlan, *Uranie* (Hazan, éditeur) ;

Georges Linze, *Le Prophète influencé* (La Renaissance d'Occident, Bruxelles) ;

Sidney Hunt, *Sidney Hunt, graveur anglais d'ex-libris,* par Edmond Paul, traduction H. Dort (L'ex-libris, Paris) ;

Jean Giono, *Colline* (Grasset) ;

Valentin de Manoll, *Pour une Nymphe défunte* (Le Rouge et le Noir) ;

Pierre Mac Orlan, *Œuvres poétiques complètes* (Le Capitole) ;

Jean Cocteau, *Les Enfants terribles* (Grasset) ;

Maurice Courtois-Suffit, *Le Rossignol américain* (Au Sans Pareil).

What to read

New books by some of our contributors :

Zona Gale, *Portage Wisconsin* (Knopf) ;

H. R. Hays *Strange City* (Four Seas C°) ;

Walter-René Fuerst, *Twentieth-century Stage-Decoration* (Knopf).

Blaise Cendrars, *Little Black Stories for*
    Little White Children (Payson and Clarke).

Le gerant : J. BRUNEL.

Montpellier. — Imprimerie Causse, Graille et Castelnau, 7, rue Dom-Vaissette.

September
1 9 2 9
Septembre

4

Revue Mensuelle

A monthly magazine

PRIX 6 Fr.

DANS CE NUMÉRO :

ALAIN est un des plus éminents des philosophes français vivants.

ROBERT DELAHAYE est un poète inédit, et membre de l'Académie de l'Art des Jeunes.

WALTER-RENÉ FUERST est connu à Paris comme décorateur, architecte et peintre.

SIDNEY HUNT a paru dans le dernier *Tambour.*

VALENTIN DE MANOLL est l'auteur d'une plaquette, *Pour une Nymphe défunte.*

MARIO MONTANARD a paru dans les deux premiers numéros de *Tambour.*

ALFRED NAHON est le fondateur de l'Académie de l'Art des Jeunes.

CLAUDE SYMIL est connue de nos lecteurs.

RICHARD THOMA nous donne aujourd'hui la suite de son essai sur Cocteau (voir le numéro précédent).

IN THIS ISSUE :

PAUL FRÉDÉRIC BOWLES is a Young American poet who has appeared in *transition, This Quarter,* etc...

CHARLES HENRI FORD is the editor of *Blues.*

WALTER-RENÉ FUERST is a Parisian artist and author of a remarkable book on stage-decoration.

SIDNEY HUNT contributed to the last issue of *Tambour.*

NORMAN MACLEOD is an American poet who is about to publish a new magazine, *Brogan.*

EDOUARD RODITI appeared in *Tambour II.*

JULIAN L. SHAPIRO says he would rather have written *The Idiot* than *Jean-Christophe.*

VIRGINIA STAIT is a distinguished American poetess and short-story writer.

RICHARD THOMA is a bi-lingual American poet and prosateur.

PARKER TYLER has contributed to *Blues, transition,* etc...

R. S. V. is a young American woman who here appears in print for the first time.

KATHLEEN TANKERSLEY YOUNG is an American poetess, associate editor of *Blues,* and contributor to *transition,* etc...

TAMBOUR

5

T A M B O U R

Directeur, Harold J. Salemson, Editor

5, Rue Berthollet, PARIS (V°) France)

Of this issue, 250 copies are numbered.

De ce numéro, 250 exemplaires ont été numérotés.

Interpréter le passé, c'est exprimer le présent;
exprimer le présent, c'est créer l'avenir.

To interpret the past is to express the present;
to express the present is to create the future.

PRÉTEXTE

Il y a cinq ans qu'Anatole France est mort. Et, qu'on le veuille ou non, ceci a laissé un vide. Aujourd'hui, nous lui consacrons ce numéro spécial pour essayer de faire une mise au point. Il y a deux choses qui restent obscures, aussi bien pour les admirateurs que pour les adversaires de **l'écrivain:**

I. Qu'est-ce qui a fait l'importance d'Anatole France, et qu'est-ce qui lui a valu sa place dans la littérature (car, quoi qu'on en dise, il en a occupé une)?

II. La place d'Anatole France a-t-elle été prise par quelqu'un d'autre ou reste-t-elle inoccupée?

Les divers essais et opinions compris dans ces pages tentent d'expliquer la valeur ou la non-valeur d'Anatole France; la question de sa position prépondérante dans la littérature mondiale est plus difficile à résoudre, bien que presque tangible.

Au moment où il mourut, Anatole France occupait une place unique dans les lettres: c'est cette place qu'aurait pu occuper Voltaire si l'échange intellectuel mondial avait été plus facile de son temps; c'est la place qu'aurait sans doute tenue Zola s'il avait vécu à un âge plus avancé; bref, dans l'hsitoire des lettres, il n'y a jamais eu d'homme dans la situation de France et on peut fortement douter qu'il y en ait jamais un autre pareil.

Or, nous ne parlons pas, à cet instant, de *mérite*. Là-dessus, trop de diversités d'opinion défendent qu'on ait l'audace de vouloir résumer en quelques mots la situation. Nous envisageons présentement *sa position vis-à-vis du public*.

Aujourd'hui, d'innombrables groupes de partisans littéraires s'attaquent, se sont attaqués à France: on voudrait établir posthumément la supériorité de Barrès sur tous ses contemporains; ou bien, pour mieux louer Gide, on nie France; encore sont-ce les « modernistes » qui se moquent du « bon maître » au profit de tel ou tel mouvement. On oppose, bien maladroitement, France à Proust. (Il faut noter que l'un de ceux qui ont eu le plus à faire dans tout ceci est le peu délicat M. Jean-Jacques Brousson, dont le nom-même est un si lamentable pastiche et qui pourrait tout aussi bien, et mieux à propos, s'appeler André Vide, Anatole Panse, ou Romain Roulant.) Quoi qu'il en soit, ces minorités dissidentes, et qui forment peut-être une majorité, ne sauraient pas plus que nous nier que, du point de vue de son importance personnelle, Anatole France ait été le premier homme de son temps.

A-t-il un successeur? J'en doute.

Aucun écrivain vivant ne connaît la recette de ce mélange de distinction littéraire et d'intérêt général qui fit de France l'écrivain — j'entends bon, pour ne pas dire grand écrivain — le plus populaire qu'il y ait jamais eu.

Knut Hamsun est suivi dans certains pays avec autant d'intérêt que l'était France; mais son rang n'est pas universel. Romain Rolland n'a pas su continuer sur la voie où l'avait amené le formidable succès de *Jean-Christophe*. Bernard Shaw prendra peut-être la place de France, mais il ne l'a pas encore. James Joyce et D'Annunzio sont trop « intellectuels »; de même que Gorki dans un autre genre. Pirandello, Eugene O'Neill, Ernst Toller n'ont pas encore atteint la situation qui leur reviendra peut-être; mais, parmi **eux, seul O'Neill semble capable de devenir** un jour la figure prédominante de toutes les littératures. Arrêtons cette vaine énumération qui serait susceptible d'offenser certains.

Il en ressort qu'un homme tel que France, un homme dont chaque nouveau livre est un événement d'une envergure sociale, un tel homme n'existe pas aujourd'hui.

Porquoi? pourquoi? Qu'est-ce qui distingue France des autres?

Nos contemporains les plus intéressants ont bien voulu se joindre à nous, dans ce numéro, pour essayer de trouver ce pourquoi. Je n'ai voulu montrer ici que la place occupée par France et qui me fit croire qu'il serait intéressant de tenter de débrouiller ce dilemme. — H. J. S.

———

PRETEXT

———

It is now five years since the death of Anatole France, and whether we like it or not, his death has left a gap. Today we are devoting this special number to him, hoping to clear things up a bit. Two things remain unclear, for the admirers of the author as well as for his adversaries.

I. What was it exactly that made the importance of Anatole France, and to what did he owe his place in literature (for, say what we may, he held a definite one)?

II. Has the place held by Anatole France been taken by someone else, or does it remain unoccupied?

The different essays and opinions contained in these pages attempt to explain the value or non-value of Anatole France; the question of his preponderant position in world literature is still more difficult to solve, although almost tangible.

At the time of his death Anatole France held a unique place in letters: it is this place that Voltaire might have held if universal intellectual exchange had been easier in his day; it is the place that Zola would probably have occupied if he had lived to a more advanced age; in short, in all the history of letters, no man has yet had the position of France, and it is doubtful whether another will ever enjoy it.

However, at this time we are not talking of *merit*. Too much diversity of opinion forbids us to risk trying to resume the situation in a few words. We are considering here only *his position in relation to his public*.

Today innumerable groups of literary partisans are attacking, have been attacking France: posthumously they would like to establish the superiority of Barrès over all of his contemporaries; or perhaps in order to praise Gide, they belittle France; further there are the « modernists » who continually deride the « good master » in favor of one movement or another. Quite clumsily Proust is pitted against France. (It is to be noted than one of those who have had the most do to with all of this, is the none-too-delicate M. Jean-Jacques Brousson, whose very name is such a lamentable pastiche, and who might as well, if not better, have been labelled André Vide, Anatole Panse, or Romain Roulant.) However the case may be, these dissident minorities, which perhaps form a majority, can no more than we deny that from the standpoint of personal importance Anatole France ranked first in his day.

Has he a successor? I doubt it.

No living author knows the recipe for mixing literary distinction and general interest which made of France the writer — I mean good, not to say great, writer — the most universally appreciated that has ever lived.

Knut Hamsun is followed in certain countries with as much interest as was France, but his rank is not universal. Romain Rolland was unable to continue the path into which his formidable success with *Jean Christophe* had led him. Bernard Shaw, possibly, will take the place of France, but as yet he has not reached it.   James Joyce and D'Annunzio are too « intellectual »; Gorki likewise, in a different manner. Pirandello, Eugene O'Neill, Ernst Toller, have not yet attained the situation which may eventually be theirs; but of these, O'Neill alone seems capable of becoming one day the predominating figure of all literatures. However, enough of this vain enumeration, liable to end by proving offensive.

The conclusion is that a man such as France, a man whose every new book is an event of social importance, such a man does not exist today.

Why? Why? What is it that distinguishes France from the others?

Our most interesting contemporaries have lent themselves in this issue to the task of helping us solve this « why ». I wished here only to show the place held by France, and which made me believe that it would be interesting to try clearing up this enigma. — H. J. S.

ANATOLE FRANCE (I)

Une autopsie cinq ans après

―――――

ENQUÊTE :

I. Vous semble-t-il que la situation d'Anatole France ait changé depuis sa mort? Si oui, de quelle manière?

II. Avez-vous changé, personnellement, d'attitude envers l'œuvre de France depuis la mort de l'écrivain? Pourquoi?

III. L'indifférence dont on entoure généralement l'œuvre de France indique-t-elle que celui-ci tombe à l'oubli ou que son sort soit réglé, dans le sens qu'il est devenu « classique »?

IV. Sur quel plan mettez-vous Anatole France? Pourquoi?

Marcel Berger:

Au lendemain de la mort d'Anatole France, consulté par la *Revue Mondiale*, je déclarais que je voyais en Anatole France « le premier des écrivains de second ordre ».

Mon opinion n'a pas varié... parce que je n'ai pas relu l'écrivain dont j'avais, comme tant d'autres, subi l'ascendant — d'ailleurs quelque peu imposé — dans mon ado-

―――――

(1) Voir, parmi les *Notes*, des détails sur les auteurs.

lescence. Mais, que je n'aie pas éprouvé le besoin de le
relire, c'est peut-être plus fâcheux encore pour lui que pour
moi.
Telle me paraît l'indifférence à son égard de la plupart
de nos camarades de lettres. Il a manqué, je le crois, de
plus en plus, à Anatole France, ce je ne sais quoi de direct,
d'humain ou de vraiment grand qui vient toucher, à travers
les temps, l'esprit ou la sensibilité des hommes. Il a été
beaucoup trop « classique de son vivant », beaucoup trop
« Académicien-type » (lui qui ne mettait jamais les pieds
à l'Académie!)
Sauf dans quelques menus chefs-d'œuvre comme *Crainquebille,* il n'a pas touché le tuf. Trop élégant, trop melliflu.
Au point de vue idées, un simple vulgarisateur d'une bonne
petite philosophie bourgeoise courante; comme styliste, un
charmant pasticheur du xvii*. Il ne s'est jamais « colleté »
directement avec la vie, avec l'émotion à faire entrer toutes
saignantes dans des mots. Un aimable petit-maître. « Le
premier des écrivains de second ordre ». Et même quand je
dis le premier...!

Jean Cassou:
J'aime trop Voltaire pour ne pas considérer Anatole
France comme un simple *poeta minor,* un agréable dilettante du genre Paul-Louis Courier. Mais en France on se
plaît tellement à tout ce qui est bijou, bibelot, émaux et
camées, article de Paris, etc., qu'on en arrive facilement à
confondre des ordres de grandeur tout à fait distincts et le
diamant avec le strass. Un certain modèle de prose molle
et bien troussée donne tout de suite l'illusion du beau style.

C'est une confusion immense que d'avoir pris pour un grand sceptique et pour un grand écrivain cet habile homme et cet amusant pasticheur à qui tout a réussi, qui a su se faire goûter de tous les milieux et jouer les révolutionnaires et les destructeurs tout en rassurant les consciences les plus pusillanimes et en donnant des gages et des satisfactions aux salons, aux académies.

Anatole France est le type du grand écrivain pour professeurs. Seul, en effet, un professeur peut s'y tromper et s'y laisser prendre.

Ceci dit, il faut reconnaître qu'il y a, dans l'*Histoire Contemporaine*, des pages très divertissantes et que *Crainquebille* est une chose émouvante, juste et forte.

Jean Catel:

On ne lit plus Anatole France? Mais on ne l'a jamais beaucoup lu. On le lisait comme certains lisaient et lisent le feuilleton de leur quotidien. Ce n'est pas *lire*.

— Pourquoi *lirions*-nous France, dites, alors que nous avons Proust, Gide, Valéry, Cocteau, Claudel? Pas le temps.

Blaise Cendrars:

Ennui, ennui, ennui, ennui, ennui, ennui, ennui, ennui.

Maurice Constantin-Weyer:

Anatole France?

Non, ce n'est pas lui qui a changé; c'est nous! Il est d'avant-guerre; nous sommes d'après-guerre. Il est sceptique; nous sommes graves.

Jérôme Coignard a fait la joie de notre jeunesse. Nous

avions appris, à son école, le goût de l'anarchie. Quatre
ans sur les champs de bataille nous ont restitué le sens de
la discipline, à tel point que, même chez ceux qui affirment
le plus hautement leur indépendance, on constate, au fond,
le désir d'être encadrés et le regret de n'être plus com-
mandés.

Cela n'empêchera pas Anatole France de devenir un classique. Au fait, il l'est déjà. Lorsque nous voulons nous
représenter les lettres françaises d'avant-guerre, c'est à lui
que nous pensons. Et c'est encore un hommage que nous
lui rendons...

Maurice Courtois-Suffit:

J'ai lu les livres de France, comme tout le monde, mais
j'ai cessé de penser à eux. Ils sont toujours là, dans un
coin de bibliothèque. Je ne les relirai point. Je suis prêt,
d'ailleurs, à reconnaître tout ce que vous voudrez sur cet
auteur qui peut tenir une place dans notre histoire littéraire.
On comprend très bien pourquoi il a des défenseurs.

Malheureusement, dès qu'on me demande mon opinion
sur France, j'ai envie de parler de Barrès. Pour ne pas
vous mécontenter, je m'abstiendrai. Et, pour ne pas occuper
trop de place dans *Tambour,* j'ajouterai simplement que
je tiens pour admirable le discours de Paul Valéry à l'Académie Française. Il répond à votre questionnaire d'une
façon magnifique.

Léon Deffoux:

Me permettez-vous de faire une seule réponse à vos quatre questions? La situation d'Anatole France n'a pas

changé. Mort comme vivant, il demeure un délicieux grand homme artificiel. Il semble avoir répété pour chacun de ses lecteurs le geste que fit la mère de Pierre Nozière quand elle lui donna, en la marquant d'un simple trait, une des roses qui décorait le papier de sa chambre. Par ce geste, ne lui révéla-t-elle pas le monde extérieur et qu'il y avait des roses sur le papier? Le génie d'Anatole France a eu, pour la plupart d'entre nous, des conséquences aussi sensibles et nous devons lui être reconnaissants de nous avoir offert, comme au petit Pierre Nozière, des roses artificielles.

Joseph Delteil:

Anatole France est un écrivain qu'on lit (et agréablement), mais qu'on ne relit pas.

Fernand Divoire:

Depuis que j'ai l'âge de 18 ans, je n'ai jamais changé d'opinion au sujet d'Anatole France.

Son œuvre n'a jamais présenté d'intérêt pour moi. (Ne voyez là aucun dédain, mais seulement une différence entre ses préoccupations et les miennes.)

Je dois dire, cependant, que certains livres auraient pu, si cela avait été possible, me rendre Anatole France sympathique.

Sur quel plan je mets l'œuvre d'Anatole France? Sur le plan des jolies choses inutiles, donc nuisibles.

Henri Duvernois:

I. Oui. Il a grandi.

II. Non. En quoi la mort d'un écrivain peut-elle changer l'opinion que l'on a de lui?

III. Je ne vois pas que l'œuvre d'Anatole France soit entourée d'indifférence. Bien au contraire.

IV. Permettez-moi de me réserver. Il y a des noms qui échappent aux palmarès.

André Gide:

J'ai déjà répondu à votre enquête, dans l'*Ermitage* de février 1905: « L'unanimité subite des louanges n'est pas une assurance de survie; ceux qui plaisent tout entiers d'abord sont ceux qu'on épuise d'un coup. Je voudrais être sûr que nous n'épuiserons pas vite *Anatole France*. Pas de pénombre en lui; je m'inquiète. J'aimerais à pouvoir penser que dans cent ans on nous accusera de ne l'avoir pas bien compris, et que son premier mot n'aura pas été son dernier. »

Et, dans la *Nouvelle Revue Française* de février 1910: « J'aimerais France avec plus d'abandon si certains imprudents n'en voulaient faire un écrivain considérable. Etc... » (V. Morceaux choisis, p. 137.)

Cette opinion, qu'en ce temps j'étais presque seul à avoir, je crois qu'aujourd'hui beaucoup de gens s'y rallient. Mais ce n'est pourtant pas une raison pour que j'en change.

Louis Guilloux:

Votre autopsie après cinq ans est-elle bien utile? Que nous importe Anatole France? Il n'y a pas un mot de vrai dans tout ce qu'il a si péniblement raconté, et il avait peur de la mort.

Jacques Heller:

I. Anatole France n'est plus « à la mode ».

II. Non. Je n'ai jamais beaucoup aimé son œuvre, hormis *Jeanne d'Arc* qui, chacun le sait, est de....... Les adorables pastiches qui ont fait sa gloire m'ont toujours paru périmés et bons pour cette partie du public qui ignore les classiques ou ne les aime qu'adaptés, arrangés au goût actuel.

III. On ne peut présumer. Cinq années ne sont rien dans l'histoire d'une littérature comme la nôtre.

IV. Anatole France a écrit de beaux vers. A ce titre au moins, il me semble qu'il aura toujours sa place « au plan » des poètes, si j'ose dire.

Constant de Horion:

I. Au point de vue de son influence éventuelle sur la jeunesse d'aujourd'hui, la situation d'Anatole France ne peut qu'empirer. La raison en est simple: il a réhabilité le doute. Il a plaidé toute sa vie pour l'indépendance de la pensée en même temps qu'il se faisait le gardien des traditions... Autant dire qu'il est aux antipodes de notre génération.

En littérature, ajoutez à cela qu'il fut dur pour les symbolistes et ceux qui en procèdent directement. Valéry ne l'appelle pas sans quelque mépris « le prophète du passé »...

Finesse, élégance du style, scepticisme empreint d'idéalisme déçu, culte de la raison raisonnante et, malgré tout, du rêve, respect de l'érudition, tels sont les piliers sur lesquels repose son œuvre. Or, tout cela s'effondre devant les brutalités et les outrances de l'idéal présent, idéal d'affirmation, d'action et d'autorité sous la dictature d'un maître ou sous le despotisme plus brutal encore de la masse amorphe et veule.

II. Mais si la foule s'écarte de lui, parce qu'il ne répond plus à ses aspirations, d'aucuns lui restent fidèles et je ne crois pas être seul à mettre le maître de Jérôme Coignard sur le premier rayon, parmi ceux dont jamais on ne se lasse.

III. Est-ce à dire qu'Anatole France est detiné à tomber dans l'oubli? Nullement. Celui que M. Bernard Fay appelle, avec quelqu'ironie, « le Maître de la Littérature Officielle en France » est aussi le « Mainteneur de la langue traditionnelle ». Et, quoiqu'en pense Jean-Jacques Brousson, à ce titre seul, parmi bien d'autres, il est passé d'emblée au rang des « classiques» .

IV. Dans quelle catégorie faut-il l'insérer? Mais à la suite des grands sceptiques, « de tous ceux qu'il vénérait en tremblant et dont il prétendait n'être que le très humble écolier, de ceux qui s'attaquèrent à tout ce qui ligotte l'intelligence et la pensée » (1), à la suite de Rabelais, de Montaigne le pyrhonnien, de Voltaire, de Diderot, de Renan... En un mot, c'est le dernier des Encyclopédistes!

Joseph Jolinon:

Pour faire l'expérience que Marcel Prévost nous conseillait dernièrement dans *Gringoire,* j'ai voulu relire la *Reine*

---

(1) *Propos d'Anatole France* recueillis par P. Gsell. Page 83.

Pédauque, livre francéen typique. Hélas! que les derniers fervents du si bon maître me pardonnent, à la page 48 j'ai capitulé. Comment dire? Je me trouvais dans l'état d'impatience d'un professionnel de la motocyclette obligé de se ballader en calèche avec ses grands-parents. Nous ne pouvons décidément plus marcher à cette allure. « Inadéquat » dirait Snowden.

Ce n'est pas tout. Trop de beautés formelles, une perfection trop égale, cette permanente confusion de l'académisme avec le classicisme... « Mon Dieu, quelle barbe! » me dis-je en refermant le livre. C'était plus fort que moi.

Or, il y a quinze ans, je l'aimais encore.

Ceci en dépit de la pitié réfléchie que j'ai toujours éprouvée pour les écrivains trop soucieux de la forme. Est-il, en effet, un art plus limité que la littérature? Que sont les moyens d'expression d'une langue, si belle soit-elle, dont quelques centaines de grands lettrés peuvent seuls apprécier les harmonies profondes? Beauté de forme d'Homère, du Dante, de Shakespeare, etc... Ce qui reste d'une œuvre. n'est-ce pas sa substance?

Et, sous ce rapport, Anatole France (Bergeret) restera, me semble-t-il, comme le meilleur peintre de la société bourgeoise française d'avant la guerre, et comme l'un des représentants de son esprit critique.

Ce qui ,enfin, à mon sens, aggrave ce cas littéraire, c'est de sentir que, par exemple, un type dans le genre de Racine, s'il revenait aujourd'hui, n'écrirait pas du Racine, tandis que lui, France, ne pourrait sortir sans un énorme dommage de sa jolie marqueterie verbale.

Combien sommes-nous de ma génération à penser de la sorte?

A vous, enquêteur gracieux, de faire le point.

Georges Linze:

I. Non.

II. Non.

III-IV. Anatole France s'évalue en fonction même de ce moyen-âge qu'est pour nous l'avant-guerre. Son élite aveugle n'eut aucun sens, ni celui du passé, ni celui de l'avenir.

Au milieu de la révolution des goûts, des mœurs, de la surprenante irruption des machines, du génie des constructeurs et des ouvriers, son incroyable statisme vaut-il un haussement d'épaules? Car le lyrisme est déchaîné et ce n'est pas la première fois qu'il trace sur le monde des signes prophétiques.

Anatole France, auteur sans disciple, sans poésie, servant d'une perfection inutile, eut bien des saluts amicaux et opportunistes aux forces politiques portées elles-mêmes par le rythme du temps.

Qu'est-ce que cela signifie? Cela ne remplace pas une dangereuse et nette découverte de l'homme le plus récent, le vrai, où sont chaque fois les espaces, les destins et toutes les villes.

Victor Llona:

I. La « situation » d'Anatole France n'a pas changé *depuis* sa mort. Elle a changé le jour même de sa mort. On a senti que le cadavre ne résisterait pas à l'embaumement.

Sur le catafalque, sous l'avalanche des discours, des fleurs et des couronnes, il s'est dissous aux yeux ahuris des thuriféraires. Il n'y a même plus de momie sous les bandelettes.

II. France a fait mes délices à cette époque de ma vie où, par dégoût du fade pédantisme des maîtres de collège, on s'aveugle avec reconnaissance sur les mérites et sur les intentions de qui vous fait la politesse de sucrer sa pilule. Mais je ne l'ai pas relu. Je n'en ai jamais eu l'envie. Cette inappétence me semble une indication précieuse. Je préfère ne pas me forcer et conserver l'illusion que l'*Ile des Pingouins* est une belle satire et *Histoire Comique* un honnête roman.

III. Classique, je n'en sais rien — bien qu'il y ait les grands, les moyens et les petits classiques. Mais je crois que les chercheurs de l'avenir auront toujours recours à lui, j'entends ceux qui n'auront pas la chance de posséder un Jean-Jacques Brousson. Car France est une inépuisable mine de références qu'il faudrait un temps et une patience infinis pour retrouver dans les bibliothèques.

IV. Ce qui précède me dispense, je crois, de répondre à votre dernière question.

Marcel Loumaye:

Anatole France n'est pas mort il y a deux ou trois ans. Son action s'est éteinte en 1914. Avec la guerre, un monde nouveau est né, dont M. Bergeret ne fait pas plus partie que Voltaire. Il est donc naturel que la jeunesse d'aujourd'hui, toute dynamique, se détourne du délicieux maître.

Verhaeren, disparu dix ans plus tôt, est beaucoup plus
près de nous.

Anatole France est réellement classique. Son immortalité
est certaine. C'est la raison pour laquelle nul ne songe à
s'en occuper.

Par son style il était en dehors de son siècle. Voyez en
ceci un haut éloge et un léger blâme. Ses idées reflètent le
temps de l'affaire Dreyfus.

La désaffection qu'on constate à l'égard d'Anatole France
a d'ailleurs des origines politiques. Les catholiques l'ont
toujours détesté. Il ne manque pas de journalistes de droite
pour affirmer que le maître est désuet, mais qu'un René
Bazin est bien vivant.

A l'extrême gauche, Anatole France est suspect. Il s'est
déclaré socialiste mais avec un dilettantisme qui dévoile sa
nature aristocratique. Quel terrible réquisitoire contre toute
révolution que *Les Dieux ont soif!*

Et puis le socialisme lui-même est fané et Anatole France
ne s'est jamais proclamé communiste. Vu de Moscou, il est
l'ennemi.

Mais l'exquis vieillard dans sa tombe fait un pied-de-nez
à ses détracteurs. Et il ne nous comprend pas, nous qui
l'aimons mais qui le plaçons exactement à sa place, en marge
de la grande vague lyrique de l'époque.

André Maurois:

Je ne puis vous répondre que brièvement, mais je crois
que le destin posthume d'Anatole France est le même que
celui de tout grand écrivain. La courbe de la gloire a ses
ondulations. Ce que les hommes ont trop aimé les fati-

gue; ils y reviennent lorsque l'oubli a rendu nouvelles les choses les plus anciennes.

L'œuvre d'Anatole France est d'ailleurs inégale. Je crois que ce qui restera de lui et deviendra classique, ce sont surtout les fragments d'*Histoire Contemporaine* et des courts récits, comme *Crainquebille, Riquet,* mais qui sait? Le goût de la postérité est quelquefois très mauvais et il se peut qu'une œuvre d'une sentimentalité un peu exaspérante comme *Sylvestre Bonnard* résiste au temps.

Paul Morand:

I. *Si la situation de France a changé depuis sa mort?*

On a un public durant sa vie ou après sa mort. Chaque entrée au Père-Lachaise, c'est un lecteur de moins pour Anatole France.

II. *Si j'ai changé d'atitude envers l'œuvre de France?*

Oui, car pendant des années je n'ai pas osé dire que je détestais son œuvre, de peur de mettre mon père en colère. J'ai écrit depuis dans *Paris-Tombouctou:* « ... France, boutiquier parisien, malin, âpre, bambocheur, que deux managers, son amie, « Madame », et son éditeur, exploitèrent méthodiquement, après lui avoir passé un habit noir. On parle toujours de la situation mondiale d'Anatole France. Cette situation n'est pas seulement littéraire, elle est, au fond, politique et tient à ce que ce collectionneur de vieilles chasubles fut dreyfusard, puis, soi-disant, d'extrême-gauche. En outre, comme son style s'inspire d'époques internationales (humanisme du XVIᵉ et surtout cosmopolitisme du XVIIIᵉ siècle), les étrangers n'eurent pas de peine à retrouver, dans ses livres, des souvenirs de leurs lectures, condition essentielle du succès. »

III. L'indifférence dont on entoure généralement l'œuvre de France est une réaction naturelle. Si ses contemporains ne l'avaient pas, par politique ou politesse, imposé comme l'égal d'un Chateaubriand et d'un Balzac, France ne passerait pas aujourd'hui un si mauvais moment.

IV. Mon avis?

L'œuvre de ce compilateur agréable, de cet aimable érudit, de ce charmant écrivain de cabinet, pourra être consultée avec fruit pour l'étude de la petite bourgeoisie française de la fin du XIXᵉ siècle, et des salons parisiens à l'époque de l'affaire Dreyfus.

François Ribadeau-Dumas:

Anatole France représente pour nous une époque morte aujourd'hui. Dieu merci! Pratiquez votre autopsie. Vous découvrirez sous un aspect vénérable et vénéré, convenable et adulé, que l'écrivain qui ne travaille avec quelque humanité demeure fruit sec.

France, styliste, compilateur, ironiste, jamais créateur et vivant dans la poussière du passé. « Oui, mais il y a la vie! » disait-on après chacun de ses ouvrages. On le répéta en suivant ses funérailles. Et France, en haut d'une bibliothèque, ne sera pas relu. Barbe blanche vénérable, barbe sénile, son œuvre est momifiée.

Ne lui jetons qu'une pierre tombale. On peut apprendre à lire dans ses livres, car pour cela le sens importe peu. Je révère Anatole France. Il est classé. « Classique »? Ah, non! j'honore trop le mot *classique*.

Jacques Roujon:

Non, il ne me semble pas que la situation d'Anatole
France ait changé depuis sa mort. Et, en ce qui me
concerne, je reste dans l'état d'esprit où je me trouvais
lorsque j'ai écrit « La vie et les opinions d'Anatole France ».

L'indifférence de la jeunesse à l'égard de ce grand écrivain date d'avant la guerre et n'a fait, depuis, que croître
et embellir. Les jeunes gens n'ont pas tort de chercher des
inspirations ailleurs que dans l'œuvre de ce maître du secp-
ticisme intégral.

Je crois que, dans quelques années, on « redécouvrira »
France et les grandes beautés de certaines de ses œuvres.
Il a poussé trop loin l'intelligence pour jamais tomber dans
l'oubli. Aucun écrivain n'a mieux que lui manié la langue
française. Il est bien difficile de le mettre sur un autre plan
que le premier.

André Salmon:

I et II. Trois ans avant la mort d'Anatole France, j'ai
publié dans *Signaux*, de Bruxelles, un *Centenaire d'Anatole
France* et c'était ma façon d'envelopper dans la pourpre ce
dieu mort; je souhaitais que fût perdue la sotte coutume de
faire de ce grand académique le « bon maître » du premier
venu. Ça ne m'empêcha point, lors des quatre-vingts ans
de France, de le saluer, à l'occasion d'une enquête de
Paris-Journal, d'un « Bonne fête, grand-père! »dont *Paris-
Soir* fit sa manchette.

III. France a représenté le goût, vertu de lecteur et non
de créateur. Rien de ce qu'a fait valoir France n'eût été

ignoré sans France qui l'emprunte aux classiques. Ce mosaïste épargne aux paresseux de nombreuses lectures classiques. L'avenir le rangera, conteur, au-dessous de Nodier. L'écrivain de l'*Histoire Contemporaine* n'aura aucun rang parmi les pamphlétaires s'il n'eut ni haine, ni foi, ni seulement vrai mépris.

Des gestes des hommes de demain dépend qu'Anatole France prenne place parmi les architectes de la cité nouvelle.

Un jeune écrivain pourra toujours tout ignorer de France sans dommage.

Akos Tolnay:

Veuillez considérer cès réponses ce que je crois être l'opinion de la majorité de ceux qui s'occupent de littérature dans mon pays (la Hongrie). Au moins, je crois ne pas avoir tort de les attribuer à la génération actuelle — aux jeunes — dont je suis.

I. Oui, on lit le Maître, on lit beaucoup les traductions — d'ailleurs excellentes — de l'*Histoire contemporaine,* de *Crainquebille,* du *Crime de Sylvestre Bonnard* et de tous les autres. Mais... mais, ce n'est plus la même catégorie de lecteurs qu'auparavant. De nos jours, on croit ne plus avoir le temps de s'arrêter à des finesses de style, et les polissonneries du vieux Coignard ou les coucheries si fréquentes du *Lys rouge* n'intéressent plus qu'un monde très restreint. Les jeunes filles des pensionnats, peut-être.

II. Non, certainement pas. Je n'ai jamais cessé d'admirer l'incomparable style, le français si pur des bavardages du Maître. Mais je n'ai jamais considéré Anatole France que

comme un dilettante, « le prince des dilettantes » — pour
m'exprimer selon Jules Lemaître. Beaucoup de mes amis
pensent de même.

III. Tous les traités concernant l'histoire de la littérature
contemporaine le classent, chez nous, entre les classiques
du style. Est-il tombé en oubli quand on a si souvent l'occasion de lire, dans beaucoup de romans modernes, des
tournures de phrase ou une idée dont l'écrivain n'a pas su
suffisamment cacher l'origine qui, quelquefois, a un parfum par trop « Bénédictin narquois ». Vraiment, je crois
que nous tous, nous écrivons un peu Anatole France, et
avec cela, je vous ai répondu à votre quatrième question.

CONCLUSIONS :

Pour tirer quelques conclusions que ce soient de cette
Autopsie, il faut ajouter à ces réponses celles des écrivains anglais et américains, données par ailleurs. C'est à
cet effet que nous les passons en revue.

Les prenant au hasard, on voit le jeune romancier Samuel
Rogers mettre France à part entre ses ancêtres et ses imitateurs et le trouver avoir une grande influence sur les jeunes.

Le très célèbre écrivain Theodore Dreiser n'a, lui, pas
assez de paroles pour louer France: *Thaïs est une des grandes œuvres d'art du monde.* France est devenu classique.
Et quant à le mettre sur un plan quelconque, Dreiser écrit:
*Sur quel plan est-ce que je mets Sophocle? Sur quel plan
est-ce que je mets Villon? Sur quel plan George Moore ou
Dostoïevsky? Celui des écrivains et personnalités grands
et immortels.*

H. L. Mencken, sans lui reconnaître de profondeur, loue néanmoins France. Et M. Edmund Wilson, excellent critique, explique fort bien pourquoi il considère France un des grands écrivains français modernes, parce qu'il a poussé l'intelligence aussi loin qu'elle se peut pousser, tandis que chez un Proust qui le dépasse, elle est déjà en décomposition.

Le grand écrivain anglais Bertrand Russell ne tarit pas, lui non plus, de louanges envers France, et Miss Zona Gale met France à une place très élevée. Bernard Shaw, d'ailleurs, fait très spirituellement de même et il prédit pour France une nouvelle vogue lorsqu'il ne sera plus nullement d'actualité.

Le jeune poète anglais d'avant-garde, Sydney Hunt, n'aime guère France et le trouve suranné. Mais H. R. Hays, aussi jeune et aussi avant-garde, nous écrit d'Amérique qu'on ne doit pas désespérer et qu'à la révolution du cycle, le grand France revivra. M. Guy Holt le trouve délaissé pour n'être plus vivant (sujet à reportages), mais il croit qu'on doit attendre qu'une génération nouvelle porte un jugement sur France pour penser à savoir s'il est immortel.

Enfin, Waldo Frank et William Carlos Williams, tous deux influencés par leur connaissance de l'opinion française, nous disent: celui-ci qu'il n'a jamais lu France parce qu'il ne l'intéresse pas, et celui-là qu'il trouve que France restera comme symbole de la fin du classicisme, mais qu'il est déjà de lecture ennuyeuse.

On voit que l'opinion anglo-américaine est assez favorable à France.

En tirer des conclusions?

A vous, lecteur. — H. J. S.

ANATOLE FRANCE [1]

A Post-mortem Five Years Later

QUESTIONNAIRE:

I. Do you think Anatole France's situation has changed since his death? If so, in what manner?

II. Has your personal attitude toward France's work changed since the author's death? Why?

III. Does the general indifference shown toward France's work mean that it is being forgotten or that its fate is settled, in the sense that it has become « classical »?

IV. How do you rate Anatole France? For what reasons?

Theodore Dreiser:

I do not agree that there has been no more discussion of the work of Anatole France since his death. Articles concerning him have appeared in this country at least.

At best all things go in waves. If there has been a wave of silence there will presently be one of discussion. He is too distinguished an artist to disappear in five hundred years, let alone five.

I. No. Considerable attention has been and is being paid to examining the data of his life. This cannot but result

---

(1) See, among our *Notes,* details about the authors.

in a higher estimate of the man as a character, as well as an artist later on.

II. It has in no way changed. I still consider *Thaïs* one of the great art works of the world.

III. I do not agree that there is a general indifference to France's work. I do agree that its fate is settled. It has become classic.

IV. How do I rate Sophocles? How do I rate Villon? How do I rate George Moore or Dostoievsky? — As great and enduring writers and personages.

Waldo Frank:

I. Anatole France was primarily a « period » writer. As such, his position is bound to change radically with time.

II. I have always liked Anatole France but never considered him a great writer. I can't say that my attitude has ever materially altered, since I first knew him. He was a writer in a great tradition: the son of « princes ». His inheritance, which he kept pure and luminous, gave him a significance in a decomposing world. For he represented precisely an integration of the French rational spirit, which has become archaic.

III. I suppose the world is more vividly aware than ever, that the rational skeptical formula of Anatole France simply does not *work:* i. e., it corresponds to none of the deeper needs by reason of which men turn to books. But how much lovelier is Anatole France than his innumerable cheap imitators — in the United States!

IV. I think he will retain a permanent place in the history of French literature, as a wondrously sweet and late example of the spirit that was Molière and Voltaire. Our sons will be able to study the strength of this spirit in this afterglow. He will remain, hence, as a symbol and as a personality. Not as a creator of intrinsically significant works. Already, the thin pastiche of his prose makes rather poor reading.

Zona Gale:

It seems to me that Anatole France's place in literature is now as secure as it has ever been. Whether security will remain to it can be known no more than for other writers. What he has written is still in the current vein. When that vein changes no one can forecast what will become of the work of any writer. Certainly it looks now as if the cleverness, the incisive quality of his comment, will always have a value as reflecting the mind of many of his time.

H. R. Hays:

I think the silence after his death a fairly normal thing. It seems to me that when any rather big writer dies the floral pieces are so heavily perfumed and elaborately constructed that there is bound to be a reaction. And when a flock of ratlike biographers has gnawed and chewed the great man's slippers and dressing gown to its heart's content and the last bastard has been unearthed the public palate is pretty well dulled. I'm afraid five years is too long after for a post-mortem and not long enough for anthropological excavations. After all, France contributed to the literature of ideas and ideas go in cycles. Flesh and blood character has a steady appeal but it seems to me that France's people as characters are little better than lascivious puppets. If, however, his ideas are important and I think that they are, he'll probably be revived with another turn of the wheel. And so I say, let him be temporarily forgotten, our children or grandchildren will have the thrill of digging him up and finding the corpse miraculously preserved.

Guy Holt:

I. Do I think Anatole France's situation has changed since his death? If so in what manner? If by situation you mean has his reputation altered, I think the answer is obviously yes. There is an apparent tendency on the part of a good many critics to regard France's work as less important than it appeared during his lifetime. I speak now only of Americans whose opinions I have encountered either in print or in conversation. Insofar as France's popularity here is concerned, I think he is as widely read now as he ever was, but on this point I have no definite knowledge.

II. My personal attitude toward France's work has not changed since his death beyond the fact that I am no longer stimulated to read him by the appearance of new books from his pen.

III I would think that the factor indicated in my answer to Question II contributes in large part to the lack of present day discussion of France's work. He is no longer writing: therefore as news he no longer exists. His work has been amply discussed contemporaneously and little can be added to that discussion during the lifetime of people who read his books as they were written. Another generation will have occasion to appraise his work in the light of its value to them, but only that later generation can say whether or not his work will seem to merit appraisal.

IV. I must beg off answering this question. I abhor categories and shun the making of comparative judgments whenever possible.

Sidney Hunt:

I. (a) Yes. (b) See III.

II. (a) No. (b) See IV.

III. Classics is as classics forgot.

IV. (a) As a gentle ironist he fought the good fight but not nearly hard enough. Garrulous. Cud-chewer. As an artist did not meet reality half way. A laughing willow, rootless, headless. So not very high.

(b) I do not like studious musers, or that « irony like the gentle play of summer lightning ». And because I consider Picasso an artist, and Matisse not.

His nineteenth-century rationalism and backward glances to Greece, serene gods (ah! and cruueeell!) now out-of-date, as also rodinesque haunches of venus.

H. L. Mencken:

I see no change in the general view of Anatole France. Those who liked him while he lived still like him, and those who had doubts about him still harbor them. As for me, he seems to be one of the most amusing writers that ever lived. I see nothing profound in him, but profundity is certainly not the only thing that is valuable. I know of no other modern French writer who is more entertaining or who shows a more civilized and stimulating spirit.

Samuel Rogers:

I. I gather that it has suffered the inevitable reaction that follows the death of men, especially writers, very highly acclaimed during their life-time.

II. No.

III. Perhaps it means that, for the time, it is being forgotten by the younger generation which does not realize its influence upon their own work.

IV. I consider him a writer of great talent and charm. No one of his aspects, considered in itself, shows particular depth or originality; but when his work is taken as a whole it stands out sharply both from the writers in the past to whom he is most indebted and from his various imitators.

Bertrand Russell:

I. People are occupied with urgent problems, and forget dead men quickly. Who remembered Voltaire in 1794? Fewer than now.

II. No.

III. Anatole France has, I should say, become « classical ». But his brand of cultivated scepticism is out-of-date, alas! Modern scepticism is either ignorant or directed against

Science in the interests of religion. Moreover he believes
in reason — oh fie!

IV. Very high. Reasons given under III.

Bernard Shaw:

I. The situation of all authors is changed by death. There
is a descent into hell followed by a resurrection even with
the greatest of the immortals.

II. No.

III. As he is dead his books are less advertised by the
publishers, who have to concentrate on new works and
leave the old ones to take care of themselves. That is all.

IV. This is not a reasonable question: Anatole France
cannot be disposed of in a sentence. His books seem to me
likely to survive as Sterne's have survived in England;
but just at this moment his XIXth century anti-clericalism
« dates », as we say, very badly. His failure with Jeanne
d'Arc eclipses his success with la Reine Pédauque. People
want to find a way out of Penguin Island: they are out of
patience with the Voltairean pessimism of his conclusion
of its history. But when this phase passes, and his works
are read disinterestedly as entertaining literature his vogue
will revive; and he will take his appropriate place among
the classics.

Edmund Wilson:

In answer to your questionnaire, I should say that (I)
Anatole France since his death has gone completely out of
fashion. That is, that, though he is widely read by the
general public, he is either belittled or neglected by people
specially interested in literature.

That (II) my own personal attitude towards France's work has not changed since his death. I greatly admired him before he died, and still admire him as much.

That (III) France has probably not merely gone down never to be heard from again, but, as you suggest, become a classic — though there are classics and classics — and the reputation of a given classic may do a good deal of rising and falling.

That (IV) I consider Anatole France one of the great modern French writers. He is a sort of flowering and summing up of a whole side of French culture. He is like an embodiment of the French intelligence after it had assimilated Voltaire, Stendhal, Flaubert and Renan. France, in fact, carried *intelligence* in literature almost as far as it can go, and though he was perhaps less original than any of the older writers I have named, he certainly had a wider range both of feeling and of ideas than any of them. But it is precisely because he is a culminating figure that the world has lost interest in him since his death. By the end of the War, there had come in French thought a great reaction against all the sort of thing that Anatole France represented. He had come to seem to people facile, and it is true that he did have a facile side. Some of his last books, « La Vie en Fleur » and « Le Petit Pierre », for example, are largely mere literary confectionery· It is true that he had learned all too well, as he set out to do when he laid siege to the Academy with « Le Crime de Sylvestre Bonnard », how to please the French bourgeoisie: he made it possible for them to absorb painlessly Renan, Flaubert,

Stendhal and Voltaire. The youger generation objected to him, also, on the ground that he led nowhere, and it is true that France does not lead anywhere. He really, by the time he died, believed in nothing except art, and that all too much of the time from the rather dispiriting point of view of the collector of objets d'art.

Yet it is curious to think of the tremendous reputation of Proust, which has been increasing almost in exact proportion to the decline of France's reputation.   There is nothing very different in Proust from what we find in France. He has mastered the Symbolist technique, which lay outside of France's range. He has assimilated the Symbolist writers just as France had assimilated almost everything up to them. But Proust's point of view is, at bottom, almost exactly like France's. His own admiration for France was extreme, and his whole tragi-comic point of view about love, for example, may be found in France's « Lys Rouge » and « Histoire Comique », and, like France, he believes in nothing but art. France had already, before Proust, some phrase about believing in nothing but « the succession of phenomena and the relativity of things ». Proust does not even pretend, as France did, to interest himself in politics. He has carried the literature of the pure intelligence even farther than France, and in Proust it has already begun to decay. I think that both these men were great writers, but I have a good deal of sympathy with the generation which is tired of the sort of thing they represent.

William Carlos Williams:

Since I have never read anything that Anatole France has written I cannot answer your questions.

Of course I know very vaguely something of his style and once I dipped into The Revolt of the Angels which my mother had been reading.

Perhaps it might be along the line of your inquiry to have me say why I have never felt impelled to read Anatole France.

As near as I can get to it it is because I have somehow received the impression that though France has been directly interested in life to the fullest and most uncensored degree he has written of it indirectly almost if not quite in an allegorical manner and allegory means nothing whatever to me. In fact it is directly repellant. So is involved symbolism. In fact so is all symbolism.

But this is pure nonsense since I do not know what I am talking about. Yet I have tried to be of assistance to you.

CONCLUSIONS:

To the answers given us by English and American writers, we must add,to have a complete view of the situation, the opinions in French. With this goal in mind, we will here pass in review the French answers before coming to any conclusions.

Taking these judgments at random we have Louis Guilloux, a young novelist, and Jean Catel, French authority on Whitman, telling us that France's work is dead and that we have no time to read it; on the other hand, Léon Deffoux, the well-known critic, proclaims his admiration for France and ends: *we must be grateful to him for having offered to us, as to little Pierre Nozière, artificial roses,* referring to the gesture of Pierre's mother making him a present of the wall-paper flowers.

Paul Morand thinks that France is merely a dilettante, a good writer but not a great one, but he considers his work as having an importance, since it is a document for writing the history of the end of last century. André Maurois, who admires France, thinks that only parts of his work are immortal. However, the playwright Henri Duvernois sends us the most enthusiastic answer of all: Since his death, Anatole France *has become greater... There is no indifference about France's work. Quite to the contrary.* And he refuses to rank France, for *certain names are above lists.*

From the young novelist Jacques Heller comes the most unexpected answer: France has an importance only as a poet, but he was a great one.

Fernand Divoire, literary critic, and Maurice Courtois-Suffit, the young novelist and story-writer, are and always have been indifferent to him.

Jacques Roujon, author of a book on the life and opinions of France, finds it natural for him to be temporarily forgotten but does not doubt he will soon be *rediscovered.* As for Joseph Delteil and Blaise Cendrars, the first says one takes pleasure in reading France but never rereads him, and the second sums him up in one word, *ennui.* Victor Llona sees his only importance in his compilation of clas-

sical references, and André Salmon thinks his main asset
was taste, virtue of the reader not the writer, in the light of
which he avers that young men will always be just as well
of if they ignore France.

Joseph Jolinon, the Renaissance-Prize-winner, finds
France too interested in form to appeal to the men of today,
but priceless as a chronicler of the time of the Dreyfus Case.
The young François Ribadeau-Dumas calls France absolutely dead and gone. The Goncourt-Prize-winner, Maurice
Constantin-Weyer, feels that France is no longer what men
of today want but that he is certainly a classic.

André Gide recalls to us past opinions of his about
France, to the effect that France, too easily understood, is
immediately exhausted, and he concludes against him. The
young novelist and playwright Marcel Berger also finds
him doomed.

The young Belgian writers Marcel Loumaye, Georges
Linze and Constant de Horion disagree about France. Loumaye considers France above his assaulters, while Linze
thinks him entirely uninteresting and out-of-date. Constant
de Horion, however, places France's works in the first row,
among books one can never be tired of. For Belgium, the
ayes have it.

A young Hungarian novelist, Akos Tolnay, gives us what
he thinks is the general opinion among the younger generation in his country: France, admirable dilettante, is a
remarkable stylist, and one cannot call him forgotten when
in most modern novels one is struck by the phrases and
ideas that recall him.

And finally, Jean Cassou gives us a beautiful page about

Voltaire and France. A great admirer of Voltaire, he dislikes France for his fragileness as compared to the other's strenght. But he does admit that some fragments of his work may last.

As the reader will see, there is a much greater diversity of opinion in the French answers than in the English ones. Rather than content myself with merely counting the raised fingers, and afraid of betraying the truth through the prejudice of my own opinion, I will leave to the reader to decide if Anatole France has been condemned or acquitted with praise. — H. J. S.

LES DIEUX ONT SOIF
II: PROMENADE PUBLIQUE

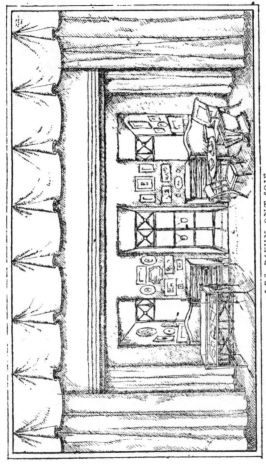

LES DIEUX ONT SOIF
II: A L'AMOUR PEINTRE

(Dessins de Walter-René Fuerst)   (Drawings by Walter-René Fuerst)

LES DIEUX ONT SOIF
III: CHEZ GAMELIN

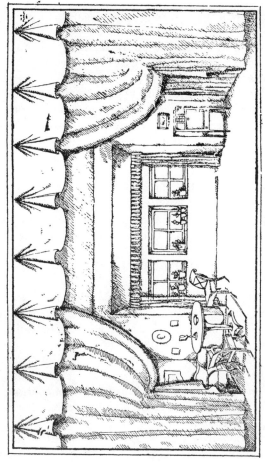

LES DIEUX ONT SOIF
IV: LA CHAMBRE D'ELODIE.

(Dessins de Walter-René Fuerst)   (Drawings by Walter-René Fuerst)

NOTES SUR ANATOLE FRANCE

Il est clair que, depuis la mort d'Anatole France, l'influence littéraire d'icelui n'a cessé de décroître et qu'elle tend de plus en plus vers zéro. Non qu'il y ait quelque rapport entre la disparition de l'écrivain et le silence dont on entoure son œuvre : de son vivant même, à peu près depuis le début de la guerre, l'auteur du *Jardin d'Epicure* n'avait plus droit qu'à l'indifférence des jeunes lettrés.

D'abord, la perfection même de son art, le rendait stérile. Comment eût-on pu, je ne dis pas faire mieux que lui, mais seulement l'égaler dans le domaine où son génie l'avait fait roi? Il a eu de pâles imitateurs. Mais — comme Racine et pour des raisons analogues — il était impossible qu'il laissât derrière lui aucune postérité. Et de fait, il n'en a point eu.

Il était, d'autre part, l'ultime représentant d'une philosophie qui, selon toute apparence, est aujourd'hui défunte; il se trouvait au terme extrême de cette lignée de rationalistes, issus de Descartes, pour lesquels le doute demeurait le seul moyen d'atteindre à la vérité, qui se souciaient moins de croire que de connaître et de comprendre, et à qui la pensée apparaissait comme « la plus grande des aventures humaines ». Lorsque le mouvement anti-intellectualiste eut proclamé la faillite de ces conceptions et la prééminence du sentiment et de la foi sur les valeurs purement logiques, Anatole France vit se détourner de lui les générations nouvelles. Son scepticisme parut démodé, sa connaissance du monde trop étroite, sa spéculation sans portée profonde. Cet esprit incomparable, on le considéra

comme un dilettante, un ironiste sommaire, une espèce de
jongleur superficiel et plat. Bientôt il devint odieux, et son
œuvre chut dans le discrédit. Il semble, en d'autres termes,
qu'on doive tenir France pour la plus symbolique et la
plus illustre victime de l'anti-rationalisme contemporain.

Depuis que n'est plus celui qu'on appela si longtemps « le bon maître », les mêmes causes continuent à
produire les mêmes effets. Sans doute on le lit encore. Mais
on ne le relit guère. Au moins chez les littérateurs, on n'en
éprouve pas le besoin. Et peut-être cela vaut-il mieux:
lorsqu'on voit de quels sarcasmes et de quelles ordures le
couvrent la plupart des jeunes écrivains actuels, lorsqu'on
entend M. Paul Valéry reprocher à l'auteur de l'*Histoire
Contemporaine,* la clarté de sa pensée et de sa langue,
et soutenir « qu'il y avait dans ses livres un art consommé
de l'effleurement des idées et des problèmes les plus graves », on en vient à se demander si notre époque est encore
capable de comprendre vraiment l'œuvre de France.

■   ■   ■

Pour ma part, et bien que je ne lui voue pas une admiration sans réserve, je persiste à considérer Anatole France
comme un très grand écrivain. Cela tient à ce que je ne
donne ni dans le pragmatisme, ni dans le mysticisme du
siècle, et à ce que je refuse d'admettre, jusqu'à preuve
du contraire, que l'intelligence soit une tare.

■   ■   ■

Il se peut que l'œuvre d'Anatole France soit, en effet,
« classique ». Mais, outre que ce terme demanderait à être

défini, car il offre plusieurs acceptions assez différentes, on ne saurait, il me semble, juger du classicisme d'un auteur sans un certain recul dans le temps. Ce pourquoi il ne nous appartient pas, à mon sens, de décider si France est classique ou non. Je ne crois pas, néanmoins, qu'il tombe à l'oubli. Pour les raisons indiquées plus haut, le prestige de son œuvre subit en ce moment une éclipse; *mutatis mutandis,* il arrive à l'auteur de la *Rôtisserie* une aventure analogue à celle de Ronsard au XVII° siècle. Combien de temps cette éclipse durera-t-elle, c'est évidemment imprévisible. Ne nous inquiétons pas cependant du sort que l'avenir réserve aux ouvrages de France. Le jour ne peut pas ne pas venir où on les situera à leur vraie place, qui est très haute, et où on les honorera comme les fruits les plus parfaits de la culture.

■   ■   ■

Tout ce qui précède suffit, je crois, à expliquer pourquoi France, à mon avis, doit être mis au rang des génies de notre littérature. Il y a quelques années, M. Benjamin Crémieux prédisait à l'auteur de *La Vie en fleur,* « à cheval sur le XIX° et le XX° siècle, une place analogue à celle qu'occupe Diderot au XVIII° ou encore, mais un degré au-dessous, à celle de La Bruyère au XVII° ». Le « degré au-dessous » mis à part, cette opinion me paraît assez judicieuse.

Fernand Ferré.

MARCHING ON

The reputation of Anatole France is passing through a phase of partial eclipse — so much, I think, is sure. Still, I should be surprised to learn that there has been any great falling off in the popular demand for his works. The advance-guard of literature has far outpaced him, but Anatole France is no weakling to fall by the wayside, and, when the pioneers decide to stay their progress for a while, to take breath and stock of themselves, I think they will see, far down the road, a sturdy John Brownish figure, bearded and erect, « marching on » towards them.

Pre-war novelists, realistic or romantic, French or Anglo-Saxon, were interested above all in appearances, *parade*. « No more Parades », we heartily agree with Mr. F. M. Ford. The literature of appearances is dead — for the present generation at any rate. Anatole France, whatever his limitations may have been, made war on the meretricious, whether realistic or romantic. Since I am invited to state my « personal attitude » let me say at once that it is a feeling of obligation to the witty ironist who did so much to free his generation fromt the shackles of national self-complacency, of racial and social antipathies, and from all the harpies of Mother Grundy's brood.

« *M. Bergeret* », his creator tells us, « *jouissait de l'indé-*

*pendance véritable, qui est toute intérieure... Il n'était pas
triste parce que sa sagesse approchait de la bienheureuse
ataraxie, sans toutefois y atteindre. Et il n'était pas gai
parce qu'il était sensuel et que son âme n'était point
exempte de désirs et d'illusions.* »

It is easy to understand that the present generation has,
for the most part, little use for a M. Bergeret. « Ataraxia »
seems to them not a « blessed » but a damnable state.
Taraxia, or (to « recondition » an ancient vehicle for modern use) perhaps I should say *taxitaraxia,* is more in their
rhythm.   M. Bergeret's sensuality, too, has been jazzed out
of all but the most provincial alcoves.   The « roses and
raptures of vice » have gone the way of the little blue
flower and the green carnation.   Modern love is like a trip
in a racing plane, over almost before it has begun, and,
sensually speaking, the tardy hippopotamus is an anachronism.

Literature, too, is being «speeded up » by the machinists
of realism, just as the « movies » have been ousted by the
more lifelike « talkies » (and very soon, I suppose, we shall
go still one better and crowd to eye, ear and nose the
« *smellies* »). For the moment, then, the slow, leisurely,
unrealistic yet (from a modern standpoint) little imaginative France is forgotten and interred in the classical mau-
soleum. But the illustrious dead have a habit of « walking »
and rejoining the ranks of the quick at their appointed
season.   Already there is a movement towards a new form
of literature which promises not only to give us back our
dreams but, revitalizing language, to open new horizons of

emotional experience. It will no be an easy prose, that
he who runs may read, like the magazine story or publicity
page, and to enjoy it the reader will need to close his ears
against the din of modern life. Thus we shall relearn the
virtues of ataraxia. And though, stylistically, the work
of Anatole France will be at the opposite pole from the
neo-idealistic prose of the near future, I think that his
spirit — of intellectual independence, ironic calm, humane
sensuality, contempt for active politics — will come into
its own again and that the rising generation will rate Anatole
France, as I do, among the great humanists of European
literature.

Stuart Gilbert.

OPINION D'UN JEUNE [1]

Vous remettez en scène Anatole France. Vous avez bien raison, car « si nous ne parlons pas de lui, nous y pensons toujours ». Cet écrivain, qui fut et restera discuté servira toujours de cible à tous ces « princes des nuées », rêveurs pâles qui s'accrochent désespérément à la remorque de la littérature. Mais tout homme a ses défauts, un écrivain plus que les autres sera sujet à critiques — (souvent oiseuses) — Anatole France surtout, parce qu'il est *grand*. Styliste remarquable et classique jusque dans les moelles, il distille une prose élégante qui, sous une apparente facilité, cache un « métier » et une maîtrise incontestables. C'est une continuelle musique que ses phrases légères, ironiques, musquées — sans grande portée philosophique, je l'accepte, mais d'un « bel esprit », un peu pédant, un peu simiesque, non dépourvu de grâce. C'est le marivaudage savant, les brocarts, les effets, la pose parfois, mais tout cela agréable aux yeux et doux au cœur. On a dit, le plus sérieusement du monde, que ses œuvres étaient des pastiches, voire des plagiats de Rabelais ou de Racine. Mais non! Il s'agit de contacts, d'affinités. Anatole France les subissait parce qu'il était de la lignée de ces deux génies. Qui donc pourrait le nier? Et soyez sûr que si l'on se tait sur Anatole France, c'est qu'on en a déjà trop parlé et trop écrit, mais en dehors de ces bavardages, l'œuvre est là, solide et ferme. Nos neveux et nos arrières-neveux sauront lui redonner un éclat passagèrement terni.

Valentin DE MANOLL.

---

(1) Nous avons cru bon de donner à part cette réponse, destinée à

ANATOLE FRANCE
AN ESSAY

It is fashionable to say: « Anatole France, oh well! »
It is fashionable to say: « Anatole France, oh hell! »
It is fashionable to say: « Anatole France, oh well, it is just Anatole France, oh hell! »
The time has now come when we must explain: oh well, oh hell. Because, in spite of oh well, oh hell, Anatole France was a good writer; and it is now time for us to explain why Anatole France is not a great writer. Good writers pass with the past, great writers remain in the present.

Anatole France is not a great writer because Anatole France wrote for the sake of writing; not out of necessity, but out of a desire to prove that he was clever. He was quite content to write: « La Marquise sortit à cinq heures », or « Posez la douille sur cette table », or even « Le moignon d'Albert guérit très bien », because such sentences all helped to prove that Anatole France had great powers of observation, and could be very natural when he wished, and, in fact, that Anatole France was a very clever man possessed of considerable genius but who could put his clerverness and genius to any purpose he chose.

Anatole France was also very gaulois. « Encore une œuvre de cet odieux génie qui a inspiré Rabelais, Voltaire,

---

notre *Autopsie,* car elle est symptômatique et elle montre que les jeunes dont les œuvres sont parfois si loin de celles de France ne le méprisent pas pour n'avoir pas écrit comme ils le font. — H. J. S.

4

Jean La Fontaine, (and Anatole France, Louis Bertrand, Léon-Paul Fargue (since he has been compared to Rabelais) and the immortal Colette) commenté par M. Taine (and the late, very late, Paul Souday). Printanier, l'esprit d'Anatole. Charmant, son amour. En voilà de la peinture à l'émail! »

This gallic humour can only produce thoroughly dead and classical writers. Rabelais and Voltaire are great, but the others are mere literary artificers, and their work nearer related to the decorative arts (l'art dans les salons) than to that class of art which is generally considered immortal.

Anatole France has failed. He did not create life, nor even living characters; he always took the attitude of a sceptical outsider, and wrote satirical comments on all those things from which he considered himself, a superior being and an intellectual,entirely detached. He helped in many ways to create the superior-intellectual fallacy which is such a poison to modern creative thought.

The characters in the works of Anatole France — especially Bergeret for whom our Anatole France had such a Narcissian affection — spoke of life and of the reality-which-is-not-realism-but-life in the terms of dust-born dust-bred and dust-dead scholiasts rather than in those of active, living, and creative men. They do not even seem to have ever lived in the author's imagination otherwise than as dressmaker's busts on which to drape the precious tissues of his own sophistries. And the obscenity which made our elders find Anatole France a synonym for Satan the Tempter is not the vigourous and healthy obscenity of a Petronius, but a sort of fashionable and accepted convention, like certain charmingly-libertine, rustic, and thoroughly fatuous prints of the 18th century (Le Mari dupe et content), in which the treatment and the subject are not as obscene as the ideas which one naturally associates with the title, and which, in spite of a ludicrous stylization, was the original, though purely artificial, intention of the artist. Thus the description of Madame Bergeret being surprised in the arms of Roux contains no deliberate, outspoken obscenity, but, beneath the polished style, and the fashionably-conventional attitudes, lie hidden the bait and the hook with which Anatole France hopes to draw the fish of obscene thought out of the dark pools of his reader's mind. And this is an unpleasant, sneaking type of pornography which cannot even invoke the protection of Nature, that dea ex machina who has so opportunely saved so many pornographists from condemnation, but only that fat and inflated old maid, Art, whose elephantiasis is expected to hide all crimes, and whose fetid breath   is proclaimed to transmute the lead of vice into the pure gold of virtue.

Yes indeed Anatole France has his faults but we must not forget Anatole France's style we must not forget lest we forget, lest we forget that Anatole France was a born stylist.

We must not forget to include in our anthologies and our text-books some charming delightful and typical piece of Anatole France's exquisite and highly-polished prose.

Yes indeed and we must not forget to buy a complete bound set of Anatole France's complete works and we must not forget to place them in a place of conspicuous honour in our libraries and to cut the pages and we must not forget to lend them one by one please return volume two *Le Lys Rouge* and I will give you volume three *La Violette Jaune* to our more cultured friends.

We must not forget finally and we must not forget that we must be very careful not to be led into the erroneous theory that Monsieur Bergeret is a prophetic vision of Paul Valéry in private life because we must not forget that Paul Valéry has written *Le Cimetière Marin* which is a living poem wheread Bergeret only wrote scholiastic commentaries on the Aeneid and the Iliad which scholiastic commentaries we must forget together with their scholiastic author and the scholiastic author of their scholiastic author whom we must forget.

Edouard Roditi.

ANATOLE FRANCE
CROYANT ET CRÉATEUR

Ce n'est pas à vingt ans qu'on renie son époque. Mais, quelques raisons que nous ayons par ailleurs de l'aimer, il nous faut bien lui reprocher l'étrange discrédit dont elle entoure la mémoire et l'œuvre d'Anatole France.

A première vue, ce discrédit apparaît comme paradoxal. On peut s'étonner qu'un temps qui semble avoir érigé en principe la recherche de la jouissance soit hostile à celui dont toute la vie ne fut qu'un long hymne à la volupté. En réalité, jamais écrivain ne fut victime d'une plus formidable méprise.

Comment interprète-t-on son œuvre, et quelle philosophie, croit-on qui s'en dégage? Les plus indulgents diront: « un scepticisme élégant »; c'est l'étiquette consacrée. Les catholiques vouent France à l'exécration des siècles, pour ce scepticisme qui ruine les fondements de la religion; par un dogmatisme identique, les gens d'extrême-gauche le réprouvent; quant aux hommes d'action, à qui toute littérature semble vaine — comme si la pensée n'était pas la génératrice de l'action — ils se contentent de l'ignorer; s'ils le lisent par hasard, ils le rejettent aussitôt à cause de l'*apparence* statique de son art. Et tous d'accabler le grand écrivain sous la même dédaigneuse formule: « un scepticisme élégant ».

Or, — et c'est en quoi gît la méprise inique — RIEN N'EST

PLUS FAUX QUE CETTE FORMULE. Nous en sommes restés à
l'opinion que pouvaient se faire d'Anatole France les jeunes
générations de 1900 à 1910. On conçoit que les nourritures
spirituelles d'Anatole France aient paru par trop délicates
à des hommes épris de réalisations immédiates, qui s'en
tenaient uniquement au positif. Les gens de valeur qu'ils
comptaient dans leurs rangs ont proclamé bien haut leur
désaffection pour le vieux maître. Et la guerre est venue. Les
générations cadettes, occupées d'autres soins, hélas! plus
pressants, n'ont lu France que partiellement et distraite-
ment; elles s'en sont tenues à la lettre, et, pour l'esprit, elles
ont paresseusement adopté les opinions de leurs devan-
cières. Somme toute, elles n'ont lu France, *que pour trouver,*
dans leurs lectures, *la confirmation d'idées préconçues.* C'est
donc à nous qu'il appartient de reprendre, avec l'œuvre
d'Anatole France, le contact direct; c'est à nous qu'il appartient aussi de redresser l'erreur monstrueuse. Ce n'est pas la
seule affaire où les nouvelles équipes auront à infirmer
les conceptions des équipes aînées, d'ailleurs sans esprit de
dénigrement systématique, et surtout sans prétention à l'in-
faillibilité.

On reproche à France d'être sceptique et destructeur. Non.
ANATOLE FRANCE CROIT et CRÉE. On a pris ses tâtonnements
pour des assurances définitives, ses railleries légères pour
des arguments massifs. « J'ai regardé plus d'une fois, je
l'avoue, du côté du scepticisme absolu, dit l'écrivain. *Mais
je n'y suis jamais entré.* »

Dans les limites de ce bref témoignage, nous ne prétendons pas donner un portrait achevé d'Anatole France; il

y faudrait plus de temps et de réflexion, et nous aurions, nous aussi, à formuler des réserves: car nous n'avons point l'admiration béate, ni le jugement entier. Nous voudrions seulement exposer à grands traits ce qui nous paraît être la véritable philosophie du père de Crainquebille.

« Moi, dit-il quelque part, j'aime la vie, la vie de cette terre, la vie telle qu'elle est, la chienne de vie ». L'amour de la vie, des choses et des créatures, le goût du désir et de la volupté, et concurremment, cette large pitié humaine de qui a vécu, donc souffert, — voilà le fond du génie d'Anatole France, voilà ce que porte en lui cet homme qu'on dit sec et sans bonté. Mais toutes ces vertus se tempèrent et se trouvent naturellement éloignées des excès, grâce au contrôle vigilant d'une raison admirable, d'un sagesse culturelle jamais en défaut. Sans doute est-ce le rationalisme de France qui l'a desservi. Les hommes de notre temps, si peu maîtres d'eux-mêmes, si abandonnés aux instincts, et aux impulsions affectives, n'admettent pas volontiers qu'on puisse exercer sur soi-même une discipline. A leurs yeux, Anatole France est apparu comme le champion de la Raison pure, — cette Raison tant honnie. Les aveugles! La page magnifique qui termine *Les Opinions de l'Abbé Jérôme Coignard* leur est-elle donc demeurée lettre morte?

« Les vérités découvertes par l'intelligence demeurent stériles. Le cœur est seul capable de féconder ses rêves. Il verse la vie dans tout ce qu'il aime. C'est par le sentiment que les semences du bien sont jetées sur le monde. La raison n'a point tant de vertu... Il faut, pour servir les hommes, s'élever sur les ailes de l'enthousiasme. Si l'on raisonne, on ne s'envolera jamais. »

Pour nous, cet appel nous touche. Nous allons vers celui qui, bien que pessimiste — mais le pessimisme est une forme de la bonté, et c'est l'optimisme qui est égoïste — nous enseigne à aimer la vie, les hommes, la beauté. Et nous ne croyons pas que cette leçon puisse être stérile. Elle nous apporte une certitude, elle nous enjoint de vivre, — et vivre c'est créer; elle est un principe de foi et d'action.

Telle est, encore que sommairement exprimée, la philosophie d'Anatole France. Nous la méconnaissons avec une sereine impudence. Mais redoutons que l'avenir, vengeant ainsi le grand vieillard, n'aille confondre nos injustices et nos débilités.

23 Octobre 1929   Francis Ambrière.

UTILITY OF ANATOLE FRANCE

I doubt whether there is any author whose case is more complex than that of Anatole France. For if Anatole France has many admirers, he has had, during the last years of his life and since his death an unbelievable host of enemies. And it is these enemies that afford one of the most curious elements of the France case.

This introduction may sound incomprehensible, so let us in a few words sum up the facts relevant to what we should like to bring out: France's enemies, almost without exception, are old admirers of the master who, at some moment, for one reason or another, turned against him. Among them, scarcely any one has constantly disliked France's work since he was old enough to have opinions for himself. Of course, we have today some of the younger men who have obstinately refused to read France, either admitting it openly or convincing themselves that he was of no interest to them, but this is because the younger men have been influenced by those of their elders who, having undergone the evolution of first admiring and then often hating the work of France, try to impress upon their sons and younger brothers that they need no waste their time upon him.

But, I say, these men, who have not allowed others to tell them whether or not France is worthwhile reading but have inquired into the matter for themselves, unless they await an age much too advanced, are bound, experience seems to prove, to have a great admiration for the author of *Penguin Island.*   In many cases, this admiration lasts a lifetime — and France's staunch idolizers are innumerable — but in just as many it wanes. And when it does, the natural reaction is a hatred for France, as violent or more than the previous admiration, for it is rare that upon the first reading one remain indifferent to this writer.

One may believe that the above statements are pure fantasy and that I have no basis for them. However, it is from the opinions generally expressed by admirers and enemies of the author that I have drawn these conclusions (1). I believe therefore that one may express almost as an axiom: Every human being of normal quality, if he read Anatole France, must necessarily either conserve a lifelong admiration for him or else pass through a « France period » during which the work of Anatole France will be required for his well-being and meet with his greatest enthusiasm.

The great charm of France's perfect style and refined humor make it almost inevitable for every man to undergo at some time such a period of admiration; but what it is that determines the exact moment of this subjugation and the time of life at which it generally takes place, may show some interesting points for the comprehension of France's sophisticated literary potion.

As soon as I advance the theory that to those who do not have recourse to his work all their lives, Anatole France is *necessary* during some period usually occuring in extreme youth, I see the numerous enemies of Monsieur Bergeret jumping to their feet, their faces distorted into

---

(1) Further illustrated by several of the answers to our *Post-mortem*: Victor Llona, Joseph Jolinon, André Gide, etc...

a half-gleeful smile, half-frown of despair: despair because
I call France necessary, glee because if he is necessary, they
aver, I have lost myself by saying the time one calls upon
him is in extreme youth. In extreme youth, they say, one
does not know his own mind and aversions or enthusiasms
are of no importance. But it must be taken into consideration that when any number of men who today declare
no use for France, admit that during their youth he was one
of their favorite writers — and usually *the* favorite — there
must be some other reason than mere chance. Here can
be no coincidence. Obviously France does exert a distinct
attraction upon young minds in the forming. And that is
not because they are incapable of a sound choice.

I have tried elsewhere (2) to demonstrate that France is
not the mere imitator of the classics that some have made
him out to be. In my estimation, there is a great part of
distinct *modernism* in his work. As I explained it in my
other essay, the modernistic side of France takes in his
method of exposition, his taste for the curious but useless
detail, his treatment of certain subjects common to the outstanding writers of our time, and so forth.

On the other hand, we have France's style which offers
absolutely no element of innovation — except a great faci-
lity for adopting slang and common talk, which must be
proclaimed in his favor. But it is exactly because France
united this classical style with an entirely contemporary
conception that he has so great a charm and so undeniable a value.

---

(2) *Anatole France, moderne,* in this issue.

To every young reader and to a great many more advanced ones, France offers a definite element which is of the utmost necessity to them. In his work, they find in the first place that background of culture — his knowledge of everything that has ever been said, written, or done, is a unanimously recognized fact — which is indispensable as an immovable criterion toward which anything more advanced must be reverted. This culture, and with it France's profound respect and upholding of the perfection of the classical style, provide the basis, the fundamental element from which any innovation (whether it be that of the creator or the educational advance of the reader) must necessarily take its start. Next to these ingredients of foundation, one finds in the books of France the reflection of the general trend of thought in his time (*Penguin Island* and *Contemporary History*) as well as the adaptation of an excellent mind to what it realized would be the conception of the future (notably in *A Mummer's Tale* and *The Revolt of the Angels*). These are not only of a precious guidance but also enrich the mind profoundly. And further, there is to be seen in these books the work of a virtuoso such as there had been none in a long time and has been none since (particularly in the execution of such works as *Thais, the* perfect novel, and *The Queen Pédauque*). From this viewpoint France is not a disciple or an imitator of the classics, but one of the utmost among them. His craftsmanship had rarely been equalled before his time and never since.

These aspects of his work give a sufficient idea of the justification of his necessity from an intellectual attitude.

Beyond that, we may add that the cutting humor of his satire and the rare plesantness of his novels merely increase the reasons why his work should have a definite place and utility.

But for several generations already the books of Anatole France have been among the preferred reading-matter of the younger groups. And they bid fair to continue. The reasons stated above, of course, hold good for explaining the favor with which readers of any age greet his work — when they like it. They are part of the explanation for the particular appreciation of him by the younger readers. But for this case an extra element must be joined to the preceding points.

Anatole France has an exceptional quality for remaining young. His adaptability to the trend of the times is well seen in the vast change of outlook that characterizes the author at the different periods of *Sylvestre Bonnard* and *The Revolt of the Angels*. At sixty, France was younger than when his years totalled half of that number. For his theory of light-hearted scepticism had reached its final complete stage and left him so doubtful about everything that nothing could touch him. He had the carefreeness of a boy. And it is this carefreeness — arrived at after a half-century of meditation — that makes his mind so adequate to constant communion with the minds of youths still carefree for not yet having been adulterated by society. Anatole France, the man who has been called a mundane snob, reached through reflection the state of primitiveness to which his admiration for Rousseau led him. He thought man was good, and in order to prove it, purged himself of every impure element until he *became* good.

Now, Eugene O'Neill in his *Great God Brown* has pitted Brown against the artist Dion (who might also be called The Great God Pan, or further Peter Pan). Dion, simple in his genius, is good; and Brown is the polluting effect of Society opposed to him. Dion is man in his primitive form, because he never grew up too much and not quite enough.

It is thus with the men who proclaim to have gone beyond being able to like France. They have grown up too much to have for his carefreeness the brotherly feeling of the carefreeness of youth. But, oh! how quickly most of them would affect a warm feeling for him, if they could realize that saying they like him no more is equivalent to saying: Yes, I have grown up, I am no longer interested in this childish merriness, but I have not grown up enough to have returned through philosophic attitude to the sincerity of youth. That I repeat, is what France did, as Voltaire had done it. He went beyond ordinary maturity to that state of serene detachment in which his ultimate pondering completed the cycle and brought him back, having tried and found the vanity of everything, to the primitiveness of childish inexperience.

A good reader might follow that evolution himself all through the work of France and in his own mind enact the various stages the author went through until he too reached similar conclusions. But there are so few good readers!

So, it appears for the present that Anatole France's chief

utility is as a companion to youth, bringing to it after years of mental discussion a confirmation of its own love of living. Perhaps some day many men will have accomplished the circuit of thought France experienced, and at that time France's place in letters and in society will merely go up and up. Until then, France has a distinct utility, outside of his literary perfection, and his place, secure though stationary, is far from being a low one.

Harold J. SALEMSON.

ANATOLE FRANCE, MODERNE

Comme je demandais à un de mes amis, qui, d'ailleurs, n'aime guère Anatole France, pourquoi, selon lui, les jeunes écrivains délaissaient le maître, il laissa tomber sans penser ces mots: « Ils lui doivent trop pour pouvoir le reconnaître ». Quelques années se sont écoulées depuis lors et j'ai souvent été tenté d'établir un parallèle entre France et la « littérature moderne », voire de montrer France fondateur des écoles contemporaines de littérature iconoclaste.

Dire que France ait réellement *fondé* le mouvement moderne des arts serait sans aucun doute exagérer (1). Cependant, si nous voulons bien essayer de définir les plusieurs éléments qui prêtent à des œuvres ce qu'on appelle le modernisme, on pourra peut-être en tirer des conclusions intéressantes et qui montreront chez France un côté assez inattendu.

On s'accorde pour voir en lui un descendant des classiques: les uns le disent aussi grand que les classiques, les autres ne lui voient qu'un intérêt de pasticheur. Toutefois, on ne peut oublier le « tout ce que l'on voudra, mais d'abord, Anatole France a préservé la langue française »

---

(1) D'ailleurs, ceci demanderait des explications beaucoup trop longues et une étude détaillée que je n'ai jamais pu prendre le temps d'écrire.

de Maurice Barrès au moment où la politique mettait
celui-ci aux antipodes de l'auteur de *L'Ile des Pingouins.*
(Barrès lui-même aurait peut-être ri de la supériorité qu'on
revendique aujourd'hui pour lui sur France.) Et, si on peut
discuter qu'il soit absolument nécessaire aux jeunes de lire
l'œuvre de France, on ne peut nier que cet œuvre, s'ils le
lisaient, les dispenserait presque à jamais de lire les classiques.

Mais ceci est acquis : presque parmi nous, Anatole France
reste le dernier des classiques; plus, il est un pont. Ce
pont ne serait-il bâti que d'un seul côté? J'entends, France,
dernier rejeton malheureusement sans héritier légitime
des classiques, s'arrête-t-il là? Comme *pont,* ne le voit-on
pas aborder de l'autre côté en se rattachant, s'il ne leur
jette pas réellement leurs fondements, aux contemporains
dits *modernes?* Pour ma part, il me semble que France n'a
guère moins d'importance comme prédécesseur des hommes
d'aujourd'hui que comme successeur de ceux de jadis.

Pour expliquer cette phrase qui peut paraître pour le
moins paradoxale, il importe de mettre au clair les signes
distinctifs des modernes, comme je le disais pour commencer.

En premier lieu, rappelons l'idée de Baudelaire, si souvent
reprise depuis, selon laquelle la surprise formerait un des
éléments principaux de la littérature de notre siècle. Baudelaire, comme à son habitude, avait vu juste, et je crois
que ce ne serait que prolonger sa pensée sans nullement la
trahir que d'ajouter au mot surprise le mot détail. En
effet, la surprise, dans la littérature contemporaine se com-

pose surtout de rapprochements inattendus, non de gestes, mais de mots. Chez les écrivains qui ont été ou qui sont encore de l'avant-garde ces vingt dernières années, ce n'est pas l'inattendu de l'action qui est le plus singulier, mais bien les accouplements extraordinaires de mots, de phrases dont le rapport est bizarre ou imprévisible. Ainsi, pour prendre un seul exemple, il est évident que, dans le vers de Max Jacob,

> *Dahlia, ô dahlia, que Dalila lia!*

l'étonnant n'est pas le fait que Dalila ait lié les dahlias, ce dont elle fut sans doute fort capable, mais plutôt la juxtaposition sans raison apparente des mots phonétiquement similaires, mais qui ne suivent aucun ordre *inéluctable.*

Telle est une forme de l'inattendu verbal. L'autre est dans le détail, tout aussi surprenant, qui nous frappe non par son invraisemblance mais par l'irrélévance et l'inutilité qu'il montre dans sa banalité. Ce sont là les deux éléments de la surprise, et cette seconde forme se rencontre chez Anatole France (et *consciemment,* loin de la banalité persistante mais non voulue de François Coppée) alors que chez aucun de ses prédécesseurs ou de ses contemporains, une telle tendance ne m'a frappé.

Je n'ai pas relevé tous les exemples de ce détail amusant mais apparemment inutile que j'ai trouvés chez France. Je me contenterai d'en signaler un seul. Dans *La Révolte des Anges* (édition originale, page 336), Maurice a été blessé dans un duel par Arcade, son ange gardien. Celui-ci, sur la prière de Maurice, est venu le voir avec Gilberte des Aubels, pour qui ils se sont battus.

— Mon ami, dit Arcade, j'étais innocent. Je me suis fait homme. Aussitôt j'ai fait le mal. C'est ainsi que je suis devenu meilleur.

— N'exagérons rien, dit Maurice, et faisons un bridge.

Mais à peine le malade avait-il vu trois as dans son jeu et annoncé sans atout, que sa vue se brouilla; les cartes lui glissèrent des mains, sa tête alourdie retomba sur l'oreiller et il se plaignit d'un grand mal de tête.

Si ceci n'est pas du « modernisme », je ne sais comment je l'appellerais. D'abord, l'apport tout à fait imprévu de l'idée de faire un bridge, puis la suite. Je ne vois guère un Balzac, un Flaubert ou même un Zola (2) écrire cette dernière phrase sans la réduire à quelque chose d'aussi banal que « à peine le malade avait-il ramassé ses cartes, que sa vue se brouilla, etc... », si toutefois ils avaient l'originalité de faire jouer au bridge leur personnage souffrant. Je puis certes me tromper, mais j'attache une grande importance à ce bridge et à ces trois as qui firent que Maurice annonçât sans atout.

Il est vrai que la surprise, le détail (3) (même étant

(2) Ne pas confondre, d'ailleurs, avec les détails excessifs et inutiles des écoles réaliste et naturaliste qui, devenant un système et une méthode, perdent toute valeur de surprise, partant de modernisme.

(3) Cependant, à ce propos, il est intéressant de noter que le héros (ou un des héros) du livre le plus « moderne » qu'il y ait, Léopold Bloom dans *Ulysse* de James Joyce, « s'intéressait surtout aux détails mineurs de la connaisance humaine » (je cite de mémoire), tout comme le fait son créateur et comme le fit plus que quiconque Anatole France. D'ailleurs, un des plus grands écrivains vivants et le plus « moderne », justement James Joyce, a bourré ses livres de détails inutiles mais cocasses ou extraordinaires, et c'est par suite de l'éxagération qu'il fit de cette méthode et de ses autres (notamment le dédain et la haine qu'il porte au style classique et au langage ordinaire, ce en quoi il diffère évidemment de France) que j'ai moi-même été amené, malgré la grande admiration que je professe pour lui, à attaquer sa nouvelle œuvre.

donné que j'aie remporté ce point) ne forment pas tout
le modernisme. Un autre élément important, bien que relativement récent, est l'innovation dans le style. De ce côté-là,
il serait injuste et inutile de demander quoi que ce soit à
France, car c'est précisément son traditionalisme linguis-
tique qui le rattache aux classiques.

Par conséquent, il me semble avoir démontré que, dans
le domaine de la forme, France, tout en restant fidèle
au classicisme le plus pur, jette aux modernes de sérieux
points d'appui et constitue un vrai pont entre les deux
manières. Après le style reste, pour être très sommaire, la
conception littéraire, la matière, et finalement le point de
vue idéologique. Et, sous ces autres rapports, il me semble
bien que France est plus un précurseur des contemporains
qu'un retardataire poursuivant l'œuvre des classiques.

Quant à la conception littéraire, je ne veux   prendre
comme exemple que *La Révolte des Anges,* dont la forme et
la façon s'apparentent à toute une grande partie des œuvres
de nos contemporains par la conception graphique,   ou
mieux cinématographique. En effet, dans ce roman, plus
de *littérature.* L'auteur a écrit un scénario. Nulle exposition de raisonnements *per se,* mais toujours une traduction, parfaitement réalisable à l'écran, des idées en actions.
La phrase citée plus   haut en est elle-même un   exemple
frappant. Le fait d'avoir mentionné les trois as évite tout
besoin de sous-titre. Les gestes tiennent debout: c'est du
cinéma.

Ceci me fait songer à une phrase que j'ai écrite et qui
a fait sourire bien des gens. Parlant de la *Frédégonde* de
Jean Cassou, écrivain tout-ce-qu'il-y-a-de-moderne,   j'y ai

dit que cette vie imaginaire me rappelait encore plus un
conte philosophique de Voltaire ou de France qu'une œuvre
d'un de nos contemporains. Mais il y a peut-être plus de
rapports entre les deux qu'on ne le croit généralement.
(D'ailleurs, le propos de Cassou lui-même, qui m'a dit:
« Voltaire, c'est du surréalisme », prête encore de la matière
à réflexion sur ce point.)

Cependant, on me fera observer que *La Révolte des
Anges,* n'ayant paru qu'en 1914, a pu être influencée par
l'œuvre des premiers « modernistes ». Ma foi, Anatole
France n'a certainement pas cessé de lire en vieillissant et
il a dû être fort au courant des faits et gestes de MM. Apollinaire et Cie, mais je crois que la démonstration que j'ai
faite autour de la *Révolte* servirait tout aussi bien pour
L'Ile des Pingouins ou mieux encore *La Rôtisserie de la
Reine Pédauque.* On doit avouer que presque tout l'œuvre
de France est étonnant de logique visualisée, si je puis dire,
d'illustration de l'idée par la vie, même si cette vie n'est
que celle de pantins, comme on l'a voulu.

Néanmoins, si on ne veut pas se rendre à l'évidence de
cette conception cinématographique, au moins dans certaines œuvres de France, je ne saurais relever tous les
points qui entrent dans la formation des œuvres contemporaines pour essayer de les rattacher tous à France. Mais
deux des écrivains que l'on considère parmi les plus formidables de notre siècle ont traité d'une certaine matière
qu'il est intéressant de retrouver dans l'œuvre de l'auteur
du *Lys Rouge.* Je parle de Gide et de Proust — et je dois
dire que je considère ce dernier l'écrivain le plus important qu'il y ait eu depuis France. Le sujet qui est commun

à ces deux auteurs, et dont ils ont été les deux plus grands
analystes, c'est, on le sait, l'homosexualité. Or, l'auteur du
Lys Rouge — je cite ce livre-là à dessein — a écrit aussi
Histoire Comique, parue, si je ne me trompe, à la fin du
siècle dernier, par conséquent avant les œuvres de Proust
et de Gide, et qui épuise en quelques remarques — d'apparence légère, comme il se doit — tout ce sujet d'homosexualité que l'on devait plus tard discuter péniblement. Monsieur
Gide y trouverait même l'opinion que les mœurs qu'on a
accoutumé d'appeler anormales sont aussi *normales* que
les autres. Ce en quoi *Corydon* n'aura fait que répéter ce
qu'avait déjà dit France par boutade après les anciens.

Et finalement, je voudrais soutenir l'opinion que France
ne manque pas de passion et qu'il sut prendre parti. On a
dit de lui que son scepticisme fut à tel point exagéré qu'il
mena à l'inaction totale et que ce paisible vieillard, avec ses
doctrines, paralysait la volonté. Comme il faut avoir mal
lu France pour dire de pareilles choses! L'auteur d'*Histoire contemporaine,* homme d'inaction? Vous ne le voudriez pas. Car, M. Bergeret, lui-même, a su se prêter avec
violence à certaines causes. Mais il est trop facile d'accuser
de lâcheté la personne qui est raisonnable et se lève contre
la violence.

Ce qu'il faut comprendre, c'est qu'Anatole France a mis
tout autant de violence à combattre la violence que s'il
avait lui-même opté pour un mouvement quelconque. Le
raisonnable sceptique qu'il fut a su être violent pour combattre toute violence s'opposant à sa raison sceptique. Il
a su, comme on dit, tremper le nez du chien dans sa

propre marchandise. Mais ce n'est évidemment pas au chien lui-même qu'on doit demander de le reconnaître.

Enfin, on me viendra dire que je n'ai montré que certains côtés de France et qu'il y a encore ceci, cela de répugnant. Ce à quoi la réponse est d'autant plus accablante qu'elle est simple. Si Anatole France a été scénariste dans *La Révolte des Anges*, parfait romancier dans *Thaïs*, conteur admirable dans *Balthazar*, critique littéraire fort respectable dans *La Vie Littéraire*, satiriste dans la meilleure veine traditionnelle dans *L'Ile des Pingouins*, moraliste (ou immoraliste) dans *Histoire Comique*, et différent encore dans chacune de ses autres œuvres; c'est qu'Anatole France a été peut-être le dernier de ces grands virtuoses dont Shakespeare a été le meilleur modèle, tellement puissants que n'importe quoi les tente, capables d'exécuter n'importe quelle œuvre même avec la forme et le sujet imposés, et jusqu'au bout des ongles artisans purs, sachant vraiment ce que veut dire le mot *écrire*.

Oui, sachant ce que veut dire le mot *écrire*. Car nous devons rendre cet hommage à Anatole France (que nous ayons ou non senti après ces pages qu'il a quelque chose de « moderne »): il a été, pendant sa vie, l'homme nécessaire à chaque génération pour lui rappeler comment s'écrit le français, l'homme à qui tous ses contemporains se rattachent parce qu'eux, les innovateurs, ont besoin d'un point immuable qui sauvegarde pour eux les règles qu'ils briseront. Un tel homme, nous en avons un parmi nous aujourd'hui, et de tels hommes restent des monuments pour toutes les générations futures. Voilà pourquoi j'ose dire qu'Anatole France, incomparable successeur aux classiques, n'a cependant pas peu fait pour instituer la « littérature nouvelle ».

Et il me semble que je vois France, ayant lu ces pages, sourire et dire:

— Tout est possible, dans le meilleur des mondes.

NOTE A

Il est une autre chose qui prête un étonnant modernisme à l'œuvre de France.

Chaque homme, quels que soient son éducation, ses opinions personnelles, ses points de vue littéraire, politique ou autre, passe par une « période France ». Il est un moment dans la vie de chacun où l'œuvre de France lui est nécessaire. Et il me semble particulièrement important de noter que cette époque, lorsqu'elle ne se prolonge pas sur toute la vie, se place dans la jeunesse, au moment où l'esprit se forme. France nécessaire aux jeunes, France plus amusant à un certain âge que n'importe quel fantaisiste, ce France-là me paraît indiscutable et surtout très « moderne ». Si je n'en ai pas parlé dans cet essai, c'est que je lui consacre tout spécialement quelques pages en anglais par ailleurs.

NOTE B

Je retrouve dans de vieux papiers — vieux de trois ou quatre ans, à peine — une préface que j'avais faite, étant très jeune, pour une œuvre future. Aujourd'hui, cette idée me fait un peu rire, et craindre aussi que si je la réalisais je fâcherais plusieurs personnes. Je projetais alors de réunir des essais sur cinq hommes, dont France le premier. Le lien que je trouvais était celui-ci: il s'agissait d'Anatole France et de ses quatre héritiers: Paul Valéry, l'héritier académique; les héritiers littéraires, Proust et Paul Morand (puisque France préfaça le premier livre de Marcel Proust et celui-ci le premier de Morand); finalement, l'héritier « gardien de la langue française » (toujours le mot de Barrès), Jean Giraudoux.

Et ce qu'il y a de plus curieux, c'est que j'arrive toujours à faire s'accorder la grande admiration que j'ai pour ces cinq écrivains tellement différents, cinq de mes auteurs préférés.

Harold J. Salemson.

NOTES

LACUNES

Certaines lacunes se produisant dans ce numéro, nous tenons à dire que nous eussions préféré voir notre *Autopsie* donner une coupe absolument complète de l'opinion actuelle mais que, certains écrivains, comme M. Marcel Prévost par exemple, s'étant prononcés sur le sujet dans d'autres publications dernièrement, nous ne leur avons pas adressé notre questionnaire, d'abord pour ne donner que de l'inédit et ensuite pour ne pas les forcer à se répéter. Que nos lecteurs nous en excusent.

ABSENCES

The absence of the opinions of certain men will be noticed by our readers. Many outstanding literary figures answered our questionnaire either by modestly saying they considered their opinions could be of no importance, or sending us letters of which the contents of the following extract form a typical example:

« ...No I cant write an article about him for that number nor can I even answer the questionnaire because *ah for gods sake dont say that, no you dont mean it, oh its too much really, aw go on, pshaw, out on ye, fie, for shame, bologna, tripe, yaw kiddin me,* I never read a line of the gentleman. Am I supposed to hang my head under my arm, crawl on my face and vitals down a ten-mile track of ground glass rusted tacks torn tin cans and breadcrumbs, hang a crepe around my neck and a lot of other junk, or may I retain my smile, may I whisper occasionally, ah may I live? You went further than most other people. *You assume that Ive read france.* Others *ask* me. And when I honestly come out with it, they tie a look of blank disdain and shock on their mouths and shake their heads as who should say *My boy youll con.e to a bad end, a bad end.* To tell more truth, Ive made several attempts with the books that have the best reps and find that I simply cannot drag myself into them more than a page or two. I dont pretend that Im right; the fault may be in me. Furthermore theres a sonofabitch in this country I hate like poison and he just dotes on france and by jesus what he likes I hate, hate, *hate.* Have you ever felt that way about anybody? I admit its childish, but I cant do anything about it. It transcends passive contempt. Of course, Im intensely sorry that his stupid judgment coincides with yours, but no matter how he formed it, he has it, and it gets in my way... »

Others having lately written upon the subject elsewhere, we refrained from sending them our questions.

CONTRIBUTORS-COLLABORATEURS

Francis AMBRIÈRE, auteur d'une vie de Joachim du Bellay à paraître sous peu, a été un des premiers collaborateurs de *Tambour.*

Marcel BERGER est un écrivain français connu. Il a écrit: *L'amour sans l'amour,* etc...

Jean CASSOU est un romancier et critique qui est rapidement devenu une des grandes figures de notre jour.

Jean CATEL est l'auteur de trois volumes sur Walt Whitman à paraître chez Riéder.

Blaise CENDRARS, romancier et poète, a déjà collaboré à *Tambour.*

Maurice CONSTANTIN-WEYER a obtenu le Prix Goncourt 1928.

Maurice COURTOIS-SUFFIT, auteur de deux romans et un recueil de nouvelles, a collaboré au premier *Tambour.*

Léon DEFFOUX est un critique littéraire connu.

Joseph DELTEIL a obtenu le Prix Fémina 1925.

Fernand DIVOIRE est un critique et poète très distingué.

Theodore DREISER, is one of the leading American novelists.

Henri DUVERNOIS est bien connu pour ses romans et pièces de théâtre.

Fernand FERRÉ collabore à diverses revues, mais il ne livre pas volontiers ses œuvres au public.

WALDO FRANK is one of America's most distinguished novelists and critics.

ZONA GALE, widely known novelist and critic, has previously appeared in *Tambour*.

André GIDE est un des écrivains français les plus discutés de notre temps.

Stuart GILBERT, story-teller and authority on Joyce, appeared in *Tambour* I.

Louis GUILLOUX est l'auteur d'un excellent roman, *La Maison du Peuple*.

H. R. HAYS, known to our readers, is the author of a book of verse, *Strange City*.

Jacques HELLER a écrit un beau livre, *Nord*.

Guy HOLT is an American critic and publisher.

Constant DE HORION est un critique belge.

SIDNEY HUNT, English poet, artist, and critic, is familiar to our readers.

Joseph JOLINON est le lauréat du Prix de la Renaissance 1929.

Georges LINZE, poète et critique belge, a collaboré à *Tambour* III.

Victor LLONA, romancier, traducteur, critique, est un des plus forts traits-d'union franco-américains.

Marcel LOUMAYE, professeur, poète et romancier, est Belge.

Valentin DE MANOLL est un jeune poète connu de nos lecteurs.

André MAUROIS est l'auteur d'*Ariel* et d'autres grand succès littéraires.

H. L. MENCKEN is of course the editor of *The American Mercury*.

Paul MORAND est un romancier et poète fort connu.

François RIBADEAU-DUMAS est secrétaire de rédaction de *L'Européen*.

Edouard RODITI, bi-lingual writer, has already contributed to *Tambour*.

Samuel Rogers is a novelist,author of *The Sombre Flame* and *Less Than Kind.*

Jacques Roujon est l'auteur de *La Vie et les Opinions d'Anatole France.*

Bertrand Russell is one of England's leading sociologists and critics.

André Salmon est connu pour ses poèmes, ses romans et ses reportages.

G. Bernard Shaw is one of England's leading playwrights, to be sure.

Akos Tolnay est un jeune romancier hongrois de grand talent.

William Carlos Williams is a radical American critic and novelist.

Edmund Wilson is one of the editors of *The New Republic.*

Readers are requested to note that although the number of pages has not been increased, the smaller type used in this issue of *Tambour* affords a much greater amount of reading-matter.

Les lecteurs sont priés de remarquer que, bien que le nombre de pages ne soit pas accru, le caractère utilisé pour ce numéro de *Tambour* offre une quantité beaucoup plus grande de matières.

Le gerant : J. BRUNEL.

Montpellier. — Imprimerie Causse, Graille et Castelnau, 7, rue Dom-Vaissette.

ANTHOLOGIE

Revue Internationale

Abonnements : **3 belgas**

||||||||||||||||||||||||||||||||||||||||

RÉDACTION :

Georges LINZE

104, rue Xhovémont, LIEGE, Belgique

ADMINISTRATION :

Constant de Horion

288, rue Mandeville, LIEGE, Belgique

REPRÉSENTANT EN FRANCE :

P. FLOUQUET

64, Boulevard Verd Saint-Julien, Meudon PARIS

REPRÉSENTANT EN ITALIE :

Nenè CENTONZE

17, Viale Umbria, MILANO

November
1 9 2 9
Novembre

5

ANATOLE FRANCE

Revue Mensuelle

A monthly magazine

PRIX 6 Fr.

5

ANATOLE FRANCE

DANS CE NUMÉRO – IN THIS ISSUE

TAMBOUR

6

T A M B O U R

Directeur, Harold J. Salemson, Editor

5, Rue Berthollet, PARIS (V°) France

Of this issue, 250 copies are numbered.

De ce numéro, 250 exemplaires ont été numérotés.

Interpréter le passé, c'est exprimer le présent;
exprimer le présent, c'est créer l'avenir.

To interpret the past is to express the present;
to express the present is to create the future.

ESSENTIEL : 1930

(*Note:* Tel est le titre d'un manifeste que nous publierons dans notre prochain numéro. Le poème qui suit en est une sorte de préambule.)

Parenthèse.

Bris de vaisselle,
Bruit de lessive,
Ordures ménagères.
Coups.

Parenthèse.

Lumière, obscurité,
Forme, anti-forme?
Idée, pensée, formule,
Essentiel: 1930.

Un point.

Harold J. SALEMSON.

ESSENTIAL : 1930

(Note: This is the title of a manifesto we will publish in our next issue. The following poem is a sort of preamble to it.)

Parenthesis.
Smashing dishes,
Crash of washing,
Household garbage.
Blows.

Parenthesis.

Light, darkness,
Form, anti-form?
Idea, thought, expression,
Essential: 1930.

Period.

Harold J. SALEMSON.

ONAN [1]

OU L'AMOUR EST NÉ PARFAIT

C'est cette minute d'éveil qui m'a
donné la vision de la pureté.

Une Saison en Enfer.

Seulement, voici ce que j'ai trouvé,
c'est que Dieu a fait les hommes
droits, mais ils ont cherché beaucoup de détours.

Ecclésiaste.

Alors Juda dit à Onan: Va vers la
femme de ton frère, prends-la
comme beau-frère, et suscite une
postérité à ton frère. Onan sachant
que cette postérité ne serait pas
à lui, se souillait à terre lorsqu'il
allait vers la femme de son frère.
Ce qu'il faisait déplut à l'Eternel
qui le fit aussi mourir.

Genèse.

---

(1) Je ne voulais pas publier *Onan* parce que cette œuvre ne m'est
plus rien. Je l'avais commencée à Paris en 1926, je l'ai finie au Maroc
en 1927 et à ce moment j'avais raison devant moi-même. Et puis,
d'autres décors et d'autres personnages m'ont occupé, et de ce moment
j'ai rejeté tout ce pessimisme, pour préparer une venue... Maintenant
le lyrisme d'Onan m'est odieux, je préfère un autre lyrisme, aussi
je demande que l'on considère *Onan* comme l'œuvre d'un écrivain
mort. — M. J. A. (*Paris, 1930*).

I

1) *Un personnage extérieur au drame ou, mieux, un simple haut-parleur devant un rideau blanc.*
(Les paroles qui suivent sont dites avec emphase.)

Onan est seul!
Ecoutez la parole de ses âmes.

(Le décor est constitué par une portion de sphère blanche avec des paillettes de métal; comme fond, une toile d'un bleu froid et aveuglant. L'éclairage s'effectue par le haut, de sorte qu'il n'y a pas d'ombre.)

Onan I (purement explicateur: rôle de définition, de construction dans l'espace; il danse autour d'Onan II une danse circulaire et qui devient immense. Ce n'est pas un personnage — c'est une voix, un moule qui donnent leur forme aux deux Onans. Sa voix provient de partout et de nulle part, elle occupe toute la scène. Quant à Onan II, il reste immobile jusqu'à « Tu portes tes mains... » Alors, seulement, son geste le distingue du décor, en même temps qu'apparaît l'outre.)

Le ciel bleu est trop bas pour y élever ton regard
sans l'attrait d'une découverte.

Onan!

Tu es parmi tes brebis une outre
vide et bienheureuse.
Les autres hommes vivent, travaillent et peut-être
    souffrent, et tu es là
tel qu'autrement je ne te saurais concevoir,
avec la seule volupté du soleil

faisant danser des ronds derrière tes paupières closes.
Le chemin blanc n'est pas fait pour toi:
jamais tu ne seras voyageur

l'ombre factice des toits de pierre sèche t'offense et
t'oppresse.
Onan!
je te vois éternel sur le sol aveuglant.
Que dire de la fusion de ton âme stupéfiée,
dans le bourdonnement des insectes et de tes oreilles?
Tu n'es plus. As-tu jamais été?
La peine, devenue souffrance, de ta jambe
sous toi inconfortablement pliée,
te lie seule à ton troupeau.
Adolescent,
tes veilles diurnes sont muettes,
et la louange de Javeh inconnue à ton âme.
Tes yeux sont clairs et pleins de rêve,
mais tu ne rêves pas.
Ta bouche
n'a cependant pas le rafraîchissant sourire de l'idiot,
ni aucun pli douloureux.
Mais,
voici que ta quiétude n'est plus l'égale de ton rêve.
D'incertains désirs sourdent en toi que tu cherches à
glacer dans la lueur des étoiles. Un inexplicable
inconnu fait ta chair toute moite par moments,
et le souffle te manque.
Tu portes tes mains vers ta gorge,

et ton geste
se brise.
Tu hais
le soleil
et
tu attends le soir.

Onan II:

   J'ai soif.   (Geste vers l'outre.)

3) (Soir — le chemin vers le puits est visible, et la poussière est
   bleue.)

Onan II (il fredonne stupidement — pas de paroles — des sons
         faux et qui n'amènent ni plaisir ni douleur) :

   La la la la la la la la la, *etc...*

Onan I:

   La vaine tâche d'assembler le troupeau docile est
      accomplie,
   Et tu voudrais savoir des chansons
   pour contenter ton abattement.
   Les chiens hurlent mieux. (Onan se dresse vers le ciel et
                                    se tait.)
   Tu te tournes vers l'Eternel
   mais on n'apprend pas aux simples
   de paroles pour appeler l'Eternel,
   rien
   que son nom et sa demeure.

Onan II: (uniquement parce que c'est le soir, grégaire — nulle
passion, nulle attente: un éternuement — encore celui-ci
serait-il nécessaire et inéluctable):

Javeh!

Onan I:

Ce ne sont que deux syllabes — même pas un nom —
vides comme une ville morte;
comme si tu parlais soudain ta complainte creuse.
Ton âme prête pour adorer ne frissonne pas.

Onan II:

Javeh!

Onan I:

Ton cri demeure sans écho — tu ne sais même pas
prier,
toi qui soupçonnes la prière.
Tu te contenterais d'être, mais ces heures sont nouvelles, et tu te fuis —
depuis que l'eau du puits t'a montré ton visage.

Onan II:

Javeh! Ce mot qu'ils disent n'a rien derrière lui que
je voie;
mon père Juda chante des psaumes où il proclame
retremper sa force.
Javeh, l'Eternel!

Le ciel est froid et m'apaise
je veux...

4) *Onan II:*

> Tel qu'en ce temps où j'étais un petit enfant,
> tout nu dans la poussière, la nuit venait m'y faire voir
>   des choses,
> ma soif étant morte aux premières étoiles.

Onan I:

> Une femme passe —
> qui bouleverse le soir de son geste diurne,
> Tamar, épouse d'Er ton frère.

Onan II:

> Est-elle la réponse à mon appel muet?
> Mon corps est lourd
> et s'enfièvre.
> Mais c'est un délice quand mes yeux sont sur elle.

Onan I:

> Tu tends les mains...
> Dieu découvert?

Onan II:

> Vois femme!
> Mes paumes s'élèvent vers toi dans un geste accompli,
> et mes regards s'y reposent.
> Tu es loin,
> mais le soir est muet,
> et ma voix s'adoucit:
> il me semble que je chanterais.
> (complainte)

> Mes mains —

tu es sous mes yeux
ta forme blanche passe,
Mes Mains
moulent le vent. Tu es près de moi,
Mes Mains
dans l'air
l'air
sur mes mains.

Onan III (Faiblement entrevu, voix musicale et monocorde. Il
            est nu et beau selon l'idéal de chaque homme):

Bientôt
ton corps sera *seul* assez parfait pour te recevoir.
            (Mais il n'est encore qu'un état d'âme passager, et il
            n'est plus.)

Onan I:

Ton corps n'est plus veule,
des frissons le parcourent.
Tes mains sont des oiseaux
Tu découvres des anges
Tamar
Sera-ce un nom rival de Javeh
dans les chants de tes soirs.

Onan II: (complainte)

Mes Mains
et les souffles de la terre
mes mains
riches de présent
de futur

mes mains...   (infiniment)

Onan I:

La loi, Onan.
« Nul de vous n'approchera sa parente »
Tamar, épouse d'Er ton frère.
Tu as levé les yeux sur elle.
Crains le courroux du Dieu que tu n'as su trouver.

Onan II (le chant continue, irréel, peu importe: il y a sa voix
et son âme):

Elle repasse
lourde de l'outre fraîche.

Onan I:

Elle n'est pas la chair de ta chair,
l'esprit de ton esprit,
pour que tu lèves les yeux sur elle,
Tamar, épouse d'Er.

Onan II

(le chant continue, mais il vient d'autre part):

. . . .

5) *Onan II*

Mes mains tiennent ta forme prisonnière,
Tamar,
tu m'apaises
et je suis hors de moi

j'ai vu ses yeux sous ses paupières
et

j'ai tressailli dans leur miroir.
J'ai vu...

Onan I:

Voici que tu hais en toi-même
l'eau profonde des puits,
brouillée d'herbes.

Onan II:

Tes yeux
où j'ai vu ma beauté.

Onan I:

Tamar,
épouse d'Er!

Onan II:

Mon inquiétude est morte
et je tressaille
au murmure qui emplit mon oreille.

Me revoir en elle-même!

Onan I:

Tes nuits seront bruyantes
par le cortège de ton désir.

Onan II:

Javeh!

Onan I:

Ta voix s'épouvante!

L'eau du puits respectait ton calme.

Onan II:

Javeh!

6) *Onan I:*

Et ta nuit s'écoule,
à d'autres dans le futur pareille,
animée de réveils qui te font te dresser.
Onan,
ta beauté naît.

LE SOMMEIL D'ONAN:

(Musique — un sommeil inquiet et plein d'égarement,
constellé de mains infiniment célestes.)

II

1) *Onan III:*

J'ai trouvé tout délice en ma beauté.

Onan II:

Le monde est un désert vide,
trop imparfait maintenant pour me recevoir.

Onan III:

Le monde
est beau parce que tes yeux sont beaux,
nécessaire,

ondulant au rythme de ta main,
riche
en lueurs éblouissantes
à des moments où tu mourrais.

Onan II:

Joies!
O minute solitaire où je m'étreins,
Presqu'en des pleurs
je me résume,
délicieusement élues
et souffertes.

Onan III:

Seul dieu
que je me révèle
aux caresses que je me donne
religieusement.

Onan II:

Les mots sont morts
quand suffisent à me bercer
les sons.
Je suis un stylite impérissable.

Onan III:

La vie est
notre adoration.

2) *Onan I:*

La loi justifie tes désirs, Onan,

le vœu muet de ta chair,
la vie s'est ordonnée merveilleusement.

Onan II:

Un miroir seulement
et rien d.: plus!
Je ne cherchais que tes yeux
où voir ma beauté.
Ma chair
douloureuse s'exaspère,
mais ce m'est un délice.
Tamar
Tu te courbes sous mon désir pressenti,
ton attente m'enfièvre —
Tamar
JE ME SUIS VU DANS TES YEUX.

Onan I:

Susciter une postérité
à Er ton frère.

Onan III:

Chant des chères pensées d'Onan:

Des rêves,
des rêves,
j'avais formé,
pour les unir à la vie;
si beaux, qu'ils furent seuls.
Un jour,

je devins lumineux
au point de m'éblouir moi-même,
et je ne fus plus qu'allégresse.
Je me plongeais dans mon amour
comme en une eau très pure,
et toute volupté était en moi;
ruisselante d'amour,
que mon âme était belle!
Je chantais les courbes corps
et mes chastes baisers,
tel un enfant nu
joue dans le sable
constellé de merveilles —
mes yeux avaient des regards
lunaires où se baigner.
J'ai renoncé à tout
qui n'était pas moi-même
et la joie de moi-même.

Oh!

la brûlure délicieuse de mes regards,
ardent du désir de moi-même.
Je me suis bercé au son de mes paroles,
au chant de moi-même.
Mon amour et moi.
Tous mes gestes
je peux les dire
à m'enivrer.
Mes jambes gonflées d'ivresse

dans l'air qui les bat.

Toute ma vie
pour chanter
ma beauté perpétuelle,
sagement ivre d'être moi-même.

> (Apothéose d'Onan III: toute la
> mesure de son allégresse, et puis
> il ne peut plus être.)

Onan II:

Tes yeux,
ce sont seuls tes yeux.

Ma vie est imparfaite si tu ne la précises.

Je suis le spectateur de toutes mes minutes.

En toi je m'éblouis,
Soleil recréé,
en toi je lis plus
que tu ne saurais jamais dire.
C'est un lourd et merveilleux poème
Que celui de tes regards.

L'Eternité se ride
et un dieu qui est à mon image
s'y révèle.

Tout cet hymne qui s'éveille muettement,
les mots que je manque à trouver,
ils sont dans tes regards vides
que je peuple.

Je suis né,
ma solitude grandit,

je suis,
et le monde est en moi.

Onan I:

Pour toi
ses lèvres distilleront le miel.
Voici!
ta chair et ton corps se consommeront!

Pour toi
elle parfumera
de myrrhe, d'aloès et de cinnamone
sa couche où s'enivrer d'amour jusqu'au matin.

Onan II:

Tes yeux,

les eaux dérobées sont douces,
à ton regard semblables,
plein du mystère que j'y sais trouver.

Onan I:

La vie est telle.
Tu succombes au désir de l'autre.

Onan II (fatigue, amertume: il revient au pâtre grossier avec
      en plus la bouche pâteuse des lendemains de beuverie):

Je hais le désir reconnu chez elle
parce que j'y disparais.

Ses yeux n'ont plus que la couleur de caresses
que je récuse.

Subir —
ce sont ces minutes brutales
l'orgueil de beauté
meurt —

souffrance de l'absorption
qui me fait résorber.

En d'autres temps tes lèvres
auraient été joies contre mon corps —
et puis,
la honte d'avoir oublié mon corps,
dans la seule attente d'un écho
Et ma divinité.

Onan,

j'étais Onan;
me voici,
chair assouvie
qui pantèle.

Irrémédiable et j'ai perdu l'attente bienheureuse
et cette douleur de mes refus,
exquise.

Onan I:

Onan,
la vie est encore un jardin
où chantent

des oiseaux possibles,
où mûrissent
des fruits à cueillir peut-être,
et des parfums probables à respirer.
Rien n'est mort
pour être maintenant différent.
On naît,

Onan,

on oublie,
on renie
et l'on recommence.

Onan II:

Mon beau désir
il n'y a plus d'anémones
mon beau désir
la pluie c'est tout juste de l'eau
on inventera des mots nouveaux
pour mon désespoir
mon beau désir
qui me trahis.
Une image
pour mouvoir mes mains
qui me fait vomir.
Une image
je suis aveugle pour moi.
Ma solitude est une grande tour
avec des lézardes
et mon soleil est à nouveau le soleil.

Mon beau désir
que j'ai perdu.
Oh! moi!

glâneur de dégoûts,
dépassant mon désir,
j'ai bestial voulu
de ma dent le fruit avilir
révélant impuissant
l'inconnu de son amertume
à en mourir.

Onan I:

Ta chair honteuse n'a pas de miroir
et tu peux croire encore à ta beauté infaillible.

Onan III (faiblement):

Chercher où est Dieu!   (évanouissement)

Onan II:

à en mourir!

Javeh!

Onan I:

Ta prière est vide
et tu retourneras à l'eau du puits.

Onan II:

Javeh!

III

1) *Onan I:*

Le ciel bleu est trop bas pour y élever ton regard
sans l'attrait d'une découverte

Onan!

Tu es parmi tes brebis une outre
vide et bienheureuse.
Les autres hommes vivent, travaillent et peut-être souf-
frent, et tu es là
tel qu'autrement je ne te saurais concevoir,
avec la seule volupté du soleil
faisant danser des ronds derrière tes paupières closes.
Le chemin blanc n'est pas fait pour toi:
l'ombre factice des toits de pierre sèche t'offense et
t'oppresse.

Onan!

je te vois éternel sur le sol aveuglant.
Que dire de la fusion de ton âme stupéfiée,
dans le bourdonnement des insectes et de tes oreilles?
Tu n'es plus. As-tu jamais été?
La peine, devenue souffrance, de ta jambe
sous toi inconfortablement pliée,
te lie seule à ton troupeau.
Adolescent,
tes veilles diurnes sont muettes,
et la louange de Javeh inconnue à ton âme.

Tes yeux sont clairs et pleins de rêve,
mais tu ne rêves pas.
Ta bouche
n'a cependant pas le rafraîchissant sourire de l'idiot
   ni aucun pli douloureux —

Onan !

corps rôti par le soleil
dédié à l'abrutissement bienheureux.

2) *Silence devant le rideau blanc.*

Michel J. ARNAUD.

FROM THE CHINESE

A LONG CLIMB

In a sharp gale from the wide sky apes are whimpering,
Birds are flying homeward over the clear lake and
*   white sand,*
Leaves are dropping down like the spray of a waterfall,
While I watch the long river rolling on forever.
I have come three thousand miles away. Sad now with
*   autumn*
And with my hundred years of ills, I climb this heights
*   alone.*
Misfortune has laid a bitter frost upon my temples,
Heartache and weariness are a thick dust in my wine.

                                              TU FU.

THOUGHTS OF OLD TIME ON THE CH'U RIVER

A cold light shone on the gathering dew,
As sunset faded beyond the southern mountains;
Trees echoed with monkeys on the banks of Lake Tung
*   T'ing*
Where somebody was moving in an orchid-wood boat.
...Marsh-lands were swollen wide with the moon,
While torrents were bent to the mountains' will
And the vanished Queen of the Clouds left me
Sad with autumn all night long.   MA TAI.

TURKESTAN

Faithful to their vow that they would conquer the Hun,
On the desert, clad in sable and silk, five thousand of
*   them fell...*
But arisen from their crumbling bones on the banks of
*   [the river at the border,*
Dreams of them return, like men alive, into rooms
*   [where ladies lie sleeping.*

CH'EN T'AO.

GENERAL KÊ SHU

This constellation, lofty with its seven stars,
Is Kê Shu lifting his sword in the night:
And no more barbarians, nor their horses, nor cattle,
Dare cross the river boundary.

ONE AT THE WESTERN FRONT.

MEMORIES OF EARLY WINTER

South go the wild-geese, for leaves are now falling,
And the water is cold with a wind from the north.
I remember my home, but the Hsiang River's curves
Are walled by the clouds of this southern country.
I walk, I weep till my tears are spent.
I see a sail in the far sky.
Somebody tell me where the ferry is...
It's growing rough. It's growing dark.

Meng HAO-JAN.

A SPRING MORNING

I awake light-hearted this morning of spring,
Everywhere round me the singing of birds
But now I remember the night, the storm,
And I wonder how many flowers were stricken.

Meng HAO-JAN.

ON RETURNING AT THE YEAR'S END TO CHUNG-NAN MOUNTAIN

I petition no more at the north palace-gate.
...To this tumble-down hut on Chung-nan mountain
I am banished for my blunders, by a wise ruler.
I am sick all the time, I see none of my friends.
My white hairs hasten my decline,
Like pale beams ending the year.
...Therefore I lie awake and ponder
On the pine-shadowed moonlight in my empty window.

Meng HAO-JAN.

ON FINDING A RECLUSE ABSENT FROM HOME

When I questioned your pupil, under a pine-tree,
« My teacher », he answered, « went for herbs,
But toward which corner of the mountain,
How can I tell, through all these clouds? »

CHIA TAO.
Translated from the Chinese by
WITTER BYNNER and KIANG KANG-HU.

Jeanne MILLAS : Rue Froidevaux

LA NAISSANCE DE VÉNUS

A Jean DESBORDES.

Pour ce soir-là le monde était barré par une toile de fond représentant une marine froidement colorée par la lumière des étoiles qui dirigeaient leurs faisceaux blancs sur cette évocation.

Puis on entendit les notes sanglotantes, ironiques et désabusées d'un jazz hawaïen qui glapissait des charlestons de doute, cependant qu'aucune tête glabre ne se montrait.

Les lupanars demeuraient invisibles.

Tout à coup j'aperçus dans la mer artificielle du décor une femme qui, au rythme athlétique d'un crawl, nageait vers le rivage. Elle toucha terre et je vis qu'elle portait un maillot de soie blanche, sur lequel s'inscrivaient les initiales d'un club inconnu. Ses cheveux étaient dissimulés par un bonnet en caoutchouc.

Elle s'avança vers moi — sa démarche faisait gonfler sous sa peau des muscles puissants — ses jambes longues ne semblaient pas connaître la fatigue et ses seins étaient des coupes nouvelles inventées pour de troublants cocktails.

Sa gueule avait la personnalité d'une Marie Laurençin.

Elle me tendit la main, je voulus la baiser et déjà je sentais sur ses doigts un parfum pénétrant de Coty, lorsqu'elle arrêta mon geste d'un vigoureux shake-hand.

Elle parla d'abord en plusieurs langages que je ne comprenais pas, elle devait être polyglotte.

Elle regarda autour d'elle, et, apercevant très loin l'enseigne lumineuse des Folies Bergères, elle se présenta en français:

— Vénus; et vous?

— Moi, je suis *l'éternel masculin*.

Alors elle me proposa d'être ma compagne. Et c'est pourquoi nous arpentons tous deux le xxe siècle.

Fin

Valentin de Manoll.

POEMS

TO THELMA, DEDICATION OF A NEW NOVEL.

> You, you have given me this second summer
> When frost bit at the root;
> And still under the warm of you there ripens
> The unexpected fruit.
>
> Even as under your cherishing hands the flowers
> In the window of a room
> Lift bravely into the chill of a stern November
> New buds and second bloom.

Ludwig LEWISOHN.

HYMN

SO EARLY IN LIFE
IVE NEVER SEEN ANYTHING LIKE IT
BIRDS MAY STILL KEEP THEIR NESTS IN THE TIPS OF THE
[WIND
FRAIL FOLK IN THE SLUMS MAY CONTINUE POURING GLUE
[IN GRUEL
BUT THE WILDERNESS REMAINS LIKE AN APPLE UNTOUCHED
[TO ME

FORESTS MAY TURN GREY
CHEEKS MAY BECOME DISCONSOLATE
STUPID FOLK MAY COUNT THEIR BEADS IN CHURCHES
DISCOMFITURE REMAINS A BAUBLE TO ME AS OF OLD

OBELISKS MAY WHIRL POINTEDLY INTO TORNADOES
GREY DAWNS OF SODOM ON THE PLAIN MAY DISSEMINATE

PYRAMIDS OF BAROQUE INANITIES MAY CLODDISHLY LIE
THE WIND STAYS A RED POOL OF MOTION HERE

WHEN SPIDERS FIND MY BURIED HOPE
PRAY GODS THEY MAY NOT DIVULGE ITS SECRET
PRAY GODS THEY WILL RELINQUISH IT
AND NOT CAST IT UP INTO BEIGE SANDS TOO SUBTLY FOR
                                              [HUMAN EAR

OH SPOTS OF GREEN IDOLATRY
OH BROKEN PANES OF GLASS
INTO BRAZEN URNS THEY POURED THE LAUGH
AND INTO MINE THE WIND CAME UP

                                        Paul Frederic BOWLES.

AMERICA

    The ribbed glass chambers where we live
    Our voluntary crystal shells
    Who is there here to complain?
    The white light of our flimsy prison
    Where we all lie languidly on taupe matting
    Hearing the scraping of dry fronds at the screen
    Where no insect flies nor scaly serpent moves
    The satin coverlets on our beds
    The rows of bottles with brittle stoppers
    Our windows with tiny panes
    Who is there to rebel?

                                        Paul Frederic BOWLES.

SUMMER DAYS ...

        Summer days are a garden
        full of glory

and idle joy:
hours of thought perch
meditatively
like doves
in porcelain
calm and unhurried.
There is no place for you...

Vera FANCOTT.

SHAFTING SUNLIGHT ...

Shafting sunlight rapierlike through
flowering casements.
Lighting on black coats
cast on brass bedsteads
like seaweed on a ridge of rock;
and drowsy heads laid on relentless pillows;
light taps and shy doors
half opening, temptuous buds...

Vera FANCOTT.

QUERY

you love me then
                    in cups
                            alone at night

or
    with other bodies
                        playing
                                counterpoint
    is it fair

                    to dare
                              to care:
                    to tell me
          :: caring ::
                         that you care

          i do not care: you care: who cares

          slobber no more before me
          such cheap litany:
          ask the response

          look ::
                    see
                         my eyes

          are you so blind

          not i ::
                    no :: not i ::
                              not i
                                   shall word

          what you
                    yourself
                         should say

                                        Richard JOHNS.

MEXICAN DANCING : 5O YRS. BACK

     Indians and Spaniards in a melting pot
     of blood wombed from the course of time.
     Mexicans after a pattern of mountains,

the grief of skyline within their body
crystallized in dactyllics.
No other nation for each so separate occasion
a poem.
At a Mexican dance one night,
a wall-flower because I composed
no Spanish runes
asking these splendid dress and satin
configurations, for the favor of waltzing.

Norman MACLEOD.

CHELSEA EMBANKMENT

Like hard knife-blades
the seagulls' wings
carve air.
      Their cries
are sharp.
      The wind
bites.
The housetops
cut the cold sky.

A. S. J. TESSIMOND.

A FLIGHT OF STAIRS

Stairs fly as straight as hawks;
or else in spirals, curve out of curve, pausing
at a ledge to poise their wings before relaunching.
Stairs sway at the height of their flight

like a melody in Tristan;
or swoop to the ground with glad spread of their feathers
before they close them.

They curiously investigate
the shells of buildings,
a hollow core,
shell in a shell.

Useless to produce their path to infinity
or turn it to a moral symbol,
for their flight is ambiguous upwards or downwards as you
please,

their fountain is frozen,
their concertina is silent.

A. S. J. TESSIMOND.

MAZURKA

> In a flurry of silk
> frothed in white lace
> she goes sedate
> with the fan
> reproving
> inviting.
>
> The blush becomes her
> (practised so long
> before the tall mirror
> after she had curled her hair).

Play
    delicately
        hands grazing the keys
a Chopin mazurka.

A. S. J. TESSIMOND.

COLLOQUY

Funny little schoolhouse
  Topping the hill,
What have you done
  For good or ill?

I have taught the farmer's boy
  How to read and write.
I sheltered melody and joy
  On a winter's night.

I started many marriages
  In the month of May.
I smiled upon some raw recruits
  Before they marched away.

Scribbler asking questions,
  What are you worth?
Just a hapless song or two,
  And a little earth.

Joseph UPPER.

DAISY FIELD BY MOONLIGHT

Silver fingers of a dead queen
Touch yellow-ripe, white-robed hearts

Where a new generation of virgins
Waits like an expectant victim
For the high priest of seduction
To begin the disappointing sacrifice.

Joseph UPPER.

D'UN PAUVRE CORPS

Ciel! elle a été battue. Qui donc a osé? Mais son corps est marbré comme un ciel peint tout fait qui nous vient d'Amérique aux premiers froids! Qui donc? Mais celui pour qui son corps est le ciel de tous les jours. Rien ne peut la changer. C'est toujours elle, avec son ciel fait comme un lit de tous les jours. Elle a froid, ses mains se ternissent dès qu'elle aperçoit seulement des pierres bleues, mais l'aquilon est fait pour chasser le nuage. Et lui, il est loin encore de la chasser. Il la repousse pour mieux l'attirer à soi. Un bel apache! Bien qu'elle se déhanche trop déjà pour être une statue de marbre. Nul ne l'adore hors moi, qui sors, en hiver, sans chapeau. Aux premiers froids, les plus beaux, les plus dansants, se calfeutrent chez eux. C'est à croire que la rue aux pierres plus bleues, aux pavés plus gris, restera déserte pendant de longs mois.

Que m'importe! En toutes saisons, je suis enrhumé; mon corps frissonne doucement comme un étang d'automne pas encore glacé; ma figure se creuse de petites rides, mais c'est quand je ris.

Tout cela s'arrangera en hiver à la terrasse d'un café de Paris. Il y aura des braseros ou pyrogènes.

Sept. 1929.

HENRY-FAGNE.

THE CORNCRIB

Every individual lives at a certain tempo and that of David Cossum was exceedingly slow. He thought slowly, every idea taking a good while to penetrate and every decision being mulled over in a hesitating way. He worked slowly and methodically, generally evolving out a system or ritual for every task and following it with the devoutness of a monk. He even ate slowly, shovelling in his food in large placid mouthfuls.

It was perhaps the only remarkable thing about him, for he was a quiet colorless man, one of those remnants of English colonial stock, degenerate, forgetful of tradition, almost sunk to peasant level.

A small dairy farmer is his own master and speed amounts to little as long as he works faithfully and asks for little return, but with the advent of Jessie, a new rhythm was introduced into the well organized andante of David's life. He had never thought of it that way when, after his father's death, he began to look about for a wife. She was pretty and a good teacher. He liked the disciplined way she ruled her schoolroom and the neat freshness of her person. He needed a woman in more ways than one and she had no desire to teach school the rest of her life; but when the stiff formalities of the little country wedding were over, and his large wrists were free once more from the restriction of white cuffs and she was established in his home, he began to realize what he had done.

She had cast one glance over the bachelor disorder of the house, had put on her apron and said smiling happily,

« Now David things are going to be different ». Her school mistress mind desired first of all order, everything must be in a certain place, the washbasin on the bench outside, his boots behind the stove, the milkpails hung on their private nails like neat rows of figures to be added or divided. For five years she had been scolding, cajoling, and stimulating her pupils to pass from grade to grade till she was wrapped up in the idea of advancement and progress, and David's ways worried her from the first. He had no particular ambition. He was satisfied if things went on without too much difficulty and he had a certain inarticulate liking for his fields and his stock. It was enough if they and he were well fed and comfortable.

So she began to nag. All the energies of her restless executive nature were devoted to speeding him up, forcing him to make decisions. She refused to let him be slovenly, she tried to break up his wasteful rituals and he opposed her with a leaden obstinacy. The tempos of their lives conflicted yet neither could overcome the other and so they dragged along in a halting rhythm now faster now slower. David it is true became somewhat inured to her constant prodding, although sometimes a dull resentment and annoyance rose within him all the more bitter because unexpressed.

The two children came and she renewed her efforts. She nagged him into building a new barn, into buying pure

bred stock, into adding to his farm where he could. She
read agricultural bulletins and prodded him into trying new
rations, and keeping records. He felt no gratitude for all
this. Rather his resentment stored up within him and at
times he would have liked to brush her aside like a
persistent mosquito with its irritating and continual hum.

There was one thing however in which she had never
been successful.

The old corncrib was a ramshackle affair, slatted to let
in air on the damp new grain, and raised a foot or two
from the ground by four posts which theoretically prevented
the entrance of rats. Actually they took their toll every
year, and the white litter of dust in the empty bins was
always mixed with the little yellow crescents of the grains
from which the fastidious animals had bitten the succulent
heart, the embryo plant. Patiently and futilely David
nailed tin over their numerous holes. Each year they
gnawed new ones and every crevice was scarred by the
hieroglyphics of their sharp rodent teeth.

The corncrib became almost a symbol of everything in
David against which Jessie struggled. The yearly waste
although it was not very large, maddened her. She figured
it out over and over again. She showed the results to
David; she argued and scolded.

« Two pairs of shoes for the children we could have
bought with the grain the creatures eat », she would say.
« And you let it go to waste. I've figured it out. You cut
a few logs and take them down to the mill and for about
fifty dollars get enough lumber for a new crib, counting the

shingles. You could build it in spare time and raise it on iron pipes. I saw plans for one like that in the farm paper. Why don't you do it this year David? With the children going to High School we need all we can get. »

He grew more and more obstinately set. He wasn't going to be bothered. The old crib was good enough. Unconsciously for him too it had become a symbol, a symbol of his easy-going life before he married her and submitted himself to her eternal nagging. The corncrib became a matter of continual bickering between them. Although they did not really quarrel, they irritated each other continually. There was not much to distract them and to provide an even balance in their lives. He was up at five to help the man with the milking and when the last slow-moving black and white ruminant had filed out into the pasture he swung the heavy collars on the team and drove them out to the potato patch. Their heavy feet thumped dully on the hard turf, the trace chains clanked, their legs moved in a ponderous rhythm. Somewhere in the orchard an oriole whistled a little questioning sequence, and one of Jessie's much prized roosters flapped his wings and crowed. David was not listening to the bird, he was thinking that his team looked well. He liked his horses and there seemed to be a sort of kinship between them. They were large patient and strong like himself and they moved in a slow heavy tempo — his tempo.

Jessie would be getting the children off to school, finding their books, scolding them, insisting on washed hands at the last minute, giving the youngest a quick decisive kiss.

Then the chickens must be fed, a mash for the growing broilers.   They were sturdy, well feathered.   Two little cocks erected their ruffs and attacked each other, bounding and striking with unspurred feet in mimic warfare.

On the way to look for a stolen nest she passed the corncrib. It was getting worse and worse. Why it looked ready to fall down. It made her feel angry and helpless. David should have more regard for his children than to waste money like that.   It was a disgrace.   Her firm mouth tightened.   She'd make him get rid of that tumbledown thing if it was the last thing she ever did.   Strange how he was so stubborn after all these years. Sometimes she almost wished she hadn't given up school-teaching.   It was hard work raising children, keeping up the house, energizing David.   Still she had accomplished a good deal. The boys were in High School, Henry was clever, he might even want to go further with his education.   All the more reason not to waste money.   That corncrib!

She bustled about a thousand tasks.   The milk pails and strainers to be washed and scalded till they gleamed thru a mist of steam. She hung them up neatly.   Then she swept with short angry strokes as if she had a personal animosity against dust.   When the house was in order she sat down to peel potatoes for dinner.   In her hands the knife flashed briskly and the naked white balls stripped of their earthy jackets dropped into the kettle of water with quick splashes.

At noon David returned plodding behind the team with the bent-kneed shuffle of the field laborer, his shoulders a little stooped. He looped up the reins, fed the team and went to the well for a drink. Slowly he rinsed the dipper, refilled it and drank, pausing a moment between each swallow. His arms were burnt a dark brown as was his face and around the edge of his hair was a lighter streak of skin showing a recent haircut. His faded blue overalls were bagged at the knees and his shapeless shoes ran over their soles. He slumped into his seat at the kitchen-table hungrily.

« David please wash your hands ». For years she had said this and for years he had slouched unwilling to the basin outside. It was typical of her that she never abbreviated his name to Dave. She hovered about setting food on the table.

The years had dried her, David thought.

Her hair was getting thinner and sometimes hung in wisps about her cheeks. Her mouth had always been firm but the little creases at the corners had deepened. No matter what she had been doing her apron was clean.

She sat down at last and ate hastily not bothering to taste her food. She was too much occupied with what she intended to say to David. He as usual was eating in large mouthfuls, pausing and laying down his fork while he chewed. It never failed to irritate her vaguely.

« David », she said, « I've talked enough about that corncrib. You can see for yourself that it won't last much longer. I read in the farm paper today about an all steel crib you could get for two hundred and fifty dollars. You could pay for it in a few years with the grain that's wasted the way it is. »

He began to be annoyed at once. Only a few days ago he had said positively he wasn't going to do anything about it, and she was beginning again.

« I said I ain't going to do nothing and I ain't ». He reached for more potatoes. Let her nag. He was used to it. It was almost a pleasure to balk her on this point.

« It's a shame to waste money this way. Henry needs a new overcoat. As far as I can see you'd let the children go ragged. You don't seem to care. Why won't you do as I ask you? »

She had stopped eating altogether and was fussing nervously with her fork.

David seemed to ingore her. He chewed in silence. This woman who hectored him, he thought, how strange it seemed that he had once desired her intensely. But long since the physical bond had died out between them. She was a gadfly, a continual urge to do things that did not interest him, always prying him out of his easy-going comfort. The wisps of hair were hanging about her face again. She looked flushed and worn.

His silence maddened her. She had a queer illogical notion that a certain wrinkle of flesh at the back of a rather thick neck was the seat of his obstinacy. At least it always seemed more noticeable when he was heavily defiant.

« If I'd known what a slow shiftless man you were, I'd never have married you, David Cossum », she burst out angrily. « You haven't any more ambition than a nigger. If I didn't push and push and slave and scrape I'd like to know where you'd have been. You're enough to drive a woman crazy! »

She had said it all many a time before but for some reason he was less patient than usual. It was as if the suppressed resentment stored up within him were beginning to exceed bounds. The continued whine of the mosquito was more and more galling.

« You be quiet », he enunciated thickly, a dull red suffusing his face.

« Don't speak to me like that », she cried shrilly. « I'll say whatever I have a mind to. »

« I said, be quiet. Shut your mouth. » The unaccustomed loudness of his voice shocked her into silence. He finished his pie and pushed his plate away resentfully and stumped slowly and heavily out. He heard her footsteps cross the floor, quick sharp, angrily tapping. « I'll have my way », they seemed to say. His own plodding footfalls answered « No-no-no ».

A tension was building itself up between them, a queer unnatural tension. He was beginning to be sick of it, he reflected. She never let him alone. It was enough to drive a man mad. As he passed the corncrib, he spat, deliberately, determinedly.

Jessie's nerves were like overstretched violin strings. She spent the afternoon hoeing the garden, striking viciously at plantains and sorrel. She killed beetles with malicious energy. She determined that David must not bully her in

this. The new barn, the stock, the silo, point after point
she had gained by consistent nagging, fretting and wearing
away his passive resistance. The corncrib was bare of
paint, shingles had fallen from the roof; there was even a
board or two loose from the siding. It was only to spite
her that he refused to put up a new one. Another plantain
fell a victim to her angry chopping hoe, which rose and
fell in a nervous rhythm. Out in the lot David tramped
unceasingly up and down the rows after the team, slowly
and steadily. The peaceful monotony of the work was
soothing but for once he was not soothed. His mood was
strangely unquiet. Twenty years of farm-work had
hardened his muscles, roughened his hands and bent his
shoulders and now suddenly he was tired of it all.

Grasshoppers impinged against the leaves of the potato
plants in a little pattering rain. The dry earth poured
from the culitvator teeth in miniature landslides. From
endless depths of blue sky a hot sun poured down relent-
lessly. From the cross of his suspenders a dark line of
sweat gradually widened on his blue shirt. The salt taste
of perspiration was on his lips. Back and forth he tramped,
swinging the cultivator about at the end of each row.

Forces seemed to be at work within him, strange seething
forces. It would be pleasant to strip and plunge into cool
deep water, shedding his farm, his identity, himself. Plunge
and swim for a blessed eternity of freedom. Farm-work
was hard enough without being ceaselessly driven on to
attempt more and more projects. He leaned on the cultivator handles to rest, muttering gloomily to himself.

As the sun sank imperceptibly lower and the shadows of
the fence rails lengthened the patch was finished.   He
unhitched the team, hooked up the traces and once more
plodded back to the house behind them.   Once more he
passed the corncrib.

He looked at it and the muscle that ran over the edge of
his square jaw bulged.

Once more he drank slowly at the well.   Then he chopped
an armful of kindling, leaned the axe against the doors
while he dumped it into the woodbox.

He was heavily silent at supper.   When Henry punched
his brother slyly and the younger boy whined, he told him
savagely to shut his mouth.

Jessie eyed him determinedly.   She was not going to be
beaten.   The tension between them seemed to grow.

« If you've got over being mad maybe you're ready to
talk about the corncrib », she said finally.

« I ain't and I ain't goin' to be. »   His voice boomed
out so suddenly that the children were startled.

It only aggravated her. « David Cossum », she began,
« you ought to be ashamed. »

He had risen suddenly. « Will you shut your mouth?
Another word and I'll... », he did not finish.

« I'll say what I please », she shrilled.

Something seemed to snap in his head.   His eyes glared
inhumanly; his face was twitching.   His eyes rested upon
the axe leaning against the doorway.   In another moment
he had seized it in a sudden, unwontedly swift movement.

Jessie shrieked as did the children. When he advanced toward her in a strange savage way, she eluded him and ran out of the doorway.

After her he pounded, panting, gasping, his eyes murderous.   It seemed a ghastly undignified parody of a child's game of tag. The terrified woman shrieking with fright, the man silent and relentless as a beast of prey. Halfway round the house he stopped suddenly. He looked at the axe in a dazed sort of way and allowed it to fall from his hands.

An expression of horror spread itself over his face. Then he turned and began to run, stumbling, uncertainly, toward the dark woods behind which the round red sun was just slipping out of sight.

H. R. HAYS.

NOTE SUR DES RABACHAGES A PROPOS DE LA RÉVOLUTION

On conçoit facilement la Révolution comme un rapport concret, matériel, de l'homme et des hommes avec un état de choses donné. Cette Révolution se justifie, s'explique, prend toute sa force en présence du concret, elle colle à l'événement et ne vit que par lui.

On conçoit aussi l'idée révolutionnaire ou, je dirai mieux, l'esprit révolutionnaire. Il naît de la nécessité, de l'imminence et de la possibilité de la Révolution. Il prend donc, lui aussi, toute sa force dans le concret. Il peut, sans doute, acquérir une certaine autonomie et vivre par lui-même chez des êtres qui, à un moment donné, se trouvent voués à la Révolution. Mais il n'existe, pourtant, que parce que la Révolution est là, possible, imminente, nécessaire.

Il y aurait enfin (selon une phraséologie souvent employée maintenant), « l'idée de révolution », ou encore, « la Révolution permanente ». Si je comprends bien, ce serait une position de l'esprit, en dehors de toute justification ou de toute exigence du concret : une attitude de l'esprit, rien d'autre. Je vois mal comment cette attitude de l'esprit se distingue de la position anarchisante ou même de certaines positions mystiques, de celles qui, par exemple, font trouver à certains racistes allemands « un gage d'éternel salut dans la guerre ». Cette position de l'esprit ne s'inquiète ni des classes, ni des conditions humaines, ni de l'ensemble des faits qui pèsent sur les hommes et, pour moi, elle n'a, avec la Révolution qu'un rapport verbal et qu'une incidence momentanée.

Je dirai donc, pour conclure et pour rendre tout clair, que la Révolution est pour moi tout autre chose : un rapport de l'esprit et du concret, un jugement de l'esprit sur les faits et sur les événements, la naissance d'une volonté justifiée et qui, en rapport avec les choses, se sent nécessaire.

Ni les ouvriers, ni les paysans ne me paraissent devoir devenir révolutionnaires par d'autres démarches que par celles-là. Si un intellectualisme ou, pour mieux dire, un rationalisme sévère et scrupuleux peuvent amener des hommes qui ne sont ni des ouvriers ni des paysans à concevoir la Révolution, comme cet acte grave, exigé par les choses, et non pas comme une aventure ou une exigence gratuite de l'esprit, il faut en conclure que la référence au concret, le souci constant de ne pas faire fi des choses de tous les jours,— le pain qu'on mange, la famille qu'il faut quitter pour des combats que votre vie ne justifie pas, le labeur trop dur pour que l'esprit et le cœur y restent libres, — est peut-être ce qui donne aux hommes l'unité la plus profonde et la plus réelle.   André CHAMSON.

TERPSICHORE ON THE NEVSKY PROSPECT

Piotr, directs the teacher, play a slow walk, and piotr searches his ragged folios for a chopin nocturne. It is played intelligently and with fine spirit, but with somewhat too much feeling for the occasion, andante sostenuto, sombre in the sullen colours of a moonless night. You can almost see the pompous cadaver heavily in its formaldehyded coffin. You are impressed; you are moved. It is your feelings that are tampered with as piotr reads his personal sadness into the necklace of notes strung out before him. He is interpreting, you know. The chorus of sound he produces is a parabasis in pure subjective lamentation, a romantic view wherein there is no external reality but that you cannot splash it with all the intrinsic slop you own. Piotr is russian, with his deep causeless universality pervading the pores of the world, shuttling his essence to the core of the atom, behaving like an electron.

Piotr has gone greek. That is why he is here, to awaken the greek dead with romantic noise. Piotr is a moujik at heart.

Andante, that serves the purpose; inappropriate to the style of dance, of course. *That* would be greek; or greek in intention; or greek freely intermingled with cream of tartar, cossack flash and colour, shaggy screaming ponies, glaring short swords and the usual sweeping lip-hair like black water furled under a keen prow, clay under a ploughshare; or greek in full motion and yelling itself hoarse.

She might have chosen bach or any other in a not too remote classic mode, but nominates an incurable byronizer as accompaniment to classic movement, motion that is not motion. Chopin, as near the spirit of greece as glinka or moussorgsky, worlds in between. But admitting an error, as of requiring a hornpipe to albeniz or a gavotte to god save the king, admitting a primary wrong, what then. Your preceptress out of soudeikine or is it bakst would seem not to concern herself with the anachronism, but to wish merely to give a selected group of young women a barefooted grace they have never known before, to revitalize an interest in the beauties of their form, an interest which that or any other music must demand, even chopin on a dithering boston piano. Her point is simple, just to surprise a grace supposed to be inherent in every animal.

She fails of achieving her point for the same reason she fails in her selection of accompaniment. You cannot find a greek rhythm in chopin; you cannot read it in.

No more can there be a dance that you do not see. Your subjective treatment of music, while it has more than one argument to support it, proves a mediocre dodge for dance. You can see only the dancer. That is why I say that dance essentially fails, requiring as it does the rude interposition of a fat slug between music and appreciation. In dance there is inescapably too much person, too much saddle between the rider and the horse. If you concede a restricted sense of the term, you may shut your eyes to sound, but not to *motion*. At chamber music, it is customary, often infinitely desirable, not to stare at the little bald beetles scratching their black and golden brown jackets, sawing themselves in two, embarrassing contortions. Or when your soloist unmistakably evinces the pain wrought in his tender soul by the music that he plays, rocks precariously in a horrible emotional agony, juggles his eyeballs and shoots his cuffs in a dizzy drunken orgasm, call it a violent solo, you may nullify your own discomfort by closing your eyes to the annoying vision *without denying the music*. But you must *see* a dance to possess it, and when you see a herring-fed interpreting, forcing her paltry soul into movement before you, as a sensible man you experience a sudden overwhelming disgust that can never be surmounted, become aware that souls have dimensions, some puny, some great. From then on you are but wasting your time. When from the scarcely obscuring folds of her orgiastic regalia comes a flaccid burst of obscene fat, you cast about for a cuspidor, you want to get your hat and coat, you even have leisure in which to think of asking for a refund of your money.

But it is the teacher's idea that everyone *being an animal, you know* has a certain animal grace. Her clever and rare figure for that would be, *as graceful as a panther.* Her careful observations at the zoological gardens do not deceive her. No one denies a panther its grace, but the simile is not allowable in relation to man. You may confidently suppose that the teacher would never say, *with the grace of a man,* or, *as graceful as a woman.*

The teacher is trying to relocate the grace. She is an integral part of the new movement among the tenants of carnegie's olympus, among the bats in carnegie's belfry, a movement to stalk insensibly back over the accretions of time and relive the greek, to implant it in themselves after so many years of petrouschka and borscht. At least petrouschka has a limited appeal. Greece is a multi-fingered prong bounded on the north by fourteenth street, the proletcos cooperative cafeteria restaurant, oh yes, by the workers bookshop now, where gorki and london rub dust-jackets on the significantly empty shelves, but he told me they'd soon fill the caverns, yes, wo'n't be long before we're full, the new republic?, fifteen cents, please. Union square. It is confidently greece to an ill-concealed balalaikan lilt, but greece none the less, and greece sub union square jams the angled corridors of upper carnegie to seek out the middlemen who are eager to cull a bumper crop from this neo-muscovitic whirlwind assailing its putative pedal erudition. Lizaveta's bacchic yowl spirals the air like a projectile and you run headlong for the notion stores that stink like massachusetts cotton mills, lint-filled air choked with the stench of cheap dry-goods sprayed with machine oil, all the stuff exudes it, heavy barrel grease, stores packed with burlap-skinned women clamouring for thus much nile-green gauze and a yard or two of washline please to catch it up in attractive folds.

Then you're almost ready. Black hair damp with self-dew, you pin it behind your ears, you forget the fried herring you had for breakfast and await the slow walk the teacher orders, piotr and his chopin nocturne how pretty andante sostenuto.

Bodies, very eager and conscious bodies, stretching out in love, also in melting strawberry and retching pistache, move gapingly across a shadow-turning floor. With them, the reek of sweat drying cakingly with aged dust on the soles of flat feet, swollen, ridged with redoubts like a battlefield, smeared with bright splotches of rouge on coldly distressing heels, feet with giant tossing nails, yellowed, cracked and sharply splayed out. Then up the crutches to the flatiron bulge of the calf *say brightly, it is the cloven hoof, the clean and the unclean.* Up, but roughly as over a dangerous way, to the bulbous knee, flanked by welts and lumps. For beauty's sake, don't stop. The thigh, long triangular tendons rearing out of drooping flesh from kneecap to crotchcrease, all of it is ugly. Ten bodies disturbing fetid moisture, every window slammed to, no air save the old and smelldry; nothing new, fresh, but fresh pleural fiilth sifting through pendulous gasping lips, gasps, wet stale gasps, remember the herring now, gasps and grunts. I forgot to say that an artist is here, the kind who wears a wide black wilted bow-tie and a big rusted black velour. He is graphing your discernible souls with a fountainpen on wrapping paper. Your souls are out. Beauty is in the eye of the beholder, that's the gist of it, is it not?

A schumann skip, piotr, she waves as they cavort sweatily, stickily, by. Like sacks of stuff kicked about, they skip. They tremble the floor. The merry farmer, please, piotr. Spontaneous combustion. One wonders why the sweatdust doesn't explode; they'll flow the walls out. On attic hills in the great, great long ago. Take them away; their soles are tough enough. Sell them for something, glue, leather, who cares what, but away, that's all. Idiotic girlish laughter floats across the room as they misperform a simple variation, dirty, dirty, they attempt the dieaway and flop like lumps of hillside when the smoke clears away. They plump leadly, thickly, fully, with grace just outside the door, just outside, too bad. Hair now whirling in self-created cyclones, riding the wind they doubtless think, souls about to take flight. Especially that simpering fake, the one who said she loved *simply loved* to dance, who asked me here to observe proof of her limitless devotion. Unbearably affected, she dances logically, deliberately, carefully with her head. A fake walk, badly disguised as a writhing supple glide, my tight-tendoned one. Canting your head like a snake, your hair sleeked blackly back like its smooth scales, with a viscous disgusting glaze it flows coldly back in a deep black tide, you booby-bird with your scrawny throat aslant. There's agony in your eyes. You have nothing and you so much beg for favour. Music is noise, admit it. You must take something to it, a brain or a soul, and what have *you?* For the one a bone-incrusted whorl of greyish phlegm; for the other a loud protestation.

Say, give me my hat. Julian L. Shapiro.

AMOUR DU RAYON
Courte tragédie en cinq actes

(*Note.* — Nous avons extrait et sommes heureux de publier ce fragment
de la pièce inédite *Amour du rayon*. Il est le seul qui, malgré les coupures,
supporterait d'être figé par l'imprimerie sans nous faire encourir le courroux de la censure. — H. J. S.).

ACTE V

Intérieur d'un réveille-matin. S'y trouvent le
Subconscient de la Lectrice, les Muscles du Sportif,
et le Visage du Politique.

Lectrice: Arriverai-je à arrêter le réveil avant qu'il
ne sonne?

(Le réveil sonne. Les Muscles se contractent,
le Visage baille).

Sportif: Oh! confort d'une position insolite, vieille
habitude morte...

Politique: Tristesse de la source tarie.

L: Je crois avoir été contrariée.

P: Il n'en est rien.

S: Simple habitude à prendre. Pourquoi toujours
penser à ce qui aurait pu être; ce n'est pas là le secret
du bonheur. Dites-moi, Lectrice, pourquoi n'ai-je pas
de subconscient?

P : Pardon, il neige du subconscient.

L : En tout cas, ça n'est pas moi.

S : Fleurs mauves du présent, grandes azalées virginales...

P : Serres chaudes des amants empressés et des chemises empesées ! O ! serres chaudes !

L : Beaux diamants des faux-cols glacés.

P : Merci du compliment.

S : Mais c'est à moi qu'il était destiné et s'il me plaît de le considérer comme une injure, croyez bien que je n'en ferai rien.

L : Je me condense autour d'un noyau. Un fait positif a eu lieu. La maison où nous sommes a sonné. Il n'était pas absurde à un certain moment de supposer...

S : Continuez, je vous prie...

L : ...que cela ne pouvait arriver. Or, maintenant cette hypothèse est tout à fait exclue. Le temps est un menteur.

P : Oui, le temps ment et ses mensonges nous rongent le fond de l'âme. Leur alluvion est le contenu de nos journées vides. Oh ! temps perdu ! temps perdu !

S : Je vous demande pardon mais la porte cochère vient de s'ouvrir. Il serait temps de profiter du prin-

temps. Fleurs mauves du présent, grandes azalées virginales. L'air est étouffant à l'intérieur, le chant des
oiseaux révolutionne la Nature. Ne ferait-il pas beau?
Il est moins absurde de le supposer que cela n'en a
l'air.

L: Le temps aurait-il quelque influence sur vous?

S: Les mélancoliques prairies pleines de vaches et
d'enfants furent toujours pour moi un précieux auxiliaire. Elles me faisaient comprendre les mécanismes
subtils de l'intérieur de notre réveil. Mais la gravitation est venue tout gâter.

P: C'est le chant de la gravitation, c'est le chant du
printemps revenu, c'est le temps du plain-chant du
matin!

L: Je suis d'avis d'envoyer tous les champs paître.
Il vaut mieux parler d'un gradient de gravitation, et
du petit déjeûner du matin. Quant aux rouages de ce
réveil, je ne saurais assez les remercier de tourner à la
vitesse dont vous vous rendez compte et qui m'empêche,
moi nébuleuse, de me dissoudre aux alentours de cette
colossale montre verticale.

P: Vertébrale, mademoiselle.

S: Verticale et vertébrale. Je suis d'ailleurs d'avis
que les noms désuets des 4 points cardinaux devraient

être remplacés par les initiales grecques des héros morts au champ d'honneur, alpha, gamma, béta, delta, je les vois ainsi. N'êtes-vous pas de mon avis, Politique?

L: Il me semble que quelque chose se contracte par ici.

S: C'est moi.

L: Vous comprenez la plaisanterie.

S: Il est vraiment peu charitable de votre part de me mettre ainsi dans une situation ridicule aux yeux du P.

P: N'ayez crainte, cher ami, ceci n'aurait pu vous rendre plus ridicule à mes yeux.

L: Au lieu de vous chamailler ainsi, Monsieur le P, vous feriez mieux de faire attention à ce que vos yeux ne tombent pas par votre cou. En voilà un d'ailleurs qui git lamentablement par terre, aplati et réflétant le dernier paysage aperçu au moment de passer outre.

S: Sotte légende!

L: Vous confondez sans doute avec le rayon vert.

S: Je me comprends, je sais très bien ce que je veux dire.

P: Poème!

(Son oreille gauche ramasse son œil et le remet en place).

L : Vous retardez, cher. Quand avez-vous connu Picabia? Il m'a été présenté par une ammonite que j'ai trouvée dans ma salade. Les temps ont bien changé.

> (Nouvelle sonnerie du réveil. Le Visage du **P** descend lentement et disparait).

S : Une petite explication sentimentale? J'ai toujours prisé d'être à couvert pour ce genre de sport.

L : Je fonds d'amour.

Voix du V du P : Allons, les enfants, ne vous excitez pas.

L : Heureusement qu'il ne peut plus que roter.

> (A ce moment P rote. Et de la fumée monte à l'emplacement de son Visage), etc...

Thomas Yung ZERDLIK.

A FAIRYTALE

Sunday, no pecuniary duties, no petty commercialism, no diplomacy to get the best of the next one, and I diverge from materialism to sentimentality. By force of inspiration I decide to go out to look for the enjoyment of somebody's company or to give somebody a chance to enjoy mine, upon which I have often been complimented.

The weather is delightful, the atmosphere bewitching, and without realizing it, I walk far, far away, and there comes the fairytale. I behold a scene which is beyond description: under a large tree, rich with branches and leaves, sits a charming maiden with half closed eyes and with a book in her lap, — seems lost in her enticing dreams. Her exquisite figure and her spirited face, a rare combination, enchant me and I am magnetized. Neither thought of withdrawing nor strength to do so, but I come nearer and nearer, and my approaching awakens the Fairy. She opens her eyes — what eyes — she looks, she stares, and for a moment we look into each other's eyes without words.......... I found myself and say: « I greet you, my dear lady, and implore you to forgive my intrusion ». Her genuine purple lips move, exhibiting the most marvelous mouth and teeth, and compassionately say: « Welcome sir, be seated, sir ». Our ensuing conversation and actions are neither to be described nor divulged...

Apostles assure us there is a god, and some even are certain there are three gods. As long as god there is, there must be heaven for the simple reason that god could be nowhere else; he cannot be photographed, he cannot get a passport, without a passport he could not get visas, he has neither old nor new money and could not travel without. Besides, to my knowledge, god was never interviewed by reporters, and this makes it axiomatic that god is in heaven, the entrance of which is strictly prohibited to reporters.

Thus, contrary to all philosophy, we must accept that heaven there is. It goes without saying that the intimacy of my newly acquired young beauty elevated me to a position in heaven, and there we landed. Whether heaven's surface is measured by yards, lots, acres or miles I am not aware of, but Apostles are certain god is all over there, and naturally the first we met was god himself. He gave us a hearty welcome and I was delighted with the reception, in particular with the informality; no questions as to whether we carry booze or smuggle diamonds, passport, visas, marriage license,

nor to our guilt of the Allen Law. God, who knows
everything, not only suspected, but knew of our intimacy and seemed to approve a fact which is natural
law and harms no one. So far so good. Then god addressed us as follows: « The hospitality of heaven is at your
disposal but the one thing I do not tolerate is idleness,
and you must contribute by efficient work; nature gives
you everything free, and you have to give something in
return. » In perfect harmony with god's ruling, I
applied for assignment, and I was appointed as god's
recorder of prayers — who and how anybody prayed.
A radio instrument was handed to me and I listened:
Prayers — various languages and intonations — then
I heard: « I, your servant, John the horsethief, come
to beg of you, dear god, to help me ». I could stand it
no longer, and appealed to god. « Even as a god, the
personification of tolerance, how can you endure the
prayer of a horsethief, the lowest creature in mankind
to implore you to help him steal horses, and to get
away with it? » God smilingly looked me over and said:
« I see now I was mistaken in assuming that you, young
man, are above the ordinary human being; you and all
others of flesh and blood are limited in idealism; you
condemn the guilty without mercy; you punish many
who are not guilty at all; you spread sorrow and grief

to the innocent dependents of the convicted; and you even go so far as to take life which should be inviolable. I, god, know as well as you do that John is a horsethief; I even know that John aspires for help with the hope that after accumulating what you call wealth, he will change his profligacy to an honorable life, and he might do so and might not; I not only tolerate his prayers, but encourage him; the only shining candle in the miserable life of John, the horsethief, is called HOPE, and I, god, the arbiter, have not the heart to deprive John of that glimmer. »   Leon LAIT.

NOTES

(Harold J. SALEMSON)

___

BOOKS

To begin the new year correctly, it might be a good thing to say a few words about the last books we read before the old year's end, and clear away some of those that an anticipated New Year's resolution made us read despite our having neglected them when they first appeared.

Among the novels that the end of 1929 brought us, several are of a really high caliber. *Low Run Tide and Lava Rock* (two novels in one volume) (Liveright) by Elliot Paul, for instance, is a thoroughly interesting book. The author's power for story-telling remains as great as it was when he wrote *Indelible*. And that means something. Why, then, is this new book less *complete* than his previous ones? I take it that his period with *transition* has had an effect upon him and, although his new novels are no more radical than the others, I believe his vanguard affinities are playing a rôle, in his makeup, which is not yet clear. And, if I read this book with interest, I am certainly awaiting his next with impatience.

A thoroughly *modern* novel, on the other hand, is *The Eater of Darkness* (Macaulay) by Robert Coates. The author, also a contributor to *transition,* has written one of the most interesting works that advanced contemporary literature has produced. This debauch of writing merely for the sake of writing (and laughing) this headless-tailless parody of a detective-story, is the most merry, the most skillful, and the most fascinating thing we have read in a long time. And next to it must be put two volumes from Macaulay's excellent *Transatlantic Library: Last Nights of Paris* by Philippe Scupault (translated by William Carlos Williams) and *The Black Venus* by André Salmon (translated by Slater Brown). Both of these books are among the significative works of modern French literature, and both translations delightfully readable.

Another book that comes to America from abroad is *The God Who Didn't Laugh* (Payson and Clarke) by Gleb Botkin, a young Russian refugee who writes directly in English. Had his birth not placed his among the Czar's intimates, this young man should probably have been in quite a different Russian camp than he is today. He writes well, and his satire, his exposures of the corruption among the ascetic monks of the Orthodox Church lead us to believe we are in the presence of an intelligent person. His book is one to be read for enjoyment, education and complete satisfaction. Not so good is *Brother Anselmo* by Dorothy Glaser, brought out by the same publishers in the special *Two Rivers* collection opened by a volume of Gertrude Stein. Miss Glaser's book is about monks too, but the four insipid tales it contains are powerless pastiches of Anatole France or even Thornton Wilder.

For strength, one might look into either of the three following books: *River House* (Scribners) by Stark Young, *Red Ending* (Liveright) by Harry Hervey, or *Passion Is The Wind* (John Day) by Bridget Dryden.

Stark Young's book is of the same type as his preceding novels, and in its homely simplicity it attains to real heights. One is struck by the introduction, in this volume, of the outside world into the Southern family-life the author had heretofore portrayed. His novel gains through this innovation and we are before a poignant drama, masterfully handled, that definitely consecrates an important figure in American fiction.

As for Harry Harvey (a young archeologist, we are told), he works entirely in depth and plays upon the psychological mannerisms of his characters. His book tells the tragedy of a woman engrossed in her love for one of her sons, and of her other son who dies because of the coldness around him. Dominy! Dominy! The name of the preferred brother rings symbolically! *Red Ending* is a powerful study which promises that its author may some day write a great book (this one falls down only by its melodramatic end which is a sort of compromise with the commercial demand).

Bridget Dryden, too, has great power; so great, in fact, one is astounded that a woman should possess it. Her novel is centered about the life of a great department-store and all the characters live their intimate drama in the shadow of this overpowering force. For sheer narrative and for capturing the inner psychology and reactions of her characters and her main personage — the store — Bridget Dryden is to be highly lauded. Moreover, her book is so perfect a blend of true literary value and the finer points of the wide-appeal category that it is hard to imagine how she achieved it: most likely she did it unconsciously, and that is perhaps another point in her favor.

A great American novelist and thinker, Ludwig Lewisohn, has made his first appearance in French with *Vérité et Poésie* (Truth and Poetry), a selection of his finest passages translated by Régis Michaud and Franck L. Schoell. In this excellent choice from his many works the French public will have an introduction to those of his books which are about the appear in complete translation. And Paris will not be long in recognizing the profound values which intelligent Americans have been admiring for years.

Among the poems that have appeared lately, we have found nothing to dissuade us from thinking that since the death of the 1912-1920 (?) Renaissance no great luminaries are brightening the American poetical firmament. Ralph Cheever Dunning dates from before the free-verse bloom and is outside it, men like Harry Alan Potamkin and a few others have not published any volumes as yet, and a Norman Macleod is a solitary figure. Still there are some excellent lines in *Strange City* (Four Seas), a slim volume (!) by H. R. Hays. The talent is still young, but is promising, although perhaps more in matter than in manner, and for his matter H. R. Hays has an excellent prose medium at hand. This does not go to say his volume is not interesting, but I see more in his future as a prosateur than as a poet.

R. Ellsworth Larsson in *O City Cities* (Payson and Clarke) has some passages, too, that are exquisite poetry, but his form is so modern that he must be careful. When one fails to achieve perfection in modernistic verse, the effort is infinitely more of a flop than when a cut-and-dried classical form is used. Larsson has written a fine suite of poems, except for very occasional flaws, and he seems to have a spark of real poetry in him.

Not so Le Roy Mac Leod, whose *Driven* has been published by Covici, Friede. Someone has compared his poetry to that of Hardy, and though he does not quite deserve this derogatory judgment, his book is fairly flat. Neither form nor matter are attractive and it is hard to take an interest in these poems. The only poem in which Mac Leod attains to real feeling, *Sequoia*, is drowned in the remainder of the book.

George O'Neil, author of *God-beguiled* (Liveright), is the only poet we have read lately — among new poets of course, for there are always those one rereads — who seems really to have something in him consistently. Every poem in his book vibrates with a very certain poetical value and, although no one piece stands out, the ensemble is of the very highest caliber. From this regular altitude, I am awaiting the rare occasion upon which George O'Neil will soar just a little higher; he writes good verse now, then he will be a great poet.

And to finish this list and have a clear slate for the first publications of 1930 in our next issue, we will note two good volumes published by Horace Liveright. The first, *A Night Among The Horses* by Djuna Barnes, is an enlarged re-edition of her first collection of short stories, *A Book*. The stories, in themselves for the greatest part very interesting offer as a whole a synthesis of a very curious psychology. Miss Barnes, a wellknown figure of Bohemian life, seems to react energetically against this and proclaim the utter failure of it. Almost everyone of her stories is of a morbid character and most show the dire results of high and Bohemian life. Thus stated, this sounds puerile, but the book has its importance.

The other volume is *They Still Sing of Love,* a collection of musical criticisms, essays and fantasies, by Sigmund Spaeth. As a straight critic of music and particularly upon the subject of the importance of jazz, Spaeth holds a distinct place not to be denied. But when he tries general artistic theories (as, for instance, in the essay *The Artist and His Public*), he contradicts himself and is somewhat weak. Still, this book has high spots.

To terminate: The masterpiece of 1929 was probably *Colline* by Jean Giono, awarded the Brentano Prize. Jacques Le Clercq's translation should be good — we have not seen it — though is was a nearly impossible task. The English title is *The Hill of Destiny*. Read it.)

Les Livres

Eussions-nous donné un Prix Tambour, ce ne serait ni Georges Bernanos (qui n'a nullement mérité son Prix Fémina), ni Marcel Arland (valait-il bien le Prix Goncourt?), ni Marcel Aymé (qui lui, cependant, a été justement récompensé par le jury du Prix Théophraste-Renaudot) qui l'aurait eu, mais Jean Giono, dont *Un de Baumugnes* (Grasset) vient remarquablement succéder à son premier livre, *Colline*. Dans son nouveau roman, notre collaborateur garde ce sens profond de la Nature, de sa toute-puissance, qui avait prêté à *Colline* un charme si étrange et qui en avait fait un livre si captivant. Aujourd'hui, Giono traite un drame beaucoup plus humain. Les hommes n'y sont pas complètement écrasés par la grandeur du Monde,

mais les sentiments tellement idéaux que dépeint Giono, l'amour,
l'amitié, la vertu poussés jusqu'à un tel point deviennent eux-mêmes
des forces naturelles et ne sont plus des caractéristiques d'hommes. Il
est impossible de dire l'attrait hallucinant, l'attachement inévitable
qu'on sent pour l'œuvre de Jean Giono.

Autre livre qui fait suite à un précédent: *Les Confessions de Dan
Yack* (Sans Pareil) de notre collaborateur Blaise Cendrars. Voilà la fin
du *Plan de l'Aiguille*, et je crois que ces deux volumes forment le
chef-d'œuvre de l'auteur. Le second a quelques mièvreries, dans « Les
Cahiers de Mireille », mais l'ensemble est un des plus beaux romans
de notre temps. Analyse, psychologie, aventure, et enfin, vie, y sont
si savamment entremêlées que de classer cette nouvelle œuvre de
Cendrars dans aucune catégorie serait une erreur certaine. Cendrars
est très personnel, et je me méfie de ceux qui expliquent leur sentiment envers son œuvre: on l'aime ou on ne l'aime pas, mais sans raison
raisonnante.

Quant à *L'Heure d'allumer les lampes* (Renaissance du Livre), par
Léo Gaubert, je le trouve être un roman adroit et même passionnant,
mais j'en suis mauvais juge, car la question dont il traite — le conflit
de la Science et de la Religion — me semble pour ma part résolue
d'avance. Cependant, ce volume apporte quelques idées nouvelles au
dossier du problème et la lecture en est captivante. M. Léo Gaubert
est un excellent romancier de grand avenir.

Dans un roman paru voici bien des mois, mais que nous venons
de lire, M. Jacques Chardonne a traité une sombre histoire à la
Mauriac. En deux mots, *Les Varais* (Grasset) est un livre de Mauriac
en moins bon. Ce qui laisse tout de même à Jacques Chardonne
un rude talent.

Du côté amour, deux romans: *Amour nuptial* (N. R. F.) de Jacques
de Lacretelle est le récit de la vie conjugale de l'auteur de *Silbermann.*
Ceci gêne un peu, car on s'imagine que l'auteur se raconte, mais
comme roman, ce volume se place très haut. Ecrite dans le style
sobre, mais nuancé de l'auteur, l'histoire est ici aussi placide que
dans ses autres livres. Il est inhérent à Jacques de Lacretelle, quels
que soient l'état de surexcitation de ses personnages ou la vitesse de
l'action, d'écrire toujours à la même allure, pacifique et nullement

pressée. Cela vous donne une impression de connaître votre auteur qui ne peut que faire plaisir. Mais alors que Jacques de Lacretelle écrit d'un amour tout légitime, Mme Marguerite Grépon, dans *Poursuites* (Ferenczi), traite l'amour extra-conjugal, et elle étudie cette question négligée quoique fort importante, le droit d'une femme laide à l'amour. Son livre est adroit et révèle développées les qualités que nous remarquions déjà dans *La Voyageuse nue*. Cependant, ce n'est pas encore le *grand livre* que nous lui demandions déjà l'année passée. Il ne nous reste qu'à attendre. Attendre aussi pour voir ce que nous donnera, à l'avenir, Jacques de Lacretelle. Tout ce qu'il a fait jusqu'ici a encore été l'œuvre du jeune homme qui écrivit ce chef-d'œuvre *Silbermann*. Mais bientôt, son esprit devra nécessairement prendre un tournant nouveau et il sera curieux de l'épier.

Comme poésie, nous avons les premiers volumes de trois nouvelles collections. D'abord, aux Editions des Revues, *Poèmes révolutionnaires* d'Alexandre Pouchkine, traduits de main de maître par Valentin Parnac, nous révèlent l'œuvre poétique trop ignorée hors de Russie d'un des grands génies de la littérature mondiale. A la fois Victor Hugo et Byron, Pouchkine a aussi su être Voltaire, et pour avoir joint Racine et Dostoïevsky dans une œuvre comme *Eugène Onéguine* nul ne lui niera une place immense en littérature. Malheureusement, cette collection n'est pas aussi bien présentée qu'elle le pourrait être.

Le premier livre de la maison Fourcade est plus beau, s'il est moins important. Sous une couverture neuve et charmante, nous avons ainsi pu lire *Mes propriétés* de Henry Michaux. Ces proses et ces poèmes atteignent, me semble-t-il, à l'imitation la plus parfaite que nous ayons du langage de la folie. Ces courtes histoires fantastiques, mais pleines de détails incongrus, sont d'exactes reproductions de manuscrits d'aliénés. Qu'importe si ce fut ou non le but de l'auteur! Ces pages qui ne manqueront pas d'agacer bien des lecteurs sont soutenues par une verve et un lyrisme qui dévoilent un vrai poète. Peut-être n'utilise-t-il pas au mieux ses dons? C'est une autre affaire.

De Belgique nous viennent les deux premiers volumes de la collection « L'Ecrou », *Pont* de Georges Linze et *Poèmes de Guerre* de Marcel Loumaye (Anthologie, Liége), poèmes en édition très restreinte. Cette collection se compose de reproductions de manuscrits reliés avec un

boulon. La forme est originale; la poésie de Loumaye, un choix de ses
livres précédents, est excellente; celle de Linze est, me semble-t-il, de la
grande poésie. Un George Linze, en français, un Norman Macleod en
anglais, voilà les jeunes poètes qui ont recréé la simplicité chinoise de
Tou-Fou. Dénués de « poésie », leurs poèmes atteignent la vraie
grandeur, car leur lyrisme ne réside ni dans la forme ni dans l'image
acceptée. Ils *sont*. Et c'est pour cela qu'ils sont poètes.

Restent quelques documents: le *Shakespeare* de Maurice Constantin-
Weyer (Riéder) nous montre le plus grand artisan qu'ait jamais eu
la littérature, sous un aspect qui est sans doute son jour véritable.
Monsieur Constantin-Weyer qui *sait* lui-même remarquablement
écrire nous apporte une courageuse étude sur l'homme qui, mieux que
quiconque, *savait* écrire. Le *Manifeste du surréalisme* d'André Breton,
qu'ont réédité les Editions Kra, nous semble un peu amusant après
ces cinq années, mais dans les poèmes de *Poisson soluble*, il y a de
belles pages. De belles pages aussi dans les chroniques littéraires que
réunit en volume M. Emile Dantinne, *Les Idées et les Livres d'aujour-
d'hui* (La Gazette de Huy, Belgique). Les pages sur Valéry sont fortes
et justes, et le conte qui termine le volume est excellent. André
Thérive a eu raison de louer la critique qui se fait en Belgique.

Enfin, quelques traductions intéressantes: des contes d'animaux
curieux, *Voisins mystérieux* (Stock) de C. G. D. Roberts (traduit par
J. Delamain), deux livres de W. H. Hudson, remarquablement traduits
par Victor Llona et sur lesquels nous reviendrons, *Un Flâneur en Pa-
tagonie* (Stock) et *Vertes demeures* (Plon); et *Vérité et Poésie* dans la
collection des « Ecrivains et penseurs américains », pages choisies de
Ludwig Lewisohn, traduites par Franck L. Schoell et Régis Michaud.
Cette bonne traduction présente pour la première fois au public
français une des figures les plus importantes de la littérature américaine d'aujourd'hui. On ne saurait exagérer la valeur de Lewisohn,
critique, romancier, homme d'idées. Ses œuvres dépassent le cadre
d'une littérature et sont d'importance internationale. On ne tardera
pas à le reconnaître en France.

Et voilà qui nous laisse le champ libre pour attendre les dévelop-
pements de 1930.

Cinéma -Théâtre

Aujourd'hui que le cinéma parlant est venu pour rester, qu'on en soit adversaire ou partisan, on ressent un attachement curieux au cinéma muet. Pour cette raison, le Gala Méliès, qui a eu lieu à la Salle Pleyel le lundi 16 décembre 1929 n'aurait pu tomber plus à propos. Cette soirée, organisée par la direction de l'excellente salle Studio 28, nous a permis de faire ou de refaire connaissance avec les films fantastiques faits par Georges Méliès, inventeur du spectacle cinématographique, entre le début du siècle et 1912. Nous y avons reconnu bien des éléments qui sont devenus plus tard les ressorts constants du cinéma, surtout du cinéma comique. Et nous aurons toujours plaisir de voir ces films ainsi que *Forfaiture,* le premier film dramatique, qui a clôturé la séance.

A ce propos, on se doit de louer l'initiative de la Salle des Agriculteurs, où Mlle Myrga et M. Tallier, déjà directeurs du Studio des Ursulines, ont installé un cinéma de répertoire. On peut aimer ou ne pas aimer les films qu'on y donne, mais ce cinéma de répertoire nous permet actuellement et, espérons-le, nous permettra toujours, de revoir les vieux films de valeur. Le répertoire se compose aujourd'hui surtout de films d'il y a quelques années, *Club 73* (*Dressed to kill*), *Moana, Les Nuits de Chicago* (*Underworld*), *Nanouk,* etc..., mais lorsque le choix se sera un peu plus étendu sur toute la production cinématographique, les Agriculteurs seront le type de ces cinémas que toutes les grandes villes devront avoir et qui permettront désormais aux bons films de n'être plus relégués à l'oubli après leur période de nouveauté.

Mais le cinéma parlant pose aussi la question du théâtre. D'aucuns croient que celui-là avalera celui-ci, mais parmi les nouvelles pièces que nous offre la scène parisienne, il y en a au moins une qui pronostique encore de beaux soirs pour le théâtre en chair et en os. Elle nous apporte une preuve définitive du grand talent d'Henri Jeanson. Car cette pièce, *Amis comme avant* au Théâtre Antoine, ne laissera indifférent aucun spectateur. L'auteur y a campé un drame si simple, si émouvant que les acteurs et les spectateurs en sont entraînés à oublier le monde et à ne vivre que les moments des personnages. Cependant, ceci est si sobrement fait qu'à aucun moment la pièce ne touche au mélodrame, et c'est une belle victoire pour l'auteur, pour les jeunes, pour la littérature, et enfin, pour le *théâtre.*

AWARDS-PRIX

The Witter Bynner Undergraduate Poetry Prize for 1929 has been divided between Elder James Olson (whose remarkable poem *Two In a City* appeared in our first issue), Miriam Cosland and Dorothe Bendon. The judges were our contributor Witter Bynner (the donor) and Eunice Tietjens.

Among the stories listed by Edward J. O'Brien as The Best Short Storie of 1929 appear, marked by the three stars of exceptional merit, *The Count* by Samuel Rogers (*Tambour*, n° 2) and *A Necessary Dismissal* by H. R. Hays (*Tambour*, n° 3). *The Whispering Pagoda* by Stuart Gilbert (*Tambour*, n° 1) was also listed.

Le prix des Muses, décerné cette année pour la première fois, est venu très justement récompenser l'œuvre de notre ami André Chamson. On se rappelle que nous avons écrit: *Chamson est la figure la plus importante qui soit apparue en France depuis Marcel Proust.*

Revues

Parmi les pages les plus intéressantes que nous aient apportées les revues ces temps derniers, il convient de citer celles extraites de *Vent du Printemps,* la prochaine œuvre de Jean Giono, publiées par *Europe.* L'excellente revue *Bifur* a donné aussi des choses remarquables, particulièrement un conte de Jean Giono, des pages de Cendrars, un article de Philippe Soupault, et de bonnes traductions de l'américain: *Des Collines comme des éléphants blancs* par Ernest Hemingway, *La Lune des Antilles* par Eugène O'Neill, et des lettres de William Carlos Williams et Jean Toomer.

Signalons encore les premiers numéros de *Notre Plume,* organe de l'Académie de l'Art des Jeunes, qui se défend, mais dont le directeur a malheureusement cru devoir reproduire sans le signaler des poèmes déjà parus ailleurs; ceux de *Bravo,* l'excellent hebdomadaire du théâtre qui a pris d'emblée une place importante et qui s'améliore constamment; enfin, ceux de *La Revue du Cinéma* qui paraît transformé, aux Editions de la N. R. F., qui contiennent d'excellentes choses: un numéro consacré à Georges Méliès, le scénario du célèbre film *Un Chien andalou,* et des articles où Jean-George Auriol et ses fidèles collaborateurs, particulièrement J. Bernard Brunius et Michel J. Arnaud, continuent à s'éloigner de la littérature pour « parler cinéma », ce qui est excellent.

Magazines

To be noticed:

The first two issues of *This Quarter* edited by E. W. Titus, which group the outstanding names of contemporary letters;

Close Up, which continues as the most important review of the cinema published in English, with an excellent article in each issue by H. A. Potamkin;

The Morada, the first issue of which promises us a particularly good new magazine of advanced letters;

Blues, transformed, appearing quarterly, with some fine contributors;

Poetry, which remains the leading American magazine of verse, just where it should be between the modernists and the reactionaries.

Musique

Bien qu'on ne puisse parler dans *Tambour* de toutes les manifestations musicales intéressantes, il en est qui commandent quelques mots. Tel, le concert qui a regroupé les Six (Honegger, Milhaud, Poulenc, Auric, Durey, et Germaine Tailleferre), après dix années d'efforts individuels. D'un point de vue documentaire, cette soirée marque dans l'histoire de la musique et bien que comme compositeurs les Six soient de valeurs inégales, le spectacle de Honegger à la tête d'un orchestre ou de Poulenc au piano est quelque chose qu'on n'oublie pas. Par surcroît, le parrain du groupe, Jean Cocteau, a prononcé quelques paroles assez étonnantes sur l'art de demain. Ce ne fut pas le moment le moins intéressant de la réunion.

Montpellier. — Imprimerie Causse, Graille et Castelnau, 7, rue Dom-Vaissette.

Le gerant : J. BRUNEL.

BRAVO
tous les spectacles

◇◇◇◇◇◇◇◇◇◇◇◇◇

Jacques THÉRY

d i r e c t e u r |||||||||||||||||

◇◇◇◇◇◇◇◇◇◇◇◇◇

La Vie
est un spectacle

**LE SPECTACLE DE LA SCÈNE
LE SPECTACLE DE L'ECRAN
LE SPECTACLE LITTÉRAIRE**

tous à travers les textes des meilleurs écrivains
de notre temps et de l'illustration actuelle :
le Document Photographique

Tous les Vendredis
1 fr. 50

SPECIMEN GRATUIT SUR DEMANDE

PARIS, 5, Place Clichy (17me)

February
1 9 3 0
Février

6

....

Revue Mensuelle

A monthly magazine

PRIX 6 Fr.

6

DANS CE NUMÉRO — IN THIS ISSUE

MICHEL J. ARNAUD, admirable poète, est aujourd'hui un des principaux espoirs du cinéma français.

PAUL FREDERIC BOWLES is even younger than the editor of *Tambour*.

WITTER BYNNER is one of America's outstanding poets.

ANDRÉ CHAMSON est l'auteur de *Roux le bandit, Les Hommes de la route, Le Crime des justes,* etc...

HENRY-FAGNE est un poète belge de 23 ans. Il a deux volumes qui paraitront sous peu.

VERA FANCOTT, 21-year-old English poetess, here appears in print for the first time.

H. R. HAYS it a frequent contributor to *Tambour*.

RICHARD JOHNS edits *Pagany*.

KIANG KANG-HU is a distinguished Chinese scholar.

LEON LAIT writes us: Even sophism originates thinking, and that result is worth while.

LUDWIG LEWISHON wrote *Up Stream*...

NORMAN MACLEOD edits *The Morada*.

VALENTIN DE MANOLL a déjà collaboré à *Tambour*.

JEANNE MILLAS a collaboré à *Tambour III*.

JULIAN L. SHAPIRO, of the bar, bars no innovation.

A. S. J. TESSIMOND is one of the most interesting of the younger English poets.

JOSEPH UPPER has contributed verse to a number of leading American magazines.

THOMAS YUNG ZERDLIK est un jeune écrivain et photographe arménien. Il écrit directement en français.

TAMBOUR

7

TAMBOUR

Directeur, Harold J. Salemson, Editor

■■■ 5, Rue Berthollet, PARIS (Vᵉ) France) ■■■

Of this issue, 250 copies are numbered.

62

De ce numéro, 250 exemplaires ont été numérotés.

Interpréter le passé, c'est exprimer le présent;
exprimer le présent, c'est créer l'avenir.

To interpret the past is to express the present;
to express the present is to create the future.

ESSENTIEL : 1930

(MANIFESTE)

...chercher notre nouvelle direction
sur un autre chemin. Ce chemin sera
la Révolution de l'Idée, le nouveau
point de vue, une attitude entièrement
rénovée, purement idéologique, qui
pourra être juxtaposée à la Révolution
du Verbe et à la Révolution du Geste,
mais qui sera indépendante de toutes
les deux. (H. J. S.)

Dans l'histoire des arts, le seul divorce d'avec le **genre** classique fut le romantisme. Tout modernisme **n'a été** qu'une variation sur le thème romantique: à savoir, pour le classique, l'œuvre seule existait; pour le romantique, seul existait l'artiste; pour les modernes, quelle que **soit** leur tendance, l'art n'est qu'une projection de la personnalité de l'artiste dans le monde qui l'entoure, ou, si l'on veut, une interprétation du monde extérieur par **rapport à** l'artiste. En ceci, le modernisme n'a été qu'un **romantisme** qui se distinguait par sa forme.

Première conclusion: Le modernisme n'a été qu'une variation de forme.

Or, les mouvements les plus nouveaux du modernisme ont mis à notre disposition toute la gamme des **anti-**formes. Les modernes, prétendant se désintéresser de la forme, ne se sont occupés que d'elle, et ils ont atteint un classicisme de l'anti-forme. Celui-ci est autant à éviter **que** celui de la forme. Si l'on n'a rien à dire, que **peut-on** attendre des formes nouvelles?

Deuxième conclusion: Le modernisme, recherche de forme, est épuisé.

Par conséquent, il est une nouvelle voie à **chercher.**

Cette voie doit ignorer la forme, puisque toutes **formes** et anti-formes sont à sa disposition. Elles attendent qu'on les utilise.

> (Mais une poésie adéquate
> revient au monde
> et comme un rire (aha!)
> comme un rire
> juge déjà les événements. — Georges Linze.)

Ces formes n'ont plus droit qu'à une considération secondaire.

(On avait oublié qu'on avait une peau, pour ne penser qu'à ses vêtements. — Ralph Cheever Dunning, en conversation.)

La première place doit être donnée au fond.

(L'art n'est pas un paradoxe, l'art n'est pas un jeu d'esprit, ni une mode plus ou moins spirituelle, ni une pose... C'est un phénomène aussi complexe que la vie... — Blaise Cendrars.)

Mais le mélange de la forme et du fond doit être savant.

(En ceci comme en toutes choses humaines un équilibre est nécessaire. — Bertrand Russell.)

Troisième conclusion: Aux formes que le modernisme a données, il faut attacher un fond.

Pour arriver à ceci, il est nécessaire de nous débarrasser de certaines choses, et d'en embrasser certaines autres.

Il faut supprimer non pas le poncif démodé, mais celui qui n'exprime plus notre temps. Car l'essentiel est d'arriver à exprimer la force, la beauté, le dynamisme, et les autres ressources, actuels, sans pour cela créer de nouvelles phrases passe-partout telles que la « mythologie contemporaine » ou le « fabuleux mystère de notre temps ».

(Amour, science, ambition, religion, beauté, mon effort prisonnier n'est que l'essai d'un élan vers le ciel, une rechute en terre. — René Glotz.)

Il faut renier à la fois classicisme et romantisme, et pour ce faire prendre un nouveau point de vue.

(Est classique qui a oublié les classiques. — Sidney Hunt.)

Quatrième conclusion: Pour trouver le fond nouveau, il faut une nouvelle attitude, un nouveau point de vue.

Pour tout dire, nous ne voulons plus de l'œuvre seule des classiques, ni de l'artiste seul des romantiques. Quant à la moderne projection de la personnalité de l'artiste dans le monde extérieur, nous y susbstituons le monde sans l'artiste, le monde tel qu'il est en 1930, monde que devra recréer l'artiste (ce qui ne suppose nullement un réalisme obligatoire), selon la façon contemporaine d'envisager les choses.

Autrement dit, nous demandons à l'artiste d'envisager son temps avec le point de vue de son temps, tel qu'il le comprend, et sans nous y faire sentir sa présence. N'exprimer ni une œuvre ni un homme, mais un monde.

Dernière conclusion: L'Essentiel: 1930 *est d'envisager le monde avec des yeux actuels, pour dire quelque chose, quelle que soit la forme qu'on préfère.*

Harold J. SALEMSON.

NOTE: Ceci n'engage en rien le programme de *Tambour* ni le choix de ses matières. Seuls sont considérés être liés par cette doctrine, le signataire de ce manifeste, et les adhérents dont nous donnerons les noms dans nos prochains numéros.

Dans notre prochain Numéro:

Nous résumerons les divers mouvements de presse soulevés par notre enquête sur Anatole France, et nous publierons message de Claude Bordas, des poèmes de Jean Mariotti, Robert Radelet, Richard Thoma, Valentin de Manoll, Claude Symil, Walter Lowenfels, etc...

ESSENTIAL : 1930

(A MANIFESTO)

> ...seek our new direction on another
> road. That road will be the Revolution
> of the Idea, the new point-of-view, an
> entirely renovated outlook, purely ideo-
> logical, which may be correlated with
> but will be independent of both the
> Revolution of the Word and the Revo-
> lution of the Act. (H. J. S.)

In the history of the arts, romanticism was the only
divorce from the classical trend. All modernism has been
but a variation on the romantic theme: to wit, for the
classic, the work alone existed; for the romantic, solely
the artist existed; for the moderns, whatever be their tendency, art is but a projection of the artist's personality into
the world about him, or, if we wish, an interpretation of
the outside world as related to the artist. In this, modernism has been but a romanticism distinguished by its form.

*First conclusion: Modernism has meant only a variation
of form.*

Now, the newest movements of modernism have provided
us with the entire scale of anti-forms. Claiming to neglect
form, the moderns have been wholly occupied with it, and
they have achieved a classicism of anti-form. This classicism is as much to be avoided as that of form. With
nothing to say, what is the use of new forms?

*Second conclusion: Modernism, a research of form, is
exhausted.*

Consequently, a new path is to be sought.

This path must ignore form, since all forms and anti-forms are at its disposal. They are waiting to be used.

> (But an adequate poetry
> is coming back
> and like a laugh (haha!)
> like a laugh
> already is judging events. — Georges Linze.)

These forms have no longer a right to more than a secondary consideration.

(People thought so much about their clothes, they forgot they had skins. — Ralph Cheever Dunning, in conversation.)

The first place belongs to ideas.

(Art is not a paradox, art is not a pastime, nor a more or less witty fashion, nor a pose... It is a phenomenon as complex as life... — Blaise Cendrars.)

But the mixture of manner (form) and matter (ideas) must be well-wrought.

(In this as in all human matters a balance is necessary. — Bertrand Russell.)

Third conclusion: To the various manners given us by modernism, we must add matter.

To arrive at this, it is necessary to relinquish certain things, and to embrace certain others.

It is necessary to suppress not vocabulary which is out of style, but that which no longer expresses our time. For the essential is to succeed in expressing the force, beauty, dynamics, and other contemporary resources, without however creating new formulary phrases such as the « contemporary mythology » or the « fabulous mystery of our time ».

(Love, science, ambition, religion, beauty, my captive effort was but the attempt of a start toward the sky, a fall back to earth. — René Glotz.)

It is necessary to disavow both classicism and romanticism, and to do this, to take a new point-of-view.

(Classics is as classics forgot. — Sidney Hunt.)

Fourth conclusion: To find the new matter, a new attitude is needed, a new point-of-view.

In short, we no longer want the sole work of the classics, nor the artist alone of the romantics. As for the modern projection of the personality of the artist into the outside world, we replace it by the world without the artist, the world as it is in 1930, a world the artist must recreate (which does not suppose any obligatory realism) according to the contemporary way of seeing things.

In other words, we demand that the artist look at his day with the point-of-view of his day, as he understands it, and without making us feel his presence in it. Neither a work nor a man are to be expressed, but a world.

Last conclusion: The Essential: 1930 is to look at the world through contemporary eyes, in order to say something, whatever form one may prefer.

Harold J. SALEMSON.

NOTE: This in no way changes the program of *Tambour* nor the choice of its features. The only ones considered to be held by this doctrine, are the signer of this manifesto, and the adherents whose names we will give in our coming issues.

BOTTLES

Whether they be new or old
Bottles are designed to hold
Vintages until the day
Someone pulls the cork away.

What have we, then,
to do with patterns or with fashioners
of newer bottles to contain the old
most potent vintage men
have ever striven, unsuccessfully,
to hold?

What scaffolding man fosters
And sundry forms invents
To make a bid for greatness
And hide his impotence.

A half a hundred bottles
Of intricate design
Cannot increase the power
Of unfermented wine.

To him who captures streams of liquid fire
Out of life's press, comes no uncertainty,
But from the bottles on the table he
Selects according to his heart's desire.

Or, finding none of suitable attire,
Forgets them all and deftly, skilfully,
Builds one of yet another symmetry
Such as his potent vintages require.

And yet, opposing forces seize upon
The question: Is the fluid in a cask
More powerful than in a demi john?
Forgetting, in their eagerness, to ask —
What of the bottle when the wine is gone?
What of the wine that never leaves the flask?

Frederic COVER.

TWO POEMS

ETERNITY

Love lived beyond the grave in Greece
And thus
One urn held mixed the ashes of
Achilles and Patroculus.

The Romans would not say farewell
But sucked the breath
Of dying friends
And cheated death.

So Aucassin once gaily set
His face toward hell with Nicollette.

But we, my dear,
How can we use such shifts as these
To hide the face of fear?

COWARDICE

I shall pretend I have not heard
And tremble at the whistle of each new bird.

I shall not walk where yellow willows rise,
Before the new green leaves, I'll close my eyes.

And I shall turn in silence from your lips —

Lest spring should prove to me
Less of a challenge and my pulse
A fraction slower than it used to be.

H. R. HAYS.

POÈMES ITALIENS

Qui es-tu?

Qui es-tu? Le nuage frisé
Qui rassérène les espaces bleus
Et, au soleil qui le salue,
Reluit chargé de topaze?

Ou la rose qui éclate par-delà le mur,
Que le passant devine mais ignore,
Et qu'ingénu et muet il adore,
Parce qu'elle enchante son matin pur?

Ou l'étoile verte qui, la première,
Pique le ciel de l'angélus
Et pénètre dans le cœur et le lime
D'une nostalgie inconsolable?

Qui es-tu, Poésie?

Angiolo Silvio Novaro.

Vitres

Toutes les vitres de cinquante maisons
pauvres et riches, toutes,
au vrombissement qui éclate
se brisent.

Alors, hors des accrocs
des accrocs des cinquante vitres
commence une fuite de choses.

Oiseaux délivrés
fragments de rêves
ambitions en essaims

perruques chauve-souris amours
croix péchés dépits fards
exhalations d'âmes
haleines de corps chauds de corps glacials
flèches-pensées haillons-soupirs
les passés les avenirs
pauvres et riches, de cinquante maisons
agitent de voiles pâles et évaporent
Sur les silex du trottoir
la grêle des vitres sèches
tinte au froid qui se taît
car dans le ciel poussent les premières étoiles.

Massimo BONTEMPELLI.

Dans le train

Un amandier en fleurs dans un jardin,
entre deux noires statues mutilées
qui regardaient là-bas la mer en bourrasque,
m'accompagna, pendant tout le voyage,
de sa joie blanche et parfumée,
à travers les plaines, les monts et les villes,
comme s'il était collé sur la vitre.
Jusqu'à la petite gare de campagne,
frémissante de sonneries:
où il amincit ses rameaux
en une grisaille de cheveux,
se fana rapidement,
se recueillit et sourit tristement
dans le pâle visage de ma mère,

qui toute seule m'attendait
et me donna sur le cœur un saint baiser
qui sentait la cendre et les larmes.

Corrado GOVONI.

Notre peine

La vie s'échappe de nos mains
comme le torrent des rochers immobiles,
et le cœur émigre ébahi et sans armes,
de ciel en ciel, aux sommets lointains.
L'amour raille les désirs humains
par son double visage pareil aux hermès,
et nos âmes inquiètes et malades
tendent toujours vers les rêves vains.
Ne pas pouvoir se soustraire
aux lois supérieures et inconnues du destin,
c'est bien notre constante angoisse terrestre;
ne pas pouvoir fixer en des formes éternelles
la joie changeante du chemin,
c'est notre peine antique et désespérée.

Giuseppe VILLAROEL.

Delta

La vie qui se brise dans les transvasements secrets,
je l'ai liée à toi:
celle qui se débat en soi-même et semble presque
ne te connaître pas, présence étouffée.
Lorsque le temps s'engorge dans ses digues
tu accordes ton sort au sien, immense,
et tu affleures, mémoire, plus évidente
de l'obscure région où tu descendais,

comme maintenant, après la pluie, s'intensifie
le vert aux branches, et aux murs le cinabre.

J'ignore tout de toi, hors le message
muet qui me soutient sur le chemin:
si tu existes, forme ou fantôme dans la fumée
d'un rêve, te nourrit
la rivière qui s'enfièvre, toute trouble, et gronde
à la rencontre de la marée.

Rien de toi dans le vacillement des heures
grises ou déchirées d'un éclair de soufre,
hors le sifflement du remorqueur
qui des brouillards aborde au golfe.

Eugenio Montale.

Le seuil

Dans l'azur taciturne du soir
les flèches des rayons du soleil
changent le silence en tourbillon:
la terre met des ailes à sa peine
semblable au prisonnier
qui brise ses chaînes,
chaque chose s'envole avec elle dans le ciel.
Notre àme seulement, au fond de nous-mème,
s'alourdit d'une obscure douleur,
et nous nous arrêtons muets,
sur la limite d'un seuil inattendu.

Nicola Moscardelli.

Tombé pour toujours le soleil

tombé pour toujours le soleil
le long de son chemin

les derniers hommes passèrent
en courant vers la mort —
la terre resta vide
avec sa grande rumeur
d'eaux et de forêts
à tournoyer dans le temps;
il resta des routes et des ponts
des maisons des portes et des fenêtres:

dans la ville une poupée
sur une terrasse.

Giacomo PRAMPOLINI.

Lux

Je regarde en la nuit les clartés allumées par les hommes
    et, là-haut, celles qu'alluma l'Eternel.
Leur lumière est de même essence, mais au ciel elle brûle à
    l'état d'esprit pur, alors qu'ici bas sur la terre il lui
    faut, pour s'exprimer, tout un prolixe appareil de
    matière.
Où vas-tu, lumière, lumière, lorsque, l'appareil s'arrêtant,
    tu t'éteins aux yeux des mortels?
Il semble que tu t'éteignes dans le noir même de la nuit,
    mais voici que soudain la certitude me vient que là-
    haut l'attirèrent les étoiles, tes mères.
O âme, la plus belle des flammes, toi aussi allumée ici-bas
    par une fragile et caduque combinaison de matière,
    réjouis-toi, exulte...
Car si la même loi divine régit les esprits et les astres,
lorsque les sens inertes sembleront t'avoir éteinte à jamais,
tu seras transubstanciée en un immortel rayon de lumière...

Garibaldo ALESSANDRINI.

Grand'maman

Ma mère vint au devant de moi par son escalier
pour embrasser mon fils.
Et moi, je m'arrêtai dans un coin
pour ne pas voir ses larmes, pendant qu'elle l'embrassait
— Grand'maman! dit-elle, elle qui toujours avait dit:
— Maman!
Je compris que moi, moi seulement, en revenant à sa maison
l'avais tellement vieillie.

Ignazio DRAGO.

Soie

Vitrines des merciers.
Aquarium de zoophites.
Merveilles de profondeurs marines.
Les cravates précieuses allongent en spirale
leur tige chatoyante
sur les rocs glacés des cols empesés.
Tout le fond scintille
de nacres et de coraux
taillés en boutons de manchettes.
Les tendres méduses des foulards
ouvrent leurs parasols roses.
Richement gaînée
tranche la jambe tronquée
d'une belle noyée
à laquelle font couronne
de transparentes chemises
d'anguilles voluptueuses:
les bas de femme.

Giorgio FERRANTE.

Avenir

Ce sera dans dix siècles, dans cent.
Un matin éparpillant des roses d'argent
sur la ville
aux gratte-ciel d'acier.

En flânant parmi les femmes, gai,
sans but,
l'avenir rencontrera
— fil qui entre dans l'aiguille —
une absolument
identique, identique à toi.

Sans même y donner d'importance
il pourra écouter une voix qui sera la tienne,
boire à une bouche qui sera la tienne,
se mirer à l'éclair de tes dents, les tiennes!
Puis,
s'en aller, sans nulle surprise.

Mais moi je l'aurai reconnue, semblable à personne,
et serai triste de n'être que poussière,
à jeûn depuis des siècles,
de ne savoir que me dissoudre
en froufrous aériens, labile survivance!

Et de ne pas pouvoir — hélas! —
habiller de fraîches chairs mon absence,
pour étreindre cette Une
qui sera toute toi!

Lionello FIUMI.

Mirages

Lorsque la lune confie ses mystères muets
à l'oreille tendue du silence,
des choses terrestres bondissent des ténèbres
pour ravir cette magie.

Au fond de la chambre le miroir d'absinthe
peuple d'un phosphore de pensées
son ennui rectangulaire.
Des rails chevauchant les distances
veulent aussi se parer
d'éclairs d'élégance.
Les étangs anachorètes,
derrière les cils des roseaux,
ne sont que des yeux qui épient.

Indifférente, la lune laisse faire.
Déjà, elle lève l'ancre vers des plages d'elle seule connues,
parmi des mystères que nul jamais ne connaîtra.

Les choses terrestres demeurent là,
déçues comme des mains vides.

Lionello FIUMI.

(Tous ces poèmes ont été traduits par Lionello Fiumi et Eugène
Bestaux).

TWO POEMS

To The Dead

What message is this written here
on your white lips
on your cold brow?
What is written, cryptic, terse,
on that bosom, stilled by death?
Is it a warning cold and clear
sounded in silence?
I defy
the power that made you minion to
the nothingness that claims us all.
I am I.
What I have been
shall live forever.
When the dust has cast its thrall
o'er all its own,
these, my arms, shall even then
hold fast some truth, some throbbing song.
Coward you,
who silently,
bowed to the summons, relinquished all.
I shall hold fast nor ever free
this life, this fact, this mystery.
God gave me life,
not as a loan for some brief time,
but as eternal surety
that I am I...
so long as He is He.

To The Living

This is our comfort in the dark:
some faint contact in the mist,
some defiance-mockery
that dares to laugh and to resist.

Shadows in shadow, form in fog;
gray in gray from dust to dust.
Yet touch my hand and kiss my lips.
This, if we're to live, we must.

This alone can ease the longing,
this, to truth, the brave reply.
This is all that we can win to.
This is all... until we die.

Romola S. Voynow.

MAGIE

Comment se fait-il qu'une humble lumière — si petite et si timorée — puisse tenir tête à toute la nuit rapace?

Un point de joyeuse clarté, une flamme qui saute sur place, et voilà de la vie qui vient, de la confiance, un imprécis bonheur qui suffoque.

Une lueur... et c'est une forme grise, toute bienveillante, qui trottine dans un pays immatériel de cendres quiètes où l'on s'étonne soudain de rencontrer ce qui fait la paix de chaque jour.

Une lumière placidement accrochée au-dessus de ma tête... et c'est tout un jardin de joie qui se coule dans ma chambre, l'envahit, la noie sous une retombée folle de jeunes feuillages.

Et le feu... quand c'est le maître-feu amoureusement blotti au giron de la cheminée! Voilà fadets et farfadets et d'autres encore dont on ne sait pas les noms. C'est leur ronde pourpre qui se noue et se déchire, c'est leur chœur où crépite le rire complaisant des grosses bûches...

Défi, raillerie, insulte à la nuit rapace qui se vautre dehors et glisse sous ma porte ses doigts sorciers.

Claude Symil.

BEAUTY PASSES

BEAUTY PASSES

Mock not those, dear, romantic women,
Louise Labé and Gaspara Stampa,
women who loved once
and then withered
when love passed.

They are trailing vines;
they fall from the trellis and die
when the roots are cut.

Yellowing age is spent
in amorous reflection
and beauty
passes with the loving of men.

CONTRAST

I am softer, rococo,
lethargic, given to dreaming,
while she is straight as a menhir,
and breastless,
eager for life and more life
till too much living will kill —
wounded she will not be
and never tamed.

Quick eye,
brow like the new moon's thread,
alizarin mouth so readily
showing white laughter!
(My pale smile too languid,
unsure.)

Black, red, sable.
So is she, but painted more strangely
mysterious totem pole
alone on the plain.

Let winds sweep over
prehistoric prairies —
prairies of America —
giving more life!

Arabella YORKE.

A TOULON...

A Harold J. Salemson.

Serre-la dans ton cœur cette simple romance,
émouvante comme un aveu,
qu'un marin fredonnait sur le quai de Toulon.

Elle sentait la mer et l'amour, elle était
vive comme si elle partait en promenade
un jour de beau temps.

Une fille s'est retournée
pour l'entendre jaillir des lèvres du marin;
un brun rose qui marchait en se balançant...

Et tout à coup je t'ai revue...
Et j'ai pensé qu'aucun poème de moi
n'aurait eu le pouvoir de t'accrocher le cœur ....
aussi bien que ce chant sans paroles
qu'un marin fredonnait sur le quai de Toulon!

Mario MONTANARD.

3 SONGS OF DEPARTURE

IN MEMORY : NORTHERN NAVAJO

> like no other people to say
> beautiful to things not quite understood.
> between birth and four days of mourning
> lonely beneath a scarlet cliff
> the color of independent grief
> there such for singing,
> the days are a requiem
> to be intoned softly:
> beautiful.
> it is better, the story that is told.
> it is better for the sadness
> of comprehension.
> the days are grey as sand.

FARTHER THAN THE DESERT GOES

> past all belief that this should happen so.
> the universe is atmosphere of snow
> and kosharis ride to messenger the day
> that speaks of nothing in the sun to say.
> always the memory of what I speak
> renders the earth dull, the cañons bleak
> and the wind is the sound

of a deserted hogan found
covered with death on an alien ground.
for a lifetime I go among my race
with a mask of sadness upon my face.
only in me to live,
you find reflected incident:
death is a sieve.

SONG TO BE SUNG AT DAWN

it is true what no man believes,
death will separate the navajos
one from another.
upon the frail likelihood of my living
depends the unity of day and night.
otherwise the world has no meaning,
beautiful as a chant at night.

Norman MACLEOD.

ART MODERNE

Au fond du puits de nos larmes
la grenouille lèpre mouvante
tel un arc-en-ciel d'émeraude
se projète du nord au sud

     Pour annoncer le baptême du ciel
     des étoiles comme des clochettes.

Quelle rumeur le cœur de l'homme
si l'acrobate à bout de forces
au creux de son aisselle cherche
les secrets de dieu sans amour

     Mais la folie aux longs mirages
     chancelle sur son socle et choit.

Et l'écheveau des lampes
sous le vent qui tremblote
au jeu quotidien des ombres
ferme un œil et la nuit.

               Nino FRANK.

ALASTAIR

Nero was a monster. This was his heritage. He delighted
in the bloody combats of the gladiators. He gloated over the
spectacle of death in its most tortured forms. He thrived
on the food of vampires. But he was also a clown. And
this was his doom. For a monster alone may yet be delicate, but when a monster is also a clown, then his acts
are tainted with the poison of burlesque and travesty. They
are corrupted with parody and cheapened with caricature.
The obvious is present in large quantities and the spectator
is invariably rewarded with ennui. That is why Nero was
commanded to die.

Fortunately for him, Heliogabolus came later. So late,
in fact, that it may be remarked that he had predecessors
but no descendants. It gave him background. He was no
teratological mountebank, intent on pastiche insincerities,
but a serious dilettante, bent on exquisite refinements.
Where Nero had been merely bloodthirsty, Heliogabolus
was cruel. Where Nero had been crude, he was supremely
elegant. In the night of the unpolished grossness of his
antecedent, the excellent discrimination and surpassing
taste of Heliogabolus shone with a peculiar brilliance.

The drawings of Aubrey Beardsley would have pleased
Nero. Only the drawings of Alastair could have satisfied
Heliogabolus.

For Alastair is impersonal and detached. His touch is
lighter than a butterfly's wing. He is not interested in criti-

cizing the book he illustrates. Never does he descend to
satire. He has no use for wilful anachronisms. His object
is to present a period by evoking the colour and the perfume that it has left behind. Thus the costumes and the
decors come to life of themselves; even the emotions and
expressions suggest their own renascence. For these last
change as often as do the decorations. Each age has had
its predominant emotions, its hegemonical facial expressions and gestures. Of all illustrators, Alastair alone is
aware of this. It is on him alone that disappeared ages have
left the impress of their forms and movements. His graphic
realization of dead gestures is infinite, his depiction of them
is vivid. The reason for this, if there must be a reason,
is that his men and women are never distorted cows, as in
the work of several contemporary artists, nor distorted
gods, as in the work of the Japanese. The beauty that
Alastair creates is due to his restraint, his lack of exagge-
ration, his use of the subdued gesture and the apparent calm
of his objectivity. It is the manner in which beauty should
be created. And, of course, Alastair, in the subtle psychology of his skill, proves always more cruel in his illustrations than his confreres of the cattle or giants. He definitely
arrives at more Brobdingnangian conclusions than those
of which the others even dream.

It is perfectly true, as the Comtesse de Noailles has
already pointed out, that Alastair achieves his greatest
success through the combination of tragedy and falballa.
The spectacle of tragedy is always more moving when it

appears to be the disintegration of beauty. We may shudder
when confronted with sin and death in all their ugliness,
but it is with horror and disgust. We look away quickly and
forget rapidly. But let us meet with these same vices, with
the identical terror of the supreme moment, in a setting
of lutes, waxen white camellias, powdered wigs and stiff
brocades, and the effect is immediately one of poignancy,
evocative of the infinite and the absolute and the despotism
of the tyrant with a scythe. And after all, in this age of
misguided charities, we are only too apt to forget that the
pains and torments of the canaille are also the sufferings
of the enlightened. There are too many communists in the
world of art. We need more exquisites.

Alastair is an exquisite. For this reason, he is never obvious, nor are the characters in his drawings ever vulgar.
They are never given to rude emotional displays nor to
crude tempers. They vibrate only to subtle, secret stirrings
and seem disposed rather to physical inertia than to violent
exhibitionism. But their thoughts are quite revealed so that
we always know their plans or fears. In one of his illustrations for Salomé, Alastair shows us the Princess of
Judea tempting the prophet Iokanaan. She is crouching
behind him. His back is turned to her, but his eyes are
staring wildly over his shoulder. From the expressions on
their faces, we know that Salomé is already planning the
prophet's decapitation and that Iokanaan has seen the gates
of his Heaven open to receive him. Yet there is no movement in the drawing, nothing but uttermost calm. Salomé
has assumed a feline pose, indeed, she looks like a cat,

while Iokanaan is standing straight as the cross. Both are watching, looking before them, fascinated by the approach of the imminent end. Each is thinking of himself. Neither is mentally present, except in a sense of awareness. It would have been a simple matter to invest this illustration with movement, to make it a purely physical thing. But Alastair's drawing board is not the opera house of Charles Garnier, nor is it the stage for amateur theatricals.

Alastair is calm, critical, cabalistic. There is nothing of Art for Art's sake about his work. Gertrude Stein and James Joyce claim to have restored to the word « reading » its original sense. One reads their works for reading's sake, without interest in what the words may say, if they say anything. In their books one reads purely to read, not to learn or be informed, or pleased or annoyed. Many artists have done the same thing with their pictures. One looks merely to look, not because one wants to see anything, recognize a person or a place or an object. This is called modernity and is really no older than protoplasm or fig leaves. Lovers of this sort of thing will be disappointed in Alastair. He does not use colours merely to make spots on his drawing paper: children do that. But no one can reproach him with drawing through his eyes. He draws with his imagination, with his intellect, with his urbanity.

It is an error to believe that the surrealists, the cubists, the impressionists, the futurists, the symbolists, the expressionists, the vorticists, the pandemoniumists, the suridealists possess imagination and superhuman powers of interpretation to the exclusion of all other schools of art. Imaginative drawing must of necessity take definite form.

Imaginative drawing without harmony of line, co-relation
of detail or concrete form is no longer imaginative drawing,
but a sort of plastique colour movement, an artistic chaos.
This is especially true of cases where the artist is desirous
of picturing people with whom we are personally unac-
quainted. One can never believe in people who do not look
outwardly like human beings, no matter how attractive
they may be as monsters, and, invariably, one connects the
physique of the artist with that of his creature creations.
I once told a friend of mine that I had just seen Marie
Laurencin. « Has she a nose? » he queried. Undoubtedly,
human anatomy as we know it must serve as the foundation for imagined graphic characters.

In *Le Coq et l'Arlequin*, Jean Cocteau writes: *Que pense
la toile sur laquelle on est en train de peindre un chef-
d'œuvre? « On me salit. On me brutalise. On me cache ».*
Is this a criticism of contemporary painting, or a criticism
of the enemies of contemporary painting? At any rate, I am
convinced that if Alastair's drawing paper possesses the
power of thought, then its thoughts, when Alastair takes
his pencil in hand, must run like this: My nakedness is being
covered at last. I shall be able to appear in public, now.
Tonight, I will go into the world and command attention
by my beauty.

For some artists, the war was a cruel thing: Some died;
some crawled through it; some escaped with minor wounds.
The work of most of them has suffered since then. The
crash of the guns, the roar of motors, the reverberation of
machinery, all have saturated their pages and covered their
canvases. For a few years, the world was one huge machine,

and all human beings who came into contact with this machine were either broken by it or made to worship it. They saw Machine, they preached Machine, they produced Machine, they became Machine. Science progressed, science swept the universe like a plague. What was not Machine, died. Machine triumphed. And then Machine went mad and embraced the Roman Catholic faith.

But there are still some spirits who never came under the rule of Machine, who, in the words of Ludwig Lewisohn, never succumbing to Machine, never, reacted from it, and through war, peace, and reaction kept their heads. These are the intelligent. They are the elect. They are the artists. For science is not intelligence, but an indifferent brutal, irresistible Force. Machine is inferior to Nature, since it depends on Nature for its progress, but Art is superior to Nature since it is not concerned with Nature. The scientist exists by will, the artist by divine right. When the two forces meet in one person, the result is shock, the shock of irresistible force against immovable object. Science and Art. And the work produced is cataclysm.

The artist is always final. He stops at the end, not in the middle. Further than the artist, no one can go, save the critic. The critic begins where the artist leaves off. Naturally, he cannot go to the same place as the artist. He goes further, but to a different place.

Distance lends perspective, you say. I answer: Distance borrows perspective, trains it in the circus and exhibits it at Paul Guillaume's.

The public believes that beauty is easy to achieve, since beauty is always simple and direct. The vogue accorded to hideous deformations in all forms of art is not a manifestation against aesthetics, but the applause of a public which believes that only tortuous ugliness is difficult to prepare.

A beautiful drawing is nothing more than a series of lines meeting in the right place. This statement withdraws nothing from the inspiration which causes these lines to converge beautifully. Inspiration is not a tenth part of genius. Genius is the application of inspiration. Without inspiration we have only geometrical and mathematical patterns. Inspiration turns logic into art. The modern cry for a marriage between logic and art is not an echo of ancient Hellas, but of modern Italy. And Marinetti is its prophet. When such a marriage is consummated, the result is complete sterilization.

Alastair knows that all things are not equal in value to each other. He knows how to choose the true from the false. He never mistakes quartz for gold, nor glass for crystal, nor figures of earth for gods. In his Crucifixions, which are the most wonderful in all the world, he never gives us a Barnabas for a Christ. He knows that if there is to be a victim, it is never Barnabas but the Christ. In these drawings, there is none of the sickly pious quality so frequently encountered in the work of the Renaissance masters, none of the heavy gloom of the Flemish school. The Christs of Alastair are martyrs who were born of the Cross, they are the fruit of that lonely tree. Never are they victims of Pontius Pilate, but always of Jehovah, suffering intensely without comprehending, despairing but never resigned, wise, mad, defiant.

Alastair does not achieve beauty merely by making use of beautiful things. He draws beautiful things, but they attain beauty because Alastair gives them character: because they are in character: because they are characteristic. They are never superficial, even in part. Their beauty does not detract the attention from the central theme of the drawing. In Alastair's work, everything is complementary, everything makes for the perfect whole. Every line is architecturally necessary. Remove the slightest of them and the drawing will dissolve into nothingness. For the same reason, nothing is merely decorative. Change the pattern of a gown, replace a bouquet of camellias with a cluster of chrysanthemums — your drawing will no longer be by Alastair.

Alastair is not only an artist but also a theatre. A theatre inhabited by ghosts, but none the less real for that. Here, all the fripperies, all the horrors, all the passions of the past are on view in a combined tragedy of extraordinary splendours and starry destinies. The settings, the costumes, the impersonations, are all by Alastair. Even the tragedy is by Alastair. This play does not recognize the confines of three or five acts. It is bound only by Time and Space. Only Alastair could have imagined it and it will never be produced by the Moscow Art Theatre nor staged by Max Reinhardt.

The curtain rises on a decor of poisoned flowers and

deadly serpents, the characters appear and speak their
parts with the scornful lips of gods who know they will
not ever be believed, and the tragedy begins. Not one of
these players wears a mask, not any one of them has a
shadow. They are all selfish and cruel, depraved and vicious,
cynical and wise. Before our eyes we see them pass, more
real than ourselves, greater, more imperishable, arrogant
in their freedom, despising our applause, scornful of our
censure, approving only those of us who witness their parade unperturbed, calmly, with detachment. They pass and
on a perverse music and the tragedy of life and the tragedy
of death descends a curtain of red moons and green moons.

The sun gives a poor light. One has only to look at a
canvas of Claude Monet's to realize it. Besides, Art is, or
should be, the arch-enemy of Nature. Art strives to interpret Nature, not to picture it; the latter is left to cameras.
Again, Nature is constantly active, never at rest, and abhors
death. That is why we cannot look at the sun. It fatigues
us with its permanent restless fire. Nature is ashamed of
the moon. It is her one failure, since it is dead, gives no
light of its own and yet remains undestroyed by Nature.
The moon is an inexplicable phenomenon. It is Art in Nature. It is therefore the only thing in Nature of which an
artist should make use.

The moon is not made of silver, nor of green cheese.

One never encounters the sun in the drawings of Alastair.
He is perhaps the only artist who does not depend on light
contrasts and shadows to illuminate his drawings. In fact,
I have never seen a figure cast a shadow in a drawing of
Alastair's. There are no shadows in Art. Everything is clear,

decisive, concrete. Even when Alastair employs the moon, he does not use it as light, but as a decoration. It is sometimes green, sometimes red, and serves merely as a background for his fantastic designs. Yet the drawings of Alastair burn brightly. Their fire is magic.

Magic is green. Everything else is dead. The drawings of Alastair owe their life-like qualities to the mastery of his thaumaturgy. These drawings do not come from a machine, but from a witch's cauldron. Theirs are no common ingredients, but rare, fantastic, baroque. The snake in Genesis knew their secret. Certainly, Hecate possessed the formula. Perhaps Salammbô read it in the stars. Only two artists have ever divined it: Alastair and Gustave Moreau. This is the magic that makes the unicorn more real than the horse, that makes the moon more vivid than the sun, that gives a consciousness to dreams.

Was Cleopatra a legend, Sappho a myth, Balkis a fable? What does it matter so long as Alastair gives them life? To the dreamer, all dreams come true. In the faery land, Alastair walks with a sure step, touching here and there a dim shadowed figure with his magic wand, summoning from the deep gloom of legend's limbo the familiar Queens and Gods, commanding from their tombs the dead to rise. We know these figures, we recognize them, to us they prove the reality of dreams. We call to them; they smile at us in greeting. For they know us even better than we know them. They have been waiting for us for centuries. To dreams, creators of dreams are born.

The artist is always sacred and profane. He destroys temples to erect altars. He rejects creeds to foster cults. To the artist, crucifixion is no proof of divinity. Therefore, he does not put Lucifer before Christ. Nor is virginity a proof of innocence. To the artist, the worshippers of Cybele are no less virginal than the maidens of Vesta. Love and lust are the twin children of religion. Both are born pagan; neither attains virginity. One remains mentally innocent. The other is always physically corrupt. Neither is superior to the other, but each reviles the other and their mother disclaims them both. The artist effects the reconciliation.

Immorality is positive, morality is negative. The artist is always positive. Immorality is constructive, morality is destructive. There are no ruins in art, save those achieved by Time. The corruption achieved by Time is constructive in that it adds the perspective of the ages to each particular work of art.

Poetry is the only art. By poetry, I do not mean verse alone. Verse is only one way of capturing a poem. Poems are caught as well in a novel or in a play, in a drawing or in a block of marble. Music, painting, sculpture, the dance, verse and song are but mediums for poets.

Even poor poetry is superior to trees.

Alastair is a poet of the graphic arts. By this I do not mean that the drawings of Alastair are odes or eclogues or sonnets, any more than that the Imaginary Portraits of Walter Pater are paintings of the Dutch school. Such contradictions in terms are ridiculous. What I do mean is this: The drawings of Alastair possess all the attributes of true

poetry in that they give one a sense of infinity and comple-
teness and understanding. They give one a sense of pier-
ceing at once the Veil of the Temple and the Veil of Isis;
we seem to penetrate at once with Istar to the Seventh Gate
and with the Prophet into the Seventh Heaven; apparently
we read the riddle of the Sphinx and the secrets of the
Apocalypse are immediately ours.

The aim of the poet is to compose a poem. To do this, he
must overcome innumerable obstacles. He must fight
against things as they are. He must defeat convention and
tradition. He must waylay the future. He must continuously
strive against uncomprehending contemporaries, for only
the dead and the unborn can understand him. The world
he lives in will always treat him as Punch, but he must
know that he has created, in himself, another Hamlet.

One cannot make a Hamlet without breaking eggs. The
result is solitude: The world resents having its eggs broken.
But to the artist, there exists no solitude. There exists only
isolation. Enough broken eggs will fill a moat. Alastair has
broken all the eggs behind him. The world tries in vain
to put them together again, while the mocking laughter of
Humpty-Dumpty grows into a whirlwind which will destroy
the past. And Alastair stands alone upon a solitary peak.
In the wide heavens above him wheels the feathered
Simorg-Anka.

Richard THOMA.

MES STATUES

Maintes années ont passé depuis qu'un milliardaire,
chez qui j'avais habité à New-York, m'offrit une statue
d'Apollon, pareille à celle du Belvedère : il paraît que
c'est la mienne qui est authentique, et que celle qui se
trouve au Vatican n'est qu'une excellente copie de
l'œuvre de Léochares. Un autre Américain que je
connus peu après à San-Francisco, ne voulut pas être
moins généreux que son compatriote, et il me donna une
Niobé entourée de ses quatorze enfants. Par la suite,
j'achetai d'occasion un condottière à cheval du XVe siècle, qui était peut-être de Verrocchio, et, longtemps
après, une ou deux années après la guerre, le maire
d'une commune de l'Italie du nord, dont j'avais sauvé
quelques fils au cours d'un incendi (je ne le nommerai
pas), m'exprima sa reconnaissance en m'offrant un
grand Humbert Ier debout, qu'on n'avait pas pu inau-
gurer à cause des querelles locales, et qui avait dû
rester caché dans un magasin. Je possède également un
scribe égyptien qui me vient d'un héritage ; et le gros
lot d'une loterie me procura un chasseur de chamois,
un rocher sous ses pieds et un fusil entre les mains,
dont l'auteur est inconnu mais sans aucun doute pos-
térieur à 1880. Toutes ces statues sont de grandeur

nature, hormis l'Apollon et le Humbert Ier qui sont plus grands. Et comme il me faut les garder dans ma chambre, elles m'encombrent un peu.

Par je ne sais quelle fatalité, toutes mes statues sont en marbre, à l'exception du scribe égyptien, qui est en granit, mais très clair. Fait remarquable, elles deviennent toujours plus blanches, ce qui les rend encore plus encombrantes.

Ma chambre est assez grande, mais ces statues l'ont rendue tout à fait disproportionnée. L'Apollon dépasse de son cou et de sa tête les étagères. Chaque fois que je vais de ma table de travail à mon poêle pour y mettre du bois, je ne fais pas attention aux bras tendus de Niobé et j'y cogne avec ma tête. Le condottière à cheval, j'ai dû le mettre devant le piano, si bien que je ne peux plus en jouer. Le panache de Humbert Ier arrive jusqu'au plafond, et ce roi prend toute la place où je tenais autrefois une armoire à linge qui m'était sans aucun doute plus utile.

Le chasseur de chamois est la première statue que l'on rencontre en entrant. Le facteur des recommandées, en attendant que je signe le reçu, pend toujours sa casquette au canon du fusil que le chasseur tient couché en joue.

Depuis que j'ai chez moi ces statues, presque personne ne vient plus me voir. On a peur.

Et cependant, on ne les a vues que le jour.

* * *

A la lumière naturelle, le jour, mes statues ont un
air recueilli et hypocrite. Elles semblent même plus
petites. Elles sont dures, plus fermes. Mais la nuit, leur
tempérament se manifeste tout entier. Je crois que le
jour elles ne voient rien. La nuit, oui, elles voient; mais
je pense qu'elles ne s'aperçoivent ni de moi ni des
choses qui m'entourent. Elles voient toujours au-delà
ou en-deçà de moi qui les regarde et essaie de me faire
regarder par elles. Elles contemplent. Elles contemplent d'autres choses, d'autres personnes, d'autres vies.
On peut causer avec un arbre, avec une chute d'eau,
avec un fauteuil; mais nous ne pouvons pas nous entre-
tenir avec les statues. Voilà pourquoi elles nous semblent immobiles. Je crois, par contre, que la nuit, lorsqu'elles voient, elles bougent aussi; mais leurs mouvements se déroulent selon des dimensions que nous ne
connaissons pas; de là l'air égaré qu'ont toutes les
statues la nuit.

Cependant, suivant la lumière que je leur accorde, —
je parle toujours de la nuit, — je crois que je peux avoir
une certaine influence sur leur façon de se conduire.

Lorsque j'allume les trois ou quatre lampes électriques qui se trouvent à différents endroits de ma chambre, toute la place est aussitôt encombrée par les ombres de mes statues. La chambre s'agrandit, mais cela ne suffit pas; elle s'efforce de les contenir, mais les ombres s'y sentent toujours mal à leur aise. Elles montent le long des murs, se replient sur le plafond; elles s'enflent et se courbent; chacune d'elle voudrait être seule et se jette à travers les autres, elles s'entrecroisent et s'embrouillent, s'entrecoupent et se volent réciproquement la vie et la liberté. Cette cohabitation d'ombres gigantesques se condense en une lutte sourde et parfaitement immobile, de même qu'il arrive que le nœud de deux grands lutteurs frise l'immobilité dans les moments les plus dramatiques.

Alors, dans ma chambre, il n'y a de vie que pour cette énorme lutte frauduleuse, qui ne sera jamais résolue, qui envahit toute la place, si bien qu'il ne m'en reste, à moi, presque plus et que je dois me recroqueviller ici ou là-bas, dans les très petits intervalles que les ombres m'abandonnent. Lorsque une raison quelconque m'oblige à traverser l'une ou l'autre de ces ombres, bien que je saute ou rampe le plus vite possible, je perçois leur contact noir qui, si j'hésitais un instant,

m'absorberait; et qui laisse sur mon corps un goût de
velours, qui me remplit de frissons.

Entre temps, les statues dont surgissent ces ombres
essaient de s'agrandir pour lutter avec elles : la masse
noire du piano disparait tout à fait derrière le cheval
du condottière du xve siècle; le roi Humbert Ier se raidit
encore davantage et son panache s'écrase contre le plafond; les bras de Niobé ont l'air de vouloir s'étendre
jusqu'à toucher le fusil que le chasseur de chamois
couche en joue. Il n'y a que mon collègue égyptien qui
garde ses proportions, cependant son front se fait
plus obtus et obstiné. La petite cape d'Apollon devient
un mac-farlane gigantesque et blanc.

A ce moment, les visages de toutes les statues rayon-
nent et jouissent, avec une sorte de satisfaction éton-
née, de la lutte sourde des ombres. Elles n'ont plus rien
de frauduleux. La parole de leurs figures est maintenant nette. Elles ont l'air de gens qui ont respiré après
l'asphyxie. Leur blancheur prend des nuances violettes,
comme si un sang nocturne affleurait de leurs corps, dès
qu'à la lumière de l'air succède la lumière des lampes.

Les ombres tendues et énormes semblent souffrir de
cette joie.

Une nuit qu'elles me parurent souffrir plus qu'à
l'ordinaire, j'en traversai trois ou quatre, puis j'étei-

gnis soudain les lampes et ouvris toute grande la
fenêtre.

* * *

Un gel surhumain m'investit tout à coup. La nuit
était pleine de lune. Les constellations avaient disparu
du ciel : seules, quelques étoiles éperdues aux extrêmes
bords se penchaient pour mendier, et personne ne les
avait chassées. Toute la face du ciel était exsangue. Une
stupéfaction mortelle parcourait l'espace et descendait
baigner les terrasses désertes. Une égalité infinie
démembrait le monde, poussière insensible et blanche
tombée des siècles consumés sur la terre.

Effaré, je me retournai pour regarder ma chambre.
Mon frisson fut tronqué d'un coup par une peur
immense que je sentis jaillir de mon cœur. La blancheur de la lune pressait la blancheur des statues, elle
se moulait sur leurs formes, adhérait à leurs figures,
comme si elle voulait leur retirer un masque. Mais les
statues se sentaient vivantes : une horreur macabre
montait de leur cœur à leurs visages, qui allaient se tor-
dre tous et crier au secours, et ne le pouvaient pas
encore, comme quand on dort sur le cœur. Ceci dura
quelques secondes ; puis je sentis que cet effort les
aurait fait bouger, que sans doute mes statues allaient

faire des gestes et se mettre à parler; alors, plein de désespoir, je brisai leur affolement et le mien en jetant un éclat de rire grand et puissant et en criant:

— Non, non, assez, ce serait idiot, don Juan Tenorio, vieille histoire, ballet russe; allons, allons; — et je fermai d'un coup les volets, si bien que la chambre piqua une tête dans les ténèbres et dans le silence. J'attendis immobile, serré dans mon coin. Je sentais dans cette obscurité la présence de mes statues. L'obscurité était pleine de statues. Quelques autres secondes s'écoulèrent. Et l'obscurité se gonfla de mouvements réguliers, égaux. J'eus de la peine à les saisir. Puis je compris. Mes statues respiraient. Elles respiraient très lentement, comme la mer; et toute l'obscurité recueillait ces halètements dans une douce palpitation qui arrivait à moi comme à la plage, et serrait à présent mon cœur, m'opprimait, jusqu'à ce que mes sentiments se ternirent...

Lorsque je me ressaisis, autour de moi le silence était compact et libéré. Un rayon luisant entrait d'un joint d'un volet et perçait la chambre. Je me levai pour ouvrir les volets, le soleil entra. Mes statues avaient repris leurs dimensions normales et l'aspect inexpressif et frauduleux du jour.

*
* *

Je ne sais pas du tout comment cela finira, si je n'y
mets pas bon ordre. J'avoue qu'il ne me déplairait pas
que mes statues se décident à devenir vivantes. (Je
serais curieux de voir si le fusil du chasseur devient
aussi un fusil véritable et s'il est chargé). Car alors,
un jour ou l'autre, à un moment donné, elles s'en
iraient : toutes les choses vivantes s'en vont.

Mais je doute qu'elles deviennent vivantes, ou alors
il y faudrait Dieu sait combien de temps ; et moi je ne
peux pas vivre au milieu d'un tel encombrement, dans
un pareil effroi. J'ai l'intention de me débarrasser le
plus tôt possible, d'une manière quelconque, de mes
statues.

Massimo BONTEMPELLI.

(Traduit de l'italien par Nino Frank et Philippe P. Datz).

STRINGS

« No, don't tell me about the story called The String, by that French writer. Of course I have heard of it; I read some, having the time now, but mine has no more to do with his — Look at what I have had, thousands, and that man had just one.

« *My strings?* And me? The first thing I remember was standing on a street corner and wishing for a black ginger cake in the window near me. *Wishing.* Then a big man slapped me on the back and said, — Move on. What you crying for? Nobody on earth wants tears.

« I put up my hand and felt my face was wet. I didn't know it was till then. I moved on, but I haven't cried many tears since that time. The next thing I remember was fighting a bigger boy to get near an ash can. He was picking out a piece of string. I got my place and we picked together a few months. What did we get? *Don't you know?*

« I thought everybody who had ever lived would know what was to be found in ash cans. Ashes, for one thing, and lots of paper, bones, buttons, rags, shoe soles, potato peelings, entrails, a cent or two sometimes and — sometimes — a crust. We separated them and sold them to the jobbers. When I had twenty-five cents I was on my way to fortune.

« I must have been nearly seven at that time, but knowing a much about my sort of work as boys of thirteen. It was then I rentend a closet, eight by eight. I remember measuring it, because I knew men didn't grow over six feet and I wanted it big enough to lie down in when I was grown!

« My blood? Where I came from to know so much? Born in America, but back of me there's a Scotch line strong enough to pull up America by the roots, and a few drops of French blood. That's the reason I'm telling you this. Scoth blood couldn't, American wouldn't give adone way or the other, but French blood — You know what it is, you have its essence and I just enough to know when the spirit would speak for the flesh.

« What do you suppose I gave for that closet? Fifty cents a month, and I had to hustle to get the money. When I bought a one burner oil stove and a five cent frying pan, I knew how Midas felt! The rags I couldn't do one thing with I used for clothes and bed. After two or three months of ash cans I got to be a regular rag picker. Did you ever step from a low business to a high one? It makes you *feel* like a red toy balloon *looks!*

« I didn't have any help to speak of — unless you count it help when I knew a few houses that always allowed me to have their rags. I didn't want any either, just my two hands and — plenty of rags. I was born independent, Scotch blood is rich with it and French blood — I would guard their high silence, too.

« There was one old lady I never will forget. She'd send for me twice a year, before Christmas and in June. She had one son, just about my size, and she would have a closet full of things to sell. 'Twas like going to a store and seeing everything you wanted to buy, and getting'em! For her things meant my bread and herring — and tea, sometimes. Her son's clothes — The day I felt rich enough to keep a coat and trousers of his there wasn't a millionaire in New York could compare his feelings with mine!

« Forgotten how I sort clothes? Does a man ever forget the color of his skies, the land of his blood, his first child? You go through the pockets first of all, and this is the most careful exciting work. For sometimes valuables slip through a hole, down in the turn-up of the outer stuff.

« A rag picker keeps what he finds; when you buy you buy outright. But I always returned rings, if I knew where the came from. The first money, outside of rags, I ever made came that way. 'Twas a plain gold ring and it came from the house of the old lady I told you about. I looked at it a long time before I decided. I hadn't had anything but two slices of bread for two days and the thought of a hot herring and a cup of tea made me dizzy.

« Course I was going to sell the clothes, but you get nearly double for them if they are worth fixing and these were worth it. I never lost ten cents by being in too big a hurry to make it. At last I rolled the ring up and started. 'Twas before Christmas, the wind blowing and snow falling like needles. When I got to the back door I could smell turkey and coffee. I was turning away — it decided me on the herring — when the cook spoke.

« — You want to see Mrs. Forrest? Well, stand outside. I've just cleaned up that hall.

« Mrs. Forrest came and I showed her the ring.

« — 'Twas in the pocket of the gray dress, — I said.

« — Yes, it's mine, — she answered, and then she looked at me. I hadn't gotten to shirts and rags were wrapped around my feet for socks.

« — Jane, — she said to the cook, — cut him some meat and bread while I get my purse.

« Jane grumbled after Mrs. Forrest turned away, but she gave me two thick slices of bread, thicker than I ever cut in my life, and Mrs. Forrest came back with a dollar bill. I had never taken bread from anybody before, but I thought this time I had earned it and — I don't believe my hand would have let go if my tongue had refused. And I know I never could have got to a place where they sell food if it hadn't been for that bread. That was the only time that I was ever given food that I remember.

« You would think I was dirty, living in that pig sty with those rags. I wasn't! I fixed me some wires, like a fence, and they separated the colthes from me. And I cut a window above, and night and day the air blew on them — 'twas before the days of fumigation. And I had the biggest tin pan you ever saw, it hung on a nail outside my door, and no end of wash rags! I always picked the best end of the best towel for my rag, but I never used one for drying. That would have been extravagant. In five minutes my warm body dried me — clean.

« But I was telling you about sorting rags. All the best things were put together, cleaned, gone over with dye, if it would help, matched with buttons and sold to the second hand dealer who would give the most. Till they were sold they were separated, as tidily as in any store. I put up hanging shelves and I could find any pile I wanted in the dark, from shoe strings to an overcoat, though for overcoats I'd rather have looked for snakes in Ireland!

« Well, I got along, I was *bound* to. A spelling book and reader came in one lot of things and I learned to read. A Jew taught me writing letters. I worked one hour a day for a week — scrubbing floors on my knees it was — and he paid me by writing down one letter. But he never had to show me twice and I learned how to join them up.

« When I was about fifteen I had two good sized rooms rented to store my rags in. I had cleared them out of my little hovel and now had that to myself. Talk about luxury! I never imagined anything like the sumptuousness of having a clean change of clothes hanging up one side of that eight by eight room, and me in a tub of water the other! From that time on I prospered, but as I did not spend — unless you count herrings and bread — I was compelled to make.

« When I was nineteen a man moved in the same block I was in and opened a hot dog place. Poor! I thought I had been poor but he was poorer — going down hill like a hoop. Drinking, poor devil. His wife was dead, but he had one little girl. She did not know her age but she must have been twelve though she looked about nine. Thin as a wafer, with big gray eyes that seemed like they were always hunting something to eat.

« First time I saw her she was sitting cross-legged at my door, watching me at dinner, like a hungry dog that follows every morsel from your hands to your mouth. I had turned around to get my tea and when I turned back there she was.

« — Now you just clear out, — I said, going to the door,

for I made it a rule children and dogs and cats shouldn't
hang around.

« — It smells good, — she answered, but she got up and
backed away, one hand reaching out to ward off a blow.
She thought that was what I was going to do.

« — Hungry? — I said, but I might as well have asked
if she was cold. One was as plain as the other. She did not
say anything, just looked at me, but now she had both arms
up to protect her face. 'Twas easy to see what she was
used to.

« I went back in my room and put the bit of herring on
the stale bread I was going to eat. I always bought old bread,
it was cheaper and lasted longer. She seized it and started
away. The next day, same hour, there she was and I —
seemed like I just *couldn't* finish my bread. I had enough
when I was half done. She got the rest.

« The next day I was trying to clean a spot of grease off
an old army coat I had bought for twenty-five cents. Mostly
the spots would come off in a jiffy, but this one stuck.

« — I bet I show you, — said a lively little voice behind
me and there was the girl, Em they called her.

« — Well, take it, — I said, and I stood over her to
take the coat away if she tried any tricks. But she didn't.
She scrubbed for all she was worth, rubbing it the right
way too, so as not to strain the goods.

« Then she held it up and gave me her first grin.
— You bet, — she said.

« She was always around, specially at meal time, and
you might as well have told your own dog to go home as
told Em. First thing I knew she was working for me, about

half the day, and getting for it just as much bread and
herring as I had, and that was just enough to keep me from
starving. One loaf of bread a day and three herrings. That
was what we divided between us. The bread was six cents
and a herring two cents.

« After this had been going on for some time and I saw
what the little thing could do — and she told me she had
more to eat than she had ever had — I said, — Em, if you
want to keep on helping me I'm going to see your father
and make a bargain with him.

« Em just clasped her hands together and looked like she
was praying. — Tell him you'll feed me and give me a coat
sometimes. If he knowed you give me this five cents he'd
have it for drink or kill me.

« That was the first time I felt sorry for her, up to then
I'd been thinking she was doing well for herself. I'd had it
so much rougher. 'Twas about the first of December I saw
her father, a drunken hog who didn't have so much longer
to swill.

« — I'll be damned glad to get rid of her, — was all he
said. I went to my nearest rag room and hunted about until
I found a child's pair of shoes that would almost fit her and
a nearly worn out dress. She was so glad she would stop
work and smooth her hands over the dress like it was
something alive, and then stoop down and pat her shoes.
When she came to work the first morning she had a newspaper pinned from her neck to her heels, to save the dress,
and she carried the shoes in her hand!

« At the end of five years Em's father died. He had held

on, beyond the belief of my own eyes. He was in debt for
his last meal, in debt for everything he could be in debt for,
from his medicine to the straw he lay on. He was not
buried before a rat of a lawyer was there, and in less time
than it takes me to tell you the little room was stripped by
his creditors. They cut the glass out of his window and took
the bricks from his hearth. I gave the money for his coffin
and when we got back from the funeral Em had no place
where she could go — she had gone to him when she was
through working for me.

« I haven't told you about those four years. Em took
over one room and I another, where the rags were kept,
you know, and she beat me hollow on everything! She was
there from dawn to dark and she could buy better, clean
better, *sell better* than I could. I taught her to read and
by and by she taught me; some good books came our way.

« I used to plan about bigger rooms, having more help,
doing this and that a little closer and then — a home to
live in with a tree in front. Em always helped me plan
until I got to the home. She never would say a word about
that.

« I was paying her a little something from the first and
she saved every cent, except what she had to spend now
and again for her father. That's the way things stood until
he died. When we came back from the funeral she waited
at the door of my room, like a child uncertain what to do
next. Till then it had never crossed my mind that her
home was gone.

« — Em, — I said, — where will you stay?

« She just looked at me and didn't say anything. I don't believe it had crossed her mind until then, having no floor to lie on. She had saved up a little money and so had I, but both of us together could not have rented her a regular room, even in that poor neighborhood. And we knew it.

« — You stay here, — I said, — and I'll find out how things run in New York. — For an idea had crossed my mind that I thought would be cheap. It seems queer now, but until you face starvation day and night you don't know how every thought is wrapped up in it.

« I had a friend, a policeman, and after I had explained matters he said it would be easy, only I must not tell anybody I was just marrying the girl until she could afford some place to live in, when I would get a divorce.

« — Preachers don't marry for you just to get a divorce, — he said, — unless, of course, you has money to burn.

« He told me what to do and I went back and told Em, explaining all about the divorce we would have as soon as I could afford it. The blood burned in her face like flame.

« — You sure you want it this way, now? — she asked. — Because I could — there's always the river —

« — I am *sure* — I said, for she looked exactly like the child who had sat on my door step four years before.

« We got married and everything we did prospered. But when my little girl was born, and that was ten years after, Em left me, for always. Before she went, *long before*, I had learned to love her and she — That's too close to tell, even now. But she had other things to eat besides herring and bread. You mustn't think...

« But the strings I started out to tell you about, you seeing me pick up this long piece and wondering — Little Em is good to me, but she don't know what strings mean, the ones I find and the ones from the bundles that come to my house now and that I collect. In the early days when I had no light, after the sun went down, I would lie on my bed and knot strings and wind them into balls. They brought two cents more for a pound ball that way than they did sold loose. The second hand dealers bought them to tie up their bundles.

« And now that I am an old man and things too easy, sometimes, for memory to rest, I lie on my bed and knot the strings for the old days' sake. Little Em does not like for me to do it, but when you've been through the fire some of the ash will always be yours.

« Sell them now? Yes, it's hard to break old habits and after dark — that's for Little Em, too — I go around to a second hand dealer — it's a merciful long way now — and he gives me the same price. Five cents a ball. It goes in the savings bank. For Little Em? Can you ask with my Scotch and French blood! *Don't you know?* »

Virginia Stait.

IL N'EST PLUS DE CRIME
DE LÈSE-LITTÉRATURE

A Liang-Tsong-Taï.

La gloire littéraire, cette fameuse chose immortelle, n'a plus qu'à se répandre en pleurs. Il n'est plus de crime de lèse-littérature. Et voilà la vérité qu'il faut commencer par établir — accepter ou renier — avant de pouvoir entreprendre aujourd'hui une discussion sur quelque proche sujet que ce soit. Car, à un tournant de chemin, on me trouverait toujours là qui répéterais: Définissez vos termes! Il n'est plus de crime de lèse-littérature.

Si on recherche les causes et les origines de la mort de ce forfait, la source principale se trouvera évidemment dans le domaine de la littérature moderne. D'ailleurs, la littérature n'est pas seule dans ce cas, et tous les arts connaissent de pareilles situations. Mais, alors qu'en peinture, qu'en sculpture, qu'en musique même, on a pu admettre l'art nouveau tout en disant: Ceci est en désaccord avec les principes fondamentaux et classiques de l'art (principes tangibles — critères vérifiables), mais ceci est tout de même plaisant, ou émouvant, ou puissant, ou bouleversant; il n'en est pas de même en littérature. Là, si nous admettons aujourd'hui, et c'est bien la moindre des choses, que l'avènement de la nouvelle conception de l'art a amené la nécessité de reviser toutes les valeurs et nous permet de discuter librement n'importe quelle gloire acceptée, si de certains mettent le prodigieux Rimbaud au-dessus de Racine (pour moi la comparaison n'existe pas), il n'est plus raison aujourd'hui d'en être choqué. Ce nouvel art, dis-je, a aboli le crime de lèse-littérature.

Cependant, dussions-nous en rester là, nous occuperions une position d'équilibre bien instable. En effet, toutes les valeurs seraient remises en cause et les partisans d'un chacun naguère accepté comme compte en banque seraient tenus de justifier la part d'admiration qu'ils réclameraient pour leur idole. Et s'ils s'y mettaient par voie de clichés critiques, comme nous le faisons tous, en invoquant les phrases creuses qui semblent décrire un point d'importance littéraire, ils me trouveraient encore à un coude dans leur chemin, qui leur crierais: Définissez vos termes. Et voilà peut-être où j'en voulais venir.

Si nous revenons à notre comparaison de tout à l'heure, que trouvons-nous? Indubitablement, ceci: la musique connaît une gamme positive de sept notes différentes, sans compter les divisions de notes (et je néglige volontairement ceux qui aujourd'hui tentent la musique polyphonique, jusqu'à nouvel ordre); cette gamme est positive, partant tangible. Abstraitement, chacun de ses éléments existe autant que n'importe quoi peut exister hors du cerveau humain, mais enfin existe. De même en peinture, il est une gamme de couleurs. Ce sont ces gammes de couleurs ou de sons qui avaient, jusque voici un certain nombre d'années, jusqu'à l'avènement des conceptions dites modernes de l'art, régi le sens de l'harmonie et de la valeur. On disait: telle note harmonise avec telle autre; telle couleur jure avec telle autre, on ne jure pas. Et on se le tenait pour dit. Puis sont arrivés un Debussy, un Cézanne (ou un Gauguin).

Après eux, le musicien ne chercha plus, non seulement à
se contenir dans l'harmonie classique, mais encore à soutenir un rythme égal, accepté — classiquement parlant,
la musique devint inharmonieuse et saccadée; le peintre
ne chercha plus, non seulement à se servir de couleurs
harmonieuses, mais encore à reproduire fidèlement la forme
de son modèle — la peinture était devenue sans harmonie,
et, dit-on, sans talent. Et pourtant, les opinions ont changé,
et les plus récalcitrants ont accepté la forme nouvelle, et
on se demande aujourd'hui comment on pouvait, il y a si
peu de temps croire si ferme en des critères qui ne paraissent plus exister.

Or, étant donné que les étalons absolus qui ont existé en
d'autres branches de la création et surtout de l'appréciation
artistique, ont complètement flanché et qu'il n'est plus de
règle pour mesurer la valeur d'une œuvre — car, comme on
a accepté que le peintre interprète son sujet, le spectateur
doit interpréter le tableau — que doit-on penser du cas de
la littérature où il n'a jamais existé de gamme tangible, de
forme nette qui distinguât entre le bon et le mauvais?
Etant donné que le génie a toujours échappé à tous les
cadres, puisque le génie d'aujourd'hui fait les cadres de
demain, comment s'attend-on à savoir qui est génial? Et
encore faudra-t-il que je m'explique tout à l'heure sur ce *on*
que je viens d'employer inconsciemment.

Mais en attendant, depuis qu'un James Joyce a atteint
par son dédain complet de la forme classique, un classicisme de l'anti-forme, toute l'étendue possible du langage
semble à notre disposition, sinon tactilement, du moins

sciemment. Tout est par conséquent admissible, et il n'y a rien à y opposer. Pourtant, ceci nous montre combien certains domaines encore peu explorés de la littérature sont en dehors des critères qui régissaient les valeurs classiques. Et il nous apparaît de plus en plus visiblement que la valeur littéraire ne réside ni dans la construction grammaticale, ni dans la construction phonétique, étymologique, ou autre, mais bien dans la trame invisible d'un fil qui remonte par-dessus un mot et passe sous un autre, et qui forme finalement la grandeur littéraire. Pourtant, si l'on changeait un peu la forme, tout en gardant les mêmes éléments, il arriverait ce qui arrive lorsqu'on imagine une cinquième dimension: deux et deux ne feraient plus quatre, mais trois et demi ou cinq. Et en littérature ceci est d'autant plus grave que nous n'avons jamais su si deux et deux faisaient bien quatre. Nous avons cru, à ce sujet, un Voltaire, un Sainte-Beuve, mais c'est parce que nous le voulions bien.

Et puis, quand je dis, nous le voulions bien, j'exagère. Je le voulais bien, oui; mais vous, je ne sais quelle a été votre attitude. Car, de critères il n'est pas tellement important qu'il y en ait, autant qu'il importe qu'on sache pour qui ces critères doivent servir d'autorité. J'écrivais, il y a un instant: « Comment s'attend-on à savoir qui est génial? » Mais d'abord, qui est *on?* Le *on* important, dira l'un, c'est la postérité. Mais l'autre répondra:

— La postérité est toujours une masse, une majorité. Or, l'opinion de la majorité est d'importance nulle en ce qui concerne les valeurs artistiques. Sinon, pourquoi croire plutôt la masse future que la masse présente? Pourtant, celle-ci se trompe presque toujours.

— D'accord. Mais alors, l'artiste ne travaille pas pour la masse. Il travaille pour une élite.

— Mais, une élite, c'est bien vague. Il y a mille élites, et l'élite de chacune d'entre elles. D'ailleurs, comment savoir où est l'élite?

— L'élite se compose des hommes qu'on accepte comme autorités.

(Ici, j'interviens de nouveau pour demander que celui qui parle définisse ses termes).

Je lui dis:

— Quel est ce *on* qui doit accepter l'autorité de l'élite? Et il me répondra:

— Mais c'est justement l'élite, enfin les hommes d'élite qui reconnaissent la supériorité d'une minorité d'entre-eux.

Mais de fil en aiguille, on arrive à voir qu'il n'y a pas d'élite, puisque l'élite n'est pas la même pour moi que pour vous. Et, à supposer que deux personnes qui discutent arrivent à être d'accord que tel critique fait partie de l'élite, qu'adviendra-t-il ensuite? Les deux hommes, qui ne sont pas partisans des mêmes gloires littéraires, seront tombés d'accord parce que le critique de leur choix admire à la fois l'un et l'autre de leurs dieux. Mais l'un continuera à dire:

— Un tel est un grand critique, un homme perspicace de la vraie élite, à cause de ce qu'il a écrit sur Valéry et tant d'autres. Mais, justement, j'ai toujours été d'avis qu'il se trompait en prenant France pour un écrivain.

Et son interlocuteur ne manquera pas de répondre:

— Pour ma part, j'ai toujours confiance en ce que dit Untel. Mais, dans ce qu'il a dit de Valéry, il s'est incontestablement trompé.

Où ceci nous mène-t-il? Tout simplement à la constatation que l'élite pour moi, c'est moi; pour vous, c'est vous; et pour un tiers, c'est lui. Mais, n'est-ce pas Anatole France qui a écrit dans ses critiques du *Temps* qu'il n'existe pas de critique objective? Nous voyons, en effet, de plus en plus, que toute critique est subjective. Cela sous-entend que pour la création il en est de même. Et c'est une chose que peu de gens songeraient aujourd'hui à nier; quittes à déplorer ensuite l'excès de subjectivisme qui amène un écrivain à ne travailler que pour lui-même. Le cas existe: c'est la fin lamentable de James Joyce. Mais là où un créateur qui s'y laisse prendre aura besoin de se contenter de se passer de lecteurs, un critique totalement subjectif ferait figure de fasciste. Car, l'essence même du critique est d'expliquer à son lecteur les qualités d'une œuvre.

Pourtant, ces qualités qu'il essaie d'expliquer, existent-elles? C'est ce dont je me permets de douter. Il est évident que le critique qui aime ou qui n'aime pas une œuvre, essaie de trouver, autant pour lui-même que pour son lecteur, les raisons de cette attitude. Il invente donc des qualités ou des défauts. Car, s'il ne les inventait pas — lui ou un autre dont il vole l'invention, évidemment, — ces qualités et ces défauts existeraient abstraitement. Il y aurait des critères positifs. Or, il n'en existe même pas de négatifs. S'il y avait des critères, ils existeraient quelque part. On n'est pas d'accord pour dire que la masse les detienne, ni qu'ils soient l'apanage d'une élite déterminée ou d'un seul homme. Il ne

reste, à ce que je vois, en dehors de cela, que deux possibilités: soit, l'Académie (ou l'Université, enfin l'instruction
publique) connaît les *vrais* critères, soit, alors, ils appar-
tiennent à un ou à plusieurs hommes de goût (c'est-à-dire,
des lettrés, mais pas nécessairement des critiques).

A la thèse que l'instruction publique connaît les critères
littéraires, on se doit visiblement d'opposer que bon nombre
des plus grands génies que nul ne songerait aujourd'hui à
contester sont restés méconnus pendant des périodes qui
ont parfois couvert des siècles et que, par conséquent, des
génies plus grands encore sont peut-être ceux, morts ou
vivants, qu'aujourd'hui on tient pour médiocres, franchement mauvais, ou qu'on ignore totalement. Et puisque, en
fin de compte, l'opinion de l'instruction publique se modi-
fiera selon les ondulations de celle des hommes que suivant
les périodes elle prendra pour chefs ou pour compétences
extérieures, on en vient aisément à conclure que ce n'est
pas elle qui détient les critères absolus. (Car, voici un mot
que nous ramenons sur le tard dans ces pages, mais un
mot qu'il faut garder présent à l'esprit: *absolu*, telle est la
qualité que nous demandons aux critères littéraires pour
les reconnaître. Nous aurons l'occasion de revenir sur leur
relativité).

Donc, il reste l'idée que ce sont les hommes de goût qui
connaissent les valeurs véritables. Il faudrait, évidemment,
composer un aréopage d'hommes de goût pour dire que tel
écrivain est grand, ou simplement important, et que tel
autre ne l'est pas. Mais, pour constituer cet aréopage les
suffrages seraient de nouveau divisés. Pourtant, Anatole
France est peut-être le seul homme que tous, depuis ses

plus fervents admirateurs jusqu'à ses ennemis les plus
farouches, seraient d'accord pour reconnaître comme un
parfait homme de goût. Or, non seulement ses détracteurs
mais encore beaucoup de ceux qui le considèrent un écrivain important, se trouvent ne pas partager ses opinions
sur un Mallarmé, un Moréas. Et dès l'instant où l'on n'est
pas d'accord avec lui, du moins pour ceux qui ne parta-
gent pas son avis, ses critères perdent leur qualification
d'absolus. C'en est fait de l'autorité de l'homme de goût.

Et il ne reste qu'une alternative, celle que nous avons
supposée déjà: mes critères sont pour moi absolus, les
vôtres le sont pour vous, et ainsi de suite. La critique est
donc toute subjective, et toute discussion littéraire est inutile. Je répète, si je ne me suis point fait bien comprendre
auparavant, que la discussion littéraire est inutile parce que,
lorsque je vous demanderai de définir les termes que vous
avez employés pour dire la grandeur de tel écrivain, vous
aurez beau chercher le mot, la tournure, la phrase, la page
même qui vous sont preuves de la « profondeur », de la
« psychologie », de la « beauté », de « l'exactitude », invo-
quées. Si ces qualités existent, elles existent à l'état de parfaite intangibilité. Et c'est pourquoi il n'est plus de crime
de lèse-littérature.

Cependant, on pourra contester que ceci amènerait une
parfaite anarchie dans les lettres. Je n'y vois aucun incon-
vénient. Car, pourquoi faudrait-il que deux ou plusieurs
soient d'accord et qu'ils se groupent?

On dira encore que cet état d'anarchie serait regrettable.
Je le veux bien. Et on ajoutera qu'il n'y a qu'à accepter des
valeurs universelles et arbitraires. C'est en somme ce qu'on
a toujours fait jusqu'ici. Mais il restera toujours ceux qui

ne voudront pas accepter ces valeurs arbitraires, et nous ne
pourrons plus invoquer les mythes passés du jugement
absolu pour les faire rentrer dans le troupeau. C'est encore
eux qui seront l'élément le plus objectif, puisqu'ils essaye-
ront d'atteindre une vérité au-delà des critères subis par un
commun consentement mais sans bases profondes.

Je crois que toutes les possibilités sont ainsi passées
devant nous et qu'aucune n'a résisté à l'épreuve. Pourtant,
je ne veux pas croire que je n'ai dit que des choses destruc-
tives. Il n'y aurait là aucun mérite. D'autant plus que la
valeur littéraire existe, relative il est vrai, mais existe tout
de même. On ne la touche pas du doigt. Et peu importe.
Car nous ne savons rien de la réalité, mais si nous admettons que celle-ci existe, un des mille et un critiques dont
les opinions sont toutes différentes est sans doute en train
de dire vrai, de toucher à cette réalité, sans le savoir.

Le philosophe d'aujourd'hui qui mérite peut-être mieux
que quiconque le titre de « plus grand » (ceci n'est, évidemment, que mon avis personnel), Julien Benda, vient d'écrire
que ce sont les idées que les hommes se font des réalités
qui sont importantes puisqu'elles sont elle-mêmes des réalités. Encore faudrait-il s'entendre sur l'expression « les
hommes ». De nouveau, nous arriverons en fin de compte
à la conclusion que pour chaque homme il y a une idée de
la réalité et que chacune de ces idées est une réalité. Comment saurions-nous si l'une d'entre-elles est la vraie réalité,
la réalité abstraite, à supposer encore que celle-ci existât?
Nous touchons là à la relativité pure. Même la réalité abstraite n'est plus *vraie,* relativement à d'autres dimensions,
à d'autres éléments. Et il en est ainsi en littérature. Le

critère absolu ne peut exister ou, s'il pouvait exister, ne pourrait s'atteindre consciemment.

Ainsi, à toutes les occasions où j'ai fait œuvre de critique, je reconnais moi-même avoir fait comme le font, consciemment ou inconsciemment, tous les critiques, c'est-à-dire, avoir trouvé d'abord une sympathie ou une antipathie pour mon sujet et avoir ensuite essayé de justifier cette sympathie ou cette antipathie par le fait que ce sujet remplissait ou manquait à remplir à des conditions que j'exigeais consciemment qu'elle remplît. Cela ne voulait dire après tout que ceci: *Moi*, j'aime cette œuvre ou je ne l'aime pas. Et je n'aurais cherché à convaincre quiconque ni à lui faire accepter mon jugement.

Pourtant, l'idée d'écrire un essai totalement destructif ne me plaît guère. Même les choses inutiles sont préférables à rien du tout. Et celui qui détruit sans chercher à reconstruire est un gêneur. Donc, j'inscris ici en conclusion la seule qualification qui me paraisse résister aux assauts et être à la base de toutes mes décisions: bien que le degré d'indifférence, d'antipathie ou même de sympathie puisse varier — et sans que cela ait aucune importance, — les œuvres et les hommes importants, qui sont les chefs-d'œuvre et les écrivains vraiment grands, sont caractérisés par ceci, qu'ils sont des *forces qui existent*. Et c'est peut-être parce que ces forces, qu'elles soient dans le style, la pensée, la psychologie, ou même la typographie, toujours intangibles et indéfinissables, qu'on les discute autant qu'on voudra, elles n'en existeront pas moins; c'est peut-être pour cela que j'ose énoncer si calmement, *il n'est plus de crime de lèse-littérature.*   5 - 8 février 1930.   Harold J. Salemson.

N O T E S

(Harold J. SALEMSON)

A POWER

A man has come to light within the last few months, in American letters, who has shown himself immediately to be one cι the most important powers in that field. I mean Mr. V. F. Calverton. He had already published *Sex Expression in Literature* and *The Newer Spirit* and we knew he was no mean critic. And his remarkable book *The Bankruptcy of Marriage,* of which I have previously spoken, is one of the best that exist upon the subject. But now, he has confirmed his sense of initiative, already obvious when he founded *The Modern Quarterly* and later became Book-review Editor of *The Book-League Monthly,* by several new exploits. One after the other, we owe to him the symposium *Sex in Civilization* (Macaulay) which he edited, the symposium upon the Revolution of the Word which he gathered together in *The Modern Quarterly,* his masterly *Anthology of American Negro Literature* (The Modern Library), and finally his first book of fiction, *Three Strange Lovers* (Macaulay).

Sex in Civilization, edited by Calverton in collaboration with S. D. Schmalhausen, is one of the most monumental books we have in the quest for a greater happiness through a better outlook upon the problems of sex. It comprises thirty-two essays by the world's most distinguished critics, doctors, psycho-analysts, and specialists on all subjects pertaining to this momentous issue. For, in truth, every aspect of the problem is here taken into consideration, and one may say without fear that the publication of this book has meant an immense step in the direction of human enlightenment. As for the symposium on the Revolution of the Word, it brought together six essays by Calverton, Jolas, Sage, Gilbert, Gorman and Loving which have done not a little to make that movement more clear and to establish an impartial attitude toward what Harry Hansen calls « The Wordy Revolution ». One is tempted to agree more with the liberty advocated by those who are for the new word than with its adversaries, but even here Calverton in his essay has stated pro and con more clearly than anyone else, albeit his conclusion is against the renovated vocabulary.

In the *Anthology of American Negro Literature,* V. F. Calverton has at last achieved a complete cross-section of the production of America's colored inhabitants. And in so doing, revealing a master-touch in the selection of material, he has been guided by past works on the subject, while adding a sufficient originality and a preface of enough strength and direction to make the composite product purely a result of his own affinities and aims. The poetic section, for example, is happily reminiscent of Countée Cullen's *Caroling Dusk;* and as a whole, each selection is a gem in itself. Calverton stresses the *typical* value of each selection, but he seems to overlook the literary merit of each in itself. No doubt, when one knows the anthologist, it is useless to say that each choice would have such merit.

Now, V. F. Calverton is, I believe, a member of that « 99 » which I have had occasion to mention before as distinctly different from my own generation. And, in *Three Strange Lovers,* it is that which recalls Calverton's *class* that appeals to me the least. There is an attitude toward life, among his characters, which we find in all the important works of that generation, an attitude derived from the influence of André Gide, or earlier Oscar Wilde. The character of the first story of this trilogy is an esthete who cannot bear to think that his beloved will be withered by age and enters into a suicide pact with her. But when her beauty has become eternal through death, there it that trait also Gidian, the lack of decision on his part to end his own days. He is awaiting a chance to do that *in style.* The other two stories are marked by analogous characteristics. What, then, makes one feel that in this book Mr. Calverton has not only gone deep into human psychology, but also created a work of great modern fiction? I believe it is that in him which belongs to no generation: his sturdy grip of his art, his profound knowledge of humanity, his enthralling story-telling, and above all his will to understand men, better to serve them.

Mr. V. F. Calverton is a writer whose handshake can bridge any gap, of time or of space.

Les Livres

Le « triomphe » de la saison est donc, d'après les annonces, *David Golder* (Grasset) d'Irène Némirovsky. Peut-être le livre s'est-il en effet bien vendu. Mais, littérairement, quel ruisseau grondant! On peut croire à la force psychologique, mais c'est qu'on aura oublié Stefan Zweig. *David Golder* est un feuilleton. Pourtant, la même maison donne deux nouveaux volumes dans sa collection « La Vie de Bohême ». Un agréable *Verlaine* de Marcel Coulon; et un *Monticelli* d'André Negis qui nous fait connaître et une personnalité d'artiste trop ignorée et un biographe au rude talent. On voudra connaître autre chose de M. André Negis.

D'ailleurs, toujours chez Grasset, il est d'autres livres intéressants. *Hans le marin*, de M. Edouard Peisson est un roman qui se lit agréablement quoiqu'un peu mince, et *Un Homme vint de l'Orient*, d'Elian J. Finbert est presqu'un livre important. Malheureusement cet Oriental qui « découvre » la France la connaît déjà trop bien. S'ensuit dans sa description un poncif gênant. Lorsque M. Finbert en sera revenu, quel talent que le sien!   ,

Mais parmi les rares livres qui semblent importants, lus dernièrement, il faut mettre au premier plan *Sodome et Berlin* (Emile-Paul) d'Ivan Goll. C'est un bien curieux roman de notre temps, mettant en scène l'inflation allemande, et dû à la plume d'un romancier poète particulier qui chevauche les civilisations allemande et française. On ne saurait trop le recommander.

Sur le même plan est ce *Grand homme* (Kra) que nous donne Philippe Soupault. Il arrache au clair-obscur de notre temps des personnages qu'il fait se mouvoir un moment dans Paris et en France, puis il les rend à l'infini. Philippe Soupault est bien loin d'avoir abandonné la littérature pour le feuilleton comme l'ont dit certains. Il reste une des forces de l'époque actuelle.

Et dans ce sens Joseph Jolinon s'affirme lui aussi. *Les Revenants dans la Boutique* (Riéder), est une peinture à la fois féroce et véridique de notre après-guerre. Et l'auteur y ajoute quelques prédictions sur la *prochaine*. Espérons qu'elles ne se réalisent pas et n'y voyons qu'une preuve nouvelle du talent remarquable de Joseph Jolinon.

Quant à René Glotz, je viens de lire son livre paru voici bien des mois, *A mon gré* (Sans Pareil), et je suis tenté de dire qu'il a redécouvert la prose. Combien plus passionnantes sont ces simples écritures diffuses que bien des romans qui cherchent à vous retenir par leur intrigue. J'attends beaucoup de René Glotz: oui, une œuvre.

Par contre, une œuvre réalisée est celle de G. Ribémont-Dessaignes, dont le nouveau livre, et un des meilleurs, *Frontières humaines* (Carrefour), vient de paraître. On a parlé de sadisme à froid au sujet de cet auteur, et c'est assez approprié comme titre pour le détachement avec lequel il plonge dans son monde irréel pour y élaborer les histoires les plus fantastiques qui soient. Ribémont-Dessaignes est tellement à part dans la littérature d'aujourd'hui qu'on ne peut que lui donner une admiration béate. Il tient une place propre et qui n'a jamais été ni ne sera jamais à aucun autre. Aux mêmes éditions, *Hebdomeros* de G. de Chirico nous rappelle que celui-ci est un peintre remarquable.

J'avoue ne pas comprendre l'engouement de Valéry Larbaud pour *Ceux d'en-bas* (Fourcade) de Mariano Azuela, traduit par J. et J. Maurin. C'est un roman excellent de la révolution mexicaine, et c'est prenant. Mais ce n'est pas grand. Ne l'est pas non plus le petit tableau de mœurs spéciales qui s'appelle *Kate* (Kra), par A. Jullien Du Breuil. Mais je suis assez étonné aussi du fait que le prix Gringoire ait été décerné au *Premier Homme que j'ai tué* (Renaissance du livre), de Marcel Sauvage. Des contes excellents mais qui n'atteignent pas encore le niveau qu'on voudrait croire celui des prix littéraires.

Du côté poésie, *Poèmes*, de O.-W. de L.-Milosz, paru chez Fourcade, nous permet de mieux connaître un grand poète. Oui, grand:

> Tous les morts sont ivres de pluie vieille et sale
>
> Au cimetière étrange de Lofoten,
>
> L'horloge du dégel tictaque lointaine
>
> Au cœur des cercueils pauvres de Lofoten...

n'est-ce pas?

Aux mêmes éditions, *Ulysse bâtit son lit* de Jean de Bosschère nous permet de préférer les dessins de celui-ci à ses vers; et *Jeux cosmiques* de Pierre Guéguen nous permet de constater que l'excellent et original critique des *Nouvelles littéraires* n'a peut-être pas tort d'être surtout critique (tant pis! je sais que c'est dangereux de dire une chose pareille d'un monsieur haut-placé).

La Viole d'ombre (Le Rouge et le Noir), de Raoul Raynaud peut s'apparenter aux poèmes de M. Guéguen puisque les deux poètes accusent des admirations analogues. M. Raynaud a un talent point négligeable s'il n'est pas de la plus haute originalité, et ce que j'aime peut-être le mieux de lui est:

Là-bas, l'indéfinissable Corbeau

Croasse noir, et dit des choses...

Il n'est plus de couleur aux roses:

Tu dors au fond de moi comme au fond d'un tombeau...

Tout autres, les *Poèmes d'ouvriers américains* (Les Revues), traduits par N. Guterman et P. Morhange, sont, de ce que j'ai lu depuis longtemps, ce que je mettrais le plus près de Milosz, par exemple. Seul, en français, un Francis André arrive à une telle grandeur comme poète prolétarien. Dans ce petit volume se révèle à la France la corde chantante d'un certain nombre de poètes ouvriers américains, Martin Russak, notre collaborateur Norman Macleod, bien d'autres, et à côté d'une conscience de classe qu'on peut ne pas totalement goûter, on trouve un lyrisme et un talent constants qui sont à la fois un enseignement et une promesse.

M. Jacques Baron, qui vient de publier *Paroles* (Cahiers du Sud), va progressivement, lui, d'une attitude créatrice surréaliste vers une attitude communiste. Dans ces poèmes l'inspiration surréaliste subsiste encore, ainsi que l'incontestable talent de Jacques Baron. Ce talent, qui va croissant, n'est pas servi au mieux par ces poèmes transitoires, et Jacques Baron « nouveau style » est un poète que j'attends avec une délicieuse anticipation. (En passant, signalons *Un cadavre,* journal surréaliste, dont le premier numéro fut consacré il y a cinq ans à Anatole France, et dont le second vient de paraître, consacré à André

Breton. Des surréalistes indépendants, — il ne s'agit pas d'un groupe nouveau, — Baron, Leiris, Vitrac, Desnos, et d'autres, signifient à M. Breton en des termes parfois peu polis, leur mépris et leur rupture définitive. Nous y reviendrons à l'occasion de la réponse de Breton).

Pour ce qui est du théâtre, tant joué qu'imprimé, deux talents immenses viennent d'y donner deux œuvres qui doivent décevoir un peu: *Amphitryon* 38 (Comédie des Champs-Elysées — Grasset), de Jean Giraudoux, et *La Voix humaine* (Comédie Française — Stock), de Jean Cocteau. La pièce de Giraudoux n'est pas ça, mais c'est la brèche qu'il faut attendre dans n'importe quelle *grande* œuvre, et il nous est permis de penser que le prochain livre que l'auteur nous donnera sera d'autant plus fort. Quant à l'acte de Cocteau, malgré l'interprétation formidable de Mme Berthe Bovy et malgré le texte tout plein d'une sensibilité extrême, le sujet n'est peut-être pas à la hauteur des sujets précédents de Cocteau. On a parlé d'une humanité nouvelle chez lui; hélas, non! *Orphée* est combien plus humain! Mais Cocteau ne suit jamais une piste très longtemps. Ceci n'est heureusement qu'un petit écart.

BOOKS

There are several people who create dates in history when they publish a new book, and among them, uppermost perhaps, is Eugene O'Neill. His latest play to appear is the last one given on Broadway, *Dynamo* (Liveright). Unfortunately, space does not permit us to deal with this volume at as great length as we might wish. However, in a few words, it is short, more compact than any of the author's previous works, and a more concise expression of his thought than he had yet given. For that reason, it will remain as one of the keystones of his work. And since it is to be followed by two new plays which will in. a way complement it, we will have occasion to mention it many times again.

Another event, *Marriage and Morals* (Liveright) by Bertrand Russell, is also somewhat, the closing of an epoch, for it resumes and concludes almost all the threads found in Russell's earlier books, that have to do with marriage, morals, or ethics. The world as Russell sees it is something of a paradise, for it is rid of hypocrisy and sham. But his theories have a practical aspect which makes of them a set of morals which might be followed, and may have to be followed, and it would be no pity.

As for verse, Judas seems decidedly in honor. Both Lola Ridge, in *Firehead* (Brewer and Warren), and Robinson Jeffers, in *Dear Judas* (Liveright), have not only used him as a character but even in a way vindicated him. Both see him ineluctably doomed to betray, the tool of a Fate which only Christ could stay, and which he did not. Neither of these poets needs our recommendation to reënforce the reputation of his gift for prosody. But I believe Miss Ridge's book is in all manners more momentous than that of Jeffers, no mean achievement either.

The prosody of Walter Lowenfels, author of *Finale of Seem* (Heinemann, London), on the other hand, demands more discussion than the content of his verse. For that prosody is so modern as to intrude upon the reader's appreciation. I do not dare say I have mastered the trick of Lowenfels' prosody, nor even of his typography. But what does seem clear is that he, with Wallace Stevens, wants « be (to) be the finale of seem ». Then, one might think he would avoid images. But they are the chief richness of this chant of love. Still, there is something metaphysical about this poet, which, in spite of his mature talent, he unfortunately did not bring home to me.

There is enough of metaphysics in Mr. R. D. Norton's *Poems and Translations* (Medici Society, London), too. But this is Rimbaud, this is Valéry, rendered into English, and into an English that is legible. Some parts of the translations in this volume can vie with the finest toward the perfect ultimate renderings of *Le bateau ivre* or *Le cimetière marin*. No one man could achieve the perfect translation of either of those poems.

Let us end by mentioning *Grotesques* (Living Art), a collection of short stories by G. L. Van Roosbroeck, illustrated by Matulka. Some of the stories may be banal, but none are trite, while some have a deliciously ironical savor.

Les Revues

L'excellente revue de gauche, courageuse et indépendante, *Les Humbles*, (4, rue Descartes, Paris V), lance un appel et ouvre une souscription en faveur de l'écrivain Henri Guilbeaux, condamné à mort et exilé, dans des conditions, hélas! trop connues, pour ses opinions pacifistes. (Adresser souscriptions et demandes de renseignements au directeur, M. Maurice Wullens).

Anthologie, la revue que dirige à Liège notre ami Georges Linze, fête son dixième anniversaire. Dans son numéro le plus récent on trouve de belles pages de Pierre Bourgeois sur la poésie, de Georges Linze, un poème de Paul Frédéric Bowles, etc...

Europe publie, depuis février, *Destin du Théâtre,* perçant essai de Jean-Richard Bloch dont on connaît assez l'acuité et la sage logique. Cet essai, sur le théâtre, est parsemé d'excellentes notations diverses dont celle sur M. Gide n'est pas la moins exacte: Gide qui écrit « le roman du romancier en train d'écrire son roman ». Le personnage que fige ainsi Jean-Richard Bloch ne peut plus nous intéresser.

Signalons enfin la transformation de l'hebdomadaire *Bravo* qui devient mensuel. Dans cette formule nouvelle, la revue qui est désormais la revue française du spectacle affirme ses tendances: donner un coup d'œil sur le monde entier, sur le spectacle dans toutes ses formes, par les admirables photos qui sont l'iconographie de notre temps. A côté de ces documents, ce n'est pas un hasard qui nous fait relever au bas des textes les noms de Jules Romains, d'Henri Bidou, de Marcel Pagnol, d'autres encore parmi les écrivains significatifs de ce jour. En supplément, *Bravo* donne chaque mois une pièce complète, dont la première a été *Le cocu magnifique* de Fernand Crommelynck et la seconde *Amis comme avant* d'Henri Jeanson.

Livres à lire

Quelques nouveaux livres par des collaborateurs de *Tambour:*
Françis AMBRIÈRE, *Du Bellay* (Firmin-Didot);
André CHAMSON, *Tyrol* (Grasset);
Jean COCTEAU *La Voix humaine* (Stock);

Maurice Constantin-Weyer, *P. C. de Compagnie* (Riéder);
Joseph Delteil, *Les Chats de Paris* (Montaigne);
Waldo Frank, *Nouvelle Découverte de l'Amérique* (Grasset);
Joseph Jolinon, *Les Revenants dans la Boutique* (Riéder);
Georges Linze, *Pont* (Anthologie);
Marcel Loumaye, *Poèmes de Guerre* (Anthologie)·
Paul Morand, *New York* (Flammarion).

What to read

New books by some contributors to *Tambour:*
Maxwell Bodenheim, *Bringing Jazz* (Liveright);
Witter Bynner, *Indian Earth* and *The Jade Mountain* (With Dr. Kiang Kang-Hu) (Knopf);
Countée Cullen, *The Black Christ* (Harpers);
Bertrand Russel, *Marriage and morals* (Liveright);
Joseph Upper, *Walking Shadow* (Bozart Press).

In our next issue :

*We will review the various impressions made by our symposium
on Anatole France, and publish* Two Stories *by James T. Farrell,*
Modern Flemish Writing *by H. R. Hays,* Towards an Epoch *by Georges Linze,* The Wheel *by Romola S. Voynow, poems by Edouard
Roditi, Max Reynolds, Joseph Upper, etc...*

Montpellier. — Imprimerie Causse, Graille et Castelnau, 7, rue Dom-Vaissette.

Le gerant : J. BRUNEL.

April
1 9 3 0
Avril

7

....

Revue Mensuelle

A monthly magazine

PRIX 6 Fr.

7

DANS CE NUMÉRO — IN THIS ISSUE
L'ITALIE :

GARIBALDO ALESSANDRINI est le poète ardent et mystique de *Rythmes d'infini.*

MASSIMO BONTEMPELLI, fondateur de 900, poète de *Pur-Sang,* et romancier très original.

IGNAZIO DRAGO a révélé une sensibilité très fine dans ses recueils, *Un cœur pour tout le monde; Signes,* etc...

GIORGIO FERRANTE s'est fait récemment remarquer par *Cœur de givre.*

LIÓNELLO FIUMI, le poète de *Pollen, Mousselines, Les yeux à la ronde,* et *Tout en cœur,* est aussi auteur d'une remarquable *Anthologie de la Poésie italienne contemporaine* (en français), éditée à Paris.

CORRADO GOVONI est le poète le plus imagé d''Italie. Il a publié une douzaine de volumes.

EUGENIO MONTALE est l'auteur du recueil très remarqué, *Os de seiche.*

NICOLA MOSCARDELLI, romancier fécond, est poète dans *Tatouages, Le Pont,* etc...

A.-S. NOVARO est un des doyens de la poésie italienne; ses principaux recueils sont *Le cœur caché, Le forgeron harmonieux,* et *Le petit Orphée.*

GIACOMO PRAMPOLINI a donné à ce jour *Du haut silence.*

GIUSEPPE VILLAROEL est l'auteur très en vue de *La palette et le hautbois, La beauté entrevue,* et *Ombres sur l'écran,* qui vient de paraître.

NINO FRANK, poète et prosateur bilingue (franco-italien), collabore à divers journaux et revues parisiens. Secrétaire de la rédaction de *Bifur.*

MARIO MONTANARD est candidat au titre du Parfait Poète Paresseux.

CLAUDE SYMIL, très jeune poétesse française a fait ses débuts dans *Tambour.*

FREDERIC COVER has contributed verse to *New Masses, Morada,* etc...

H. R. HAYS is a constant contributor to *Tambour.*

NORMAN MACLEOD is one of the really original elements among America's younger poets. He edits *The Morada.*

VIRGINIA STAIT has previously appeared in *Tambour.*

RICHARD THOMA is a bilingual poet and prosateur. He has contributed to *Blues, The Morada, Janus,* etc...

ROMOLA S. VOYNOW is a young Chicago woman whose talent has long been kept from print by a modesty at last fortunately vanquished.

ARABELLA YORKE, born in Pennsylvania, lives in Paris where she is engaged in the translation of French books into English.

TAMBOUR

ERRATA

Dans ce premier numéro de TAMBOUR,
lire à la page 4, les 12ᵉ et 13ᵉ vers du poème
CONFIDENCES :

Sur nos chaises-longues de toile,

Devant la blanche lisse du pont,

Sur le dos de la couverture, lire les deux
premières notices :

André SPIRE est l'auteur de plusieurs
volumes de vers (**Versets, Poèmes juifs, etc..**) et
de prose (**Quelques juifs et demi-juifs, etc..**).

Son poème dans ce numéro sera dans le
recueil **Poème de Loire**, à paraître chez Grasset.

Philippe SOUPAULT a écrit plusieurs
romans excellents (**Le bon apôtre, En joue !, etc..**)
et quelques volumes de vers.

T A M B O U R

Directeur, Harold J. Salemson, Editor

▬ 5, Rue Berthollet, PARIS (Vᵉ) France, ▬

Of this issue, 250 copies are numbered.

De ce numéro, 250 exemplaires ont été numérotés.

Interpréter le passé, c'est exprimer le présent;
exprimer le présent, c'est créer l'avenir.

To interpret the past is to express the present;
to express the present is to create the future.

ARRÊT PROVISOIRE

Les revues d'avant-garde, comme les transports en commun, connaissent parfois des arrêts. *Tambour* peut se vanter d'avoir échappé aux vicissitudes presque nécessaires aux publications de son genre. Pourtant, des circonstances en dehors de notre contrôle le veulent: ce huitième numéro, clôturant notre deuxième série, ne sera pas immédiatement suivi d'un autre.

Que nos lecteurs se rassurent! Le caractère provisoire de cette interruption est indéniable. Nous pensons, d'ores et déjà, pouvoir affirmer que *Tambour* recommencera à paraître vers le début de 1931. Ce ne sont, en effet, pas les difficultés habituelles qui nous bloquent le chemin, mais d'autres, moins prévisibles et plus paralysantes: notamment le départ pour l'Amérique de notre directeur au début de l'automne.

Ainsi, en remerciant nos abonnés de l'assiduité et de la fidélité qu'ils
nous ont témoignées jusqu'ici, nous leur adressons nos bons vœux
jusqu'au moment, très proche sans doute, où ils seront avisés de la
reparution et de la publication plus régulière et plus satisfaisante de
Tambour, dans des conditions que nous leur indiquerons alors.

(*Note:* Puisque nous ne pourrions donner la liste complète des adhé-
sions au manifeste publié dans notre numéro précédent, nous ne
donnons point non plus celles, déjà nombreuses, qui nous sont parve-
nues jusqu'ici. Un jour, plus tard, peut-être, pourrons-nous en publier
la liste complète.)

CARS STOP HERE

Little reviews, like public conveyances, are sometimes obliged to stop.
Tambour may boast of having escaped the vicissitudes which are
almost necessary to publications of its type.   However, circumstances
beyond our control will have it so: this eighth issue, closing our second
series, will not immediately be followed by another.

Our readers may feel certain that the temporary character of this
interruption is undeniable.   We already feel in a position to assure
them that *Tambour* will re-appear toward the beginning of 1931. As
a matter of fact, it is not the habitual difficulties that are
blocking our path, but others, less predictable and more paralyzing:
particularly, the departure of the editor for the United States, in the
early Fall.

Thus, thanking our subscribers for the assiduousness and faithfulness they have shown us, we can merely offer them our good
wishes until the time, in the very near future, when they are informed
of the re-appearance of *Tambour*, under conditions that we will then
indicate.

(*Note:* Since we should not able to give a complete list of the
adherents to the manifesto published in our last issue, we will forego
giving the names of those who have already replied. Some day, later,
perhaps, we will be able to publish all the names.)

POÈTE

Non je n'ai pas le courage
De créer les mots
En arrachant, en découpant
Mon corps de chair.

Il faudrait faire
Saigner, meurtrir, tailler,
Un peu de chair,
Beaucoup de sang,
Pour un seul mot.

Profanation des poèmes
Que l'on écrit avec la tête,
Profanation de chaque mot
Qui n'est pas une offrande
A l'autel.

Si je mets sur ce papier
Un seul mot qui fut pensé,
Un mot qui ne fut pas aimé,
Un mot qui ne fut pas baisé,

J'irai bien honteux par les rues,
A chaque mot une cloche pendue
Dira à tous que j'ai préféré vendre
                Sur le marché.

Claire HUCHET.

POÈME D'AMOUR

Nos deux corps blancs
Dorés par la lune
Descendent le fleuve lent de la nuit.
A peine le vent aux mains pâles
Soulève nos âmes.
Nous longeons les jardins de l'éternité
Où dorment les oiseaux et les dieux.
Parfois l'on entend
Une anémone s'ouvrir
Ou une étoile tomber
Comme une mouche brûlée...
Côte à côte nos corps descendent
Le fleuve de mercure
Dont on ne sait plus
S'il est la vie,
S'il est la mort.

Ivan Goll.

BEELDEKENS UIT HET LEVEN

(Poèmes en langue française)

I

La ville sous la neige
est morne
comme une poitrine blanche.

Chambre.
Le poète
promène sa prescience.

Il dit:
— femme
ta hanche est centripète.

L'instinct de la genèse a traversé ses doigts
émus
tendus par une prière
sales comme toute l'histoire
d'une machine.

Et la maison respire
voluptueuse comme une usine
elle est un poumon de la cité.

Un poète a fait un geste:
la ville est nue
et je vois battre son cœur.

La neige n'a plus
que l'adhérence de la mémoire.

Maintenant le soleil
est un peu de bonheur
qui déshabille
notre sommeil.

II

La rue est claire
de tout le bonheur
dont nos mains chaudes nous ont gonflés

nos mains
qui sont devenues simples
dans la confession
de notre chair.

La rue est vide
des découvertes
de nos corps penchés sur nous
comme une église.

Nous avons mesuré
à la prière
la pitié de notre amour

nos beaux yeux aggravés dans la douceur du ciel
tu t'es courbée
et je me suis penché

mes gestes tremblants et pieux
ont cherché le chemin
d'une étape finale au jardin de ta chair.

A la messe le prêtre ouvre le tabernacle
les fidèles ferment les yeux
penchent le front

Je n'entends plus battre les cœurs.
— Amie, j'ai dénoué ta ceinture.

Aujourd'hui cette rue est artificielle
derrière nos cœurs
qui vont à la dérive.

Un homme traverse la ville
dans une tension de tout son corps
une auto lui adhère
comm une limace.

On passe
c'est une chose sans importance.

Seule nous obsède l'heure mystérieuse
— hier vant l'émoi de ta pudeur virginale —
Où nous étions si riches
de toute otre ignorance.

Il n'y a ren autour de nous
que tes paroles simples et petites
elles soulilent encore l'étonnement :

la paix
de tous tes ours qui vont venir à mes côtés
est comme 1 trou —
parce que nus sommes si pauvres maintenant
et qu'il y a peu de choses à apprendre.

III

Autour de tes mains lentes
qui errent
sur les questions muettes de mon corps
il y a une douce et grande chaleur.

Et sur ta chair il est des pauses attentives
qui se ramifient
dans mes doigts
ainsi qu'une maturité prédite.

Pourtant tu n'as appris que de mes jeux
— hier —
l'errance de tes gestes vieux.

Doucement tes paroles viennent inutiles
sur nos lèvres qui rient sans conviction
et brisent la beauté de l'acte raisonné
où nos corps se demandent une hospitalité.

IV

Partir —
rester avec soi-même
dans les escales
du désir.

Aimer —
il n'y a de joie
que dans le silence
des paroles unies au sang.

Joie —
ton geste
a pris la forme
de mon désir.

Souffrir —
une immense nourriture
comme la succion siècle à siècle
des chairs.

Prier —
être partout
où le refus d'aimer
fige la nuit fige les corps fige la vie.

Vivre —
deux corps s'ouvrent
aux plaies humaines
amour.

Poésie —
instants tensions crucifiement spasme
conquérir l'herbier des pièges sous tes paupières
mais pas de port où l'on aborde.

Mourir —
c'est un vieux relai
d'une bienveillance momentanée
avant la lâcheté de l'oubli.

                                        Robert RADELET.

ÉVIDENCES

A André Villiers, — ce dire
est asynétiquement dédié, en
foi d'ésotérique attirance.

Le vrombissant essor des autos rumorantes
Hante le vide abscons dont mon cœur est empli,
Car la vitesse ailée exile de ses plis
Le bourgeoisisme épais des grignoteurs de rentes.

Caniculairement mon âme en combustion
Encarbonise l'air d'un rythme asynartète.
Dans les prés vagissants de verdoyants veaux têtent.
Super-film déroulé au jeu des stations !

Car la vie est ainsi, prude et taxidermiste,
Et l'auto glissera sur cet incliné plan,
Comme le veau-marin, suavement plan-plan,
Avec l'air smaragdin d'un apprenti-chimiste !

Bonheur, auto ! Oh ! tôt, bonheur ! Bonheur au taux
De vingt-six sous d'essence à chaque myriamètre,
Cubisme, Amour, Auto, mon art, mon Dieu, mon Maître,
Toto, sus au bonheur ! Tôt, tôt sus à l'Auto !

Francis AMBRIÈRE.

CIGARETTE

Sous papier blanc du tabac blond
Un bout d'or quelquefois, souvent une inscription.
    Pour toi, rêveur,
Un trésor en un cylindre long.

    Un trésor! Profanation!
Mieux: Le Bonheur.
    Bonheur frêle, mince et ténu
Ténu au filet bleu qui spire et chancelle
    Au premier souffle venu.

    Bonheur épanoui en volutes
Opulentes, nourries, puissantes, grasses, lactescentes:
    Bonheur qui dure.

    Ou bien encore...
Oui, mais c'est toujours le songe.

    La fumée bleue sinue;
Spirales longues ou brèves,
        C'est un dessin léger qui jamais ne s'achève
        Et le rêve
Suspendu au fragile tissu
    Flotte ininterrompu.

    Politique puissant,
    Commerçant enrichi,
        Poète inspiré, amoureux comblé;
Jamais n'aurez l'heur que rêvez:
    A d'autres il est donné.

Sous papier blanc du tabac blond
Un bout d'or quelquefois, souvent une inscription;
    Pour toi rêveur, le bonheur en un cylindre long
Jamais ne fit l'erreur de beaux discours
    Le bruit te fait horreur
    (D'autres le nomment son).
Il n'en est pas moins vrai que l'amour
    Te paraîtrait supportable
Si la femme n'était coupable
    De se taire pour un temps trop court.

    Rêve fumeur!
Et que le songe heureux né de ta cigarette
Erre sans heurt ni bruit, (O volupté parfaite!)
Dans le silence doux des volutes
    Planant au-dessus de ta tête.

                                    J. Mariotti,

PETIT POÈME ÉCRIT AU BAR ANGLAIS

        Au bar anglais
        Près du comptoir
        Je pensais à un Paradis
        En écrivant ce court poème
        Mon cœur
        Une fille l'a pris
        Et toujours ma cravate noire
        Et toujours mes anciens soucis...

                        Yves Chabauty-Bretagne.

POÈME POUR S. M.

Sous les beaux cieux de nuits vermeilles
Un monstre en marbre t'enlace,
Et te couvre, comme un froid soleil,
De baisers de neige et de glace.

Mais ton âme, tropicale et chaude,
Se livre aux serpents du Nil,
Et oublie, aux pays d'émeraudes,
Les linceuls de grésil.

Je suis le monstre superbement mort!

Reviens! Sans toi la lune me semble éteinte,
La nuit vénéneuse, et maladif le jour...
Mon cœur se meurt, et je me sens enceinte
De ton inconnu amour!

Richard THOMA.

OU TU ME TOUCHAS...

Où tu me touchas
s'agitent des fleurs —
de lentes jonquilles, ou de graves
tulipes de bronze...

Où tu me touchas
devint un Dieu —
émettant du pollen,
proférant la terre...

Où tu me touchas
des étoiles
        jaillissent,
dans tes temples
            consacrant —
    O Prétresse du toujours Printemps —
à l'ultime fertilité
le fruit brillant
dont la rapidité
devient
        toujours
semence.

Walter Lowenfels,
(Traduit de l'américain par H. J. Salemson.)

IMAGE PARLANTE

Vois!

Voix:

Mon dos - ah!
Mon dos - do⎫
Mon dos - ré⎭=(<u>chanté</u>)

Dans le vague - je dis: vague-
Est mon corps, mon corps beau-

Mon col lié d'un collier de
    corps - aïe!
C'est pour vous -
            vous laid
            vous bien
            vous "ter".

Valentin de MANOLL.

INDICATIVE   PEDESTRIAN

for Riva.

Irradiate
symphony of shade where
cat-pawed waters steal
into patterns of an agile silence
over a genesis of stones,

where a cool vesture invites
the contemplative cud
to new surrender of horizons:

so you
bring near the cool of Typal greens,
the purr of silences yet heavened,
the sundown blur
of shadows on a far substantial hill.

Samuel PUTNAM.

TOO MANY BOOKS

TOO MANY BOOKS

I shall drink this glass of wine
To the dregs.
I shall not stop until
Every drop is gone.

For a while I shall
    Sing and laugh and dance!

    I'll scoff! I'll ignore you!
And then when my energy
    Wanes and my brain gets tired

I'll drink another glass
And leave you
Reading your damned old book!

LOVE DISRUPTED

Dawn can be so beautiful.
It can be tranquil,
Joyous — even ecstatic.
But, my God, dearie,
Ain't it hell
When it rains?

                                        Max Reynolds.

TWO POEMS

TO A PHOTOGRAPH

Are you the sole survivor of that wreck
    Which gave my treasures to the cynic sea?
They were immured below the flooded deck,
    A priceless cargo — dreams that were, to me,
The very stuff of life. But they are dead,
    Drowned in a troubled, fathomless despair;
And you alone are left me in their stead
    For solace. Now the poisoned years will wear
My strength away with grieving and regret
    For all that wealth which nothing may recover —
Nor dredge, nor diver, nor the humble net
    Of   patient fisherman. Love from the lover
Has been abducted by the outlawed sea,
And only you remain to comfort me.

JULY NIGHT

The moon above a tall oak tree
Is an old divinity.

Fireflies in a cornfield glow —
Fairy dancers on tip-toe —

While, far off, the mountain lies
Like a dragon with closed eyes.

Wild birds chant a minstrel's praise
Of proud medieval days.

Joseph UPPER.

MOONWARD

DREAM

I sat under a tall tree with black leaves
I ate potatoes
A heron regarded me through bushes
There were kindly bees at a distance
There was no sound
No wind blew
But in a far sky a bird moved
Over hills I watched it
Over meadows with glass tops
Over forests of platinum
Over hills of steel it moved
I watched it from afarafar

In the platinum forest walked a white maiden
Slow white tones rose from her throat
She moved among the trees and sang
Where the forest white brook are
Where the wood white shadow are
Where the humming of electric wires are
Where the water white sky are

Where the long white day are
There I saw her slip between the trees and vanish
While a tone still floated in the air

SLOW SONG

There will be a time not too remotely moonward
nor yet as reminiscent of the moon's disgrace
as the bright pastures in the moonlight of your singing
or the moon's inverted canticle upon your face
when daylight over meadows and the strokes on bells
sent outward into sunlight to the banks of streams
shall settle gratefully onto the heavy grass;

shall rout no more the songless owl in moonward
                                               [dreams.

                                   Paul Frederic Bowles.

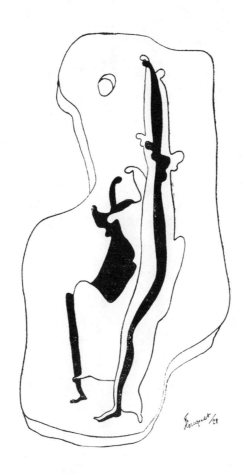

FLOUQUET : DESSIN

FLOUQUET : DESSIN

THE WHEEL

A June sun flooded the pavement as Eric trudged across the school yard. His stubby feet moved reluctantly in their thick shoes and the agony of the heat beat on his heart as on a mirror. In his pocket lay a folded square of heavy white paper on which a formidable woman had written: « My dear Mrs. Green, I am sorry to have to inform you that Eric has been misbehaving in school. I had a serious talk with him some time ago but he has persisted in his bad conduct. Will you be good enough to call on me tomorrow to discuss this matter? Yours sincerely, Miss Emma Radcliffe. »

He had watched her writing it, and read the message over her too impersonal shoulder. Once free of her, he had considered the destruction of the note. Miss Radcliffe would, however, demand his mother's presence on the morrow. It would be no better for him if he destroyed the missive. His mother, of course, would report him to his father, and his father's wrath always expressed itself in terms too concrete to be mistakable.

Eric shuffled unseeing past a game of marbles. The street stretching before him was a gray ditch banked by gray wooden houses. His mother awaited him on the front porch. « I want you to go to the store », she said in greeting. « Can't Lily go? » « Lily takes her lesson on Thursday. Run along, now, we're having company for dinner. And come right back. »

Eric traversed two blocks in a sullen reverie. The already

weighty situation had been complicated. Company for dinner! The note would have to wait until bedtime, then.

He placed his mother's list on the counter and waited. The store smelled of fresh greens and was crowded with women in aprons. Mr. Metzger, the grocer, conversed loudly with them and ignored Eric completely. Then a girl taller than Eric opened the outer door. « Lo », she said lightly. Eric felt the blood mount to his temples. This was Helen of Troy for whom all men fought. « What cha doin'? » « Oh — I'm getting some things for my mother. » « Mr. Metzger. » Helen called shrilly. He came briskly. « What is it today, little lady? » « I want you to wait on us. My friend is tired of waiting. » « Right away, miss, right away. »

Eric's admiration grew. Metzger fetched and carried for her. « Now Eric », she said graciously. « There's my list », he mumbled pointing. The bags and boxes demanded both arms when he left the store to find Helen waiting for him. « Which way you going? » He jerked his head and she fell into step beside him. « My mother lets me remember », she confided, « and so I don't need a list any more. We're going to the carnival tonight, Eric. Can you come? » « What's that? » « Haven't you seen in the vacant lot back of Johnsons'? There's booths and candy wagons and merry-go-rounds and all. Daddy said he'd take me. I wish you could come too, Eric. » « Oh, I dunno. That's mostly for kids, I guess. » Helen being older than he was too mature to take account of petty distinctions. « Well, gee, wouldn't you Like to ride on the carousel? » « Rather play ball with the fellas », he said gruffly. « Oh ». She crossed the bridge to the farther side of silence. This crushed what spirit her presence had awakened in him. What a fool, he thought, to have had this treasure within reach and to have lost it by a few careless words. He bowed his head.

Eric was conscious of someone coming towards them. « See here, what's this? » Eric lookd up to intercept a dazzling smile Helen had intended for the other boy, and to look into a pair of menacing eyes. « Why, Butch », Helen whimpered. « You said you was my girl, didn't you? » Helen lowered her lashes, but Butch was looking at Eric intently. « Then what are you walking with him for? » « I just met him at Metzger's, Butch. » « Metzger's. » Butch laughed. « Buying groceries for his mama? Well, what else can you do? »

Butch leaped and sent a fist to his jaw. In one glance Eric saw Helen back into the shelter of a tree; she held one hand over her mouth. Butch came tearing down on him like a whirlwind and his packages scattered like hail. Eric was light and slender. Butch was massive and loosely built. His arms were thick and hard, and his body had the weight of iron. Eric's breath came heavily and he closed his eyes to the assault. He was vicious as he defended himself but the other was cool in the superiority of his strength. The sun faded. Eric panted and resisted, but his lunges and blows were muffled in the bulk of his adversary. He felt the unbearable weight on his shoulders; the earth beneath him. Butch was pressing his face into the grass. « Are you down? » shouted the victor. Eric clenched

his teeth. « Are you down? » repeated Butch. There was
no answer. With great pressure Butch ground his face into
the earth. « Now », he demanded, « are you down? » Eric
could bear it no longer. « Yes, yes, yes. »

With tears in his eyes he scrambled after his bundles.
His shirt was torn, his face smudged with dirt, his cheeks
flamed and his arms were weary. Helen, under the tree,
stood looking at him. Eric turned away; tumult within.
Butch's loud laughter came to him through the still air.
A boy ran after him crying: « Butch licked Eric. Butch
licked Eric. » Others came up shouting: « Eric has a girl.
Butch licked Eric. Eric has a girl. Butch... »

The sing-song goaded him into a run. Bursting into the
kitchen he dumped the packages onto the table. « Eric,
what is the matter with you? Can't you run an errand for
me without coming home like this. Shame on you. Run up
and change your clothes before your father comes home. I
want you to set the table. » « Gee ma, can't I go play
with the boys? » « Eric, I'm surprised. I work here from
morning to night and when I ask you... » « Lily can help
you, Ma. » « Nonsense », his mother finished crisply. « It's
too near dinner time to go out now, anyway. Hurry, or I'll
tell your... mercy, what's that? »

Immaculate as a document of state Miss Radcliffe's note
protruded from the corner of his torn pocket. « Give me
that », said his mother sternly. He handed it to her and
fled. It was the inevitable.

Hot water washed away the mud, and clean clothing
replaced the torn. He reappeared before his mother with
his hair brushed neatly. She was still staring at the note

and her mouth had settled into tired lines. Eric was awed. « Ma », he breathed, « what are you gonna do? » « Set the table », she said.

Eric was seated between the two who constituted « company ». Uncle Charlie was bland, and shiny from too much soap. Aunt Emily was plump and broad, and fragrant with too much perfume. Eric glanced at his father who was carving the roast. His mother, he saw, was calm. She hadn't told him, then... yet. If the moment of doom could not be averted at least the delay was sweet. He ate ravenously and quickly, bent over his plate.

« How's the little boy tonight? » asked Aunt Emily. Eric nodded, his mouth full of food. « Answer Aunt Emily, dear », his mother cooed. Eric nodded once more. « Eric, can't you speak? » His father's voice was sharply pointed. « I'm all right », choked Eric. His father relaxed. « That's better », he said. « Next time answer when you're spoken to. »

Aunt Emily flashed her gold tooth. « I'm sure he didn't mean any harm, did you Eric? » She patted his hand with her flabby white one, and at that moment he hated her, blackly.

« Eric's a good kid », approved Uncle Charlie smugly. « How old are you, my boy? » « I'm ten. » « Well, well, quite a little man. Getting along in school? » « He'd better», muttered his father. Eric felt his mother's eyes resting on him. « What do you study now? » Charlie asked. Eric's fork halted in the process of raising its load of mashed potatoes. « Geography, spelling, arithmetic. » His uncle repeated the words. « Arithmetic, eh? Let me give you a

problem. » Eric devoured the potatoes in dismay. « If A
has two bushels of potatoes which weigh sixteen ounces
each, and B has a load that weighs forty-three ounces, how
many bushels of potatoes has B? »

Eric went on eating. As a stillness gathered around the
table he trembled inwardly. « Why don't you answer? »
roared his father. « I don't know », Eric mumbled. « Figure
it out. » Emily smiled and his mother looked troubled.
« Let him alone, father, he wants to finish his dinner. »
« He can figure a simple problem like that, I hope, Come,
Eric, what's the answer? » « I don't know. » « Think. »
« I don't want to think, papa. » « You do as I tell you or... »
« Oh, pshaw », interposed Uncle Charlie. « I don't want to
bother the lad. » « But I want him to get it », insisted his
father. « Now, Eric, before I count three. One, two, three... »
Eric looked doggedly at his plate. « Can you give me the
answer? » There was no sound. « Then leave the table at
once. I'll see you later upstairs. »

Eric pushed his chair back. For a moment he stood looking around him. Then he blinked his eyes and ran from
the house.

Down the street, around the corner, through a hedge, he
sped through the twilight. It was too much, too much. He
wondered his heart hadn't burst from the pressure. There
Helen had stood to witness his defeat, then that fiend had
tortured him, and now his father had threatened. What was
to come...

He stopped suddenly to listen to the trees as their branches bent to catch a fresh breeze. Stars began dotting the
grey sky and darkness was creeping slowly upon it. The

terror within him made him walk on, and something sprang
from the invisible to confront him. The carnival was before
him. A moustached man took his coin and permitted him
to enter. People milled around him; melodies met in mid-
air in conflict; voices shouted; cooking odors were rampant.
In a glass case popcorn had drifted like snow. A little
black dog emerged from the background to sniff Eric's
heels. Eric watched the carousel in its wild whirl. The
horses moved sedately on their brass poles; a girl held her
hat with both hands; it moved around a pillar of scarlet
and purple from whence issued music... the tinkle of a
guitar and the howl of a hand-organ. This procession passed
and repassed him until his eyes burned. Stumbling ahead
he came on a contrivance that hushed his pain.

A steel skeleton reached for the sky; it was hung with
baskets in which couples were sitting. They were as unreal
as silhouettes, but Eric heard their murmurings. A man
standing at the crank spoke to him: « One place empty,
kid, then we go. Your last chance for a ride on the world's
greatest ferris-wheel. Right this way, young man. Step in
and ride to the moon. Got five cents? »

Eric stepped into the wire basket and the man adjusted
a strap before him. He fell back to the extent of the seat.
The wheel hesitated, swung gently to and fro, then with
mighty effort took its full roll. The rush of air was like a
blessing. Darkness, with the magnitude of heaven, engul-
fed him. The sensation was delicious. The ground jerked
away, away... Below him was the carnival, a muted picture
in the glow of electric lights. People sauntered as in a
dream. The barkers' voices came to him, deadened by height

and distance. The music was as of distant trumpets. Up
he went, up. For a second he closed his eyes. When he
opened them again, he was facing the ultimate.

His neck was bared to a cool wind which caressed his
cheeks and tossed his hair. His mouth was lifted to a golden
moon and his eyes drank the immensity of the heavens.
With a rush beauty swirled around him. The blackness
was like velvet; an abyss. Within its depths struggled the
dreams of ages, the majesty of symphonies, the echo of
hope. Eric threw out his arms to it. He felt the night folding
itself therein, coming close to him. The wind played a
benediction on his brow. He was received without question
by the vast, the endless. Below him was the tinkle of a
guitar. « God », he murmured. Peace came to him, beauty
whispered to him, wonder thrilled him. He dived into the
blackness as into a pool. All bitterness, all shame, all guilt,
all sorrow, all movement, all desire were stripped from
him. He shook his very self off and entered the Nirvana of
nothingness. He saw no longer with his eyes nor felt with
his skin. He was free of them. He had gone forth to the
golden moon and the space in which it moved. A cloud
like a cobweb flecked the perfect surface of the moon. He
was still...

« Whatsa matter with you? Wanna stay here all night?
Gwan and give someone else a chance... You had your
ride. »

Eric stood on the hard earth. What lay before him was
no longer of any consequence. He started towards home.

Romola S. Voynow.

message

A René Glotz.

L'ennui... Mais qu'importe parler de l'ennui? La chose n'en vaudrait pas la peine. Pas même pour essayer de remettre à flot notre conversation morte à demi, épave déjà, qui s'éloigne à vau l'eau. Nous sommes trois ou quatre. Nous devisions. Comme la pluie d'orage abat la poussière des chemins, ainsi tout à coup n'avons nous eu plus rien à dire.

L'oiseau blessé tâche à repartir et ses ailes battent un moment la terre. Les phrases que nous échangions tout à l'heure se sont enfuies. Je ne sais quel plomb éparpilla les plumes. Il ne reste plus seulement la force de pépier un dernier appel. Notre oiseau sans doute a caché sa blessure, puis il est tombé, d'une masse, les forces épuisées. C'est tout.

Nous sommes trois ou quatre. Le silence s'est abattu. Il étouffe d'abord, tandis qu'il reste en sursaut un désir de réaction. Bientôt on n'éprouve plus qu'un sentiment de gêne. Le malaise s'appesantit et l'atmosphère s'emplit d'une buée maussade. Chacun, enfin, demeure coi. On en voudrait si l'un ou l'autre essayait de ranimer les fleurs qui dans le vase penchent la tête parce que toute l'eau s'est évaporée.

L'ennui...

L'ennui se forge à la manière d'une indécision, longue, invisible presque. Il suffirait de secouer la tête, lui dénier le droit de cette moquerie sempiternelle. Soi-même, s'éloi-

gner. Partir. Voilà tout le secret. Et l'autre s'essoufflera,
aura perdu pied, sans qu'il en demeure plus trace.
L'ennui, toutefois, est retors. Il s'avance en conspirateur;
mais il ne chante pas, comme au théâtre. Il s'apprête et
guigne sa proie. Puis l'appréhende en tourbillon. Il s'empare, harcelle, brutalise. Vous encoiffe de ses sornettes. Il
s'impose et fait en sorte de ne laisser point le répit d'une
seconde. On s'abandonne. Et la farce est jouée.

***

Nous étions trois ou quatre. A l'ombre d'un arbre arrêtés. Un arbre, j'ignore quel.
Et qui donc aurait eu ce courage de lever les yeux vers les
feuilles? Déjà, plusieurs, de la main distraite, paraissaient
préparer les osselets d'un jeu, remuant, tête basse, des
cailloux échoués entre les touffes d'herbe.

Chacun ne se souciait guère d'alentour. Je me demande
même si le bavardage subsistait, seul à seul, celui que l'on
devine à peine en soi, murmure d'intimité.

Pourtant le moment vint où m'apparut davantage le sentiment pénible de cette inhabituelle incertitude. Des mots
s'ébauchèrent aux lèvres. « Allons, regardons là-devant... »
Je crois bien que ce fut la phrase. Il me semble aussi maintenant que la parole brève naquit de mon côté, à l'écart un
peu. Je ne sais plus. Mais cela résonnait si proche.

« Là-devant ».

Il n'y eut pas un geste. Et puis les paupières se soule-
vèrent, comme à regret. Le regard s'éloigna, pensif et lourd
des heures perdues. Le papillon qui s'était arrêté sur l'om-

belle, au point rouge des carottes sauvages, reprend sa course, divague en fantaisie et se perd. Un rayon de soleil s'évertue à poursuivre les volants minuscules de soie moirée — les abandonne. Ici, l'esprit prit à tâche de caracoler d'abord auprès des rêves lointains. Et le cavalier fut désarçonné.

En tous cas, la vie s'offrait.

* * *

Nous nous avisions brutalement qu'un souffle d'air apportait l'odeur du regain des foins et j'aperçus à la branche pendant quelque poignée de pommes aux joues rouges.

La plaine rebondit outre le ruisseau, bientôt enluminée d'un bleu pâle d'ancienne miniature. Des champs ont gardé leurs blés; les épis se chevauchent et la couleur change, se bistre et s'atténue dans un rythme régulier de berceuse.

Ainsi la poitrine nue d'un malade qui respire très doucement.

Les pointes des roseaux s'agitent et se font des salamalecs. Conversations n'ont pas cessé sous le vent. Et les plumets des rouches gesticulent en raillerie.

Les saules aux faces pâles demeurent cependant plus graves. Ils branlent, discrets, à peine, du chef. Ils semblent à merveille s'accomoder du voisinage de peupliers gentilshommes qui saluent l'horizon à grands coups de chapeau. Les saules sont comme ces enfants dont la frimousse rit, mais qui ne soulèvent à contre gré qu'un petit coin de la casquette. Messieurs les peupliers ont soin du panache. A chaque jour suffit sa peine. Et les points cardinaux, tour-à-tour s'extasient devant leur politesse.

A côté, la masse des verdures s'épanouit. S'arrêterait-on ainsi de façon à considérer l'arrière-plan d'un tableau brossé à larges touches? Il suffit bien de promener ci et là toute la paresse d'un regard.

*
* *

Et le temps poursuivait son bonhomme de chemin. Nos satisfactions paraissaient se trouver repues. Quelque intérêt que nous trouvions à cette contemplation de muets, nous en avions assez pour occuper cette fin de journée. Solitaires, puisque tout plaisir en compagnie avait fait faillite.

Pas un désir qui pointât le bout de l'oreille. Le silence se prolongeait jusqu'à subtiliser des essais de rêves.

Le paysage emplissait les prunelles et le cœur. L'ennui se transformait en passivité insensible.

Le temps coulait.

*
* *

Donc les paupières un moment s'étaient soulevées — longtemps incurieuses. Mais par miracle, petit à petit, les yeux s'éveillèrent. Maintenant ils fixaient avec une étrange faim l'horizon où s'enfuyait une gerbe de soucis. Le coude avait redressé le corps qui se penchait en avant déjà.

Une apparition serait-elle advenue? Quelque chose, dans la banalité de cette lieue d'espace, dont on ignorait jusqu'à l'existence?

On gagerait que la palissade verte des bois s'entr'ouvre. Une nuée d'oiseaux bleus s'essaime peut-être vers la vallée.

Il naît une aube de mystère.
Un message parvient.
Et le voilà. Il suscite, comme un départ, l'équipée d'un vagabondage.
La plaine, du coup, perd son charme d'ensorceleuse. Les dés sont jetés. On reste par contenance à se reposer auprès des arbres câlins.
Mais il y a belle lurette que les souhaits s'évadent. Regardons là-devant ». Ce fut une diversion, une dilection désormais enfuie. « Là-devant ». Eh non! Puisque je puis apercevoir à satiété les rives proches, l'appel devra venir par ailleurs.
A peine l'alternative décidée, je me levai, pris la route à contre-pied. Je m'éloignai soudain. Le pré s'enfonçait, incorrigible, vers les profondeurs, aux chênes et hêtres. Il me fallait l'inconnu. Et je m'imaginais aussitôt le découvrir.
J'entendis un pas me suivre. Plus tard, seulement, j'osais me retourner. Aux détours de la venelle, parmi les arbres, je crois avoir entrevu des visages qui reflétaient une émotion pareille. Ainsi la voix se répète souvent aux échos.

*
* *

Nous allions du côté d'où semblent toujours apparaître les phrases inaccessibles. Du même pas, et sans qu'il soit échangé un traître mot qui eût brouillé les cartes de notre solitude.
Nous étions trois ou quatre...

Claude BORDAS.
(Juillet-août 1929).

TWO STORIES

IN THE PARK

Let the Time-Spirit record the incident in one simple sentence, and pass on to important matters; let it merely record that a young man strode briskly through an autumn park, while an aged and shabby fellow slouched on a bench, watching him.

It was a November park, peeling overtones of both gawdiness and melancholy. Leaves were everywhere; they swirled on the paths like an incessant irritation of sparrows; they wheeled and whirled on brief and dizzy flights. About the old man on the paintless bench, there was a pervasive bareness, clogged with mystic suggestions of bruised and heavy thoughts. Through a distance, framed with unadorned and irregular arrangements of trees, was a frailly breathing lagoon. Down to the right on a pretense of a hill, children were massing and unmassing in a scrub football game. And all around the far boundaries of the visible world, the sky dragged down its freighted weight, clinging to the scabby line of shrivelled bushes.

There the fellow sat, his obviously weak body slumped. His cap was a worn and dirty grey affair, rounding off the top of his long and leathered countenance. Sinking inwards, like introverted thoughts, were the gray, bloodshot eyes; slanting down from between them, was the Modigliani slice of a nose, ending but a shadow's distance from purple line of lips, now pressed tight, revealing a cheerless sort of concentration. He was practically chinless. His hands were sunk in the pockets of a frayed overcoat. The shoes were dusty; and they displayed laces that had been broken and re-tied at several points.

Momentarily, his attention roamed off towards the football game; then it directed itself at the lagoon. When a wild duck made a transient and moving pattern against the sky, he watched intently. For the rest of the time, he seemed to sit, seeing nothing.

He sat and sat, while the wind achieved greater steadiness, and increased draughts of cold; while the day sank without aid of soothing coloration from a tardy sun. He sat. When the young man passed, walking with the swift energy of a healthy body, he watched, watched until the echoes of crunched leaves and a gay whistle were gone. And he sat. The park darkened with shadows that repulsed the meagre advances of an insubstantial moon. He was there while the night grew sick with cold. Late in the evening he kicked viciously at a gathering of clipped leaves at his feet. In the morning, when sunlight began carving its way through blocks of mist that were a dirty grey and a nauseous green, the old man was there; he had not moved; he was frozen stiff.

Yet let the Time-Spirit record it simply and pass on as that young man did.

MY FRIEND THE DOCTOR

Only sick people come to see Doc; they come, spout out their troubles; and some times they forget to pay. Then, he goes up from his office, for dinner, and his wife has more troubles. She is a rip, anyway.

When Doc was a kid in a middle class Jewish home, he wanted to write. When he was a young man, without parents, slaving his way to a medical education, he dreamed of writing. When he was an interne, when he was, by necessity, in a large public health factory treating venereal diseases, he consoled himself with the intention of writing. Now a father, a hen-pecked husband, a young man forced to get the money out of a profession that is both over-crowded and threatened by the corporate momentum of our age, he is still imbued with this hope.

It seems unnecessary writing of Doc. The world is

full of his brothers; it has always swamped and swallowed the silent Miltons, the ineffective Judes. It always shall. Their story is older than the first dirty joke; and more illustrative.

Doc is a roly-poly little man. He is round-faced, with a boy's brown eyes; eyes that betray an unconcsious hurt-puppy feeling. He is stout and rotund, bald-headed. His wife is lean and tall.

Doc is writing an autobiographical novel. It is a long dull affair, a scrambled mountain of words. It tells of the spiritual history of the dreamy jew kid, of the lonely medical student, the hopeful interne, the revolting doctor of the public health institute, with his sensitivities strained through daily treatment of a disease, dirty in itself, and made worse when it has afflicted itself upon hundreds of a large city's unwashed herd, of the isolated husband, cut off from friendly intercourse, godless, seeking some personal element that will be spiritual fortification in a life that freezes around him like a blizzard. Daily he labors over this manuscript, that pile of paper, daily he strives, full of self-questiorings, shames, humiliations, the mental evils that plague any man. Throughout the world thousands are doing this. I speak of Doc because I know him; and because his dull words cannot completely obscure the spiritual bravery behind the book, the determination to face it all out, to brace oneself to whatever may come. Doc knows that the world makes every man's bargain for him, and that the world is an efficient police man in preserving the letter of these unfair bargains. Nobody starts from scratch. Doc does not whimper. Neither does his novel. It is an honest record of a life. But we have heard of that before. We care little for the history of another nameless journey through the years.

Someday the novel will be finished. But it will never be accepted. It has not the necessary spiced up interest, the verbal flexibility, the unity and force that it should. It is full of loose ends, insubstantialities, insufficiencies. It is a man's life. Even were it to be accepted, some clever squirt would have to touch it up. Doc's story is, like Ethan Frome's, a silent, lost one.

There he is, the roly-poly man, frustrated, unpropped. Sometime in the future his daughter might grow and understand what went on in his head; what tortured him to fail in giving a clarified expression of all his baffled impulses. But now, there is nobody but sick patients. And when there are none, and his wife is not too noisy, he sits writing, writing bravely, while those boy's brown eyes betray a hurt-puppy expression.

                                           James T. Farrell.

PROSES

LA MORT DE TRISTAN

Sur son cheval galopant, le seigneur Tristan traverse les bois de Cornouailles. De son amour, il ne lui reste que des soucis. Les soucis le bercent rudement sur son cheval. « Mon beau cheval ! il fuit vers la plaine ! » Le vent devant, le vent derrière, le ciel, en prennent une immortelle empreinte; pour le cavalier, les arbres poussent en beauté.

Mille signes tombent des branches, avant la chute des feuilles, mille signes dans les sentiers.

Ni les fûts mortels, ni les feuilles vertes ! S'asseoir dans une clairrière calcinée où les pluies défoncent le sol plein de pierres perdues. La soie perdue, c'est le ciel blême ou la flache verdissante, mais les plumets qui s'envolent sont des oiseaux d'hiver qui n'émigrent jamais.

Et les arbres pensants prêtèrent leurs pensées à Tristan: « Nous ne voulons pas dissiper tes soucis. Au galop des chevaux, tressautent les cavaliers. Il en est qui furent assassinés ici, assasinés.

» Parce qu'ils étaient méchants ou qu'ils ne pensaient pas selon leur âme, ou bien, parce que d'autres hommes, solitaires dans ces grands bois, étaient méchants ou ne savaient pas penser ».

Dans le grand bois qui méprise le chemin tout blanc, Tristan est assailli. Son agresseur n'est armé que d'une lance. La lance perce Tristan bourrelé de soucis. Elle lui pénètre dans l'œil et atteint son cerveau. Le cerveau reste entier. Cependant, Tristan tombe du haut de sa vie et

s'élève au faîte des grands arbres. Il en redescend le long
des fûts merveilleux. Son cheval galope dans l'air et le
mène à l'étape. Qui parle de mort ou de folie?

L'AMITIÉ AU JARDIN

A Israël,

Sous les rumeurs, allait la masse de nos pas.

Bien que je t'aie souvent rencontré dans ton jardin,
nous nous sommes rarement promenés sous tes pommiers
fleuris, sous les arbres teints de rose et de blanc. Nous
laissions la verdure au large ciel, quand il pleuvait, nous,
cherchant alors à capter les souvenirs des précieux bois
jolis qui craquaient sombrement.

Rumeurs d'une bataille, d'une longue bataille rangée,
où notre souvenir ignorant entendait seulement, parmi les
rumeurs inutiles, le bruit poignant des balles claquant
contre la crosse des fusils. Un grand-oncle à toi, que tu
avais peu connu et dont tu n'as jamais su que le rôle de
combattant, fut sauvé grâce à la crosse de son fusil, qui le
protégea à l'instant où, sentant de n'être plus entouré et
pressé par les ennemis et les siens, la fatigue enfin venue,
il se reposait, debout, derrière un buisson, affaissé sur ses
jambes dures.

Qui de nous deux resta, errant, sur ce champ de bataille.
Je crois bien que je te pris tes souvenirs de famille. L'avais-
tu senti— quand tu te levas, la pluie ayant cessé, en disant:
« Allons travailler au jardin! »

Au lieu de jardiner, tu restas immobile, l'air songeur, devant le plus beau pommier en fleurs. Sous les rumeurs du faubourg environnant, tu semblais vouloir enterrer au pied de cet arbre l'humeur qui t'avait noyé le cœur. Plein d'humour, cependant, était ce fumeur qui se campait, le torse en arrière, devant ton plus bel arbre, et qui n'en retenait que le blanc et le rose.

Quand nous nous mîmes en marche sous la double file des pommiers sans pommes, tu tentas de gravir le printemps avec, en guise de canne, le tronc de ton plus beau pommier. Blanche et rose était la fumée de ma cigarette...

Que ne s'est-elle brisée sous le coup du vent, cette fenêtre légère, dont les battants dociles battaient sur un rythme qui me plaisait, hélas!

HENRY-FAGNE.

PURPLE PERFUME

I was ten when I first smelt it. A sleepy afternoon in
sun. The soft flutter of rich old grass out there beyond the
heavy blue shadows of my tree, — a broken croquet mallet
at my side. The handsome feeling of my tired body, just
tired enough to be enjoyable, mingling with a feeling of
growth under the tonic of pure fresh air. Then the lady
came. With my mother. Through the French windows,
through the sun, under my tree of shadows, — and the
sweetness of it all about me was fortified by a sweeter
foreign sweetness that made my breath come quick, my
muscles tighten. And then I realized that it was coming
from the lady. I often smelt perfume on my mother, but
this seemed to come from within the lady, from back there
behind her clear, clear eyes. It was ridiculous to think it
came from some tiny bottle tucked away in the lady's
purse. The lady was very lovely in purple. Maybe that is
why I think of the perfume as purple: purple, light and
clear like the lovely lady's eyes. My mother told me that I
was always timid with ladies, but I am sure I was not timid
with this lady although I did not talk to her. This lady did
not squeeze my arm, or pinch my cheeks, or ask me how
old I was like the other ladies did, — like even my mother
did. She just looked at me the way a pipe organ sounds,
and all the time the smell of her was dancing up my nose,
making me very happy. After she drove away I wondered
why she hadn't taken me with her. I was very lonely. The
grass didn't smell a bit nice. The broken croquet mallet

stuck me sharply in the ribs as I rolled over on the soft
ground that seemed hard now. The sun began to lower, the
shadows broaden, while I was wondering whether I would
ever see the lovely lady again, — smell the lovely smell
of her.

I am thirty now. Twenty years have not made me forget
the purple lady. She is more vital than ever; she has inva-
ded me like strong incense. I reason that she must be quite
old now, but I am sure she is living her youth again in
someone else. I hope to find her, and make her the mother
of my children. My mother is eager that I marry a girl of
her choice. But I dislike the girl: — her eyes are not clear,
she fusses so, and she uses the damndest cheap-smelling
perfumes. Mother does not understand. She does not know
of my bondage to the lady in purple. Sometimes I could
curse her for bringing my lady out on the lawn to me that
day. It has kept me from marrying, and I want a child!

I am fifty now. My mother is dead. I have not secured my
lady. I know now I never shall. I don't mind any more
though; — I feel too old and tired to have children. It is
better that the lady stay only a dream. But I am forgetting
to tell you: — Ten years ago I saw her. In a café crowded
and mussy. The place smelt of liquor and powder and
overheated bodies. Out of the stagnant sugary pool of
odors came the perfume of my lady. I recognized it at
once, and whirled about to look into her eyes that were
clear like crystals in an ivory mold. A young girl. She was
with a young man. And she was all fluffy in purple. Then
I saw, with a hook in my throat, that those eyes were only

for him. I talked to her though. I ate into her with my eyes. I watched my chance to catch her alone, and I told her about the perfume. She was very kind, but I knew she didn't understand. I asked her where I might obtain some of the perfume, but her partner came up just then, and she was off to dance in his arms without even looking back, without answering my question. I never saw her again. I've tried every shop in town for the perfume, and I can find nothing like it. You see, I felt if I had a bit of it around me all the time, I mightn't be so lonely. She'd be with me in spirit anyway. My friends tell me I sniff and wrinkle my nose a great deal, much in the manner of a jack-rabbit. Nerves, I tell them. You see they wouldn't understand about the perfume.

Karlton Kelm.

BALLETS AND POEMS

BRITANNIA RULE THE WAVES

For Austin Coghlan.

On the island the dumb gulls laugh when the statue rises with the sun and glides across the sea towards the West. The sea-weed coils its snakes around the statue's feet; the stars weep into the sea and their silver tears fade among the waves like fins of light.

No ship... the skeletons of waves devour each other... no ship to break the monotony of waves.

A small wave deposits a dead rat on the shore of the island where the dumb gulls laugh. The statue immediately sinks into the waves as if it had anxiously been awaiting this signal.

Dumb gulls, observe the importance of the dead rat.

METAMORPHOSIS NUMBER ONE

For Hugh Speaight, this, in meagre return for Period.

There were no more faces.

One day there appeared above the western gate of the city a grey cloud like a hand. As the hand came nearer it was seen to hold a glove; and just when the hand was above the city like a dark sun at its noon, the glove fell.

Immediately all faces disappeared. A man who was buying an umbrella first became aware of this; he lifted up his head and saw that the salesman's face had been replaced by a large oval green leaf. He looked at himself in a looking-glass, and saw that his own face had also been replaced by a large oval green leaf.

The alarm was given. Men ceased to quarrel. The gold-fish in the bowl in Mrs. X's drawing-room ceased to think they were the center of the universe. Several animals were seen to fall down dead in the streets. The clock on the cathedral tower began to turn backwards. Stocks fell and there was a general panic.

Ever since that day we have all been vegetarians. But it is forbidden by law to eat the large oval green laurel-leaf.

ANTHEM FOR ROMANTICISM

For Harold Salemson.

« Tas d'œufs frits dans de vieux chapeaux,
Lys, Açokas, Lilas et roses!...»

Arthur RIMBAUD (*Ce qu'on dit au poète...*)

Economy of words no longer holds.
The flaming idiom flies again,
steel-pennanted, through paragraphs
draped heavily with damaskéd folds.

Cold white paper never laughs.
Likewise the cold white word.
Therefore we have splashed red paint,
no longer deeming it absurd.

This longing for a brighter day
at last explodes. Perhaps at night
red and green stars shall flash then fade,
or never fade — whichever may

seem more desirable to those
whose visionary song shall build
new skies, new earth: new fields where grows
something less abstract than the rose.

FROM A LETTER TO MRS. LILY TURNER.

Donne, don your black cap.
Donnish Donne, don your despair.
Judge life: its brutal stab
ruffles death's hair.

Life the murderer has left a clue.
Life the murderer has upset the chair.
The police found the room in considerable disorder.
The victim seemed asleep

only ruffled hair.

Edouard RODITI.

L'ARTISTE

Il passe toutes ses journées dans une échoppe piteuse, où s'entassent les vieilles chaussures puantes, la colle, le cuir et les formes, tellement à l'étroit qu'il lui faut laisser la porte ouverte, même en hiver, afin de pouvoir remuer le bras librement.

Il est voûté, tordu et chauve, mais sa surdité totale lui vaut une sérénité vénérable et parce qu'il réalise des prodiges d'équilibre pour disposer autour de lui des aquarelles — ses œuvres — il est très heureux.

C'est un artiste, un vrai, silencieux et contemplatif, jamais las de ses éternels paysages où les arbres jettent une ombre savante sur les champs consciencieusement labourés. Je ne me suis jamais demandé s'il avait du talent, mais je trouve qu'il dessine et colorie avec soin, une certaine grâce, et je l'admire d'employer ses dimanches à sa besogne d'art avec toute la méthode et tous les scrupules qu'il apporte en semaine à ses ressemelages.

Les conversations avec lui sont pleines d'imprévu:

« Tenez, Maurique, voilà une paire de chaussures.

— Oui, oui, dit-il de sa voix lente et unie, il **fait bien beau.**

— C'est pour les talons.

— C'est çà, un beau soleil et pas trop chaud, comme hier.

— ... les talons tournés.

— Ah! non, dimanche j'ai pas fait grand'chose. Cette petite là, tenez.

— Très jolie! mais dites-moi...

— Je les vends, vous savez, pas cher mais je les vends tout de même...

— Dites-moi si elles valent la peine...

— Non, pas possible... Je n'ai pas le temps de faire de la peinture à l'huile et puis çà coûte! Pourtant c'est beau, c'est solide. Ah! toute ma vie j'y aurai pensé! »

Je renonce à me débattre.

« Combien? — J'ai crié si fort qu'il m'a entendue.

— Les aquarelles? Oh! vingt francs, trente francs les petites, mais les grandes... »

Rien à faire. Je lui lance mes chaussures sur les genoux en hurlant: « Au revoir et travaillez bien dimanche! »

Cette fois, condescendant, il me répond:

« **Soyez tranquille, je vous mettrai du bon cuir!** »

Claude SYMIL.

TOWARDS AN EPOCH OR A FAITH OR A PURPOSE IN LIFE

Accumulated heritages are not disposed of with a wave of the hand.

The man of now who has felt, still undefinable, the coming of a new perfection, has hardly emerged from an obsessing past.

Orderless cities, singular clothes, wigs and crinolines, adequate religions, gilt edges, privileges, conventions, figleaf, a whole heredity slips over his soul like a mist.

Still, we have witnessed decrepitudes.

A secular entity, Nature is disappearing. The submissive, arranged and ornate planet reflects man.

Geometry, whose most beautiful lyricisms thus far are the Machine and the urbanized City, puts everywhere its implacable evident interrelationships, sweet with security, simplicity, poetry.

That, at the threshold of new times, people regret the touching naïvetés, picturesque disorders, savageries, causeless and lenifying dreams? What is more logical? We're selling out. The very residue will vanish. To say no weaknesses threaten us is premature.

Only one immediate certainty: the disappearance of a meditative, legendary, credulous mentality.

That that take not place without dramas, shocks and perturbations of all kinds cannot touch us before the fatality of things.

But a way of being, living, explaining, is already seeping in.

Smart guys have mentioned the imminent death of machinism, a retrogression, a renascent purity, spinning-whell, virginity, Poetry, a return to...

We'll see.

We well know there was never a SINGLE REAL RETURN TO THE PAST!

There are different speeds, invisible complexes in the subconscious of humanity.

The rest: manias of folklorists dizzy with 100 years of history.

One tangible fact, before the eyes, the heart, the intelligence: the Modern World. And graphs, statistics, figures which are not prophecies lead to irresistible phenomena.

Is it an order at last? Not regulated from behind the Earth. An essentially human order? The orderly creative plenitude of man, without the inflation of mysteries?

Man and his new violence prelude: An unheard-of

lyricism, overflows from matter still hardly born to its image.

High spectacles are in preparation and intoxicating precisions — the first — are as disturbing as truths.

Cities and Machines have found us once again simple and young. The hope laid upon them by poets hardly explains their astounding phosphorescence.

Georges Linze,
(Translated from the French
by Harold J. Salemson.)

PANORAMA de la LITTÉRATURE FLAMANDE CONTEMPORAINE

Une étude panoramique offre toujours un élément de flottaison: la ligne d'horizon.

La Flandre est avant tout un pays de peintres; talents, voire génies, ne manquent pas ici. Faut-il citer les Van Eyck, les Van der Goes, les Breughel, les Rubens; des précurseurs comme Jacob Smits, Laermans, Ensor; des modernistes tels que Permeke, Fritz Van den Berghe, Tytgat, etc...? En peinture, la tradition se perpétue sur le plan le plus élevé.

En littérature, quelques sommets seulement dominent une masse assez amorphe. Point n'est notre but de chercher les causes de cette différence, notre étude se voulant par ailleurs document plus que critique.

Un jeune essayiste écrivait à ce sujet, très récemment:

> Le romantisme est passé sur l'Europe et en Flandre, nous n'avons eu ni Gœthe, ni De Vigny, ni Shelley... Nous avons seulement un H. Conscience, un Snieders et un Van Beers, qui rima l'ode à la locomotive...
>
> Emiel Moyson ou Julius Vuylsteke sont nos premiers poètes humanitaires, mais il ne sont point, hélas! de grands poètes... La Flandre a connu la guerre et nous n'avons personne qui écrivit « Le Feu »...

Toutefois, la terre de Breughel n'aurait produit qu'un Gezelle, un Van de Woestijne et même un Van Ostoyen qu'elle aurait immortalisé la poésie. Repoussons un instant notre ligne d'horizon jusqu'à Gezelle. Ce poète est si universel, si profondément humain et si haut dans les sphères lyriques qu'il nous fait signe encore de sa génération loin-

taine. Son œuvre est trop peu connue en Europe et voici
en passant l'occasion de souligner le rayonnement limité
de la langue flamande dont la poésie révèle cependant des
richesses semantiques, rythmiques et sonores vraiment
remarquables.

Gezelle vécut de 1830 à 1899. Le mouvement des choses,
leurs demi-teintes, la sublime et simple beauté de la nature
lui ont imposé les plus purs poèmes. Il sut y mêler son
mysticisme et sa fraîche spontanéité sans être subjectif.
Gezelle est peut-être avec Albrecht Rodenbach le courant
initial de la jeune poésie flamande.

> ...Merci à la vie
> merci à la lumière
> merci à la lumière et à la vie
> merci à l'air et à la lumière
> et à la vue et à l'ouïe
> et à tout.
> Que le Seigneur soit remercié!

Nous pensons à Péguy, dont la forme et la matière ont
une résonance aussi poignante.

Un mouvement important par son idéologie, sinon par
son apport lyrique, s'affirma à la fin du siècle dernier. Il
s'agit de *Van Nu en Straks* (D'aujourd'hui et de demain).
Ce mouvement, totalement divisé aujourd'hui et diminué
depuis peu de Karel Van de Woestijne, poète délicat et critique solide, avait un programme trop peu précis; il révéla
cependant quelques talents significatifs, parmi lesquels
Vermeylen, Stijn Streuvels, Buysse, les aînés. De nouveaux
adeptes, dont Van de Woestijne et H. Teirlinck, se montrè-

rent plus libres et plus directs. Si nous aimons à signaler l'importance de ce groupe, c'est avant tout pour sa foi dans la lutte contre l'idéal académique et poncif des écrivains précédents. (Hormis le sommet que représentait Gezelle.) Ce fut une œuvre d'épuration littéraire et même sociale, dont les effets se ressentent encore aujourd'hui et dont le grand honneur revient surtout au critique et romancier Auguste Vermeylen, auteur du *Juif errant,* paru en 1906.

Et revoici Karel Van de Woestijne, dont la mort vient d'ébranler toute la poésie du monde. Ce poète est bien d'aujourd'hui par l'allure aérienne de son chant. Aristocrate de la forme et de l'image, il connaissait parfaitement la littérature française et particulièrement les Symbolistes. J'oserais même dire que son évolution avait quelques racines à la limite de cette école. Il est l'auteur de *Het vaderhuis, De Gulden Schoduw,* etc... Parmi la prose lyrique: *Janus met het dubbele voorhoofd,* etc...

Je ne puis résister au désir de transcrire ces vers extraits de *Harmonica du soir:*

Harmonica des sept douleurs, larmoyante chanson d'harmonica, air lancinant, avec tes notes comme autant de plaies; plainte qui tenaille et déchire en ce soir d'orage, si déplorablement fausse, si déplorablement fausse: pourquoi as-tu chanté, harmonica qui chantes une gaieté si triste dans le soir, pauvre harmonica comme un cœur humain, harmonica comme ma bouche amère et lasse; harmonica, ô des sept douleurs?...

De l'intimisme au grand jour, une force qui atteint à l'universel!

Nous avons dit que Teirlinck adhéra aussi à *Van Nu en Straks.* Personnalité très différente, plus fantaisiste, mais

d'un aspect non moins original, Teirlinck s'est surtout
découvert dans le théâtre. Il choisit sa matière dans le
tumulte de la ville moderne. Des pièces comme *De ver-
traagle film, Ik dien, De man zonder lijf*, sont désormais
des jalons dans l'histoire du théâtre.

La place nous manque pour parler de tous les succes-
seurs de *Van Nu en Straks*. Citons, en passant, Cyriel
Verschaere, dont la langue a quelque chose de dramatique,
le poète Maurits Sabbe (Conservateur du Musée Plautin, à
Anvers), et le romancier Félix Timmermans, auteur de
Pallieter et de *l'Enfant Jésus en Flandres*, deux livres traduits à Paris. Sa prose est vivante et alerte; traversée par
un souffle vraiment flamand du point de vue racique, elle
fait parfois penser au coloris de Jordaens et à l'humour de
Breughel. Il est également l'auteur d'une sorte de « miracle », intitulé *Als de ster bleef stille staan*, anachronisme
curieux et original.

Et n'oublions ni Joris Eeckhout, essayiste cultivé, ni
Ernest Claes, à l'humour très sain, etc...

Immédiatement après la guerre s'affirma une autre génération qui constitua des groupes plus ou moins cohérents.
On y trouve Wies Moens, Marnix Gysen, Van de Voorde,
Herreman et surtout le regretté Paul Van Ostayen, mort à
l'âge de 32 ans.

La plupart de ces poètes — cette génération compte peu
de romanciers — ne sont point étrangers aux recherches et
aux tentatives modernes. Quelques-uns restent cependant
trop romantiques. Van Ostayen fut un grand chercheur
de rythmes. Dans l'isolement de la guerre, il fut le premier

Belge connaissant les courants générateurs de l'inquiétude et de la sensibilité nouvelles. Sa poésie est basée sur une musique à échos répétés; fantaisiste en profondeur, il fut aussi l'acrobate merveilleux de sa langue. Nous n'insisterons pas sur ses calligrammes qui valent bien ceux d'Apollinaire. Aujourd'hui, son influence se fait encore sentir sur les moins de trente ans. L'extrait suivant me semble très caractéristique :

CHANT DES MONTAGNARDS (traduit par G. Marlier)

Un monsieur qui descend la rue
un monsieur qui remonte la rue
deux messieurs qui descendent et remontent
c'est-à-dire le premier monsieur descend
et le second monsieur remonte
tout juste à la hauteur du magasin de Hinderickx et Winderickx
tout juste à la hauteur du magasin de Hinderickx et Winderickx
        les célèbres chapeliers
ils se rencontrent
le premier monsieur soulève son haut-de-forme de la main droite
le second monsieur soulève son haut-de-forme de la main gauche
alors l'un et l'autre de ces messieurs
celui de droite et celui de gauche celui qui remonte et celui qui
        descend
celui de droite qui descend
celui de gauche qui remonte
alors les deux messieurs
chacun avec son haut-de-forme son propre haut-de-forme son sacré
        propre haut-de-forme
se croisent
tout juste devant la porte
du magasin
de Hinderickx et Winderickx

les célèbres chapeliers
alors les deux messieurs
celui de droite et celui de gauche celui qui remonte et celui qui descend
une fois qu'ils se sont croisés
remettent leur haut-de-forme sur la tête
que l'on m'entende bien
chacun remet son propre chapeau sur sa propre tête,
c'est leur droit
c'est le droit de ces deux messieurs.

L'almanach anthologique, publié en 1930, démontre qu'il est enfin une génération plus jeune, dont les efforts sont la preuve d'un renouveau de la littérature flamande. Tous se cherchent comme on se cherche à 25 ans. Leurs noms ne peuvent trouver place dans ce schéma qui a la seule prétention de poser l'existence d'un mouvement littéraire probablement inconnu de la plupart de nos lecteurs. L'auteur se propose d'ailleurs de parler ultérieurement dans une chronique moins sommaire et plus poétique, surtout de quelques réels talents à peine cités parmi trop de noms.

Van der Cammen.

MODERN FLEMISH WRITING

In our struggle to preserve individuality, and most of us will demand it on aesthetic grounds, at least, the product of the small nation with a long pedigree has a very specific interest. Here certainly, we should have a unity, a directness of purpose and a strong national consciousness which should result in something qualitatively vivid. We have had fads for various literatures with exotic appeal. I humbly suggest that the writing of the Dutch speaking portion of Belgium is worthy of attention.

For two reasons. Politically under the thumb of a gallic culture the Flemish peasant has revolted and demanded that his own strong, rugged vocables be recognized. He has revolted passionately and passion is the midwife of literature. In the second place the Flemish spirit draws its strength from the soil. For centuries Flanders has watched its more economically successful neighbor Holland grow and prosper. Holland is in danger of becoming effete but Flanders in the last century rediscovered its tongue. It rejected the multiple assets of modernity, simplified its inspiration and relied on peasant intuition. Flemish is Low Dutch, a near cousin of English. The new writers form their own styles, very often using diliberate archaism. The result has a flavor rather like Middle English. Imagine Chaucer living at the turn of the century. Chaucer, grown more analytic, more subtle, still heartily vulgar, still fond of the little details of living, still painting, savoring, enjoying instead of dissolving into arid doubt, and you have something very like the the Flemish literary movement.

You ahve Stijn Streuvels, who pries with searing pity into the lives of workmen. Who paints schoolboys with their bread and cheese, robbing birds' nests, stealing cherries, who can tell the story of a farmhand in a way that is somehow widely significant, who can feel for the old wife with her lace cushion and who divulges delicately a peasant girl's first communion. He is quaint, direct, earthy, yet more than earthy.

You have Buysse, a more sombre talent who cannot choke his pity for the poor into a less bitter denunciation, who dwells on brutality and animal lust because he wishes life were cast in a more delicate mould.

You have Teirlinck, a satirist and stylist who chronicles the struggles between the spirit and the flesh and who can never decide between gallic remoteness and

Flemish solidity and Timmermans, a tender rabelais, carolling nude along the canals in the morning mist.

As for poets there are the late Van de Woestijne, Edmond Van Offel, Pol de Mont, and a many more, more or less affected by French symbolism.

In them all burns a quiet realization of what we snickering call the facts of life. While the major nations attempt to be intellectualized, spinning more and more finely the delicate coccoon of words between the sensation and the expression, « Between the desire and the spasm », Flanders still knows that mud is brown soft and gritty and that wheat is made into bread.

Doubtless this is only a gesture in the face of fords, lucky strike ads and television. While it lasts it is a good gesture. We can be thankful for a group of writers as refreshing to the palate as a glass of cold beer.

H. R. HAYS.

ARTISTES

II. André MASSON

Qui peint comme André Masson? Qui pourrait peindre comme André Masson?

Car, *peindre comme André Masson* supposerait *être André Masson*. Or, il n'y a qu'un André Masson. Il n'y a pas Dieu, mais il y a André Masson. Il y a André Masson comme il y a l'homme, et comme il n'y a pas Dieu. Car..

S'il y avait Dieu, il n'y aurait pas André Masson. Il n'y aurait que Dieu. Et Dieu ne serait plus dans les livres, il serait dans les tableaux. Et Dieu serait le plus grand peintre de notre temps, de tous les temps. Mais il y a André Masson.

C'est-à-dire que, d'abord, il y a eu Breton. Et Breton a su qu'il n'y avait pas de Dieu. Alors, Breton a fort bien dit qu'il fallait devenir Dieu. Et en place du Dieu détaché de l'homme, il a formulé Dieu, cette partie prolongée de l'homme. Mais Breton n'a su que le formuler.

Puis il y a eu Masson. Masson l'a créé. Et, aujourd'hui que le surréalisme est mort (sauf dépêche: *surréalisme pas mort*), il reste un seul surréaliste. Il reste André Masson.

Et la force d'André Masson réside en ce qu'il a peint sans mysticisme. Pour lui, créer Dieu, c'était aussi simple que de respirer. Il a compris qu'il ne tenait qu'à lui qu'il y eut ou non Dieu.

Mais à quoi servirait Dieu? A quoi sert la peinture d'André Masson?

Formules: La peinture d'André Masson est l'expression
d'un Dieu humain;

La peinture d'André Masson est la force incarnée;

La peinture d'André Masson est à l'après-guerre, ce
qu'était celle de Michel-Ange, de Léonard, de Raphaël à
la Renaissance;

La peinture d'André Masson, c'est *l'Oiseau pris au piège;*

C'est chaque toile;

C'est la vie complémentaire, la vie sensuelle et intellectuelle conçue par un esprit qui pense en images;

C'est l'œuvre d'un artisan remarquable;

D'un homme qui a compris qu'il n'y avait pas Dieu;

Qui a créé Dieu;

Créé Dieu comme on fait le portrait de soi-même, comme
on se rase;

Comme on s'habille.

Car André Masson a peint sans mystique une œuvre
surréelle. Et c'est pour cela qu'André Masson est seul à avoir
compris ce qu'est l'autre partie de la vie, celle qui n'existe
pas, celle qu'on crée.

Ce qui n'empêche pas André Masson d'être un grand
peintre.

Bien au contraire.

III. TOUCHAGUES

Touchagues est aussi ridicule que le lacet de ma chaussure.

Mais je tiens à mon lacet et j'adore Touchagues, parce
que mon lacet est utile et Touchagues est important (c'est

aussi un charmant garçon). Et qu'on n'aille pas croire que je me moque de lui. Touchagues sait être sérieux. Même, il est toujours sérieux. Comme Buster Keaton, et comme Chaplin.

Ce sont les sujets de Touchagues qui sont ridicules. Parce qu'il veut qu'ils le soient. Il mord. Sa morsure est une sûre mort pour le sérieux. Mais c'est une chose tellement sérieuse.

Lorsque Touchagues mord, c'est pour de bon. Rien n'y échappe. C'est ainsi qu'il a rendu toute chose ridicule, avec un lacet.

Touchagues a commencé par faire des dessins qui étaient tout d'un trait C'était la consécration du lacet de soulier. Cela aurait dû être la consécration de Touchagues. Car il a rendu sublime le ridicule.

Mais on se tordit, et on dit à tort que c'était ridicule. Cela n'était même pas drôle. C'était triste et même d'une tristesse sublime. Il y a aussi d'autres Touchagues. Tous se valent.

Seulement, le Touchagues au lacet! Holà, c'est un artiste. Pour lui, tout avait une ligne centrale. Il a voulu que cette ligne fût le lacet. Et Touchagues est resté ce qu'il était, tout en transformant les choses qu'il dessinait.

Pour lui, il n'y a que la ligne vertébrale. Et la ligne vertébrale connaît sous ses armes les contorsions les plus inattendues. Il la noue, pour en faire le nœud central de son œuvre.

Touchagues est un type. C'est un type parce qu'il dessine, parce que la vie est son moyen d'expression et qu'il vit comme il dessine Sans desserrer les lèvres, il troue le voile, il déchire l'artifice, efface le fard. Puis il nous donne un dessin, son sujet mis à nu.

Touchagues enlève les vêtements de ses modèles pour les rendre ridicule. On voit qu'il ne reste que du ridicule. Il ne reste qu'un lacet. Alors le lacet devient un portrait de n'importe qui, une image de n'importe quoi. Il suffit que le bottier soit Touchagues : la chaussure va. On ne met la chaussure que si elle va, mais lui sait la mettre partout. Parce qu'il sait dessiner.

Or, en tout réduisant à une ligne, il a encore gardé autre chose. Sa ligne n'est pas rien qu'une ligne. Ou l'avion ne serait-il qu'une machine? La ligne de Touchagues est la ligne du rire, partant celle de la vérité. Et si Touchagues mentait, c'en serait fait de lui. Mais il ne sait pas mentir.

D'ailleurs, il ne cherche pas à faire ce qu'il fait. S'il dessine, c'est qu'il dessine. C'est tout. S'il crie, s'il hurle certaines choses, c'est qu'il les crie, qu'il les hurle. Pas d'autre raison.

Rien de moralisant, rien de démoralisant. Lorsqu'un homme voit et reproduit, il joue le tout pour le **tout. Au** jeu, **Touchagues** a gagné. Comme son temps, il a su **voir** un lacet de **chaussure. Et dans le lacet, il a su voir son** temps. Touchagues nous montre 1930 en 0391, 3910, 9103, 1039, et toutes les autres combinaisons. Comme 1929 et plus tard 1931.

Voilà ce qui est une autre affaire. C'est le message inconscient de Touchagues. Il est là pour cela. Mais le sait-on? Pour nous, il suffit qu'il dessine.
                                                                  Harold J. SALEMSON.

NOTES

(Harold J. SALEMSON)

BENEFACTORS - BIENFAITEURS

The names of the benefactors who, through their generous subscriptions, helped to permit this second series of *Tambour,* are as follows:

Voici la liste des bienfaiteurs qui, par leur généreuse souscription, ont aidé à la publication de la seconde série de *Tambour:*

> Mr. J. E. Bloom (New York City);
> Miss Berenice Davis (Chicago, Illinois);
> Mrs. Dorothea Donn-Byrne (Kilbrittain, Ireland);
> Mrs Rose B. Malkes (Chicago);
> Mr. S. G. A. Rogers (Madison, Wisconsin);
> Mr. Morris Rosenthal (New York City);
> Mme. Julia Schutz (Paris);
> Mrs. Luba Shacter (Chicago);
> Mr. Bernard Shulman (Chicago);
> Mr. and Mrs. W. H. Walling (Mescalero, New Mexico);
> Mr. Henry Weinstein (Bristol, Connecticut);
> Mr. C. D. Zdanowicz (Madison, Wisconsin).

ENCORE ANATOLE FRANCE

Comme il fallait bien s'y attendre, le numéro V de *Tambour,* consacré à Anatole France, attira sur nous l'attention de la presse universelle. L'intérêt suscité par notre enquête se refléta dans les commentaires que publièrent non seulement les journaux et revues français, mais encore ceux de la Belgique, de l'Italie, de l'Allemagne, de la Tchécoslovaquie, de la Hongrie, des Etats-Unis, de l'Angleterre, etc... Il ressortit de tous ces commentaires une chose assez curieuse et qui est, en somme, peut-être celle qui motive les conclusions que nous nous décidons à tirer aujourd'hui.

Avec un ensemble touchant, la critique, trop pressée pour lire

Tambour dans le détail, émet l'opinion presque unanime que la signification profonde de ce mouvement d'avant-garde est d'accabler la
mémoire du grand écrivain. Si nous-mêmes n'étions guère convaincus
que l'ultime direction de notre enquête fût une condamnation du
maître, les critiques l'y ont vue, et ils ont réagi avec une spontanéité
qui prouve qu'au moins chez eux Anatole France n'a point perdu de
son prestige.

Nous ne parlerons même pas de M. U.-V. Châtelain qui, dans
l'*Esprit français*, sous prétexte de défendre Anatole France, tint à
discréditer votre serviteur, pourtant un des défenseurs les plus
acharnés du maître, si je ne me trompe. Il est évident qu'étant étranger,
on n'a point le droit d'écrire *Prétexte* au lieu de *Préface,* même si l'on
a pour cela des raisons autres qu'un lapsus passager.

Quelques-unes des perles de la critique ont été fournies par l'*Ami
du peuple* (du soir) qui vit dans les réponses de *Tambour* celles d'un
« groupe d'écrivains sélectionnés »; par *Le courrier littéraire* qui, toujours sous prétexte de défendre France, opposa à *Tambour* les hommages de l'époque des 80 ans du maître — justement ce que nous
essayions de confirmer ou de démentir — et, comble d'ironie, *Un
cadavre* des surréalistes (ce pamphlet s'opposait sans doute plus à notre
enquête que les hommages déjà cités); et bien d'autres, trop nombreux
à citer, mais tant savoureux par leur parti pris, leur inexactitude, et
leurs mesquins défauts.

Seuls de rares critiques plus ou moins indépendants se réjouissaient
de la soi-disant fin d'Anatole, pour en louer d'autant plus Barrès (qui,
entre parenthèses, me semble singulièrement s'estomper ces derniers
temps). Tous les autres, du *Canard enchaîné* à l'*Action française* et de
l'*Européen* aux *Nouvelles littéraires,* se réunirent pour défendre contre
« les jeunes » la réputation de l'ancêtre — et ce sont justement les
jeunes qui l'ont défendue dans *Tambour.*

Le vrai enseignement à tirer de ceci — aussi bien des réponses
à notre enquête que des critiques des courriéristes — c'est que l'on
commence à regarder France avec une intelligence plus ouverte et
moins béatement admiratrice ou fermement antagoniste, et que la
situation du jardinier d'Epicure n'en pâtit point. La génération de la
guerre, la plus hostile, se trouve prise entre deux camps amis de

France, les aînés et les jeunes. C'est France qui en est le plus grand bénéficiaire.

ANATOLE FRANCE AGAIN

The special issue which we devoted to Anatole France caused a stir the world over such as was to be expected: the newspapers and magazines of the U. S., England, France, Belgium, Italy, Germany, Hungary, Czeckoslovakia, etc., made abundant commentaries upon our questionnaire and brought out a curious point which was one of the things that brought about our writing this final conclusion.

Long articles in *The Literary Digest, The Book-League Monthly,* and many other periodicals, as well as the deluge published in France and elsewhere, mainly aimed at defending Anatole from the violent attacks of our impudent magazine. The critics, of course in a hurry as usual, arrived much more quickly than we ourselves at the conclusion that the only result of our symposium was a rejection of Anatole France: the Americans less so than the French since a larger percentage of the answers published in English were favorable to the old man. But the press at large had a merry time putting us back into our places. And that goes to show that while that very same press did not take the trouble of trying to understand that we were impartial and not against France, but jumped at the one or two glaring adverses replies, the critics as least exhibited a certain affection for France by defending him, even if his aggressors were more or less imaginary.

The priceless gems of prejudice and incomprehension that were published would fill our small review if we were to reproduce them: we will merely point out that a slight minority of the critics attempted to prove through our so-called repudiation of France that he was dying, whereas Maurice Barrès (who, in parentheses, seems, to be rapidly fading of late) was more and more alive.

On the whole, we may conclude that the current attitude toward France shows a less serene admiration and a less intransigeant animosity, in a word that the outlook upon his work is more sane than ever. But the master's situation in the public eye is nonetheless secure.

The hostile war-generation is caught between two fires of admiration for France, the elders and the latest comers whose respect was reflected in *Tambour*. Old Anatole is assuredly the greatest beneficiary of this condition.

Correspondance

Nous extrayons, sans commentaires, les passages suivants d'une lettre d'un de nos lcteurs qui désire garder l'anonymat:

« Vous posez la candidature de M. Mario Montanard au titre du Parfait Poète Paresseux. Pour ces deux adjĕctifs, il me semble qu'aucun de nos contemporains n'est plus digne que M. Paul Valéry. Pourtant, la petite quantité de la production valérienne serait peut-être due à un mal chronique qui serait confirmée par un des ouvrages de l'académicien que je viens de voir annoncer dans un catalogue de libraires sous le titre de *Rhumes*. Si tel est le cas, plaignons le célèbre charmeur de serpents et décernons la palme à votre talentueux collaborateur. »

Les Livres

Francis Ambrière, dont les articles vivants ont été remarqués dans divers journaux, et qui a donné à *Tambour* quelques pages très intelligentes, vient de publier une *Vie de Joachim du Bellay* (Firmin-Didot). Le genre en est original et constiue le premier triomphe de ce volume remarquable: ce n'est point une vie romancée, mais un essai romancé où l'auteur a su mêler une pénétrante étude de l'œuvre du poète à sa biographie. De la sorte, cette grande poésie que le public, en général, a accepté au Lycée sans avoir jamais essayé d'en tirer la beauté personnelle et autre qu'universitaire, devient, sans être vulgarisée, à la portée de tous. Cet apport aux lectures courantes, qui ne manquera pas de rendre à Du Bellay la place qui lui est due, enrichira considérablement le stock émotionnel du lecteur. Le volume a bien d'autres qualités dont la première, et la seule que nous signalerons, est non seulement de rappeler au public l'attrait extraordinaire de Du Bellay, mais de lui révéler encore un des écrivains les plus considérables de la toute dernière génération, M. **Francis Ambrière**.

Une autre révélation, et qui ne fut pas suffisamment remarquée, est celle de Georges Reyer, dont le premier livre, *Destins croisés* (N.R.F), a paru il y a plusieurs mois. Ce solide roman annonce une œuvre durable et importante: celle d'un écrivain qui sait traiter autre chose que la courante histoire d'amour. C'est un roman de petit fonctionnaire, de Français moyen, qui a ces mêmes qualités qui ont donné une telle place à un Balzac, à un Zola, et pourtant, Georges Reyer a imprégné son livre d'une facture toute nouvelle, dénuée de plat réalisme, qui fait de lui un des artistes les plus incontestables du roman d'aujourd'hui et de demain: un *vrai* romancier.

André Berge est, lui aussi, un vrai romancier, mais qui n'en est plus à ses débuts. Son nouveau livre, *La jeunesse interdite* (Plon), second volume de la trilogie de *Bernard Bardeau,* s'il n'est pas aussi neuf que *La nébuleuse,* n'en est pas moins l'œuvre d'un bel écrivain. L'Académie Goncourt, qui a couronné Marcel Proust, devra compter avec André Berge pour son prochain prix.

Signalons en passant un livre excellent, quoique peut-être un peu mince, d'André Chamson. La valeur de l'auteur n'est plus à dire, et cette espèce de petit reportage qu'est *Tyrol* (Grasset) a, en tout cas, un intérêt documentaire dans l'ensemble de son œuvre.

Les éditions Les Revues ont inauguré plusieurs collections fort intéressantes dernièrement, dont il convient de citer les volumes. Dans la Collection Verte, *Les hommes du* 1905 *russe* de Matvéev et *Lénine à Paris* d'Aline (ceci est un nom russe et non un prénom de femme) apportent un enseignement considérable à qui veut comprendre le phénomène économique le plus important de notre époque, la révolution russe. La Collection Orange, consacrée aux questions du matérialisme, tant économique que philosophique, donne *Communisme et mariage* de Riazanov, une étude curieuse mais trop schématique des conditions domestiques de la Russie actuelle, et *Le matérialisme militant* de Plékhannov. Ce volume est un recueil d'articles polémiques sur le matérialisme philosophique et il forme à la fois une discussion intéressante du sujet et un curieux aperçu de l'auteur.

Les mêmes éditeurs viennent de donner dans leur collection Nos Poètes un recueil de poèmes de Wladimir Maïakovsky, dont le suicide a dernièrement défrayé les chroniques mondaines et assombri les cer-

cles littéraires. C'était un homme d'une grande verve et qui possédait
des dons lyriques très personnels. Ces derniers ne se mettaient pas
toujours directement au service de la Révolution, et c'est dans ces
poèmes suprêmement modernes où coule une note mordante de sub-
version jointe à une poésie très attachante que je l'aime le mieux. Il a
des images éclatantes de force et de beauté. On peut regretter en lui
un des éléments les plus vivants et les plus originaux de la poésie
moderne.

Bertrand Russell inaugure *La crise des mœurs,* autre collection nouvelle de la même maison, avec la traduction de son livre *Le mariage et
la morale.* Nous l'avons déjà dit au sujet de l'édition en anglais: ce
livre est un chef-d'œuvre.

A la suite de *Ceux d'en bas* dont nous parlions dans notre dernier
numéro, la maison Fourcade nous donne encore un roman de la
révolution mexicaine, *L'aigle et le serpent* de M.-L. Guzman. Celui-ci
est un livre d'un autre genre. Ce n'est pas un roman, mais une chronique des bouleversements mexicains. A peine le fait d'être raconté par
un des acteurs du drame, à la premièr personne, prête-t-il un léger
goût de fiction à ce volume. C'est un livre qu'il faut lire, et qui a
des chances de durer aussi bien pour ses qualités littéraires que
pour son importance documentaire.

Plusieurs autres traductions à signaler, enfin, chez Kra: la réédi-
tion de *Tristan* de Thomas Mann, dont il suffit qu'on sache que son
auteur a plus que mérité le Prix Nobel (mais la nouvelle est précédée
d'une étude sur le grand romancier par Geneviève Blanquis, étude
capitale et qu'il faut absolument connaître), et *Ile, mon île,* de D. H.
Lawrence, le célèbre écrivain anglais qui vient de mourir. La nouvelle
vaut la peine d'être lue, mais je lui reprocherais d'être seulement une
nouvelle et de ne pas mériter d'être donnée à part dans un volume
autonome. La main du maître qu'on y sent donne soif de plus que
ces 120 pages.

Signalons enfin une curieuse plaquette éditée par le Théâtre Alfred
Jarry, *Le théâtre Alfred Jarry et l'hostilité publique.* Malgré l'intérêt
de cette brochure, je n'en crois pas la publication justifiée, car ce
théâtre intermittent se complaît trop dans l'hostilité publique pour
avoir le droit de s'en plaindre. Néanmoins, le mouvement créé par

le théâtre Alfred Jarry, dont les directeurs sont Roger Vitrac et Antonin Artaud, est fort intéressant et sera suivi par cette partie du
public qui croit, avec nous, qu'il vaut la peine de cultiver parfois
l'hostilité publique.

Books

Robert Penn Warren, usually associated with a group of poets who
disdain prose but agree to write hack-biographies for opulent publishers, has published *John Brown: the making of a Martyr* (Brewer
and Warren) which, through the very enthusiasm the author has put
into it and the time it must have demanded, appears to be a sincere
piece of work. It is doubtlessly done in a most skillful manner, and
composition and execution are as impeccable as those of the author's
verse, but the prejudice in the mind of the writer, a Southerner, is
so obvious, that despite his claims of impartiality, his glee at pointing
out the pettinesses of Brown's character is often jarring. As history,
though one-sided, it may be an important book; as literature, it is
most readable.

Of an entirely different character, *Grim Youth* by John Held Jr.,
with illustrations by the author, lately published by the Book-League of
America, strikes me as singularly important. I do not look at it, of
course, from a literary point of view, for the author himself, I am
sure, has no such pretentions. It is decidedly low-brow. But it is at
the same time a document upon the mores of America's contemporary
youth which is not to be neglected. For one residing abroad the very
wealth of new slang it contains makes of it a master-work for future
study of the American language. The spirit of college-life, unique, I
believe, in time and space of history, is immortally recorded, and as
current reading it is undoubtedly one of the most amusing things that
have seen the light in a long time.

There is only one other book that I shall mention today. Offhand,
I recall having read very little new stuff, and nothing else worth
recording.

About the same time as *Babbitt* and *The Color of a Great City*
have appeared in French translation, giving Paris a view of two widely

different American talents — different both in type and value, — the
critic André Levinson has collected into a volume a score of his
articles on current American literature that have appeared in various
French reviews and newspapers, *Figures américaines* (Attinger, Paris).
The interest of these notations on some of the important writers of
today is certain, and Levinson has an acute critical mind which gives
him a definite place in our time. But, being as he is in Paris — and,
if I am well informed, never having been to the States, — his scale
of values suffers the inevitable disproportion that the distance lends.
He has great perspicacity concerning men such as Anderson and
Lewisohn, but a miscomprehension of the American civilization gives
too great a harshness to his judgment of Dreiser, too much stress to his
sense of « primitiveness » in O'Neill. But the great misfortune of such
criticism is when it deals with lesser characters. Whether Lewis comes
up to the level of the men mentioned above is perhaps open to discussion, but the importance of the « artist » Thornton Wilder or of
Anita Loos' *picaresque* novels is not hard to discredit. In such appre-
ciations we are not far from another French critic who puts Edna
Ferber in the first rank. This oblique view might give birth to some
philosophic conclusions, if one had either the time or the inclination.
As it is, it merely illustrates the value of foreign parts, « that
contemporary posterity » as a celebrated Frenchman once put it, when
great works are concerned, and its shortsightedness in connection with
the ballyhooed by-products of a world expressing itself through its
letters.

Les Revues

Europe vient de publier l'intéressante version française de Maurice
Bourgeois de la pièce d'Eugene O'Neill, *Le singe velu;*
  La Revue du Cinéma a donné, dans son numéro d'avril, *Harry
Langdon,* par Jean-Georges Auriol. L'auteur y cite J. Bernard Brunius
et formule de bonnes idées à retenir pour l'étude psychologique, voire
pathologique, des comiques américains, qu'on ne manquera pas de faire
sous peu. Très bon article;
  Contacts, dont les deux premiers numéros viennent de paraître, ne

tient pas tout ce qu peut promettre la liste des membres du groupe qui
l'a fondé, mais il y a de l'espoir.

Magazines

This Quarter publishes a sort of French anthology in its January-
February-March issue, and some excellent poems by Pauline Leader
and A. S. J. Tessimond;

Close Up, as usual, is most interesting in its numerous and varied
stills from current pictures;

Experimental Cinema, a new review published in America, might
be interesting were it not for the contributors' snobbishness concerning
the Russian cinema, excluding any points of interest from American
films — even good things can be carried too far;

The first two issues of *Pagany* promise a grand magazine of American letters: the second is so much better than the first that one is
tempted to await later developments and not speak prematurely;

The Poet and the Critic, in its first issue, has a particularly striking
essay by Clifton Cuthbert upon Theodore Dreiser's *An American
Tragedy;* it may turn out to be most interesting.

Livres à Lire

Quelques nouveaux livres des collaborateurs de *Tambour:*
Jean Cassou, *Mémoires de l'Ogre* (Plon);
Jean Cassou, *Les Nuits de Musset* (Emile-Paul);
Jean Cocteau, *Opium* (Stock);
Joseph Delteil, *Don Juan* (Grasset);
Théodore Dreiser, *La couleur d'une grande cité* (Stock);
Fernand Ferré, *Chaînes* (Collection *Contacts,* Redier);
Louis Guilloux, *Dossier confidentiel* (Grasset);
Liang-Tsong-Taï, *Les poèmes de T'ao Ts'ien,* traduits du chinois
par Liang-Tsong-Taï, avec une préface de Paul Valéry (Lemarget);

Norman Macleod, etc... *Poèmes d'ouvriers américains* (Les Revues);
Pierre Mac Orlan, *La tradition de minuit* (Emile-Paul);
Paul Morand, *Champions du monde* (Grasset);
Robert Radelet, *L'homme est à la femme comme la femme est à l'homme* (Anthologie);
Bertrand Russel, *Le mariage et la morale* (Les Revues);
Harold J. Salemson, *Où est mon père?* (Anthologie);
Harold J. Salemson et Touchagues, *Communisme de l'œil*, texte de Salemson avec dix dessins de Touchagues (Tambour).

What to read

New books by a few contributors to *Tambour:*
Maxwell Bodenheim, *A Virtuous Girl* (Liveright);
Jean Cocteau and Samuel Putnam, *Enfants terribles* by Jean Cocteau, translated by Samuel Putnam (Brewer and Warren);
Theodore Dreiser, *A Gallery of Women* (Liveright);
Stuart Gilbert, *James Joyce's « Ulysses »* (Faber and Faber, London);
Jean Giono, *One from Baumugnes* (Brentano);
Ludwig Lewisohn, *Stephen Escott* (Harpers);
Walter Lowenfels, *Finale of Seem* (Heinemann, London);
H. L. Mencken, *Treatise on the Gods* (Knopf).

(*Note:* Le premier des *Artistes* de Harold J. Salemson, dont nous publions aujourd'hui le II et le III, a paru dans *Tambour IV*. Le sujet en était: *Walter-René Fuerts.*)

Le gerant : J. BRUNEL.

Montpellier. — Imprimerie Causse, Graille et Castelnau, 7, rue Dom-Vaissette.

LA PREMIÈRE ŒUVRE

" ESSENTIEL : 1930 "

COMMUNISME
- DE L'ŒIL -
—— PAR ——
—— Harold J. SALEMSON ——

Une plaquette avec 10 dessins de
TOUCHAGUES

IL A ÉTÉ TIRÉ DE CE LIVRE UNE SEULE
ÉDITION DE 110 EXEMPLAIRES, à savoir :
10 exemplaires sur grand papier à 60 francs ; et
100 exemplaires sur alfa bouffant à 15 francs l'ex.

EXCEPTIONNELLEMENT : **COMMUNISME DE
L'ŒIL** est en vente sur alfa avec **OU EST MON
PÈRE ?,** du même auteur : Envoi des deux volumes franco
recommandé contre 20 francs, à Harold J. SALEMSON,
5, rue Berthollet, PARIS (V'), France.

Il ne s'agit pas d'un ouvrage politique